Stay Alive

Stay Alive

the life & death of Stuart Adamson

the authorised biography

Scott Rowley

new modern

First published in the UK in 2026 by New Modern
An imprint of Putman Publishing
Mermaid House, Puddle Dock, Blackfriars, London, EC4V 3DB

🦋 @newmodernbooks
📷 @newmodernbooks

Hardback ISBN: 978-1-917923-53-8
eBook ISBN: 978-1-917923-55-2
Audio ISBN: 978-1-917923-54-5

All rights reserved. No part of this publication may be reproduced, stored in a retrieval system or transmitted in any form or by any means, without the prior permission in writing of the publisher, nor be otherwise circulated in any form of binding or cover other than that in which it is published and without a similar condition including this condition being imposed on the subsequent purchaser.

A CIP catalogue record for this book is available in the British Library.

Publishing and editorial: Pete Selby and James Lilford
Typesetting: Marie Doherty

1 3 5 7 9 10 8 6 4 2

Text copyright © Scott Rowley 2026

The right of Scott Rowley to be identified as the author of this work has been asserted in accordance with the Copyright, Designs and Patents Act of 1988

Every reasonable effort has been made to trace copyright-holders of material reproduced in this book. If any have been inadvertently overlooked, the publisher would be glad to hear from them.

New Modern is an imprint of Putman Publishing
www.newmodernbooks.co.uk
www.putmanpublishing.co.uk

Printed and bound in Great Britain by Clays Ltd, Elcograf S.p.A.

Contents

1 At the End of Everything 1
2 Hurry on Boys (I: Scotland) 5
3 Richard Hell is an Asshole 23
4 So High and So Wild 45
5 Out of Town 53
6 A Mansion and a Mercedes 75
7 Working for the Yankee Dollar 87
8 Hurry on Boys (II: England) 99
9 Goodbye Civilian 115
10 Wake 131
11 The Days of Promise 149
12 We're Gonna Break Your Fuckin' Goalposts 163
13 Come Up Screaming 169
14 Everything You Ever Might Have Wanted 185
15 Wonderland 199
16 Where Did the Feeling Go? 203
17 Out of Lightness, Dark 215
18 Sometimes a Landslide Comes 231
19 The Caledonian Antisyzygy 249
20 Another Season 263
21 Paid in Tractors 275
22 Life at the Tappie Toorie 293
23 The Great Divide 315
24 Inwards 335
25 The Land Where I Lie Cold 355
26 Your Father's Hand 361

Glossary 367
Sources 371
Thank You 373

Author's Note

Big Country's Scottish identity was a huge part of their appeal and something they refused to compromise on. Editing the words of the people I interviewed for this book into standard English seemed like a betrayal of that identity, so I've kept some Scottish words and phrasings. There is a brief glossary at the back to explain any unusual words.

*'Now we play our final hand,
Move in closer, understand'*

Big Country, 'A Thousand Stars'

1

At the End of Everything

*You are on an island, in the middle of
an ocean, at the ends of the earth*

You leave the bar and get in a cab. You go to Atlanta airport and get on a plane to Nashville. You are heading home, where your son is waiting. But something stops you – and then everything stops making sense.

You don't go home. Maybe 'home' doesn't feel like home anymore and the idea of home really did *mean* something to you. You loved your home. You never wanted to leave it.

You have left several homes in the past few years. Your hometown. Your band. Your family.

What you have now – that's not *home*. Maybe it could have been. You were building something there with a woman you loved: a home, full of dogs and cats, and maybe kids one day.

You book yourself into the Best Western Hotel in Nashville and you drink. You drink downstairs in the lounge and you drink in your room. *This* is your home now.

Stay Alive

An idea forms – slowly, over days, although maybe you felt it coming, autumn changing to winter. A tectonic plate has shifted and, somewhere deep inside you, it has kicked something up. The tsunami it has created will sweep you away.

It is November 2001. The news is apocalyptic. The Twin Towers are a pile of rubble. We are at war in Afghanistan. Things are changing. The old world has ended. We are at the beginning of a new century and you are a twentieth-century boy.

In your sober moments, you make some calls. You phone Tony Butler and leave a message – one of the few times you have ever called him. You phone Bruce Watson and tell him that you love him and you have *never* said that before. Scottish men – men born in the '50s and '60s – don't say that to each other, *pfft aye right*. Scottish men don't even hug.

You phone the boys: Boabby, Pubsy, Big Slap. They don't know that people are looking for you, that people are starting to worry. The time difference is good. Evening in Dunfermline is still early in Nashville and you are relatively sober. Later, they will remember that call and wonder if it was your way of saying goodbye. They will rack their brains to think of any clues you might have given them. They will wish you'd spoken to them – you know, *properly* spoken to them, although you never really did, I mean, c'mon, who fucking *does?* – and they will wonder if they could have *done something*.

You don't know it, but your nineteen-year-old son Callum is walking the streets of Nashville looking for you. He is going from bar to bar, peering into booths, listening for a Fife accent, looking for your unmistakable frame. He could spot you a mile off. He is going to find you and help you.

You need help. You are a danger to yourself.

Your manager Ian Grant, a man you've known and counted as a friend for more than two decades, has hired a private detective to find you.

The telephone at your house rings constantly, but you are not there to hear it. Your cell phone needs charging, but you don't charge it.

You don't know it, but your wife is in hospital, fighting for her life.

You drive, drunk out of your mind, to Clarksville and back, even though you have lost your licence and are facing DUI charges.

You switch hotels, and tell reception to send up bottles of red. You should go home but it's not really home, it's just where you live.

You want to go where no one you know will find you, as far away from home as you possibly can. You want to go to the ends of the fucking earth.

And you know exactly where that is. You fly to Honolulu, Hawaii. You walk out of the airport and book yourself into the first hotel you see. You are a ten-minute drive from Pearl Harbor, three minutes away from the Pacific Ocean.

You will not set eyes on either of them. You go to your room, phone reception and ask them to send up three bottles of red.

You are on an island, in the middle of an ocean, at the ends of the earth.

It is 14 December 2001 and you have just two days left to live.

2
Hurry on Boys (I: Scotland)

The Great White North. The diamond mines of Sierra Leone. Black mambas and broken toes. Throwing stones at Eric Clapton

'I'm the only foreigner in my family,' says Bruce Watson, 'for which they rip the piss out of me all the time.'

It's a famous irony: not one of the members of Big Country – a band both beloved and belittled for being Scottish to their core – was actually born in Scotland. Guitarist Bruce Watson was born in Ontario, Canada, drummer Mark Brzezicki in Slough in Berkshire, England. Bassist Tony Butler travelled unborn inside his pregnant mother from Dominica and was delivered in a hospital in Shepherd's Bush, London – and, in April 1958, Stuart Adamson was born just a few miles from Old Trafford, the home of Manchester United.

Stuart was named William Stuart Adamson, after his father William. His mum Anne (née Muir) was already pregnant with Stuart on their wedding day in November 1957. On their marriage certificate, Anne is listed as a bus conductress and William as a colliery engineer. Both of Stuart's grandfathers had also been involved in the coal trade: Harry Adamson as a miner, James Muir as a coal merchant. William didn't want a life in the pit: he joined the merchant navy soon after getting married and, with his father at sea, Stuart and his younger sister Kim were mostly brought up by Anne.

'I think my interest in music came from my mum,' said Stuart. 'She used to work in a record shop and bring stuff like Elvis Presley and Buddy Holly home. She always had loads of mouldy old records lying about, like the Rolling Stones' first LP ...'

Anne had a great singing voice and at late-night parties, where everyone took a turn and 'one singer, one song' was the rule, she would mimic her favourites: Patsy Cline, Loretta Lynn and Brenda Lee.

Anne would send the young Stuart on errands, which included going to the record shop to buy the latest releases. 'My mum would give me six shillings to buy a single,' he said. 'The first one I bought was "Death of a Clown" by Dave Davies ...' When it was released in 1967, Stuart would have been nine years old. As well as the hits of the day, there was lots of other music in the house: 'a lot of bluegrass, Scottish and Irish folk songs – a whole complete range.'

His dad left the merchant navy for a while to run a shop in Lumphinnans in Fife where he and Anne became friends with some musicians. 'They were in a club band,' remembered Stuart, 'playing dance music, and they used to come back to the house quite often. That was great because you used to get to sit up late at night and there'd be guitars and accordions lying around.'

'From the age of eleven or twelve,' he said, 'the thing that took up most of my ambition was to be in a group. I think the idea of building up your own self-confidence appealed because I was pretty shy when I was young. In fact, I still am at times. I'm terrible at small talk.'

When Stuart was around the age of thirteen, his Uncle Drew – his mum's brother – got an acoustic guitar. 'I started messing about on it at my gran's house, learning "Danny Boy" and stuff like that to play at parties,' said Stuart. 'Then I started watching the BBC TV series *Hold Down A Chord*. I can't remember the presenter's name but I owe it all to him ...'

The presenter was John Pearse. *Hold Down A Chord* was a ten-part course for beginner guitarists, first broadcast in 1965 on BBC2. Pearse wrote a series of books on guitar playing, particularly folk and blues styles, and taught the English folk guitarist Martin Carthy. When he died in 2009, the *Guardian* said that Pearse was 'responsible for teaching a generation of British folk and blues enthusiasts how to play the guitar'.

Bruce Watson was born in 1961 in the Great White North: Timmins, Ontario, northern Canada. His parents emigrated there from Dunfermline so that his dad, a coal miner, could work in the Canadian gold mines. But when Bruce came along, his mum went off the idea. It was all right for his dad – he was working all the time – but she was stuck in a strange place with a new baby.

The family returned to the UK on the day of John F. Kennedy's assassination: 22 November 1963. His dad's job as a miner took them to Wales, then back to Dunfermline before he got a job abroad, working in Italy and Zambia. The family stayed in Dunfermline and Bruce didn't see his dad much.

'I saw him occasionally when he came back,' he says, 'but I didn't *really* see him until I was about sixteen and, at that point, it was like: "You can't tell me what to fuckin' do!"' He laughs. 'My dad just liked working in mines and that was all he spoke about.'

Bruce remembers going to see *That'll Be the Day* in 1973, a rock 'n' roll coming-of-age movie starring David Essex. 'At the end, he sees a red guitar in the shop window. The movie ends on that and it was like, "Fuckin' hell! I want one of them!"'

He got a job potato-picking and saved his money. Some of it went on Doc Marten boots, Sta-Press trousers and a Harrington jacket. With the rest, he bought a guitar and an amp from Woolworths.

For a while, Bruce lived in Brucefield in Dunfermline. Nazareth guitarist Manny Charlton lived a couple of doors up and had a brother who was in the local chapter of the Satan's Slaves motorcycle club.

'All his mates used to build these choppers, in their dirty denims, practically in our back garden,' says Bruce. One of the Satan's Slaves was a guy they called Pano. Years later, he became the Skids' first manager. At the other end of the street was Mike Baillie, who became the drummer of the Skids. Nazareth singer Dan McCafferty lived around the corner.

Manny Charlton would drive up with his family in a white BMW sports car, and step out in platform shoes, with a big fur jacket on and a woman on his arm. Bruce would see him from his schoolroom window and go, 'I want some of *that!*'

Stay Alive

Nazareth were one of the biggest names in Scottish rock in the 1970s. They had actual hit records, appeared on *Top of the Pops* and toured the US with the likes of Aerosmith and Lynyrd Skynyrd (in fact, they only narrowly avoided being in the 1977 plane crash that killed six people, including Skynyrd singer Ronnie Van Zant, guitarist Steve Gaines and his backing vocalist sister Cassie).

Nazareth named themselves after a line from the Band's classic 'The Weight' ('Pulled into Nazareth ...') and while they could have a gentle melodic side, the music that made them famous was tough, like the men who made it: no-nonsense heavy rock from the Deep Purple school.

Dropped right into ground zero of the sex, drugs and rock 'n' roll era, Naz avoided drugs in favour of booze ('I'd turn everything down,' said singer Dan McCafferty. 'I was so naive I thought I'd instantly become a drug addict'). For their first official photo shoot, the photographer took them to a strip club in London. There was hell to pay back in Dunfermline: 'When the wives saw the shots with the strippers,' said bassist Pete Agnew, 'man, the explanations we had to make ...'

Another formidable force in Scottish rock was the Sensational Alex Harvey Band from Glasgow. Dynamite performers and musicians, they were an inspired collision of prog rock ambition, barnstorming rock 'n' roll and Brechtian theatre. In Alex Harvey, they had a charismatic frontman who was a massive influence on AC/DC's Bon Scott. Just as Bon had the perfect foil in Angus Young, Harvey had guitarist Zal Cleminson. An astonishing player who painted his face like a psychotic Pierrot, he was both terrifying and technically dazzling.

As the Cure's Robert Smith put it, 'people talk about Iggy Pop as the original punk but in Britain, the forerunner of the punk movement was Alex Harvey. His whole stage show with the graffiti-covered brick walls – it was like very aggressive Glaswegian street theatre.' Nick Cave has said that his first band played so many SAHB songs it was effectively an Alex Harvey tribute band. The Skids' Richard Jobson has called Harvey 'the greatest frontman that ever lived'.

Before Harvey joined them, SAHB were a progressive rock band called Tear Gas. Their singer, Dave Batchelor, went on to produce the Skids' first album and do the live sound for Big Country. 'I loved the Beatles and the Stones,' says Bruce, 'but really it was Nazareth and the Sensational Alex Harvey Band. And what got me into the Harvey Band was the sleeve for [1975's] *Tomorrow Belongs to Me* with the giant stoneater on the front.* And they were Scottish. I fucking loved it. Nazareth were proper rock, but with the Harvey Band, there was a lot of weird shit going on.

'I probably didnae appreciate Zal's playing – or any of the guys' playing at that time. I just thought it was weird and wonderful and wacky.'

Skids frontman Richard Jobson was born in Kirkcaldy in 1960 and brought up in Ballingry, about eleven miles from Dunfermline. His older brother Francis had left-field tastes and an adventurous spirit – Francis later became a Hari Krishna monk and died on a pilgrimage to Nepal – and had a huge impact on the young Richard, introducing his little brother to music he wouldn't have otherwise heard: Frank Zappa, Captain Beefheart, MC5 and Lou Reed. 'It becomes part of your life,' says Jobson. 'Your friends at school are listening to Wishbone Ash and Genesis and you're thinking, "No, man. *Trout Mask Replica* – have you heard *that*?"'

The younger Jobson was a skinhead. 'It's interesting talking about it now,' he says, 'because people's idea of a skinhead is this kind of National Front, right-wing thug – but this was before all that. It was all about music, clothes and football. I'm from an Irish Catholic family, but where I was brought up was in a pretty hardcore Protestant housing estate. I think we were the only Catholics on it.

'The clothes, the music and the violence were part of your daily diet. As a teenager – though it's shameful to talk about it with any excitement now – it was really exciting. You weren't persecuting violence against some

---

* *Tomorrow Belongs to Me* features the song 'The Tale of the Giant Stoneater', a surreal take on environmental destruction. The album's sleeve brings Harvey's vision to life in the shape of a monstrous bulldozer.

guy walking down the street. You were fighting other gangs. But most of the time it was about music and hanging out and learning how to dance.

'I was gonna say that maybe the violence wasn't as serious as it is now, but of course it was. I got stabbed and stuff...'

Jobson went on to write poetry and to have a career in television and film. He wrote and directed his first film, 16 Years of Alcohol, in 2003. It chronicles the growth of a skinhead who falls in love with an art school student and discovers the Stooges and the Velvet Underground. His gang then turn on – and *knife* – him. 'It was pretty much as it happens in 16 Years,' he said. 'My fellow gang members stabbed me.'

So Jobson was into ska and R&B – and then Francis introduced him to Alice Cooper and the New York Dolls. 'And that was it for me really,' he says. 'I just saw something there. So there was a new thing pulling me away from ska and R&B into a world that was more alienated and lost. I think I was inclined towards that anyway.'

In his autobiography, Into the Valley, Jobson recounts how a childhood accident – he was hit by a motorcycle while crossing the road – triggered epilepsy. 'I was always a little bit ill as a kid,' he says. 'I'm epileptic, but we didn't know that at the time – and so I drifted away from people and spent a lot of time on my own. Ska was something you shared with other people, whereas Lou Reed is something you can do on your own.'

When he left school, Jobson worked at a tech company called Monotype that made PC boards for IBM, and there he became friends with Sandra Davidson.

He could tell they'd get on. Like him, she just *looked different.*

Sandra Davidson (now Adamson) was born in Newport-on-Tay, on the other side of the Tay Bridge from Dundee, in 1959. When she was four, her family moved to Sierra Leone, where her dad worked for a diamond mining company.

They lived near the mines in Koidu, where the 2006 Leonardo DiCaprio movie *Blood Diamond* was filmed. While most of the workers' kids went off to boarding school, a bunch of parents – including hers – decided to keep their children with them. There were monkeys in the trees and snakes in the grass, and Sandra and her younger brother, Raymond, had the time of their lives.

'I was there until I was nine,' she says. 'A formative period in my life. To us, it was home. We only came back because my mum was pregnant with my younger brother.'

They didn't go to school in Sierra Leone. Instead, they would play all morning, climbing on massive anthills, before joining their mother poolside at the club and swimming all day. 'It was idyllic. No flip flops, no shoes. I found it difficult to wear shoes when I came back.'

But, on the edges of this idyllic lifestyle, lay danger. 'We grew up with a rebel faction,' she says, 'and we were taught by the other adults and the Sierra Leoneans how to avoid confrontation. So it kinda gave us a head start in how to sort of manipulate, or engineer your way out of trouble.'

And there was trouble everywhere. 'There were a lot of stolen diamonds,' she says, 'and we would hear about it and then see whoever had the diamond running through the bush, being chased with machetes.'

If the diamond thief was caught, the punishment was brutal. Their body would end up being thrown in the dam.

'We saw quite a few dead bodies,' she says. 'We were not allowed to go near the dam until it was checked every day, but there were a lot of times that we saw things we shouldn't see.'

Bloated bodies were floating in their drinking water.

Then there were the snakes. If they came across a snake, they were told, they had to stand still and scream for help. 'If you moved you were at risk,' she says. 'So we were always hyper-alert.' One day, Sandra stood on a black mamba, the most feared of all the local snakes. She was running through the kitchen and someone shouted 'Stay there!' – but Sandra didn't stay, she panicked and kept on running. 'It was slithering under the sink and I stood on it on the way past.'

To this day, she can remember the feeling of that snake under her foot.

When the family returned to Scotland, it was a shock: the amount of people, the buildings, everything about it, even the smell. Those lucky feet of hers

– the feet that had never worn shoes, that had played on anthills and trampled on snakes – had magic properties. She discovered that she was great at dancing. Highland dancing, to be exact.

Highland dancing is so competitive and highly technical that today it's recognised as a sport. Sandra was a late starter, but she was disciplined and determined and progressed quickly. By the age of twelve or thirteen, just two years after returning from Africa, she was a national champion.

Then she broke three toes during a competition. Maybe those feet weren't so lucky after all.

At the time, she didn't know they were broken and continued on, doing nine more dances with three broken toes. It only made it worse. The breaks were so bad that they had altered the mechanics of her foot. She didn't dance again for a couple of years.

'Two bones had fused together,' she says. 'So, from about age thirteen to fifteen, there was nothing – I couldn't go back.' Sandra had competed in the world championships and won medals. 'It was devastating.'

Tam Kellichan, future drummer of the Skids, was born 'Thomas Kellichan' in 1954 in Dunfermline. In Scotland, the shortening of Thomas to Tom becomes 'Tam'.

Tam's dad was a miner and a drummer in a honky-tonk band that played the clubs in Cowdenbeath, so the young Tam started playing on pots and pans when he was about eight. 'And I used to get told: "Aw stoap that fucking noise!"' says Tam. So he joined a pipe band and got schooled in all that 'mummy-daddy-paradiddle stuff', but not actually on a drum. 'They widnae give me a drum. You hudtae practise fur months on mats on a table.'

So he left and learned to play from records. 'I had a wee kit,' he says, 'and I just started listening to all types of music: Deep Purple, Yes, Led Zeppelin and so on. That's how I learned tae play the drums.'

Russell Webb, the future bassist of the Skids, went to school at Bellahouston Academy in Glasgow, where he had the same music teacher as another bass player – Jack Bruce of Cream. Jack Bruce visited the school in the first flush of his success.

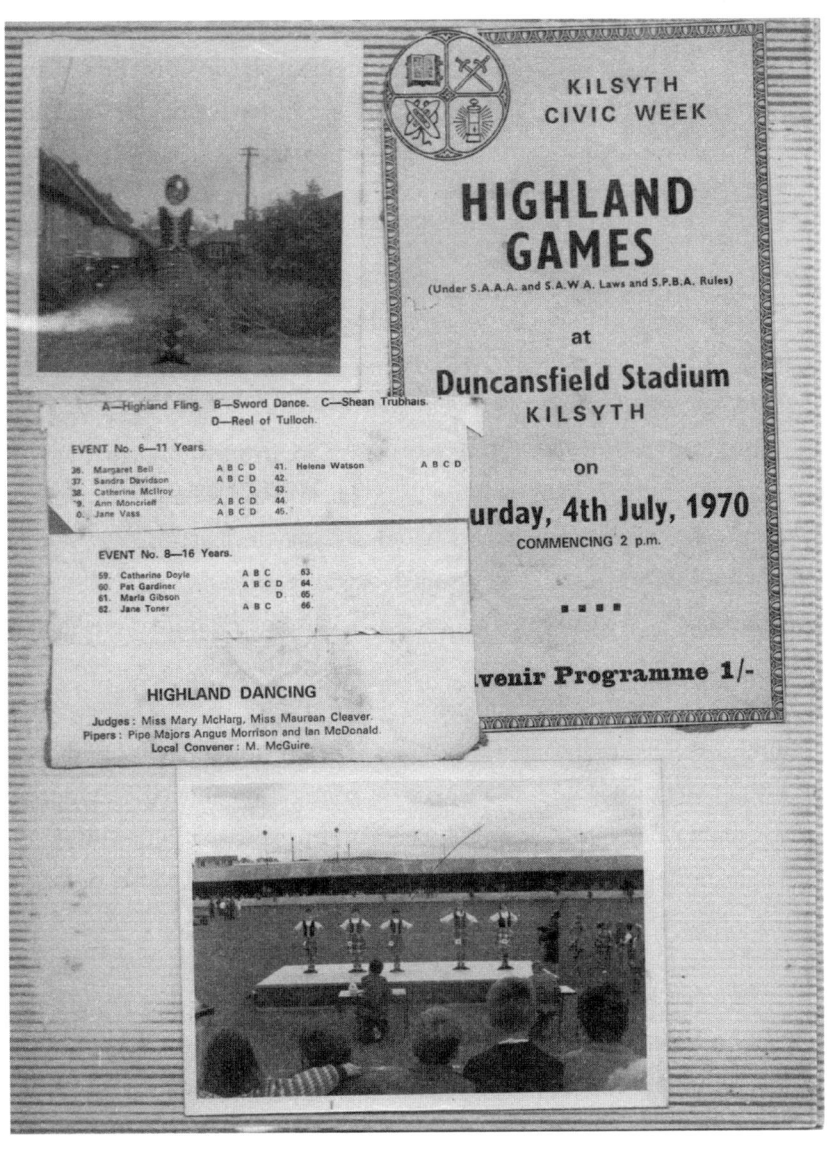

Sandra, the Highland dancer. A page from Sandra's photo album.

Russell was about eight when Cream came. He was playing football with his mates on what they called 'the plots' – the playing fields at the back of the tenements where he lived – when Jack Bruce, Ginger Baker and Eric Clapton emerged through the fog.

'It was like something out of a Clint Eastwood movie,' he says. 'These things came walking across the plots. I'm like, "What the fuck is *that?*", with their long, white Afghan coats and their curly hair and all that. Never seen anything like it. So I went up to Eric Clapton and said, "Are you a poof?" I didn't even know what a poof *was*. He just laughed and kept walking. So I threw a stone at him.

'That's my claim to fame. I threw a stone at Eric Clapton.'

Clive Ford was ten when he moved to Scotland. Clive was born in Malta and raised in Dorset. He would later become the roadie and stage manager of the Skids, but back then he was just a wee boy in a strange place.

It was the early '70s. His family had moved to Dalgety Bay, six miles outside of Dunfermline, an ancient estate that was privately developed in the '60s into an 'enterprise town' to serve commuters into Edinburgh. It was still new when Clive and his family arrived.

'We were on top of the hill that looks over the bay,' says Clive. 'There was nothing in front of us.'

On his very first day in his new home, Clive went out to explore. He was just a few steps from his house when he saw a boy hiding in a bush. The kid saw Clive, locked eyes and put his finger to his mouth in a 'hush' gesture.

'Next thing,' says Clive, 'this angry kid appears, looking for him. He sees me and – with an English accent – he goes: "Have you seen anybody?"'

'No,' says Clive.

The kid looks at him. 'You Scottish or English?' he says.

'English.'

'Oh, that's all right then,' says the kid. 'Are you Protestant or Catholic?'

Clive just looked at him, confused.

'It didn't mean a thing to me,' he says. 'Not a *thing*.'

Even as a kid, Stuart Adamson was clever, a big reader of books with an almost photographic memory. After his first year at secondary school, the school advised his parents that he should be put forward a year. They considered it, but he stayed where he was.

With his dad at sea and his mum working, Stuart's maternal grandparents played a big part in his upbringing. They lived near his school, so he'd go there on his way home. His grandad, Stuart told *Rolling Stone*, was one of the founders of the Fife Communist Party.

One day, Stuart came home from school and made a discovery that would have a profound effect on him.

Inside the house, he found his grandfather's body.

He'd hanged himself.

It was a story Stuart told a few people over the years. He mentioned it to Chris Briggs – a future Big Country A&R man and drinking buddy of Stuart's – and to Tony Butler, to Sandra and to his second wife Melanie Shelley. 'This is how I remember it,' says Melanie. 'He came into the house and his grandfather had hung himself over the stairs.'

'It was such a hard, horrible thing – and a deep trauma.'

Just weeks before Stuart took his own life, he talked to his Nashville bandmate Marcus Hummon about his grandfather. 'Stuart told me, "I found him. He hung himself in the family home." My recollection is that he was saying, "He struggled". His grandfather struggled with some of the same things that he struggled with.'

Tony Butler thinks Stuart took an even wider meaning from it.

'It was the first time in my whole life that I realised I was talking to someone who didn't have anything against the notion of suicide. He told me that his grandad committed suicide, but he didn't speak about it disparagingly. There was a positivity that he obviously took from his grandfather's actions – as in, it's okay to kill yourself, if you feel the need to do it.'

William Simpson – known as 'Bill' to most people now, but always to Stuart Adamson as 'Willie' or 'Wullie' – met Stuart at Beath High School in Cowdenbeath around '72, '73. Bill would become a founding member of the Skids, but at the age of fourteen or fifteen, they were just bonding over music and Monty Python.

'The music at the time was Roxy Music, Mott the Hoople, Bowie, Status Quo,' says Bill. 'I remember going to see Status Quo with Stuart at the Glasgow Apollo around '74. In fact, the first band I ever saw, again with Stuart, was Focus at the Odeon in Edinburgh. Rory Gallagher was a big hero of ours at the time – the *Live In Europe* album.'

Years before, Stuart's dad had bought him a Woolworths electric guitar 'which played like a plank', but he'd stuck with it. One day, he told Bill Simpson that he played guitar and invited him back to his house to show him. 'I assumed he had an acoustic and just strummed a few chords – "Streets of London" or something like that,' says Bill. 'Up in his bedroom, he gets out this kindae Flying V guitar, plugs it in and off he goes. I was blown away at how good he was. He was about fifteen. It was an eye-opener.'

Another one of their school friends was David Allen, who had first met Stuart at Beath Junior High School. 'Stuart's gran lived in sheltered housing just around the corner from my mum's house,' says David. 'Soon he was round at my house two or three nights a week.'

They were 'the proverbial fitba daft', says David. They'd play in the street and later in the school team where, he says, 'Stu was a pretty good player in midfield – good on the ball and quite strong in the tackle'.

He told David about his guitar playing and invited him to his gran's house to demonstrate. He'd set up a pretty big amp in a bedroom, along with a WEM Copicat delay pedal and a wah-wah. 'He proceeded to play "Albatross" by Fleetwood Mac, "Gimme Shelter" by the Stones and many others. I was gobsmacked – anyone could see he had real talent.' It was also very loud. 'But one of the advantages of gigging in a sheltered housing complex,' says David, 'is that the occupants don't have the most acute hearing.'

Stuart left school and started work as a trainee environmental health officer, 'doing a course in sanitary science – water sampling, shop and pub inspection, anything involved in pollution'. Bill got a job as a lab technician with the National Coal Board, analysing coal samples for sulphur. They were living the dream.

Hurry on Boys (I: Scotland)

Stuart worked with a guy who was 'a big mad drummer in a country and western group and he'd take me to see his band in his Ford Escort'. Inspired, Stuart started his own covers band. There was a guy called Iain Law – or Eetchie – on drums and a guy called Jock McMonagle (aka Paddy) on lead guitar, with Stuart on vocals and rhythm guitar. They played youth clubs and that sort of thing, but their bass player had greater ambitions: He wanted them to get into the wedding market and told the band they should learn how to play songs like 'Tie a Yellow Ribbon'.

The rest of the band were like, 'Get tae fuck. No way.'

They had a better idea. They fired the bass player.

Stuart asked Bill if he wanted to join the band. Stuart had this old bass and he gave Bill a lesson that basically consisted of 'That's a B, that's an E, that's a G …'. Bill picked it up in a couple of weeks and Stuart sold him the bass for £4. 'It took him two months to pay it off,' Stuart said later.

Bill still has a rehearsal tape from late '74 or early '75. 'We start with "Rock and Roll" by Led Zeppelin,' he says, 'then go into "That'll Be the Day", "Heartbreak Hotel", "Gimme Shelter", "Feelin' Alright" by Traffic, "This Old Heart of Mine" by Rod Stewart, "Teenager in Love", "I Love How You Love Me" – an eclectic mix.

'We'd play local discos – they weren't called discos then – they were *dances*. It was a good laugh.'

They named the band Tattoo after the 1973 Rory Gallagher album and – despite sacking their old bass player for his hoity-toity ambitions – they soon became more professional, getting themselves a mini-tour of the Scottish Highlands.

'We slept in the van with the gear some of the time,' says Bill. 'It was just fun.' They did two nights at Strathpeffer Spa Ballroom and for once they didn't have to sleep in the van. Thrilled to have beds, they were drinking and jumping around in the room in the early hours of the morning when Bill went on his arse and landed on a pint glass.

His left arm started spurting blood. Paddy was like: 'Ah, it'll be all right. Get yourself a plaster.' But Stuart realised it was serious. He and Bill went out into the night and managed to flag down a police car. The

Stay Alive

police took them to Dingwall's Ross Memorial Hospital where Bill got stitched up.

Then they had to work out how to get back to Strathpeffer. Bill remembers trying to thumb a lift – difficult at any time in the remote Scottish Highlands, but especially in the early hours of the morning when you're covered in blood.

'I can't even remember how we got back,' says Bill.

They probably walked – it was only five miles and everyone walked everywhere back then. But Stuart didn't complain or make him feel bad. He'd looked out for him.

'He was a good mate for coming with me,' says Bill.

Around this time, when she was fifteen or sixteen, Sandra and a pal went to a dance in Crossgates, walking the four miles there and back. 'That's what you did on a Saturday,' she says. There was a band playing that night, called Tattoo.

'That would have been the first time I ever saw Stuart,' she says. 'I can remember this person walking about in an Arthur Black suit. You could tell it cost a lot of money and there was a lot of effort being put in.'

Did sparks fly? Was it love at first sight? 'That's all I remember,' she says. 'Nothing else at all.'

It wasn't until much later that she even put two-and-two together.

Apart from the tapes of Scottish reels that she danced to, music wasn't a big part of Sandra's life, but she liked the glam rock she heard on the radio: Roxy Music, T. Rex, Bowie.

She left home at sixteen to work in a hotel in Pitlochry and, when she finished her shift, she'd go back to her room and listen to the radio. At that time of night, the DJ was John Peel. 'That's where I first heard the Ramones,' she says. 'At that point, he was still playing stuff like Fleetwood Mac and Pink Floyd, but there was the odd thing that you thought, "What's *that*?"'

Tattoo ended when Paddy – aka Jock – left to join the police. Bill had met the girl who would eventually become his wife and was smitten. The bad news: she was going off to Amsterdam to stay with some friends. Bill followed. He quit his job and convinced Stuart to come too.

'I stayed in Amsterdam probably for three or four months,' says Bill. 'Stuart managed a fortnight. I knew he wasn't really interested in staying 'cos he spent most of his money in the casino on the ferry.'

Bill came home, around the end of October 1976, to find that music had changed dramatically. 'Stuart introduced me to all this new stuff – the Damned, Buzzcocks, the Stranglers, the Jam etc. We went to see the Jam in Edinburgh [probably May 1977]. It was an eye-opener.'

David Allen remembers listening to John Peel's end-of-year show with Stuart. 'It was the advent of punk rock, with songs like the Damned's "New Rose",' he says. 'Stu was really galvanised by this new wave.'

Stuart had an idea for a new band. No' a covers band, playing aw that auld pish. Something *new*.

Stuart and Bill put an advert in a local paper for a drummer: 'New wave band looking for a drummer – no hippies.'

'A fucking brilliant drummer, a wee guy from Cowdenbeath, a lorry driver, a complete nutcase, turns up,' Stuart remembered later.

'A lot of people said I was like the Keith Moon of the punk rock world,' says Tam. 'I *was* a bit of a nutcase, to be honest with you.'

Tam arrived for the audition to find that there was a guy on before him and he had his kit all set up, a big Premier kit, the fuckin' works. Tam had a wee Olympic kit in his car and decided it was staying right there.

'I says tae the guy, "Look mate, is it awright if I have a shot of yours? You can go first. It would just save us having tae set up another kit."' The guy went for it and gave Tam a double advantage: not only did he get to use a better drum kit, but he also got to hear the songs and plan how he was going to play them.

Tam had been backing a one-legged accordion player, playing tangos and waltzes in the local clubs, and he was well-drilled. He got the gig. When he turned up for his first rehearsal and set up his tiny wee kit, the Skids stood around it and said, 'What the fuck is *that*?'

Later, after one of their first London gigs, Tam kicked that drum kit off the stage into the audience.

When she came back from Pitlochry, Sandra ended up working at the same place as Richard Jobson.

'So that's probably how we became friends,' she says, 'because he knew I was different.'

Jobson had a unique 'punk' look, dressing in a long, black trenchcoat and winkle-picker shoes, with his hair sculpted into a black quiff with a white stripe in the middle, like a skunk.

Sandra stood out in her own way. 'I was the worst punk,' she says. 'I always dressed like a Highland dancer should dress. I've never ever worn one item of punk clothing. I was always in a kilt or had my hair in a bun – because I was *dancing*. Even after that, I was always dressed up to the neck. I wasn't interested in punk fashion. I just liked the music. And Richard was different, obviously, the way he dressed. He was like that from the word go.'

The people who would become the Skids and Big Country were all leaving school and getting jobs. Clive Ford's family had moved from Dalgety Bay to Dunfermline. He left school at sixteen.

'In Dunfermline, you had a choice of jobs,' he says. 'It was the pit, the dockyard or the armed forces. That's all they told you about. I ended up going down the dockyard as a fitter-turner. But come 1976, '77, my interests were elsewhere.'

'I left school when I was fifteen,' says Bruce. 'I forged my papers. I got a job selling lemonade. I had to take a day off work to go and sit my O Levels. I was an Alpine juice boy.'

Alpine Soft Drinks was a fizzy pop home delivery service across the UK in the 1970s and '80s. Vans would drive around and delivery boys would jump off with bottles of limeade, pineapple crush and cream soda.

'And that's when the punk thing was happening,' he says. Bruce had been listening to Be Bop Deluxe and Led Zeppelin, and they seemed impossible to play on guitar. But this new punk music? That was different.

'Everybody's got that punk story about seeing the Pistols on TV – but we lived in Scotland. We never got that programme. You read about it in the papers.

'At the time, it was more Eddie and the Hot Rods, the first Ultravox! album, the Jam. You'd see their records inside Sandy Muir's record shop.'

Punk was easy to play. 'Not so much the rhythm and blues of Dr Feelgood or Eddie and the Hot Rods,' says Bruce, 'but when I listened to the Clash, I thought: "I can fuckin' play that! I'm never going to be able to play like Bill Nelson or Zal, but this I can do".'

When he turned sixteen, he had a choice: work down the dockyards or go down the pit. 'My dad said, "You're no' goin' doon the fuckin' pit." He'd had that many accidents with shafts collapsing, getting his bones busted up. He said, "Go doon the dockyard, have an easy life wi' yer uncles."'

So Bruce quit Alpine, got a job down the docks and started earning some money. The first real guitar he bought was in the window of Sandy Muir's shop – a red Yamaha SG500. It was his David Essex red-guitar-in-the-window moment.

'It was a real guitar,' he says. 'You couldn't get Strats or Gibsons anywhere at that time, even in the late '70s. It was all Antoria copies and stuff like that. So I saved up and got this guitar and it was *so* easy to play.'

The dockyards were full of guys in bands. 'They were all heavy metal or prog rock, that kindae stuff,' he says. 'There was 7,000 people down the dockyards at that time. You'd meet up in the canteen – and those was the days, when you could have a couple of pints, health and safety went out the windae – so I used to sit with all these older guys who were in bands and they would give me tips.'

But those older guys hated punk.

'Whit's aw this Boomtown Rats shite?'

'Well, ah don't like them either.'

'Ah like Blondie.'

'Ah bet ye dae!'

They'd give Bruce tips on the guitar and he'd pester them for more.

'How dae ye dae that?'

'Aw, ye need a wah-wah pedal.'
'Where dae ah get wan o' them?'
'Aw gonnae fuck off?'

Then Bruce met Clive Ford. Clive also liked punk and he and Bruce would chat about music in the canteen.

Bruce formed a band with his pal Raymond Davidson. Raymond's sister was Sandra Davidson. They played Ramones-y stuff, but no cover versions because, y'know, *punk*.

'It was barre chords all the way, everything in a major key, certainly nothing up the dusty end,' says Bruce. 'The dusty end' is what guitarists jokingly call the top of the guitar neck, where the difficult stuff like guitar solos are typically played. Beginner guitarists don't go there, so that end gets *dusty*.

His band was called the Delinquents. 'Which we weren't,' he says. 'We would've liked to have been delinquents, but we were too chicken shit to do it.'

Jobson was a year younger than Sandra. He was on the Youth Opportunities Programme (YOP), a state-sponsored training scheme that kept the unemployment figures down. You got a little extra on top of your dole money and, when you were fully qualified to do the job, you were let go and replaced by another YOP.

'Richard wasnae a confident youngster,' says Sandra. 'Not that I saw, anyway. He maybe appeared confident with guys, but he certainly didn't appear confident to me. But we were friends. He came in one day and said, "I've joined a band." I just looked at him.'

Sandra couldn't relate to this kid being a singer and when he said 'We're playing a gig', she thought, 'Christ. I'm no' missing that.'

One day down the docks, Clive Ford told Bruce: 'I'm working with a band called the Skids. They're playing a few gigs and they're in rehearsals.'

And Bruce said: 'Can I come and watch?'

3
Richard Hell is an Asshole

Tyre marks on the asphalt. Trouble in Alva Glen.
A maritime captain escapes.
Willie Law and the bagpipe guitar

'We didn't know each other,' says Richard Jobson. 'I went to a Catholic school and Stuart went to a Protestant school. The first time I met him was at a gig, but we were there for different acts.'

The gig was at the Carnegie Hall in Dunfermline, January 1976. 'He was there for Be Bop Deluxe and I was there for the Doctors of Madness,' he says. 'And therein laid the difference between the two of us. He was into this kind of rather melodic, romantic, epic guitar-based sound – which he kind of transmutated into Big Country – and I was into something a little bit more arty, odd and peculiar.'

It is a neat metaphor. Maybe too neat. Bill Simpson was with Stuart that night, sitting upstairs in the Carnegie Hall, and says: 'I don't recall seeing Richard there.' In his autobiography, Jobson himself remembers it differently.

Hey ho. Stories change over time. Memory is a monster.

Whether they met that night or not, the gig was a big deal for them and their age group. Rock music was barely even a decade old and already the first and second wave of rock bands seemed ancient.

'The audience was predominantly under twenty,' says Clive Ford. 'Be Bop Deluxe wasn't seen as part of the old regime. They weren't Deep Purple or Black Sabbath or Zeppelin. It was definitely something new and I think that's what the inspiration for Stuart would have been – to take it wherever you want, like Bill Nelson did.'

Stuart was looking for a singer and Jobson was already becoming infamous locally. Later, in the Skids' first interview with Dunfermline punk fanzine *Kingdom Come*, Jobson was introduced with the aside: 'You'll already know him if you were at the Graham Parker/Southside Johnny gig at the Usher Hall in March. He was the guy who jumped onstage at the end and told everyone to get GP back on for an encore.'

Jobson was a big guy, despite his young age, and he dressed distinctively, with his trenchcoat and his skunk hairdo. Stuart and Bill had seen him around and thought: 'Who's *that?*'

'When you have the condition I have [epilepsy], you tend to not look that well,' says Richard. 'And because of the influence of my older brother, I was already looking a bit punky before punk. So when everything happened, it was like, "I've been waiting for this. Where have you *been?*"'

Punk had also lit a flame under Stuart. 'I think Stuart always thought of Nils Lofgren as being a kind of punk,' says Jobson, 'which in a way he was. They were looking for a singer and the only punk in the area was me. They said, "Will you come in and do an audition?"'

The auditions were held at Cowdenbeath Working Men's Club. 'All these old miners were sitting around smoking,' says Jobson. 'The other guys auditioning all had this Bryan Ferry look – they were more into something a little bit smoother, wearing boiler suits with belts and stuff.

'It's turned into a bit of a fable that I told them all to fuck off. But if you looked at what was emerging from London that summer of '77, it was more about image than talent. I think Stuart was wise enough to understand that. He thought: "Here's this feral, mad little fucker who's got the look."'

Bill wasn't as convinced.

'We joke about this, but it's the truth,' says Jobson. 'Bill said it right in front of me. He said to Stuart, "This guy can't sing and he can't dance."

'And Stuart went: "Perfect."'

It was June 1977. Peak punk. The Sex Pistols' second single, 'God Save the Queen', was banned by the BBC but still went to number 2 in the UK singles chart, with some speculating it was held off the number 1 spot by a conspiracy.

After throwing around a lot of different names – like Dr White & the Plastic Bags and Skid Marx & the Brown Jobbies – the band settled on the Skids. The associations with 'skid marks' aside, it was a great name. Like the Clash, it implied action and danger – brakes being slammed, cars careering out of control, tyre marks on the asphalt.

They gave themselves punk stage names for a while. Stuart was Stevie Cologne, Jobson was Joey Jolson, Tam became Tom Bomb and Bill, brilliantly, became Alex Plode.

Now they needed somewhere to play.

The Belleville Hotel on Pilmuir Street, Dunfermline, hosted a Friday-night rock club, run by Mike Douglas. One of the Satan's Slaves, he was known to everyone as Pano. Pano had taken Clive Ford under his wing. 'I started going to the Friday-night rock club and I ended up on the door,' says Clive. 'I got paid in pints and I got to see bands for nothing, which was all I cared about.'

'Pano was like a big brother figure to us,' says Jobson. 'He really did help us. He was a cool guy, had a great leather jacket and the right jeans and boots, and he was part of a biker community.' The Satan's Slaves were an instant audience for the band and sometimes their protectors. 'They were interesting guys,' says Jobson, 'and they adopted us. So we had our own little gang and Pano started to look after us and got us our first couple of gigs.'

Pano had booked Edinburgh punk band the Rezillos in early '77 and the Belleville was packed. 'We were starting to get a bit of the buzz that we were reading about in London,' says Clive. 'It was starting to spread. After the Rezillos, there was a fresher audience coming in. Hair was getting shorter, jeans were getting straighter.'

Pano let the Skids rehearse in the Belleville. Clive went off hitch-hiking around France and, on his return, went straight to the club. As he walked up the stairs, he could hear the band rehearsing. He stopped in his tracks.

Pano had told him they were a punk band, but what he could hear was much more sophisticated than punk. It was brooding and melodic, and had a long guitar solo. It sounded like two guys on guitar, like he was somehow playing rhythm *and* lead. It was a song, he found out later, called 'Scared to Dance'.

'I sat on the stairs,' says Clive, 'and it started with a guitar solo and I'm going, "What *is* this?" But it was *really* good.'

He went in and sat through the rest of the set. 'Scared to Dance' was the odd one out: the rest of the set was faster and more upbeat. 'Most of the bands at the Belleville were trying to be Deep Purple – they were all trying to be *something* – and here was a band that was carving out something for themselves. They weren't trying to be anything. They had latched on to the energy of punk but they had their own thing going on.'

The Skids' first gig was on 19 August 1977. 'We had people lining up to get in,' says Clive. 'It wasn't a big room. I think maximum eighty people were allowed in there and we exceeded that.'

The band played their second gig the following day, an open-air benefit concert for the Chilean Defence League. The Skids were bottom of the bill. 'After the second gig,' says Clive, 'I turned to Tam and said, "Do you guys have a roadie?" He said no. I said, "You do now".'

'Pano and I made a decision that the band were never going to be seen carrying their gear. They were going to be totally focused on being a band.

'And Pano made them rehearse every day. Every. Single. Day.'

Clive had told Bruce Watson that he was working with the Skids and Bruce came to watch them rehearse in an old warehouse up at the top end of Dunfermline. 'I went up and Clive introduced us and they looked like the Clash,' says Bruce. 'They had the shirts with zips, and the hair, and Richard looked like a skunk with the black hair with the white bit.'

'At that time, it was all still bell-bottom flares and checked shirts,' says Bill, 'but we had all the punk gear – to a degree. Richard, anyway. Stuart was covered in zips and safety pins. We just made them ourselves. We'd get them out of charity shops. We'd look for an old man's suit with the drain-pipe trousers, a grandad shirt or something, and you'd sew zips on them, or some buttons.'

'Stuart had a Gibson Marauder at the time,' says Bruce, 'and an HH amp that was sitting on its side, with what looked like a homemade speaker cabinet. It wasnae plugged in – just to sit the amp on. It was the first time I'd seen a band play live. And they were so fucking loud.'

When Stuart realised that Bruce was a guitarist, he offered him his guitar. 'But I couldn't play it. It was uncontrollable, it was so fucking loud. Just feedback. I was used to playing in my house, but he had the distortion all cranked up and the valve sound in the amp – it was like heavy metal. I'm trying to control it and it's like, WHEEEEEEE! I'm like: "How do you make it STOAP?!"'

'Everyone talks about Stuart's use of the EBow* in Big Country,' says Clive Ford. 'But prior to him having an EBow, Stuart was a master of feedback – *controlled* feedback. Throughout that whole solo in "Scared to Dance", he would get it so that it was feeding back without being annoying. He could control it and play over it – arpeggiate over the feedback. It was really cool to hear and see.

'He loved the energy of the whole punk thing, but he also liked to bring it back a bit and just have people engaged. You couldn't go to the bar. You had to watch to see what was going to happen next.

'Stuart tried to make every note count. Even the later stuff, when it becomes a bit more musical, I think he's really trying hard – not to overplay, not to underplay – but just make sure that what he *does* play is relevant to the song. He was a very thoughtful player. The speed that they came up

---

* The EBow was a hand-held effects unit for guitar players that sustained notes. More on this later.

with things was just phenomenal. The Skids' setlist changed weekly. It was never the same. It wasn't until they were touring an album that it became a bit more standardised and fixed.'

Many of the songs that Bruce would have heard them play were never really released – songs like 'Sick Club', 'Nationwide', 'Mouth to Mouth', 'Neckshots', 'New Daze', 'Don't Want to Go', 'Hang Onto the Shadows', 'Design', 'Zit', 'London', 'Paralysed', 'Johnny Wants', 'Victims of the Weekend', 'Withdrawal Symptoms' and 'My Life'.

'"My Life" was a nice wee song,' says Bill. 'It could've been a nice single. "Sick Club" went "The catalogue boys are here tonight/They've got their brand-new outfits and they feel just right." Those were the days when you bought your clothes from a catalogue.'

Stuart's talent as a songwriter was obvious even then. 'Some people think that those songs could have been on an album before the first album,' says Bill, 'but because it evolved so quickly, a lot of that stuff was dumped. He was more talented than that.

'Myself and Tam Kellichan were a tight-knit unit but nothing fancy.' He chuckles: 'Maybe when it got to the point where it needed something more fancy, that's where it started to go wrong for us.'

'Stuart was a perfectionist,' says Tam. 'He knew what he wanted. For me, Stuart *was* the Skids. The rest of us were just ... *There*. You know? To do what he said.'

The Clash played at Dunfermline's Kinema Ballroom on 24 October 1977. Pano had helped the promoters get the gig – in return, they'd put the Skids on the bill.

'The promoters agreed to it, but nobody told the Clash,' says Clive. The headliners already had two support bands: Richard Hell and the Voidoids, and the Lou's, an all-female French punk band the Clash had met at the 1977 Mont de Marsan punk festival. So the Skids were relegated to the side stage where the DJ usually set up.

'Richard Hell didn't want us on the main stage, because they were on first, so we had to go on this little stage,' says Jobson. 'We liked Richard

Hell but he was an asshole. So we thought, "Fuck it, doesn't matter, let's do it – we're supporting the Clash!"'

'They didn't go through the main PA,' remembers Clive. 'We had our own rehearsal PA – but it was good, it was exciting and it definitely got the band on the map.'

'Mick [Jones] and Joe [Strummer] were watching us,' says Jobson, 'and it was just a wonderful thing to see them standing there. Joe said that when they were playing, they noticed these two guys jumping around down the front – me and Stuart. We were down the front.'

After that, all the local promoters were aware of the Skids. Two weeks later, they opened up for Buzzcocks. 'That was the start,' says Clive. 'It was pretty rapid from then.'

Jobson remembers the early days of the Skids as being very violent. 'This promoter would book us into barn dances in Elgin,' says Jobson, 'and then we'd turn up. So all these big Highland guys would get stuck into us. It was great fun.

'Stuart was never one for a fight and we had a lot of fights with the Skids. I mean, sometimes the whole audience would attack us. He never liked to fight. He was never there. None of them did. I did, in those days. I loved it. But they absolutely hated it.'

Bill confirms that Jobson was pretty fearless. 'Ballingry, where he comes from, is a mining village, a working-class village,' he says. 'They were all hard men down there. They were all workers, all drinkers. They hold their own. And he was in a family of five boys and full of testosterone and got up to hi-jinks. I was more your quiet, studied sort of guy. I think that was where we have our problems. Our personalities are chalk and cheese – always have been. Still are.'

Clive Ford says that Jobson has a tendency to exaggerate. 'Richard's a storyteller,' he says. 'Take everything he says with a pinch of salt. Richard used to frustrate me – and everybody who knows him – because he elaborates on the truth. But it makes it much better than if I was telling the story. If I was telling this story, it would be "And then they did this, and then they did that" and everybody would have fallen asleep.'

Stay Alive

The way Clive remembers it, the 'barn dance in Elgin' was actually 'Pitlochry and there was about fourteen people there, and they were very welcoming because no one else ever played Pitlochry.'

But he also remembers a night off at the Gartwhinzean, a hotel near Rumbling Bridge, a small village eleven miles north of Dunfermline. 'It's a hotel in the middle of nowhere. We went in there and we did get hostility. It was around the same time.'

'There wasn't as much aggression as maybe Richard's painting,' says Bill. 'It was more boisterousness. At that time, things were getting thrown at the stage, you were getting spat at, which was disgusting, and there would be the odd bottle getting thrown. There was always a bit of tension.

'It wasn't like they were *against us*, it was more like: that's what you do at a punk gig.'

'Everyone used to spit on you,' remembers Tam. 'I think that's why I'm still alive today. I've had every disease you can get.'

On Boxing Day 1977, the Skids headlined a gig at the Alva Glen Hotel in Alloa, with the Cuban Heels and the Freeze, a band from Linlithgow, just sixteen miles over the Forth Bridge from Dunfermline. Their singer was then known as Gordon Sharp. Today, she's known as Cinder Sharp, the singer for experimental noise-rockers Cindytalk and famed for her contributions to the first This Mortal Coil album on the 4AD label.

Cinder was a punk kid who saw the Skids early on. 'They were undoubtedly the best thing going on in Scotland at the time,' she says. 'Simple Minds were just starting. It took them a wee while to find their feet, but the Skids had the audience in the palm of their hand – and a large part of that was Stuart. Apart from being a brilliant musician, he was a brilliant person.'

Cinder was fifteen when she started playing in bands. Stuart seemed more mature. 'Stuart was a wee bit older. He just seemed quite sorted and helpful and very, very warm. That's the thing I remember most about Stuart – just how warm and open he was.'

On the night of the Alva Glen gig, the Freeze played and Cinder immediately ran into some trouble. 'We'd literally just come off stage,' she says, 'and I went straight to the loo. I went into a cubicle and the door smashed open on my back and six guys came in and dragged me out and kicked the fucking shit out of me.'

Clive Ford was there. 'And that's when Pano came in,' he says. 'He said, "You've gotta leave!" and we grabbed Gordon and we all ran out to the van and left.'

Anti-punk feeling was everywhere. In June that year, Johnny Rotten, Pistols engineer Bill Price and producer Chris Thomas – who would later work with Big Country – ended up in hospital after being attacked in Highbury in north London by nine men with knives and razors.

'There was a lot of violence around,' says Cinder. 'Being involved in the punk scene made us a target. We never went looking for trouble, but it certainly found us. I never had an identikit punk look. Even as a kid I was a wee bit more sort of fem-y, so I suspect that might have been why I got picked on that night.'

Alva Glen was a Satan's Slaves hangout. Possibly Cinder's assailants were pissed-up Slaves and Pano had kept the peace. You never knew where you were with the Slaves. Bill remembers them turning up at a gig down in Dumfries. 'We were thinking, "What are they here for? Are they here to beat us up?" But, quite the contrary, they were there to protect us. "Any problems, we'll sort it."'

At the end of 1977, Stuart began to encourage Jobson to write lyrics. 'Richard had lyrics – poems – which Stuart persuaded him to share,' says Clive, 'and then Stuart cut them up and made them into verse-chorus-ish, and created songs out of them.

'Richard never wrote songs, he just wrote *words*. Richard liked words. He liked changing the pronunciation of words and I think he learned that from John Lydon. He'd make a word fit and it could mean multiple things.'

'Richard had been writing poems,' says Bill. 'I wouldn't say they were lyrics because they weren't set in the usual format of a song. If you listen to the first album, songs like "Dossier of Fallibility" or "Hope and Glory" don't have a traditional song structure. "Six Times" is a crazy wee song, but Stuart managed to make something from it. Stuart was the driving force from the musical side of things. So the songs quickly evolved from the small two-and-a-half-minute, three-chord punk kind of stuff.'

'It took the Skids away from all these other bands that we were lumped in with – bands like the Ruts or the Members,' says Jobson. 'I think we were a little bit artier and more interesting than that.'

'We didn't really think of ourselves as a "punk" band,' says Bill. 'It was more art-punk. We started as a punk band in Stuart's bedroom, but it quickly evolved. Stuart knew how to put light and shade to it.

'A lot of people would come to our gigs expecting thrash-thrash-thrash – and no disrespect to the bands that did that – but it becomes a bit samey. With us, people would stop and listen. Like "Of One Skin", the stop-and-start thing, or "Scared to Dance" – a slow piece like that was unusual for a band just starting out at that time. Because Stuart was such a talented guy and Richard was an amazing frontman, we stood out.'

The first song Stuart and Richard worked on together became 'Of One Skin'. 'It's always been spelled wrong,' says Jobson. 'It should be "off" with two F's – "Off One Skin".'

In his book *Into the Valley*, Richard suggests that the song is about Stuart. The two had become close, sharing hotel rooms and working on songs together when, says Jobson, Adamson confided in him that his childhood hadn't been a happy one. 'Stuart alluded to something dark in his family life,' writes Jobson, 'and without ever getting to the absolute rub of it, it definitely had something to do with the relationship with his father.'

'We got very, very close in the beginning,' says Jobson now. It started when he told Stuart about his epilepsy. Richard was fainting and Adamson thought he was on drugs. 'He kept saying, "What's going on with you? Are you *taking* something?" People had just discovered heroin at the time. I said, "No – I've got this condition." At the time it hadn't been fully diagnosed.

'So Stuart kind of looked after me. And when you get that kind of intimacy and friendship, things start to come out. So if you look at the lyrics – "Beware little one knowledge/Inside, you seem to acknowledge/Trace the case of your family past/A maritime captain escaped the last laugh." His father was in the merchant navy. He gave me a hint of something that wasn't right. And in my own abstract way ...'

Bill admits he is unsure exactly what the lyric is referring to. 'I was a friend of Stuart's, but I only got to know him once we were teens. I didn't know him when he was young.'

Bill never had a conversation with Stuart about his home life. 'But he's obviously confessed something to Richard,' he says.

'I was at Stuart's house only a handful of times. Most of the time his dad wisnae there. It was his mum and Kim. I hardly ever saw his dad because he was away in the merchant navy. If I did see him, it was just to say hello – we were up in Stuart's bedroom, playing guitar. If Stuart did mention something to Richard, he never passed it on to the rest of us. But when you read the lyrics, you think he *must've* said something. "A maritime captain escaped the last laugh" is the obvious one.'

'Escaped' as in 'got away with it'?

'Aye.'

To understand what Richard and Bill are alluding to, we have to skip forward more than two decades to 2003.

In April or May that year, Sandra Adamson was at home when the phone rang. It was Stuart's dad, William.

It was a year and a half after Stuart's death. Sandra was still dealing with that – the death of her former partner and the father of her children, Callum and Kirsten – and supporting her kids in their grief while coming to terms with her own.

And now Stuart's dad was on the phone, saying something incredible.

'I've handed myself in to the police,' William Adamson told Sandra.

'What do you mean?' said Sandra.

'I'm a paedophile,' said William.

'*What?*' said Sandra. 'What do you mean, you're a paedophile?'

'I've been touching kids,' he said.

The following year, in February 2004, William Adamson, then sixty-seven, was found guilty of sexually abusing three children – two girls and a boy, aged between seven and ten – in the period between 1997 and 2003. He was sentenced to four years in jail.

Stay Alive

When I first started writing this book, I asked the family if anything would be off-limits. What if, for example, I wanted to speak to William?

'The old paedo?' said Callum Adamson. 'Be my guest.'

'You could talk to him,' said Sandra, 'but would you be able to believe a word he has to say?'

It was a fair point. I didn't speak to him.

I called Stuart's sister Kim. She politely declined to be interviewed.

William Adamson died in November 2023, aged eighty-six.

Kim died in June 2025.

It's tempting to look back, armed with this knowledge about Stuart's dad, and jump to conclusions. Like: Was Stuart Adamson abused by his father? Stuart was a troubled man throughout much of his adult life – insular, erratic, moody, driven to alcoholism and finally to suicide. Could this have been the root of all that?

Stuart never spoke about abuse in the Adamson household – not to Sandra or to Melanie, his second wife, to any of his other bandmates, or in any of the therapy sessions in his many later trips to rehab – so Sandra finds it difficult to believe that he would have opened up to Richard. Maybe Richard, prone to embellishment, is misremembering, filling in the blanks and retro-fitting history.

On the other hand, after the news broke about William Adamson in 2003, a family member confirmed to Sandra that there *had* been abuse of some kind in the Adamson household.

There *had* been something dark in Stuart's family life and it *did* have something to do with his father.

Stuart never discussed this abuse with anyone, outside of this conversation with Jobson, but there was abuse. Either Stuart was a victim of it – possible, but no one close to the matter thinks so – or he witnessed the abuse, or he just knew it was happening. Either way, he carried that with him for the rest of his life.

The lyrics of 'Of One Skin' are impenetrable. The young Jobson's lyrics were abstract and impressionistic, and it's difficult to extract literal meaning from them. His words are emblematic of the Skids' move away from the social realism of punk into something more adventurous and avant garde – but the result is that meaning itself is obscured and sometimes lost.

So it's difficult to decipher exactly what 'Of One Skin' is about. If it is about a darkness in Stuart's family life, it's not obvious. 'Stuart loved it,' says Jobson and maybe that's why: *because* the meaning was obscured. Later, in his own lyrics, Adamson would allude to troubled families and abusive and domineering fathers, but he would also mix these deeply personal lines with broader stories, with stuff taken from books, and then obscure the meaning further by telling journalists that the song was about the Falklands conflict or trade unionism. He was a master at deflection.

'Stuart knew it was about him,' says Richard, '100 per cent, and he always wanted to begin and end the show with it. We bookended all of our shows with it because he thought it was the first song we wrote that had some real meaning.'

Jobson's singing style obscured the lyrical meaning even further. In 1990, a TV advert for Maxell cassettes mocked the unintelligibility of 'Into the Valley', suggesting daft but plausible lyrics to the song. In the Skids' early material, with lyrics written by Stuart, Jobson's singing style is noticeably clearer. On the single version of 'Charles' – their first release – Jobson pronounces the words almost robotically. By the time of the album release, he's in full Jobson mode. It became part of their signature style: weird impenetrable verses, huge anthemic choruses.

'It's quite a talent to be able to mangle every single word that you're singing,' says Cinder. 'Elizabeth Fraser [of Cocteau Twins, from nearby Grangemouth] did that but more beautifully. Jobson mangled language in a really bizarre way.

'Maybe it's a dynamic thing,' she says. 'He was a very dynamic performer, so I'm guessing that he's taking those words and he's just *using* them. He's kind of weaponising every single one for the sake of dynamics. I don't mean that in a negative sense. It worked – Skids gigs were amazing.'

It could also be the end result of the songwriting technique: Stuart taking Jobson's poems and mashing them into 'verse-chorus-ish', as Clive says

– the awkwardness of the language informing the rhythms and phrasing of his guitar playing, the demands of structure and melody meaning that the words had to be mashed up to fit. By necessity, it took Stuart's songwriting further away from the pub-rock punk R&B of songs like 'Test Tube Babies' and 'Design'.

'But at the same time, I think that annoyed him,' says Sandra Adamson, 'because he was more than capable of writing lyrics for his own music. Not long after the Skids started, Stuart knew that there was no longevity in it because he was more than capable of writing lyrics – the way that he wanted a song to be heard and a story to be told. He had a different way of telling a story.'

'Stuart was impressed with Richard's image,' says Bill. 'He was very talented as a wordsmith. Even from people of a more mature age, you would think, "How could you write that?" Richard would say, "Take from it what you think it means", but it's difficult. A lot of the stuff you think, "What was he on about there?" but it was also impressive because it wasn't all your usual clichéd stuff.'

As the songwriting partnership took off, the bond between Stuart and Richard drove a wedge between Adamson and his old pal Bill. 'Stuart was obviously impressed with Richard,' says Bill. 'That drew me a little further away from him, which was unfortunate. Richard and I are different breeds. Richard had a vision of what he wanted to do and it wasn't something I'd ever thought about – to be "a somebody" and be down in the Smoke – and Stuart wasn't that way inclined either.'

Bill got a job as a Dutch elm disease inspector, going around forests looking for trees infected with the disease, and he got a van as part of the job – very handy. Bill, Stuart, Richard and a guy called Douglas Gregory all rented a flat in Cowdenbeath above the Junction Bar.

'This became Skids Central,' says Clive. 'Stuart also quit his day job around this time to focus on the band.'

'We were quite poor,' says Bill. 'We'd find food wherever we could.

Turnips and potatoes were quite good – there were loads of fields round about us, so you could help yourself a wee bit.'

Sandra had gone to see the Skids at the Kinema Ballroom, as a guest of Jobson, on what was probably 22 September 1977 – the band's sixth gig. 'I didn't go to the Belleville,' she says. 'The Belleville had a reputation. It was a strip club and a place where hippies went and smoked weed. It was all older, Afghan-wearing folk.'

She can't really remember the Kinema gig itself. 'I do remember a feeling I had at the time, which was: *"Jesus Christ"*. Not in a good way. And I remember thinking that he could really play guitar.'

Afterwards, Jobson introduced her to Stuart. 'I just remember Richard saying, "Stuart, this is Sandra. Sandra, this is Stuart",' she says. 'There was hardly anybody there at the time. And that's how I met Stuart.' They danced to the Bob Marley song, 'Get Up, Stand Up'.

'Sandra was great,' says Jobson. 'She was lovely, very attractive, switched on to music. It was an era where women could become your mates. That was a new thing that was happening for all of us. I think, for Stuart, it was a thunderbolt.'

Sandra doesn't remember it that way. 'It wisnae full-on or anything,' she says. She was concentrating on her dancing and had reservations about the punk scene. 'I didn't want it to affect my dancing. I didn't want to get immersed in anything, so I was quite guarded. But I did see him quite often. We went out until we thought, "Oh, that's us steady then." It just naturally happens, doesn't it?'

From the outside, it looked like they were instantly smitten. 'Stuart fell completely in love with Sandra,' says Bill. 'We were still young – she was just his girlfriend – but he was happy and he could see a future.'

For Jobson, this serious relationship was another sign that he and Stuart were on different wavelengths. 'It seemed to me that Stuart was always searching for something ... *grown-up*. There was something a little bit old-fashioned about it. You know, like, "I want stuff that my parents would have wanted."'

When they started going steady, Sandra – Stuart called her 'D', because her second name was Davidson – would go round to Stuart's house in Crossgates, or he would come to hers. He would practise guitar and she would practise her Highland dancing – and all the while he was writing songs. And some of those songs had familiar phrasings.

'I had a practice tape,' she says. 'It was a piper called Willie Law. He was just the best to dance to.'

While Sandra was practising in the bedroom, Stuart would be next door practising guitar – but then he might wander into Sandra's room, guitar in hand, and play along with Willie Law. 'He would start playing – or trying to play – some of the riffs and melodies,' says Sandra. 'He would have a laugh and play along.'

A lot of creativity begins with playfulness like this – people messing around and then stumbling across something that's actually really good. 'Or developing it from one thing to something else that you didn't expect,' says Sandra. 'That's what happened there.'

Big Country would later get tired of hearing the same old remarks about 'bagpipe guitars', but the sound of Willie Law's pipes echoed in Stuart's guitar style for years afterwards.

Sandra was a wider influence. She was driven and dedicated, and she wasn't a big fan of the Skids' music to begin with. 'I wasn't that impressed by the songs,' she says. 'I didnae feel that they were *structured*. I mean, I know punk isnae that structured, but when you heard the Clash, the way they wrote a song ... I didnae feel the Skids' early songs would have crossed over anywhere. But you could see the potential was there.

'I wasnae everybody's cup of tea,' she says, 'because I didn't give a shit about what I said to who and I didnae care if they liked me or not. If you pissed me off or I didnae like what you were doing, or I thought you wurnae of any value, I wasnae interested.'

Dancing at a competitive level had taught her a lot about what it takes to make it. 'I guess that comes from having a goal as a youngster, setting your objectives and knowing the amount of work it takes to get there. To know that at an early age is quite unique. If I found that there was complacency anywhere, I wouldnae be long in saying so.

'I can remember thinking, 'Test Tube Babies'? I found that a bit naive, even though it wasnae. I just felt it wasnae going anywhere. And my opinion was, if you put in all this effort, and you know where you want to go, then it has to be *better* than this.'

She would say as much to Stuart. Did he agree? 'Well, he could only write what he felt. There was nothing contrived about him at all. So you were battling my sensibility against his. It was his thing and he had to do it the way he felt. Any art – you do it the way you feel. Every dancer's different, every artist's different. They cannae explain how they do something. So it was just passing comments. But it was noted.'

The band continued to draw bigger and bigger crowds. The Sex Pistols were supposed to play Burntisland Half Circle in Fife, but it fell through and became a Skids gig. The venue was full.

Scottish crime novelist Ian Rankin was two years younger than Stuart Adamson and had gone to the same school: Beath High School in Cowdenbeath. 'Ian Rankin talks about the Skids being his favourite band,' says Clive. 'One time the Skids were playing the Station Hotel in Kirkcaldy, February or March, just before the band went to London.

'They were playing upstairs and the place was heaving. Downstairs in the hotel, they had these massive glass windows and they were *buckling* – just from the pressure from the floor above. There were these guys afterwards in white boiler suits, running after Stuart, wanting to talk to him. That was Ian Rankin and his friends.'

Bruce Watson would follow the Skids, sometimes helping Clive load in gear. He had another connection: Sandra's brother Raymond was the bass player in Bruce's band the Delinquents.

'My mate was called Raymond Davidson,' he says. 'Stuart was going out with Sandra Davidson. I'd been at school with them since primary.'

The Skids were playing somewhere local and Bruce asked if the Delinquents could support. 'Aye, nae problem, just turn up. You can use our drum kit as well if you want.' So the Delinquents became the support band for the Skids locally. If they went across to Edinburgh, it'd be: 'What are you daein' tonight? We need a support band.'

'Initially,' says Clive, 'there was only six of us – the band, me and Pano. But we realised that we needed some cash. The band needed some better instruments – specifically, Tam and Bill. So Pano approached Sandy Muir.'

Sandy Muir owned the record and music shop in Dunfermline where Bruce had bought his first red guitar. He was a local entrepreneur who saw money in punk: it had boosted record sales and brought kids back into his shop again. Sandy thought that a successful local band would be good for Dunfermline. By February and March of '78, it was decided that Sandy would manage the band while Pano would manage tours and get gigs.

'Sandy was in his mid-thirties,' says Clive, 'but you would have thought he was mid-fifties, the way he thought. He was very Scottish middle class. A touch of Edinburgh about him. Very straight, more of a banker. Sandy wore a suit all the time. He thought he was going to be Scotland's Brian Epstein. Not Malcolm McLaren – Brian Epstein. But, y'know, I loved him. Richard doesn't have many kind words to say about Sandy, which is a shame because I think Sandy actually tried hard to be a good manager.'

'We thought Sandy Muir should do the job because he had a [Reliant] Scimitar,' says Jobson. 'Full stop. Because he had this *car*. I mean, remember, I was younger than Stuart and Bill, so when it came to making these decisions, I always leaned on the older people. I thought that because they'd been in a band before, they had more experience. But none of us had any experience. We were making it up on a daily basis.'

The next step was to release a record, so Sandy called his mate Bruce Findlay for advice. Bruce ran a chain of record shops and had released records by the Valves and the Zones on his own record label, Zoom. Maybe, thought Sandy, he could release the debut single from the Skids. Findlay – who would go on to manage Simple Minds – advised him to release it himself. The band and Pano already had the concept and name for a label – No Bad Records – and its first and only release would be a three-track EP with the lead track, 'Charles'.

'Charles' was a step up from the simple punk songs they'd been writing. Lyrically, it took the social realism of Adamson's earlier lyrics and added a dystopian sci-fi twist. 'The other stuff was kind of clichéd,' says Jobson. '"All over the country, there's a growing fear/Of people growing up" – all that stuff. But "Charles" – those are amazing lyrics. "Charles" is a masterpiece of his writing.'

In interviews at the time, Stuart referenced George Orwell and J.G. Ballard as inspirations. Like the work of those writers, 'Charles' envisages a nightmarish future where people get so lost in their work that they become automated and mechanised: 'Charles got a job in a factory/Drilling sheet metal from six 'til three ... Got lost in his task quite needlessly.'

Soon Charles' brain is a plastic box and he can't eat lunch with his metal hands. The transformation gets more and more extreme: 'Next when I saw him, his face was gone/A stainless steel spine now instead of bone.' When Charles' wife complains to his employers that she has 'kids to keep', 'They gave her the scrap price of his machine/Last weekend Charles became obsolete.'

'It's about how people leave school at sixteen,' Stuart told Dunfermline fanzine *Kingdom Come*. 'You go to work in a factory, do a trade and you're a machine-man all your life. You're working away on these machines – before you know it, you suddenly become a total moron – you're just another part of the machine.

'I know Ultravox! have this [song] "I Want To Be A Machine", but it's not "I *want* to be a machine" – people actually get turned into machines in a factory. "We can earn so much bonus if we put more into our work." The guys would be just as well being a fucking machine, they're so much involved in what they're doing in the factory.'

The music is rigid, automated, with Tam Kellichan's hi-hat pumping like a piston. So far, so new wave. As Stuart said, bands like Ultravox! were already exploring the idea of people as automatons, with robotic emotionless music. The beauty of 'Charles' lay between verses, where the chorus would normally be. There, Adamson's guitar opens the song up with a major chord melody that seems to hint at the human struggle beneath. When Charles' story reaches its end, Stuart brings the song to a close with a grand crescendo. And, just two minutes long, 'Charles' was as economical as it was original.

John Peel played it on the radio. Things started to happen.

In February, Wreckless Eric played the Kinema Ballroom with the Skids opening. He was drunk, the crowd booed him and he was drowned out to shouts of 'Skids! Skids! Skids!'

'You could just see this momentum building up,' says Clive. At one point, Pano disappeared for a weekend. When he came back he said, 'I've got it. The Stranglers are doing some secret gigs in Scotland. They're doing one in Falkirk, at the Maniqui, and one at Clouds in Edinburgh.'

Pano had camped out in Edinburgh for three days to make the connections. The Skids had the support slots.

'All I can remember,' says Stranglers bassist Jean-Jacques 'JJ' Burnel, 'is that the Stranglers wanted to do some warm-up gigs before a major UK tour. Our profile was such that we were able to do gigs that only a few people would know about and they would still sell out by word of mouth. The band on before us was the Skids. And I happened to be on the side of the stage and I thought they were fantastic.'

'We supported the Stranglers at Clouds in Edinburgh,' says Bill, 'and JJ Burnel let me use his gear. I had a wee Selmer amp or something and JJ was like, "Nah, just plug into mine." Now, that doesn't normally happen. It was great and obviously we made an impression.'

Afterwards, JJ told the band that he'd like to be involved if the Skids were doing any recording. 'It was about the songwriting, for me,' says Burnel. 'It kept me interested. Everyone wanted to be like everyone else at the time, instead of finding their own voice. There was a bandwagon and the majority of bands wanted to be like what they were seeing on the front covers of the music press. And most of the time, it wasn't us: It was the Pistols and the Clash and bands like that.

'That whole council estate punk thing – that had to be sung about, for sure. All that had to be documented in song and in the zeitgeist. But the

Stranglers had a bit of a broader palette to choose from. We didn't hide the fact that we'd been lucky enough to get a half-decent education.'

Jean-Jacques Burnel was born in London but had French parents. The Skids felt more *European*. 'I had international connections, being a fucking frog in the UK, so y'know, I liked the Skids and their sort of more expansive *weltanschauung*. And the songs stood up.

'I was sufficiently enthusiastic about them that I mentioned it to Ian Grant, who was managing us at the time, and to Alan Edwards, who was doing our press, and I arranged for the Skids to play in London – at what you would call now a showcase.'

The Skids were headed to London in April for gigs at the Rochester Castle, the Red Cow, the Hope and Anchor and the Nashville Rooms.

In the February issue of *Kingdom Come*, Stuart and Richard were asked about the dynamics between the band members.

'Bill, to me, is a friend,' said Stuart, 'I've known him since the school. Thomas is great 'cos he's just fuckin' crazy. Thomas just doesn't give a fuck. He gives 150 per cent every time we play.'

He and Jobson, on the other hand, weren't nearly so close.

'Me and Richard don't really communicate on a street level,' said Stuart. 'We don't think, "Yeah, we'll go down to the pub and get mortal and have a good laugh." But, basically, we have the same ideas about songwriting and things like that … We communicate on a songwriting level, that's about all.'

'It's more of an association than a friendship,' said Richard.

'It's not a friendship,' said Stuart. 'Richard won't ever have friends. I think he'll commit suicide eventually.'

4
So High and So Wild

Drug busts at Phun City. Selling psilocybin.
How hair length changed the world.
London calling. Setting fire to the stars and stripes

The first time that Ian Grant got busted was in the days after Phun City, the free festival he helped organise on the outskirts of Worthing in July 1970. Phun City was the brainchild of the music journalist, musician and agitator Mick Farren, along with like-minded souls like Caroline Coon, Jeff Dexter, Sonja Kristina and Ian, who was a rising face on the scene.

The organisers had rented a house and, after the festival, the police turned up to arrest Farren. Mick was down the pub, so they pinched Ian instead. He was crashed out on the floor and woke to a pair of shiny black shoes in his face.

He looked up.

'We got you then,' said the copper.

'I don't think you meant to get *me*,' said Ian.

They nicked him anyway, for possession of cannabis.

The second time Ian Grant got busted was at art college where he helped run 'weekend drug orgies'. They'd have ESP nights: pack the venue out, put strange music on, with people blindfolded and semi-naked. On this particular Saturday, the cops arrived to find Ian selling psilocybin in quid deals. Next thing he knows, Ian Grant is sitting in a police station, tripping off his tits.

The third bust – there were five in all – led to a bit of jail time. It should have sobered him up. When he came out he was fit, having worked out in prison, and was freaked out a little by the music of the time: Alice Cooper's *Love It to Death*, Hawkwind's *In Search of Space*. Everything had become a little bit darker.

Ten days later, he was back inside. 'All I wanted to do is kick back at society,' he says. 'Kick back at my upbringing, kick back at school because I got kicked out – anything but get a real job.'

Ian Grant was born in Lancing in Sussex, just outside Worthing, in 1950. He didn't meet his dad until much later in life. 'The pattern of my life was the same as Eric Clapton's,' he says. Like Clapton, Ian grew up thinking that his mother was actually his sister; all the while, he was being brought up by his grandparents.

His grandparents were good people, he says, but they weren't quite equipped to have a teenage boy in the 1960s. He remembers a significant moment: his sister/mother came home with 'Cumberland Gap', the new single by UK skiffle legend Lonnie Donegan. 'Get that noise off!' said his gran. 'It was the first time I was aware of a generation gap,' he says, 'the first time I was aware of music. I could see something going on between my gran and my mother.'

His grandparents would play brass band music. 'My grandad was Scottish, so it'd be Andy Stewart and Kenneth McKellar – things that would drive me nuts.' When his grandad died in May '67, he says, 'I became free. I could do what I wanted. My style of dress changed, my hair grew, I went out with lots of different girls.'

Freddie Bannister, the man behind Bath Festival, promoted gigs on the south coast every week. 'So on a Thursday night you'd see the Small Faces, Hendrix, Pink Fairies, the Kinks, the Move, everybody.' He saw Cream and the Who at the Brighton Dome and it blew him away. After the Who gig, he got himself a Lambretta 150, with all the trimmings.

'It was a mod scene in Brighton. You had your hair in a mod cut with a parka and your scooter, and as your heroes evolved into dropping acid, or smoking dope, or growing their hair long – like the Who, Small Faces, everybody did – you followed suit.'

'Hair,' he says. 'Hair doesn't mean anything now. You can have short hair, long hair, a Mohican. But in those days, if you had hair over your collar, it was considered long.'

The Beatles, the Stones, the Kinks, Phil May and the Pretty Things … All that hair – it upset people. 'There was that cliché, "You can't tell if it's a boy or a girl." But it gave me something to kick against.

'The Beatles and the Stones – I wouldn't separate them, I don't think one is better than the other – the two of them were the Pied Pipers. They were the people leading the way, musically and everything else.'

A local commune asked him to get involved, purely because Ian had hair like Phil May's and looked the part. The commune was going to see Dave Edmunds' Love Sculpture and the guy who had been doing the lights had run off and joined the Hari Krishnas. They asked Ian to do it instead.

It was the psychedelic liquid lights and Ian took to it like a duck to water. 'I just loved it. I can smell it now.' By the time he was eighteen, he was doing lights for Pink Floyd at Brighton Dome under the name of Crystalline Foetus, helped by a friend of his, a local singer and songwriter called Gerald 'Leo' Sayer. (Yes, *that* Leo Sayer.)

The commune ran nights up on Cissbury Ring, an ancient hill fort first built in 250 BC. 'You'd buy a ticket and the acid tab would be stuck underneath a postage stamp on the ticket,' he says. 'It was so remote, if the cops came you'd see them, 'cos they had to come up the hill. The first time they came they brought dogs, ten of them. We stashed everything. We were all tripping, hanging upside down from the trees like bats. So these cops come with torches and don't know what to do: "Get down from that tree or … [uncertain cop voice] we'll *arrest* you."'

Ian and his friends in the commune would get up at 4 a.m. and nick bread from outside the bread shop, and the fresh fish delivery from the front of the fish shop, before the straights were up. Girls from the local convent school would come round and cook for them, before the police would take them back home and warn their parents about these dangerous hippies.

'We were scoundrels really,' he says.

Ian put on bands. Deep Purple came over from Paris for forty quid in expenses to raise money for their arts club. Then he heard about Phun City from the underground newspaper *International Times*. The cover proclaimed that 'The MC5 are coming to England'. Inside, the report said they were coming to Worthing.

'They can't do that,' he said. 'That's my patch!' A mate said, 'Ring 'em up – see if you can get involved.' The next thing he knew, he was the local organiser. He was there at the grassroots level for Phun City, dealing with the ambulance, fire, all that stuff. Apart from the small matter of being nicked for possession, it was his first real break.

He started calling the offices of Derek Savage and Dai Davies to hustle them for bands for gigs. They ran an agency and represented bands like Gypsy and Blackfoot Sue. Dai had worked at Bowie's management company Mainman during the *Ziggy* and *Aladdin Sane* era.

Ian didn't have a phone, so he'd use a callbox, send handwritten letters or turn up at their doorstep. He was representing a Brighton band called Tonge – who later became the Depressions, under the wing of Hendrix's manager Chas Chandler – and one day Derek Savage said: 'I've got all these American air force bases in Cambridge and Suffolk. They pay really well for unknown bands. I think they'd take a band like you.'

Tonge did the gigs, but Derek didn't pay up. 'He called it "Snatch the cheque",' says Ian. 'Snatch the cheque – get it first.'

So again, he hassled them: rang their offices, wrote letters, turned up at their door. Eventually, Derek said: 'Do you fancy working in London? We need a hustler like you.' And that was it. Ian had met a woman called Debbie just the month before. He said, 'I'm going to London. Will you come?' and amazingly she said yes. (Debbie became his wife – they're still married now.)

Derek and Dai formed an agency called Albion in June 1975 and Ian became an equal partner in September that year. Albion booked the bands for the Nashville Rooms in Kensington and managed a band called Roogalator – soon, they added other London venues like the Red Cow and the Hope and Anchor to their roster.

Derek asked Ian to go down to the Nashville to see a band. 'We don't know what to make of them,' he said. 'We think they're taking the piss out of us.' So Ian goes down, walks into the Nashville Rooms and the first person he meets is Brighton boy Dave Greenfield. 'What are you doing here?' says Ian. Dave had been in bands that Ian had put on in Brighton. He says, 'I'm in the band.'

The band were the Stranglers. It became Ian's job to get them gigs.

It was 1975. The Stranglers had formed the year before as the Guildford Stranglers. Drummer Brian Duffy, aka Jet Black, was a bit older than the others and owned an off-licence in Guildford, along with a fleet of ice cream vans. For a while, the Stranglers would drive to gigs in an ice cream van.

'I just hit it off with them,' says Ian. 'Hugh [Cornwell, singer/guitarist] and Dave [keyboards] were aging hippies. They were such an incongruous bunch. Jet was thirty-seven then.' That was *ancient*.

The pub rock scene was thriving. Pub rock served as an antidote to the flash of glam and the pretension of progressive rock. The bands dressed down – compared to the heroes of glam and prog, they were relatable – and they played rock 'n' roll, rhythm and blues, country and, regrettably, funk. Dr Feelgood, Kilburn and the High Roads, Brinsley Schwarz, the 101'ers, Eddie and the Hot Rods – they laid the ground for punk and Ian Grant was right in the thick of it. The Sex Pistols played three gigs at the Nashville in April 1976. AC/DC's first UK gig was at the Red Cow. The Police, the Pretenders and the Jam all went through their doors.

Albion Management had the Stranglers, 999 and Roogalator, while the Albion Agency represented the Jam, the 101'ers and Eddie and the Hot Rods. 'We had the Red Cow, the Rock Garden in Covent Garden, the Rock Garden in Middlesbrough. We were building up a network. Frankie Miller – he was our biggest catch. The best gig I booked was at Walthamstow Assembly Hall: the Stranglers, Sex Pistols and Ian Dury.

'Every day was something new. We went to the Speakeasy a lot and you'd see famous musicians. You got to talk to Jeff Beck – he's just standing at the bar. I had conversations with Mitch Mitchell and John Entwistle, them saying, "The Stranglers shouldn't be allowed!" They were anti-punk. It did threaten a lot of people at the time.'

Stranglers bassist Jean-Jacques Burnel remembers hassling the Albion Agency to represent them because of the venues they looked after. 'Our big ambition,' he says, 'was to get a residency in any of those pubs. I remember one night, in our ice cream van, passing the Hope and Anchor and Ian Dury and Kilburn and the High Roads were loading out. We said, "One day that'll be us!" When you're naive and relatively innocent, your ambitions are just one rung at a time. You don't think, "Yeah, we'll be in an arena." Or maybe kids do these days.'

The Stranglers got signed up by record company United Artists, who released their first single in January 1977. 'It was a brilliant time,' says Ian. 'My son was born on 21 January and, on the 28th, "(Get A) Grip", the Stranglers' first single, came out. It didn't chart, but then "Peaches" did in April.'

The band had a reputation of being difficult to deal with. Like, *really* difficult. 'The Stranglers didn't get to me as much as they did other people,' says Ian. 'That was why they liked me. I coped with it, but it was very stressful. Everything you did with the Stranglers was stressful.'

His first international trip with the band was to the Netherlands, for lunch with the president of EMI, their Dutch label. They were all in the record company office, waiting for the president. He arrived and they were making the introductions, when they realised that JJ was nowhere to be found. The president showed them into his office and, as he opened the door, smoke billowed out. They'd found JJ.

'There was an American flag on the wall,' says Ian. 'JJ was totally anti-American because of their presence in Japan, so he set alight to the flag. The flag set fire to the curtains. I can't honestly say that I know what happened next.'

'Well,' says JJ, like it's all perfectly reasonable, 'I mean, you turn up to see the boss of your record company and there's not a European flag, there's not a Dutch flag – there's a stars and stripes. Come on. In a Dutch room? So I've just *accidentally* set fire to it.'

'It was just part of what they were about,' says Ian. 'The press said they were a punk rock band and they weren't – but JJ was more punk than anyone.'

The year 1977 passed by in a blur of smoke and karate kicks, hit singles and sold-out gigs. And then JJ came to Ian. The Stranglers had played Scotland and he'd seen this band he liked called the Skids. 'He said to me, "Can you bring this band down to the Nashville, the Hope and Anchor and the Red Cow? I wanna produce them." So I did. John Peel was there and he gave them a session. Simon Draper came in from Virgin and he signed them. He had other ideas about producers, so JJ didn't get it.'

'I didn't actually make it to the Skids' London shows,' says Burnel. 'I don't know why. I was probably away on tour.'

He was. On 16 March, just weeks before the Skids hit London, the Stranglers played the first date of a month-long North American tour. Ian Grant was with them. JJ was arrested at the very first night at the Act One Club in Philadelphia. 'He kicked a photographer,' says Ian. 'Did a karate kick off the stage – the camera went flying. He can't go to Pennsylvania even now.'

5

Out of Town

The riot in the Glen. A terrible day at Hampden.
Some serious kickings. 'None of us talked
to each other.' Just a boy from up the toon

The Skids arrived in London in April 1978. 'The first gig was at Rochester Castle,' says Clive Ford. 'Peelie turns up and sits with the band, chatting with them forever. Then he goes away and starts speaking to his friends at Virgin.'

DJ John Peel was a fan: he played 'Charles' several times, got the band in for multiple sessions and famously once described Adamson – almost definitely with his tongue in cheek – as 'Scotland's answer to Jimi Hendrix'.

CBS were also interested, so Virgin hurriedly arranged for the Skids to play Satellite City in Glasgow, above the Apollo, with Magazine. 'That was their first gig in Glasgow,' says Clive. 'And they went down a storm.'

The Skids signed for Virgin in May 1978. It was, by all accounts, a horrible deal. 'It was for eight albums, over five years, for a twenty grand advance,' says Clive. 'That was Sandy out of his depth, I think.'

Stuart called JJ Burnel with the news of the Virgin deal. JJ said, 'Don't do it! Not yet. Maybe I can get you a better deal.' But it was already too late. They had signed for Virgin and Virgin wasn't interested in having Burnel, a United Artists signing and notorious firestarter, to produce.

'It was a shame because I wanted to help steer them,' says Burnel. 'I had a connection with the music and with them as people. I was disappointed when they didn't listen to Daddy Burnel's advice.'

Stay Alive

'Sandy Muir was a lovely man,' says Bill, 'but he was out of his depth a little. I mean, the record contract that we signed with Virgin – we should have had proper management and legal representatives advising and negotiating. Eight albums over five years. Think about that.'

It's an old story. Record companies come along when you're at your most desperate. You've been beavering away, building audiences, writing songs, improving your live performance – all the time dreaming about making the big time. And then along comes a guy with a cheque book and the keys to the kingdom. You'll sign anything – and they know it. A little voice in your head is saying, *How bad can it be? We've got a record deal!*

'We signed it as quick as we could get our hands on the pens,' Stuart told the *NME* later. 'We were just young boys down from Scotland, not expecting anything, and to come by a record deal was like being conquering heroes returning home with the FA Cup.'

'At the time, they were giving us advances to pay for recording and touring and instruments,' says Bill. 'You have to remember we were still young. I mean, Stuart was maybe nineteen. So you're getting money to tour and make albums and have a bit of a laugh. So we were okay with it. But, on reflection, we didn't really have management. Sandy just wasn't experienced enough.'

'None of us knew any better,' says Clive. 'It just moved so fast, you know. I wished the band had slowed down a bit. I wish they'd had another album out before [debut LP] *Scared to Dance* that captured all the early stuff.'

In May, the band supported the Stranglers at the Glasgow Apollo. Jobson remembers it as 'one of the most violent gigs I've ever been to in my life'. The Apollo bouncers were notoriously heavy-handed: they weren't professional security guys but local heavies who were getting some extra dosh and enjoyed beating people up.

When two fans tried to get up on the stage, the bouncers laid into them. Singer Hugh Cornwell wasn't having it. 'Hugh, like an idiot, saw the bouncers pull them away and he said, "Put the lights on the bouncers" and he slagged them off,' says Ian Grant.

After the show, a load of security guys were waiting for them. Hugh was kicked down the stairs.

Joe Seabrook, who later became the minder for both Keith Richards and Stuart Adamson, was doing security for the Stranglers. He didn't like the look of the situation and advised them to stay in the dressing room.

'I'm not staying here,' says JJ. 'I'm going to the bus.'

So JJ walked out and confronted the bouncers: 'Right,' he said. 'I'll fight you all – *but one at a time.*'

The bouncers couldn't believe it. No one took him up on the offer. 'They were just open-mouthed,' says Ian. JJ walked them out and no one touched them.

The weekend ended with JJ and Jet in the cells at Glasgow Central Station. 'It was a Saturday night in Glasgow,' says JJ. 'People were being dragged in, blood all over the place – they'd been beaten up or been in fights. It was quite memorable. I mean, we were used to violence but not on that scale.'

It was a violent time. The Skids played two benefits for the Chilean Defence League. The first was their second-ever gig in '77, the other was in the summer of '78.

'And '78,' says Clive, 'was a bit of a disaster.'

'My father was in the coalminers' union,' says Jobson, 'and he was connected to the Communist Party. Through his contacts, younger members of the Communist Party asked us if we would do a gig for Chilean refugees.

'Living in the east of Scotland at that time was a little bit like living in East Germany,' he says. 'It was like a socialist republic. You were indoctrinated with socialism, so you really believed in it. We got on the stage and I was proud as punch. It was packed. Bruce Watson was there.'

The gig was organised by the Socialist Workers Party of Scotland and they asked just one thing of the Skids: Don't play the song 'Contusion'.

'I think Richard thought of "Contusion" as an anti-authoritarian song,' says Clive, 'but it was more of an anti-communist song. Not pro anything else, just anti-that. So the organisers were aware of the subject matter of this song and they had told Pano, quite firmly, to tell the band not to play "Contusion". But Pano didn't tell the band. So they played it.'

Stay Alive

'They didn't actually appreciate what it was about,' says Bill. 'So, of course, we just ignored them. And they pulled the plug. So then there was a bit of a disagreement, shall we say, between us, them and the audience.'

'It was a hot day,' says Richard. 'Stuart looked a wee bit like Sid Vicious – he had his hair a bit like Sid and he'd taken his top off and he's a skinny guy. I was wearing a dinner suit with a collar, I think. My hair was black and white, like a ferret. Stuart went to the mic and said to the audience, "If this was a communist country, you wouldn't be allowed to watch a band like us." That was it. *Zoooompt!* Power pulled. Punches flying. Guys coming in from side of stage. *Big guys.*'

'There were glasses flying,' says Tam. 'Proper pint glasses landing on the stage. The polis were there and they were fighting with the crowd and trying to get us off stage. I'm playing away. I'm like, "Nah, I'm no' fuckin' stoapin'." Next thing he knows, there's a policeman either side of him, hauling him off the drum kit.

The 'riot at the Glen' prepares to kick off.
Image courtesy of Clive Ford

The Chilean Defence League riot cost Pano his job. The organisers had asked him to tell the band not to play 'Contusion' and he hadn't.

A week after the gig, Pano and Clive turned up for rehearsals and the band were already there. They sacked Pano and read Clive the riot act. 'That's really when the dynamic changed,' says Clive. 'It wasn't just a local band having a laugh anymore. They were signed to Virgin Records and they had to make things happen.'

One day, Sandy called a band meeting.

'Boys,' he says, 'you're going on a thirty-eight-date tour.'

'Who wi'?'

'The Stranglers.'

'You're fuckin' shittin' me,' said Tam.

Tam was not looking forward to seeing the Stranglers again. There had been an incident, back when the Skids had supported them in Edinburgh. At that gig, the Skids' changing room was literally a toilet. They had walked out of it and past the headliners' dressing room when they noticed the door was open and unguarded.

'Let's have a wee look in here,' said Tam.

Inside were six tables covered in free beers, sausage rolls, sandwiches, the fuckin' lot. Tam turned to everyone. 'Shut the door,' he said.

He cracked open a beer and stuffed a sausage roll in his gob. 'Look,' he said, 'we'll never see these guys again! Come on, let's get stuck in!'

So the cheeky wee Skids had a feast. They ate the Stranglers' food and drank their beer. And when they were done? 'We shut the door and fucked off.'

But now they were about to go on the road with the Stranglers and, more to the point, the Finchley Boys. The Finchley Boys were a crew of hardnuts who had joined the Stranglers' road crew and acted as their personal security. Maybe they were more than that. 'The Finchley Boys were the Stranglers' private army,' says Ian Grant. 'JJ was into Yukio Mishima, the Japanese poet, and he had his own private army. So JJ was mimicking him.'

The tour kicked off in Lancaster. On the drive down, they were shitting it:

'The boys were all saying, "Fucking hell! What aboot Edinburgh?"' But Tam had a cunning plan: they'd get to the venue early, soundcheck before the Stranglers arrived and they wouldn't even *see* them. Easy. But mid-soundcheck, they looked up: all four Stranglers were standing in front of the stage, watching.

'C'mere,' said Jean-Jacques Burnel. 'I want a word with you.' He beckoned for them to follow and took the Skids into the heart of the venue, upstairs, through corridor after corridor.

They were all thinking the same thing: 'We're gonna get a *doin*.'

Somewhere in the heart of the venue, JJ stopped. 'Do you remember Edinburgh?' he said. The Skids played dumb: 'Aye, I mean, y'know, *kindae*. It was a good gig, eh?'

'"I'll tell you one thing now,' said JJ. 'See that dressing room there? That's *your* dressing room. This one here? That's *our* dressing room.

'And you've got exactly the same as we had in Edinburgh.'

The Stranglers had ensured that, throughout the whole tour, the Skids had exactly the same treatment as them: the same-sized dressing room, the same amount of beers and food. 'Whatever they had, we had,' says Tam. 'Fantastic guys.'

The following year, at the Loch Lomond Rock Festival in May '79, where the Stranglers were the headliners, the Skids were playing 'The Saints are Coming' when explosions rocked the stage.

'I just about died,' says Tam. 'Almost fell aff the drum kit.'

Fireworks were exploding over their heads. 'Hugh Cornwell and Jean-Jacques Burnel had said to their pyrotechnics guy: "Light them up."'

To Tam, the Stranglers were a vision of what a band could be like: fair. All-for-one-and-one-for-all. 'Those guys were together for years,' he says. 'They shared everything they had. Split the money. That's the kind of band I wanted to be in – but I never got there.'

The Stranglers tour started in September and the Skids could feel the momentum building. 'I can always remember it,' says Clive Ford. 'Cardiff, on the Stranglers' Black and White Tour, '78. The Skids getting shouted back for an encore. It was the first time.'

Clive remembers going in the dressing room.

'Are you going back out there?'

'Whit ur ye talkin' aboot?'

'That noise is for *you*!'

The band didn't believe it. They didn't move.

So Clive went out on stage: 'Who wants more of the Skids?' The crowd went nuts.

Reluctantly, the band went back on. As Bill Simpson walked past Clive, he looked at him and said one word: 'Wanker.' Clive laughs at the memory: 'They had never done an encore up to that point.'

'Stranglers fans were pretty broad-minded,' says Burnel. 'I mean, they didn't tolerate certain things, and they let people know, but I think on the whole they thought the Skids were okay.'

In Bridlington, in East Yorkshire, there was an exception. A few guys in the audience heckled the Skids – shouting 'Get off! We want the Stranglers!', throwing cans and bottles, that kinda thing. After the gig, the band were outside chatting when the hecklers turned up.

'We started walking back to the hotel,' says Bill, 'and all of a sudden these guys pounced on us. There was a bit of a mad melee – a few fists and kicks and aw the rest of it – and I ended up on the ground getting kicked. And next thing I know, the middle finger of my left hand was broken.'

(I tell JJ Burnel this story, about Bill being beaten up by Stranglers fans. 'Well,' he says drily, 'he obviously deserved it.')

'It's still out of joint,' says Bill. 'It's always caused me a problem as a bass player. Well, that's my excuse, anyway.' They had to cancel some dates in Scotland as a result, and reached out to Bruce Watson's band to fill-in for the Dunfermline date.

'They said, "Do you want a support slot with the Stranglers?"' says Bruce. 'I was like, "Yep, I'm up for that." So I did a half-shift at the dockyard and went and set up the gear.'

The Skids' first single for Virgin was 'Sweet Suburbia'. 'I hated it,' says Jobson. 'It's just fake. Stuart was trying to write the kind of lyrics that

I wrote. He was the Ken Loach version and I was doing something entirely fuckin' weird and out there.'

Lyrically, the song is a weird mix of social realism and nihilistic poetry: people are stuck in a soulless 'hot dog life' with 'concrete days and white electric lights'. Under it all, 'remnants of the ancient heart remain', but they're destined just to 'live and live and live' and 'mate and mate and mate' and 'die and die and die'.

'Stuart's usual stuff was much more about social-realist observations of Glenrothes, these new towns and what was happening politically, and the kind of economics at the time, whereas my stuff was a little bit more like "What is this? What does it mean?" And, of course, you could throw in the word "pretentious" or whatever, but he liked it. So he had a go.'

Sonically, though, 'Sweet Suburbia' was a step forward. Paired with producer David Batchelor, the Skids sounded tight and commercial, hooky and melodic. 'I love the riff,' says Jobson. 'It was the first time I think we had ever used that open-string guitar thing. The Skids play in a different tuning, a low tuning. Everyone always thought it was because I couldn't hit the notes, but it's because Stuart wanted that drone-y effect. Initially, we didn't tune like that, but we did by the time of "Sweet Suburbia", and then we carried that into "Of One Skin".'

Stuart had started to use drone strings, a technique where you leave a lower string open and unfretted but hit it consistently so that it rings out. Often used in folk music, Jimmy Page was famous for using it in Led Zeppelin. It's also a feature of bagpipe playing. Bagpipes have at least one pipe that is not played and sounds one consistent note throughout, with melodies played over the top.

'We always played and recorded a tone lower,' says Bill Simpson. 'We played in a D tone, which gives it a lower, bassier feel. That was to assist with Richard and his vocals 'cos he was struggling to reach the higher end. When someone picks up a standard-tuned guitar and tries to play a Skids song, it's difficult. Even "Into the Valley" – it's an octave lower.'

Bruce Watson was watching and learning. 'The punk rock thing was always barre chords, but Stuart was using drone strings and I thought that was kind of amazing. I mean, he nicked it aff Jimmy Page anyway.'

Bruce actually reviewed 'Sweet Suburbia' for *Kingdom Come*: 'Not as good as they used to do it,' he said, 'far better live. "Open Sound" is far better, [it] doesn't have any weird solos like "Sweet Suburbia".'

'Open Sound' was the B-side. Inspired by a village on the outskirts of Newcastle called Wideopen (often misspelled as two words: Wide Open), Stuart wrote the words on his guitar. The phrases 'wide open' and 'open sound' resonated with his vision for the band. He wanted something unfettered by genre definitions, something big and panoramic. Just as bands from London and the Midlands were incorporating the influences of Caribbean music into their sound – ska, reggae and dub – so the drone strings and the down-tuning of the Skids combined to make a sound that was uniquely Scottish, without being twee or corny.

'No one knows of what we mean,' go the lyrics to 'Open Sound'. 'Or understand of what we do/Don't look for the easy tone/One way just restricts our view ... Open sound/That's how we are.'

Virgin released the single on white vinyl, with a sticker that said: 'This white vinyl record has a weird gimmick. You'll like it.' It was a confusing marketing message from a company known for its unorthodox promo.

In an interview with *Trouser Press* in 1979, Virgin bosses Richard Branson and Simon Draper talked about their company's fondness for coloured vinyl and gimmicks. 'We found that people are very oriented toward the look of things,' said Draper, 'and if we want to break someone – get a new single in the charts – we should give our bands an edge. I believe that packaging is important – you have to make it all hang together ... You've got to actually force those people's hands.'

'Sweet Suburbia''s gimmick was that it was on white vinyl – and you might like it. According to Draper, the single sold 40,000 copies. It went to number 70 in the UK charts.

'Sweet Suburbia' was followed in October by *Wide Open*, a four-track EP led by 'The Saints are Coming', and including 'Of One Skin', 'Night and Day' and 'Contusion'. It was released on red vinyl, with the Virgin-approved sleeve featuring a Jobson-alike character with his eyes and mouth wide open. The band hated the sleeve but, musically, it was another step forward. 'The Saints are Coming' was urgent and anthemic, tough and tender, with a melancholic intro and huge chorus.

'"The Saints are Coming" is the fastest song I've ever played,' says Tam. When it was coming up in the set he would be dreading it. 'I was going, "Fuckin' hell man. I've got to be all over this drum kit like a fuckin spider!"'

'Of One Skin' had an explosive intro and an unexpected stop-start dynamic. While the music was identifiably punk or new wave, any last vestiges of Eddie and the Hot Rods-style R&B had gone. This was something new and original, light years away from the identikit Clash-alikes of the time.

'The Saints are Coming' went to number 48 in the UK charts and the band appeared on *Top of the Pops*. In November they toured across the UK as support to their Virgin label-mates XTC.

Like 'Sweet Suburbia', the *Wide Open* EP was produced by Dave Batchelor. Batchelor hadn't been Virgin's first choice as producer. The label had put them in the studio to record demos with Gong's Mike Howlett. 'Richard and Simon at Virgin were using all their prog rock friends,' says Clive, 'giving them new gigs. Hence Steve Hillage producing Simple Minds.' To be fair, Howlett had been in Strontium 90 with Sting, Andy Summers and Stewart Copeland, pre-Police, and he went on to produce records by the Revillos, Gang of Four and the Alarm, as well as hits like 'Echo Beach' for Martha and the Muffins and 'Enola Gay' for OMD.

But unfortunately for Mike Howlett, he was in the studio with the Skids on the fateful day of 20 May 1978.

On that day, Scotland's national football team played England at Hampden Park in Glasgow. It was Scotland's last match before the 1978 World Cup finals and confidence was running high. England had failed to qualify for the second time in a row, while Scotland had knocked out reigning European champions Czechoslovakia on their route to the finals in Argentina.

It was obvious: Scotland were going to win the World Cup.

Out of Town

On 20 May, at home in Hampden, the Scots dominated play for the entire match but couldn't score. England bagged a goal in the 83rd minute and won 1–0. The band caught the match highlights on a break from recording and, on their return to the studio, took their frustrations out on the nearest Englishman: Howlett.

'Anything he suggested,' says Clive Ford, 'the band disagreed with.' The sessions ground to a halt and the band got on a train back home.

Fuck youse all!

Or at least that's the way the Skids have told the story for years. The truth, thinks Clive Ford, is a little less comical. 'When Stuart saw the Scotland result, he was just pissed off,' says Clive. 'The rest of the band too, but it really got to Stuart. When we got back to the studio, he was just moody and didn't want to be there.'

The football was only an excuse. 'In hindsight, I think Stuart wasn't really happy with the recording and how the session was going anyway, and now his mood allowed him to be vocal about it. It's funnier to say that the band got all pissed off because of the result of the game,' says Clive, 'but really it was because there wasn't any connection with the producer and the band in the first place.'

There was an extra tension. 'Stuart was really adamant about being able to reproduce the recorded versions in a live setting,' he says. 'Up to this point, all of the Skids songs were written for live performance. This was the first time the band were putting ideas down on tape before they had put them through their paces. It was definitely a learning curve.'

Scotsman David Batchelor wasn't going to fall out with the band over a football result. Batchelor had produced Nazareth's debut album and all of the classic Sensational Alex Harvey Band albums – in fact, he'd been frontman for Tear Gas, the pre-Alex Harvey version of the band. 'Simon Draper asked me which frontmen I loved,' says Jobson, 'and I said Iggy Pop and Alex Harvey. So the idea that we could work with Alex's producer, a Scottish guy, all made sense. But him and Stuart clashed pretty early on.'

Virgin sent Dave Batchelor a cassette. 'I loved it,' says Batchelor. 'The Skids just stuck out a mile. It was *more* than punk. There was a musicality to it, there was a rhythm, there was a technique, there was a skill.'

But it was still a little bit raw. 'Dave Batchelor reined them in,' says Clive. 'I can remember the first time Dave met the band. He came up to Dunfermline and he was in the rehearsal room, and he literally had been there less than five minutes. The band were doing "Into the Valley" and he goes: "Hold on a minute. Can I make a couple of suggestions?" And he just chopped the song around. And it was for *the better*.'

'The opening riff could be a four-cycle riff,' says Dave, 'but I took one of them out and we made it a three-cycle riff. The effect was that it just tore you into the next bit.'

'Into the Valley' was a hit single in waiting. Opening with a reverberating bassline and a rabble-rousing chorus, it was a perfect three-minute punk-pop song that sounded uniquely Scottish.

'An element of it was the kind of chords that Stuart used,' says Batchelor. 'In a chord, you have your major triad – your three obvious harmonies – but he very rarely had a third in there. It was all your root, your four or your five, and your octave. He carried that through in his chord changes, his riffs and his melodies. They would never go to that major third at all. It just creates a mood – there's a tonality to it.'

The Adamson/Jobson songwriting team was starting to hit its stride. 'Into the Valley', 'The Saints are Coming', 'Of One Skin': they were exciting punk rock songs with a huge wide open sound and big choruses. And if you couldn't always decipher the lyrics, they were nevertheless heartfelt and full of meaning.

'All of the early lyrics that I wrote – "Melancholy Soldiers", "Into the Valley", "The Saints are Coming" – were all about my mates,' says Jobson. 'Fife was a great recruiting ground for [Scottish infantry battalion] the Black Watch. I would never join 'cos I'm from an Irish Catholic background and, after Bloody Sunday and stuff, there was just no way you'd join the British Army – they were seen as some fuckin' dreadful imperialist force. But my mates at the time were facing either the Rosyth dockyard or the mines or unemployment, so the army recruited pretty hardcore in the estates that we lived in.

'A lot of my mates joined up to become car mechanics and engineers and, within fifteen-to-twenty weeks, they were in Northern Ireland. "Into the Valley" was about the depersonalisation of these young guys – it was originally called "Depersonalised" – about how they were thrown into the Falls Road and these places. Hell on earth at the time. And when they came back, they were changed – you would be, right? They wanted to be engineers and ended up getting spat on by kids and all that shit. When they came back, they were so bigoted and their attitude towards me changed too, 'cos I was pro-Irish nationalism and that rankled.

'"The Saints are Coming" was about one of my friends who got shot while he was in the army. He'd just had a kid and it was about a kid phoning his father. It was also about the death of my own father. The words were reflections of all that, but rather than do it in straightforward Bruce Springsteen kinda folk-tales, I chose to do it in a slightly different way. It was a time for experimenting.'

In an interview in *Record Mirror*, published in December 1978, Jobson said that he'd never written a 'happy' song. '"Hope and Glory" is about the strife of actually writing a song. It's also about getting up onstage and portraying it, feeling something for the song.'

'I have hope and glory,' go the lyrics, 'Redeeming my life's story/I have hope and glory/Dissolving all of my worry.'

'It's all about imagery,' said Stuart. 'I mean, you take what you want from the lyrics and what's behind them. It's like the lyrics are the drawing and the music's the colouring.'

The words and the subject matter of the songs – like 'Night and Day', a grim tale of a woman involved in a car accident who's then kidnapped and raped – were unsettling, even to the band. 'They make me feel anxious onstage,' said Jobson. 'I hope the audience feel anxious watching' – although even he acknowledged that 'live it's usually nothing to do with words ... It's more reliant on the music and the sound.'

The song 'Integral Plot', he told *Record Mirror* later that year when it felt like the band was falling apart, was about loneliness and backstabbing.

'The majority of my songs are about being lonely, they're all conceptual ... All my songs are about fear.'

He showed the interviewer, Ronnie Gurr, a gap in his mouth left by a missing tooth. 'I'll never get a false tooth in there,' he said, 'because every time I touch that space with my tongue, I remember that there's always someone somewhere waiting to punch you in the puss or kick you in the back of the neck.'

'A lot of the lyrics were about things that were very important to me,' Jobson told Scottish music writer Tim Barr. 'I just dressed them up in metaphor because that's the background we came from. Sentimentality and open agonising would never be accepted.'

To Dave Batchelor and engineer Mick Glossop, the recording of *Scared to Dance* seemed to be going well. Glossop went on to produce Magazine, Public Image Ltd, the Waterboys, Van Morrison and more, but in 1978 he was staff engineer at the Town House Studios in west London and had been drafted in to mix 'Of One Skin'. 'It's one of my favourite tracks of all time,' he says. 'That song is one of the most original pieces of music I've ever heard. It's so unusual, and that's Stuart at the age of, what, twenty?'

Pleased with Glossop's work on 'Of One Skin', Dave Batchelor used him as engineer on *Scared to Dance*. They recorded in Town House Two, nicknamed 'the stone room' because of its stone walls and flagstone floor. 'It was very live-sounding,' says Glossop. 'If you put a drum kit in there, you couldn't stand in the room for more than five seconds. It's where the famous Hugh Padgham drum sound came from.'*

The Skids were creating their own minor miracles in Town House Two. 'You get these magic bands that make a mark,' says Batchelor, 'that are a bit

---

* Peter Gabriel's third solo album was recorded in Town House Two the following year and is often recognised as the birth of the 'gated drum sound' that became one of the signature sounds of the '80s, used most famously on Phil Collins's 1981 single 'In the Air Tonight'. The producer was a rising talent called Steve Lillywhite. He and his engineer Hugh Padgham pushed the compressed drum sound that Lillywhite had been experimenting with on records by Siouxsie and the Banshees and the Psychedelic Furs to its logical conclusion.

special, and so you're inspired to think outside the box. I knew guitars inside out, I knew groove inside out, I knew lyrics. These guys were throwing stuff at me and it was just so refreshing on every level.'

But as the band's chief songwriter and musical director – the guy with the vision – Stuart was finding the compromises expected of him hard to deal with.

'Stuart wanted to keep things as pure as possible,' says Bill, 'to keep the recording as close as possible to what we did live. We only had one guitarist: Stuart. But obviously, when you're in the recording studio, you have to have overdubs and layers of guitars and harmonies. And he just didnae like it.'

'I'd listen to the songs,' says Batchelor, 'and I would just hear a place where Stuart could just embellish or support by doing this or that. I was never aware that he had a problem with that. I would suggest something, and he would come back with an idea – and his guitar parts were always 100 per cent. Fantastic sounds, parts that fitted so well and enhanced the song, big time.'

'It was a very difficult experience for him,' says Richard. 'They were trying to get him to change and he wasn't one for changing. "Why would I want to change the arrangement?" But the whole history of rock and pop is about people changing arrangements, y'know?

'"Into The Valley" wouldn't have been a hit as it stood. Not in a million years. "The Saints are Coming" was also changed quite dramatically. The piano at the beginning was me sitting tinkling and, lo and behold, it became part of the song.

'Stuart hated the overdubs,' says Jobson. 'He was starting to get this feeling that the music industry is just a tawdry, money-spinning capitalist thing that had nothing to do with real people or real creativity. It was a difficult experience. It should have been great fun making that album, and the fun was taken out of it because he was just like, "This is all wrong."'

'I was blown away by the way things were sounding,' says Bill. 'The songs were sounding so full and rich, and I loved all the wee intricate melodies and harmonisations that they were putting together. Dave had worked with the Sensational Alex Harvey Band and Tear Gas – I thought he was a great guy. I loved working with him, so it was a complete shock when Stuart took a kinda hissy fit. He just took off and disappeared. He went away back up to Scotland.'

By all accounts, after being asked by the producer to play a certain way, Stuart offered Batchelor his guitar and said words to the effect of 'If you want it like that, why don't *you* play it?'

And then he got on a train and went back to Scotland.

The question was a valid one: Whose music *is it*, anyway?

Stuart's reaction is not unusual, says Mick Glossop. 'That's a common, and not unexpected, type of reaction that you might get from someone who's unfamiliar with how you make records,' he says. 'But I wasn't really aware of any tensions. I mean, there were no arguments.

'The only sense of angst I ever got from Stuart was that he didn't really like being in London. He wanted to be in Scotland. So there was this sense that he didn't really like being there. And a couple of weeks before Christmas, he disappeared. Or, rather, he didn't show up.'

It left the remaining Skids and Virgin with an unfinished album. 'I remember saying to Richard, "What are we gonna do?"' says Bill. 'None of us were very proficient on the guitar.'

Glossop had the answer. In the room next door was Chris Jenkins, the chief maintenance engineer at the Town House. 'I happened to know that he could play guitar pretty well. The only thing was that Chris was very much a *rock* guitarist.'

The guitar parts already existed on tape as guide reference parts. But they were *Stuart Adamson* parts and occasionally Jenkins was, according to Glossop, prone to 'over-decorating', so they reined him in a little. 'Not only did Chris have to learn the parts, he had to learn how to play them the way Stuart would.'

'Stuart's playing was so unique,' says Batchelor. 'The tonal thing – what I was saying about the roots and fourths and fifths – that's stamped right through all the chord changes, the whole musicality of it. And this guy was just stepping out of it all the time. We worked it out.'

Later, he says, Adamson slagged him off a bit in print. 'Stuart said that he couldn't tell what he'd played and what he hadn't played,' says Dave, 'which I took as a compliment.'

'I can hear Chris's parts on the songs,' says Bill. 'A lot of people can't, but there's a fuzziness on "Calling the Tune", for example – that's Chris. He was just filling in, adding to something that was already there, an octave lower or higher, just to fill out a space. It was fine, really.'

At home in Dunfermline, Stuart heard about all this and did not think it was fine. 'When something didn't go right,' says Sandra, 'the volume that those lungs of his could put out was incredible. He would rant and rave and go on and on about something he wasn't pleased about, about a person that should have done this or that – not generally the band – and then it would be forgotten about.'

The idea of someone else tinkering with his music when he wasn't there was incredible and galling. 'I remember saying to him, "Are you going to allow that?"' says Sandra. '"Are you going to *eat* that?"'

Stuart had his own ideas and he was protective and principled about them. 'He wanted to keep it as pure as possible,' says Sandra. 'He felt that it was compromising the song. It happened later in Big Country, with other producers. He didnae like things mucked about with too much, if it wasnae a great big change or they weren't making it much, much better.'

In Richard Jobson's book, *Into the Valley*, he talks repeatedly about Stuart disappearing throughout the Skids' short career. The book paints a picture of the guitarist as moody and unpredictable, prone to leaving the band in the lurch, disappearing home at the first sign of trouble.

Not everyone agrees. 'I'm gonna touch on the disappearing thing,' says Clive Ford. 'This is one thing that's irked me a little bit, because I never saw him disappearing. I saw him *going back to Dunfermline*. But we *knew* about it. The problem within the Skids was – it wasn't just management – none of us talked to each other. I think it was typical male ego. You did not share your problems. To go back to the six – the band, me and Pano – there were four loners in that group. There was me, there was Pano, there was Stuart and there was Richard. Tam and Willie [Bill] were probably the most grounded of all.'

'I was there from '77 to January of '80,' says Bill, 'and the only time Stuart was away was *Scared to Dance*. We knew he'd gone back up to Scotland. He was going to see Sandra. He just wanted out. "I've had enough, I'm off." And we thought: "What does he mean? Does he mean 'I'm finished'? Or that he just needs to get away for a while?" And that's what it was.'

For a while, though, it really did look like the band were finished. An article by Ronnie Gurr, published in *Record Mirror* on 17 March 1979, captured the drama.

'I don't understand him, simple as that,' Jobson told Gurr. 'I think he's taking his criticisms of the rock business too far. He can't be that weak. I can't see *anybody* being that weak.' Jobson was so livid, his dreams going up in smoke, that he told Gurr that he was 'gonnae bang Adamson' (that is, give him a smack).

A few days later, calmer feelings prevailed and Jobson called Stuart 'the best guitarist around' while sympathising with his views about record companies. 'I think the biggest thing with Virgin has been the degradation of the artistic qualities,' said Jobson. 'We're not just musicians who come out with nice commercial tunes. We're artists. We think about what we do.

'I don't have the same ideas as Stuart because I like to go out and meet people. He's got a chick and I haven't and that's how he [gets over loneliness] because she is his friend. Stuart's quite right of course. He's found what he's looking for. It's just that I've not found anyone.'

In the same feature, Adamson explained that after leaving the Skids, he got 'mortal' one day and ripped up all his Skids posters and sleeves. 'So now I've got an album with no sleeve.'

As part of the story, Gurr published a letter written by Stuart on 4 January. In it, Adamson said that his unhappiness had started back with the band's very first single. 'My personal dissatisfaction began after the release of the super white "Sweet Suburbia". I just wanted to get out. I wanted to get some peace and quiet and rid myself of the disorientation

I was feeling. Meeting people you've known since primary school and not being able to speak to them just about sums that up.'

Feeling alienated when they return home is a common experience to successful working-class artists. You leave your hometown to become successful, deal with people from a different background and try to remain true to yourself. But then you return home a success and your own people look at you with suspicion – 'I suppose you think you're great?' – or admiration. Either way, you're alienated.

'Around about that time, we'd go to Edinburgh and people would recognise him,' says Sandra. 'And that kind of attention didn't sit well with him, because as far as he was concerned, it shouldnae matter. You know, "I'm just a normal human being with all the flaws that go with that, don't think I'm some kind of hero."

'I struggled with it too,' she says. 'I had people looking in my shopping trolley at what I was buying. I thought, "It's just the same thing *you're* buying!"'

Bruce Watson saw first-hand the reception they received locally. 'I loved it,' he says of the Skids' success, 'but they got a lot of abuse.' Bruce played in bands with Richard's brother, Michael Jobson. 'And he used to get some serious kickings just because people would be like "Aw, your big brother was oan the telly, what a wanker." Aw that kindae stuff.'

Michael would wear some of Richard's stage clothes around town and get chased through the streets. 'You got two or three guys jumping a young guy just because he's got a leopard-skin jacket and his brother's on *Top of the Pops*. It's that jealousy thing, y'know?

'Half the toon wants tae slap yer back and the other half wants tae slap yer face. You've no' done anything except for being on the telly.'

'Touring is the biggest pain in the arse ever,' wrote Stuart in the letter published in *Record Mirror*. 'Travelling a hundred miles to play for an hour, sleep, get up, have breakfast, travel, soundcheck, play, sleep, get up, breakfast, travel and so on, ad nauseum.'

Top of the Pops – 'the great white hope of commercial success', he called it – was similarly depressing: 'Waiting around in the TV studios watching the privileged 30 or so *Jackie* readers being herded around in front of minuscule sets. Waiting in turn behind Showaddywaddy to have your plooks [i.e. spots] "covered" up.'

But Stuart's biggest bugbear? 'Listening to people outside the band seriously talking about how to improve your songs with very little regard for how you feel the songs should sound gets depressing after a while.

'But that's how it has to be if you want to be a success. It's just another of the little compromises. Compromises like having good artwork rejected in favour of candy-striped *Carry On* characters with "wide open" eyes because it's better for marketing. A quick massage of your ego – "The tracks are bloody phenomenal!" – and the experience is painlessly completed. Won't get fooled again. I wanna be me and all that.

'It's all up to what the individual wants out of life. If someone wants to make a lot of money, rock 'n' roll is the quickest and easiest way to have a go at it. If you are determined enough, it's possible and there's nothing at all wrong with that. I'd rather just be happy with what I'm doing.

'Record companies are geared towards making money and that's all. If you want the money, grab it with both hands and good luck to you. If you're lucky, you might attain the giddy heights of critical acclaim.

'Artistic control is a joke. Unrestrained rock 'n' roll exists only in the minds of hopeless romantics. Music only exists in the free meals and handouts of high-powered business executives.

'I don't need it, that's all.'

Stuart Adamson wasn't even twenty-one and he'd already walked out of two major label recording sessions and left his band. Before he even made it – before he'd had a hit, let alone tasted real fame – he felt like he'd been chewed up and spat out.

And those coloured vinyl records that Virgin had been using to get their releases in the charts? Stuart explained to Gurr that the band didn't receive royalties for sales of coloured vinyl. And *all* of their Virgin singles – 'Sweet Suburbia', 'Wide Open' and 'Into the Valley' (released in February 1979) – were on coloured vinyl.

'Virgin have the right to sling out the coloured vinyl,' wrote Gurr, 'but, they say, due to the cost, the band can't earn anything until the black copies start selling.

'It seems the group lack sympathetic management ... The official Virgin line reads that the Skids got no royalties on 15,000 copies of "Sweet Suburbia" and will receive half the standard royalty on coloured copies of "Wide Open" and "Into the Valley".'

Has the break from the band helped Adamson get his head straight, asks Gurr? 'If anything, it's worse now,' says Stuart. 'I can't even walk around Dunfermline. It's, like, totally disorientating to be looked up at.

'It's nice to be appreciated, but not to be looked up to. It's not me. I'm just a boy from up the toon.'

Sandra and Stuart, backstage, early '80s.

6
A Mansion and a Mercedes

SS bolts. Four yokels. An explosion of YES!
Humping everything in sight.
The mansions and the Mercedes

By the time *Scared to Dance* was released on 23 February 1979, Stuart Adamson was back in the band and the drama was over.

The album's cover art by Russell Mills depicted a lone man, sitting at a table with his head in his hands, in the corner of a room with a flagstone floor just like Town House Two. In his book, Jobson says that the songs on the album were about 'feeling alienated, feeling isolated, feeling that the world's against you'. His working-class roots set him apart from many of the people he was meeting. 'How do you make a move into the arts when they're completely controlled by the class system?'

To him, the man on the sleeve is 'staring at a world passing him by' and trying to work out 'if it's worth jumping on'. It was a dilemma that he was having: 'Do you jump on and have a go? Or jump off before you get found out?'

Like much of the band's later artwork, the finished sleeve helped position the band as something a bit artier than their contemporaries – in the wrong hands, the Skids could have been marketed as rabble-rousing Sham 69 types – and its angsty imagery probably appealed to both of the band's songwriters for similar reasons: Richard Jobson, a young guy with epilepsy, lonely, on the frontline; Stuart Adamson the embattled bandleader and chief creative with the world on his shoulders.

Stay Alive

The one clear direction that Russell Mills had been given concerned the band's logo. 'The Skids logo already existed so I was asked to replicate it,' he says. He redrew it by hand, even though he was unhappy with it. 'The logo's affinity to Nazi insignia concerned me.'

The logo used 'SS bolts' – the same style of 'S's used in the logo for the Schutzstaffel, literally translated as the 'protection squad' and known as the SS, Adolf Hitler's ruthless Aryan private army. Where the sleeve's main image was sophisticated and arty, and confounded any expectations you might have about the Skids, the band's logo smacked of schoolboy immaturity and a childish desire to shock.

There was a lot of it about in the punk era. Joy Division named themselves after Nazi concentration camp brothels in which female prisoners were forced into sexual slavery to reward male collaborators.* After the death of singer Ian Curtis, Joy Division became New Order, 'coincidentally' the Nazi term for their planned redrawing of European boundaries. Famously, Sid Vicious and Siouxsie Sioux wore swastikas, while, more broadly, biker gangs dabbled with Nazi imagery as a symbol of rebellion and non-conformity. To the generation born after the war, Nazi symbolism was forbidden and therefore powerful: if you wanted to wind up the older generation, it was a sure way of doing so.

The 'SS bolts' were also used in the logo of US rock band Kiss, a band whose key members – Paul Stanley and Gene Simmons – are Jewish. In fact, Simmons' mother survived the concentration camps, having watched her own mother go to the gas chambers. To this day, Kiss can't use their regular logo in Germany because of anti-Nazi regulations.

In Britain, the Skids logo didn't cause much of a fuss. It would be used on all their singles and marketing until their next album which, ironically, would have a Nazi controversy all of its own.

---

* They got the name from a book called *House of Dolls* by Ka-Tzetnik 135633, aka Yehiel De-Nur, a Jewish Pole who was imprisoned in Auschwitz. Guitarist Bernard Sumner told Jon Savage that he saw the name in *House of Dolls* and his first thoughts were: 'It's pretty bad taste, but it's quite punk.'

'Into the Valley' came out the week before *Scared to Dance*, entered the UK singles chart at number 50 and climbed steadily, reaching number 10 in March 1979. 'Not bad for four yokels from Dunfermline,' said Jobson.

The B-side was a daft live favourite called 'TV Stars', a roll-call of television personalities and sports stars that culminated in the chorus: 'Albert Tatlock!' Albert was a character in the soap opera *Coronation Street* – a stereotypical grumpy old man.

'"TV Stars" was a muck-around in rehearsal,' says Clive. 'That's all it was and it just evolved. I think one night they threw it in the set and it became a thing. Actually, it became a thing when Jimmy Pursey cited it. At that time, Sham 69 were the spokesmen for the new London punk, and "Into the Valley" came out and Jimmy Pursey was like, "Yeah, but have you heard the B-side, 'TV Stars'? That's *real* working class."'

It became a bit of an albatross around their necks. The Skids would be attempting to make progressive experimental music – and the audience would be shouting, 'Al-bert Tat-lock! Al-bert Tat-lock!'

The Scared to Dance Tour turned the Skids into one of Britain's hottest live bands. 'I'll give you an indication of the impact the band were having,' says Clive Ford. 'On that tour, in January and February of 1979 they were playing 750- to 1,500-capacity clubs: Tiffany's in Edinburgh, Eric's in Liverpool.

'A lot of bands would get a guarantee of 60 per cent of the ticket sales, the promoter gets 40 per cent.' A 'guarantee' means that no matter the turnout, the band would have guaranteed earnings.

'Or you could do away with the guarantee,' says Clive, 'and go for 90 per cent of the door and 10 per cent of the takings. But you have to be selling out to be even considered for that. Skids went 90/10 per cent on *all* of that tour and made a ton of money. They were beating the house records everywhere they played. The only band that was close was Siouxsie and the Banshees, who had been playing the same sort of venues six months previously.

'The Skids were a fantastic live band,' says Clive. 'The record didn't capture their energy. They were exciting. If you went to see the Skids, you couldn't stop watching Richard and Stuart. There was something happening all the time. I saw *all* the bands then. The only band that got me as excited as a Skids gig was the Clash. The Skids were just a force.'

Jake Burns of Stiff Little Fingers went to one of the Nashville gigs. 'They were the first band we went to see on our arrival in London,' says Jake. 'They were always mentioned in the same breath as us, so we thought we'd check out the opposition, as it were. A few songs in, I turned to [SLF bassist] Ali McMordie and said, "We may as well go home. These are so much better than we are."'

The pace was intense. '1978–'79 was a hard year,' says Clive. 'The Skids released two albums that year and did three national tours. They were ignoring Europe. They did TV in Europe – for "Into the Valley", I think, in early '79 – but they wouldn't do any gigs. And that was Sandy, out of his depth. The tours were all over the place. They'd be doing Manchester Apollo, Glasgow Apollo, Birmingham Odeon and things like that, and then we'd be playing a cricket club somewhere. There was no continuity around and it was pretty frustrating.'

Richard Jobson says that he felt that he wasn't really being managed or looked after. On one hand, he was ridiculed as this gormless loon with a daft voice doing dad dancing on *Top of the Pops*, on the other, people were sneering at his poetry and his aspirations to be taken seriously.

Today, we talk about social media pile-ons and the dangers of being shamed and humiliated online. Back then, there was a real chance that you could be made to look like a tool by the music press. Musicians, often fresh from the council estate, were paired with journalists fresh from university, full of ideas on philosophy and art theory.

'There was no guidance,' says Jobson. 'There was no help. I always felt like I'd been thrown into interviews with people like Paul Morley, you know, and he was talking about the polymorphic delineation of organic truth in the postmodern world. And I'm thinking, *Wow.*'

There was no media training back then. No one talked about mental health issues and there were no thoughts about the record company having a 'duty of care'. The band were just left to get on with it. This was what you signed up for, man-up etc.

For the most part, they didn't even think they needed looking after. 'If you'd asked me forty-five years ago, about Richard griping about being young and nobody looking after him, we would have just ridiculed him,' says Clive. 'You think about how young you were – but we didn't think we were young. We thought we were adults and we could do anything.'

It was a different time. Bill, Clive, Sandra: none of them knew that Jobson had epilepsy.

'I was not aware of Richard's epilepsy,' says Bill. 'It was never really mentioned. We didn't talk about these things. He was in the gangs and "I'm the big man", so I don't think he *would've* talked about it.'

'Nobody really shared anything,' says Clive. 'I never knew about Richard's epilepsy. He never shared that at all. I can remember sitting with him one night in London. I thought he had taken something. I sat with him for hours, just to make sure he was okay.

'I've not spoken to him about this, but I wish he *had* shared and I might have understood. I seriously thought he'd taken something. It was odd because none of the band *did* take anything. It wasn't drugs and rock 'n' roll with them.' He laughs: 'Not a lot of sex, either.'

Tam Kellichan remembers it slightly differently. After the gigs, he would go to bars and drink with the locals, have his picture taken, sign stuff – 'and then,' he says, 'I'd pick up a girl.'

Often he shared a room with Bill, who had to put up with him coming home with one – or more – women in tow. 'I don't know how much sleep Wullie really got on tour,' he says.

Poor old Bill wasn't impressed and Stuart didn't approve either. 'He was going wi' Sandra at the time and he used to phone her every night for hours an' aw that,' says Tam. 'I was married with two kids and I was humping everything in sight.

'Stuart didnae like me for that. He kinda hated me for it. I said, "Look, son. Wait 'til you're married and you've got a coupla kids, then you'll realise what's happening in the real world." We got on great – he just didnae like it that I was cheating on my wife.'

Being faithful on the road was not something Stuart and Sandra talked too much about. They didn't need to. 'It was a given,' says Sandra. 'Stuart knew what my thoughts and concerns were.

'And Tam wasnae there later on.'

While Tam was 'humping everything in sight', the drinking was apparently at a more respectable level than you might expect from a bunch of Scottish punks on tour. 'Because of my health thing,' says Jobson, 'I never drank and Stuart never really drank. I certainly didn't do drugs. I was very anti- because I take phenytoin, which is the drug you take for epilepsy. I made a movie [about an alcoholic] *16 Years of Alcohol* and everyone always presumes that it's about me, but in fact it's about my older brother. It's an amalgam, anyway, of him and myself.'

Jobson and Adamson shared a room, so Richard saw Stuart's drinking up close. 'After the gigs in the beginning, we'd maybe have a glass of beer or something. Occasionally he got a bit drunk, but we were young guys. He just couldn't really handle it. I've seen people who can drink a lot – it seems to not really affect them. But it affected Stuart quite quickly and destabilised him into just being a bit of an idiot. So, y'know, he was wise enough. It wasn't important.'

There could be some revisionism here. Bruce Watson was stunned to hear that Richard claimed he didn't drink: 'He *did so* drink! There's loads of pictures of him – down at the Forth Bridge doing a photo session, and he's got a fag in one hand and a bottle of red wine in the other! For him to say that he never drank is an embellishment.'

Big Country's A&R man Chris Briggs told me about drinking with Stuart and Richard. 'If you went out with Jobson, by the third round he was bringing back a whisky with every pint. Stuart less so. But we did drink a lot.'

As Sandra says, 'the problem is that almost everyone you've spoken to for this book would have been drinking or on something. They're not going to remember everything accurately.'

A Mansion and a Mercedes

The difference between Jobson and Adamson was becoming more and more obvious. 'I was more out there,' says Jobson. 'Stuart was always more reserved. And I tended to get adopted by people because I was so young and feral. They were thinking, "This is what punk rock's meant to be!" Even Joe Strummer was a bit like that with me. He was always like, "You're a fucking idiot but I love you because it's just this explosion of YES!", y'know? Stuart was the opposite.

'I was going out and living a fairly itinerant life and just going for it. He always pulled back and wanted something that I couldn't even dream of having – a home and a mortgage, a car and a wife and children. I felt I had to get as much out of life as quickly as possible.'

His epilepsy hung over everything he did. 'You have a fairly existential idea that you're not going to be around for that long,' he says. 'I was having a lot of these really brutal seizures – I was very sick – but Stuart looked after me a lot. He did look after me. He wanted me to come back to Dunfermline and just get a girlfriend and calm down.

'I thought it was because he had such a stable familial life. But, of course, that's not the case.'

Jobson didn't want to come back to Dunfermline and who could blame him? He was the lead singer in a hot band and London was the centre of the universe. He was making friends with musicians, hanging out in nightclubs, exploring creativity in music, fashion, literature, wherever it took him.

'I know the view is that I was really more the disruptive member of the band, because I was in London, doing all these mad things like poetry albums, and it was driving him mad. That's not really true. We were just so different. When you get to the heart of the matter, my life was itinerant because I was just trying to squeeze every fucking drop out of it.'

So you had Jobson, this 'explosion of YES!', and Adamson, this implosion of 'Naw, fuck that'. But the two men had something in common: they were the songwriters and the two people that everyone was interested in. They were treated differently from Bill and Tam, and even their touring arrangements reflected that.

Stay Alive

'I don't know why but Richard and Stuart always shared a room,' says Clive, 'even though Bill and Stuart were school friends. Richard and Stuart shared a room, Tam and Bill shared.'

'It was because those two [Richard and Stuart] were seen as being more important,' says Bill. 'They saw themselves as the more important people driving this band. And, in fairness, that's probably correct. So I think they just wanted to bounce off each other. But it turned things with me and Stuart, a bit.'

For their second album, Jobson was keen to avoid the stress that had come with the recording of their first album. 'After the experience of *Scared to Dance*, we tried to create a kind of a situation where Stuart would feel comfortable,' he says. 'It was my idea to bring Bill Nelson in.'

The Skids had namechecked Nelson in an interview with *Sounds*. 'They mentioned me being an inspiration in the piece,' says Nelson, 'which I was quite surprised by because the punk scene was still going and a lot of those bands were dismissive of any previous generation of bands.' Nelson and engineer John Leckie went up to Dunfermline for rehearsals for a single, 'Masquerade'.

John Leckie had worked at Abbey Road as a tape op and then an engineer, working on albums by John Lennon, George Harrison and Pink Floyd. In 1976, he began a long working relationship with Bill Nelson by producing Be Bop Deluxe's *Sunburst Finish* album.

Leckie was working with Scottish bands like Simple Minds and the Associates. 'All the Scottish bands that came to London would all come to each other's gigs,' he says. 'They would all stay up all night at the Columbia Hotel, drink beer and talk. And, funnily enough, my father came from Kinross and Dunfermline, which, of course they loved.'

Nelson and Leckie went up to Dunfermline in the dead of winter. 'It must have been January or something,' says Leckie. 'It was really cold. There was ice, literally, in the rehearsal room, on the instruments. It was just like a shed, a barn with a farm door.'

'We used to rehearse at a former stable at the back of a big house in Broomhead,' says Bill Simpson. 'That's where Bill Nelson came to see us

A Mansion and a Mercedes

when we were working on "Masquerade". He must've been like, "What the hell?" The last time we'd seen him, he'd been onstage at Carnegie Hall. It was surreal.'

'Stuart had bought a guitar of mine,' says Nelson. 'The guitar that I had on the cover of the *Axe Victim* album, a white Hoyer version of a Les Paul.' Nelson had sold the guitar years before to a guy in Wakefield. When the guy re-sold it, Stuart saw the ad and travelled down to buy the guitar.

'He wanted to give me it back,' says Nelson. 'He said, "You should have this guitar." I said, "No. You bought it, you should have it."'

'Bill didn't want it back,' says Leckie. 'It was a shit guitar. It just looked good. Bill just had it for the photo session, you know. It wasn't the guitar he actually played.'

Bill has the guitar now. In 2016, when it came up for sale again, a group of Be Bop Deluxe fans pulled together and bought it for him.

Leckie was impressed by the Skids' work ethic. 'It was full-on, ten-hour sessions for a few days. Everyone was on it and dedicated. We'd party a bit, but when it came to the work and the playing, it was a full-on ten- or twelve-hour, heads-down-and-do-it. There was no messing about. It wasn't like punk rock where they would just bash it out and if it's a bit out of tune or if it goes too fast, it doesn't matter.'

For the Skids, hanging out with one of their heroes was surreal. 'I remember going down to a local pub with Bill after the rehearsal,' says Bill Simpson, 'getting him a pint, and we're chatting away and nobody in the pub knew who he was. But we did. I was a huge Bill Nelson fan – Stuart idolised him as a guitarist and I loved him. Bill and Stuart hit it off because Bill could appreciate Stuart's style.'

John Leckie was also impressed by Stuart's playing, 'in terms of the chords and the energy and the push,' he says.

'He also played this Yamaha guitar that's like a Les Paul, and quite distinctive. Stuart's was the same guitar that Carlos Santana played. It was a bit weird for a punk band to play Santana's guitar. But Bill played it and was so fascinated that he bought one as well.

'Stuart also had HH amps and they were the typical punk thing – transistor, no valve – you could throw them about and they always worked. And he also had the MXR Harmoniser, I think, a blue, rack-mounted thing which gave it the chorus. The bagpipe sound came from that harmoniser sound.'

But, says Leckie, 'the main thing with "Masquerade" is the beat. The beat was really special. I'd never heard that kind of thing before.'

'Masquerade' was another development of the Skids' sound, with call-and-response vocals and an uplifting chorus driven by a series of stuttering military drum rolls that came out of Stuart's ear for a great arrangement.

'Stuart wrote all the drum parts,' says Jobson. 'That wonderful roll in "Masquerade", that brilliant militaristic thing – he came up with that.'

Around the same time, Bill Nelson asked Tam to play drums on a song on his album *Quit Dreaming and Get on the Beam*. 'Tom Kellichan was a very un-star-like person, really down to earth,' says Nelson. 'A simple drummer but very strong, effective, and a good timekeeper. I used him on a track called "Decline and Fall" because his style suited what I needed for that track.'

Bill listened as Tam laid down a beat and then gave him some direction. 'Just like Stuart,' says Tam, who didn't mind at all. 'This is what it was like all the time. Stuart would say to Wullie, "Can you play it this way?" and then Wullie would get all tied up and Stuart would be like, "Aw, fucking hell!" And then he'd tell me what to play and I'd get all tied up again and Stuart would kick off. But that's what Stuart was like. He wanted it down to perfection.'

When the Bill Nelson track was done, Bill asked Tam what he should pay him. To Tam, it'd been a privilege just doing it. 'I just shook his hand, and said, "Bill, I want nothing for it."'

'Masquerade' went to number 14 in the UK charts in June 1979 and the band toured to support it, playing bigger venues before going into a studio in Edinburgh to start writing the next album.

'Masquerade' was the last drum part Tam Kellichan would add to a Skids recording. The divide between the songwriters and the rhythm section was getting wider. 'There was obviously some discussions about monies and all the rest of it, and that's where Tam took umbrage,' says Bill Simpson. 'To be fair, they had a publishing deal and we didn't because they were the songwriters. I didn't have any qualms with that. I was just happy to be in a successful band.'

Tam was pissed off that he and Bill were getting less. He was trying to write songs too; he wrote thirteen, in fact, but they were all turned down. Pissed off, he confronted Jobson and, says Bill, 'was told in no uncertain terms, "Well, you're *a drummer*. Anyone can be a drummer."'

Tam remembers the incident much more vividly. According to him, he and Richard stumbled out of a nightclub in London and were walking along the street when Jobson stopped and looked down at him.

'See you?' said Jobson.

'What?'

'You're fuck-all but a background boy.'

So, says Tam, 'I jumped up and fuckin' decked him. I got him on the ground, I had my two fingers on his throat, right on his thrapple, and I kept pushing and pushing and pushing and squeezing 'til he hud nae fuckin' breath left.

'And then I thought, "It's no' really worth it."'

He got up. 'See you, ya fucker?' he said to Jobson. 'You ain't worth the fuckin' bother.' And he walked away.

(Richard Jobson says this never happened, 'And could never have happened. Tam was a wee man who quite rightly had no taste for aggression of any kind.')

A little bit later, when they were in the studio rehearsing the songs that would become the *Days in Europa* album, Tam and Bill were in the booth when Stuart and Richard came in.

'Me and Richard would like a word wi' youse two,' said Stuart. 'Richard an' I have hud a discussion. I put the music tae it and he writes the words, so we'd like mair money than youse two.'

'I just sat there fucking gobsmacked,' says Tam. 'I was thinking to myself, "What you're trying to tell me is, youse two want a mansion and a Mercedes and leave me an' Wullie wi' a fuckin' cooncil house and a pushbike".'

That was it for Tam. 'I stood up,' he says, 'put my sticks on the snare drum, looked the two of them straight in the face and I said, "See youse? If money means that much to you, take the fuckin' lot. I'm off." And I just left everything and walked oot the fuckin' studio.'

In his book, *Into the Valley*, Jobson writes that 'Tom felt the band had become something he didn't really want to be part of anymore. He much preferred small-town life and would have preferred to play in a pub band, so he left.'

'Are you fucking serious, man?' says Tam. 'I'd had hit records, been on *Top of the Pops*, supported the Clash and the Jam, and I'm gonna leave for a club band? Piss off.'

He was in Italy with a woman called Charlie Green, the singer of the band Bitch, when Sandy called, asking him to come back.

'Okay,' said Tam. 'Send me 600 quid and two plane tickets.'

Sandy sent the money and the tickets, and Tam and Charlie flew back to London where Tam promptly spent all the money 'in the Speakeasy and aw that' and then hitch-hiked home.

In Dunfermline, his uncle Alec was driving for the Skids and came to take him to the studio. 'I says, "No. I said I was coming *back*, but I'm not going back to *them*."'

Instead, he formed a band called the Secrets and/or Katyn (after the Polish massacre in 1940) with Bruce Watson, Sandra's brother Raymond and Charlie Green on vocals.

'I think we rehearsed and did one gig, and then broke up again,' says Bruce. 'It's not much of a story. It fizzled out.'

When it fell apart, Tam quit drumming.

There's a rumour online that he went on to marry Charlie Green.

'Nah,' he says. 'I left her in a club in Cowdenbeath. I picked up a blonde, left Charlie in the club and fucked off with the blonde.

'The next night, she chased me, bollock naked, down the street with a poker in her hand. I was running down the street and she was right behind me, tryin' tae kill me …'

7
Working for the Yankee Dollar

Bye-bye, Bill! Catch ya later, Clive! See ya, Sandy!
The Skids go next level with Admiral Nelson,
Rusty Egan and some Nazi propaganda

With Tam gone, Jobson drafted in Rusty Egan – former drummer for the Rich Kids and one of the architects of the upcoming New Romantic scene. Rusty was perfect: he could play, he was at the cutting edge of fashion and he came armed with all the latest tech – Syndrums, a Roland CR-78 drum machine, the Simmons SDS-3 – that would define the sound of the '80s.

On the other hand, says Bill Simpson, he was 'a bit of a motormouth'.

'Rusty was from *Laahndahn*,' says Bill. 'He's some boy. But he must've thought: "What's this? Rehearsing in an old *stable*?"'

'Rusty was trouble from day one,' says Jobson, 'because he wanted to change the way our drums were. But he was *right!* He drove Stuart crazy, and Rusty and Bill Nelson clashed – but everybody agreed that what he was doing was right.'

There was a bit of a culture clash, but Rusty didn't give a shit. 'I was a working-class kid who had been through juvenile schools,' he says. 'I was used to fitting in and moving around. I was never a mummy's boy.'

Rusty Egan had already done *Top of the Pops* and toured all over the country with the Rich Kids and Bette Bright. 'At the time the Skids were recording *Days in Europa*,' says Clive, 'Rusty was also in [Martin Rushent and Alan Winstanley's] Genetic Studio demoing Visage stuff, and doing his nightclub thing as well. So he had a busy lifestyle, operating at a much faster level than the rest of the band. Everyone else was in slow motion compared to Rusty.'

Egan had been the DJ at Billy's in Dean Street which held a 'Bowie Night' on a Tuesday before it moved to the Blitz Club in Covent Garden. Blitz would help define the sounds and fashions of the '80s.

Rusty knew Richard from partying in London, thought the Skids were a great band and loved the idea of teaming up with them and Bill Nelson – especially when Nelson played them a track called 'Living in My Limousine' which he'd recorded that year and sounded not dissimilar to Gary Numan's 'Cars'. The times they were a-modulatin'.

'In 1978, I wore a T-shirt that said on it, "Kraftwerk have taken the perspiration out of drumming",' says Egan. 'By then, Mr Numan had arrived, Ultravox! and Magazine had split, and Jobson met them all at Blitz, heard me DJing and he loved it.'

'The Blitz Club scene was great fun,' says Jobson. 'I never felt part of it, but I never felt outside it. It wasn't my thing, but I kind of got it.' He went to New Romantic boutique PX and bought a load of clothes to wear on *Top of the Pops*. 'I hated what New Romantics gave us in the end,' he says. 'They killed all the urgency of punk and post-punk and gave us Spandau Ballet and Duran Duran and all that pretty-boy shit again. You could be ugly and be in a punk band and it didn't matter. Suddenly you had to have good teeth. Record companies took control again.'

'The Blitz Club was alien to me and Stuart,' says Bill Simpson. 'We were local guys. Rusty still had all the gear and the bouffant hair. He looked out of place up here and he didn't really fit in with us. I still wanted that local connection.

'Richard wanted to get away from Dunfermline from an early age. Stuart and I were quite happy to be successful – in inverted commas – and stay in our own bubble here. We were not big-city guys. I wasnae interested in that and neither was Stuart. He'd rather be up the road 400 miles. He'd get on the train any time he could.'

John Leckie had noticed it too. He knew Rusty and Jobson from latenight drinking at the Music Machine in Camden and the Virgin Venue in

Victoria, but not Stuart. 'I'll tell you one thing about Stuart,' says Leckie. 'He never really partied like that, in terms of drinking. When I found out about his death, I was really shocked because at that time he never joined the party. The others would be pretty wild – well, Jobson was. Always talking and full of himself. But Stuart wasn't a part of that.

'He wasn't shy, but he wasn't as *wild* as we were. He would always leave early. We might have three or four beers and he'd still be on his first one. So the alcohol thing – I never saw it from Stuart.'

The band went to Rockfield in Wales to record the second album with Bill Nelson. John Leckie couldn't help because he was already booked to do Simple Minds' third album, *Empires and Dance*, in the same studio.

On the first day at Rockfield, Stuart turned to Bill Nelson and said, 'Show me how you play [classic Be Bop Deluxe track] "Sister Seagull".' So Bill showed him. 'He started to play it,' says Bill, 'and I said to him, "Aw, come on. Don't copy me, do your own thing."'

Unlike the *Scared to Dance* sessions, Stuart was at ease. 'He was with one of his great heroes,' says Jobson. 'It worked. We're in Rockfield Studios, we're away from everybody else, there's no distractions. Sandra could come and stay and hang out. And we were all cool with her – everybody felt very relaxed around her – so it was all good.'

'Maybe it was different because they actually *wanted* me to be there,' says Nelson. 'They were open to ideas. I played some keyboards on the album and on one of the tracks ['Peaceful Times'] we completely reversed the backing track and got Richard to write lyrics to sing over the top. It was kind of an experimental atmosphere.'

Rusty Egan was in his element. He knew exactly what he wanted. 'On the Rich Kids album, my drums were buried,' he says. 'I wanted a clear and precise sound.'

'I'd put Rusty's impact on the Skids up there, equal to Bill's production,' says Clive. 'Did all the band like it? No. But being from the production side of it, I could see exactly what he was trying to do.' When they toured, Egan found a way to mic up the kit, connect it to the Simmons and trigger sounds from the kit. 'He did that D-Drums thing, triggering sounds, before anyone,' says Clive.

Rusty wanted drums that were 'powerful and warm and full of precision, like a machine. I felt all the punk bands needed that – Paul Cook and Rat Scabies were both precise and powerful, and I loved that. When you played with the Skids live, you could hear how precise Stuart's guitars were – the rhythms and chopping. Adding Bill Nelson and me made a sound that I felt the songs deserved. And Bill Nelson was happy to add Moog bass and sequencers.'

'The almost square four/four disco beat in "Yankee Dollar" and the roll in "Animation" was all Rusty,' says Jobson. 'Prior to that, Stuart wrote all the drum parts and all the bass parts. Bill Simpson gets credit for that wonderful bassline in the intro for "Into the Valley" – Stuart Adamson wrote that bassline. Bill Simpson never wrote anything, ever. Stuart wrote that. And he did all the drum parts. So, for the first time ever, he had a drummer who was so capable and so inventive that Stuart didn't have to do any drum parts.'

Not that Rusty couldn't take direction. He had spent three months in the summer of '76 playing with the Clash ('before suggesting Topper give them a call'). 'Joe or Mick would shout out a pattern and the notes to Paul – A-D-E or whatever – and then "1-2-3-4!" and we would just do it, so I was cool taking instructions. Once we had something, I would perfect it until we all agreed it was right. I didn't argue – it was a job.'

Rusty had a prototype of the Simmons SDS-3, given to him by Richard James Burgess of Landscape, best known for their 1981 hit, 'Einstein a Go-Go'. Egan wanted to incorporate the drum sounds from the album into the live performance. According to Clive, 'Stuart was like, "Tell him to put that fuckin' stuff away! Tell him we don't want it!"'

Rusty just ignored him.

'The problem,' says Jobson, 'was that we had to get the drum parts done fast and get rid of him because Rusty was doing our heads in. He treated us like we were provincial nobodies.'

'Richard used to take the piss out of Rusty all of the time,' says Nelson. 'He'd go off to London for the club nights at the weekend, so the band decided to booby trap his bedroom at Rockfield. They sawed a leg off his bed and then propped it up so it would collapse when he got into it. One time they sliced a loaf of bread open and hollowed it out and filled it with flies and spiders and put it back together.'

When Rusty came back, he acted like nothing had happened.

'I was a serious person,' says Egan, 'not really a joker. I came to do my job, not get drunk. I knew that punk would be short-lived and Kraftwerk were the future and here come OMD, Depeche Mode and Soft Cell. Visage and Ultravox! were starting to become one – we had already recorded tracks for Visage with the Magazine guys – and I knew Simple Minds were going to be there before us.' Time was tight and the Skids were fannying about. 'I was okay with it,' he says, 'but I wasn't really into schoolboy pranks. I was a serious young man.'

Bill Nelson was also way ahead of the pack. 'I don't think Bill liked us very much,' says Jobson. 'He was more interested in Joy Division and Simple Minds, that more synthetic European sound. But with "Masquerade", he *got* my lyrics. He didn't say, "What the fuck is this shit?"'

'Richard's lyrics were kind of opaque,' says Nelson. 'He was into left-field literature and that came across in what he was doing. The Skids had a completely personal approach to music – they weren't looking over their shoulders and trying to copy somebody else, or be somebody else. They were just themselves.'

Bill Nelson's band at the time, Red Noise, were an attempt to go beyond the trope of the guitar hero. 'I wasn't *against* guitar playing,' he says. 'I just felt that everybody was playing the same kind of thing. They had the same riffs at the same time, pentatonic scales, all of that.

'Stuart had his own approach to guitar playing. I don't know how much he realised that at the time. He was coming from a natural perspective – it wasn't contrived, it came naturally from his personality. He wasn't a straight rock guitar player. It wasn't that clichéd blues stuff. He'd got something else. Later, Big Country became more about what people call the bagpipe guitar sound, but that was just starting when we worked together.'

In 2012, Bill Nelson wrote a review of a Skids compilation and Big

Country's first album *The Crossing* for *Classic Rock* magazine. On the subject of the 'bagpipe guitar sound', he explained that 'the Eventide Harmoniser and a chorus pedal were the sonic key to it.'

'That was something that we tried out down at Rockfield,' he says today. 'I'd used Eventide Harmonizers quite a lot when they first came out. I had a thing called a Marshall Time Modulator, which was kind of a phasing unit and we used that on the bass drum a lot, so that the bass drum looped in different pitches. It gave the effect of changing the pitch of the bass drum, the sound cycling from low to high and back at a given rate. So there was a lot of that kind of stuff – trying out different effects.'

It was at that session that Nelson gave Stuart an EBow. The EBow – or 'energy bow' – was a device that worked on the guitar like an electronic bow. You held it with your picking hand over the strings of an electric guitar and it reacted with the pickups, creating a field of magnetic energy and causing the strings to vibrate. With no picking involved, the notes sounded like they were being bowed. For Nelson, it was another great way of avoiding the clichés of electric guitar playing.

Nelson used it so much that the inventor Greg Heet sent him a boxful of EBows as a thank you. 'So I had a spare one with me and I gave that to Stuart,' he says. 'I think he used it on one of the tracks on the album.'

The EBow would go on to become synonymous with Big Country.

Released in October, *Days in Europa* went to number 32 in the album charts and stayed on the chart for just five weeks, a disappointing result. Earlier in the year, *Scared to Dance* had reached number 19 and hung around in the charts for eleven weeks. The first single, 'Charade', went to number 31 in the UK charts that same month. 'Charade' was both urgent and despondent. An anthemic chorus disguised a dark lyric in which a band plays while men gamble: 'Either way, one would fail and lose.' Rusty's Roland CR-78, the first programmable drum machine, gave it a modern, futuristic spin. 'A year before OMD's "Enola Gay",' he says, comparing it to another track that used the CR-78 in its distinctive intro.

'Charade' was the only single from *Days in Europa* that was produced by Bill Nelson. Maybe its relative failure – top 40 after a top 10 for

'Into the Valley' and top 20 for 'Masquerade' – spooked Virgin. Mick Glossop, the engineer on *Scared to Dance*, was brought in to re-record 'Working for the Yankee Dollar' for single release, while 'Animation' was remixed by an upcoming producer called Bruce Fairbairn.

'Working for the Yankee Dollar' was probably the album's most obvious single, an anti-war mutant funk song about American imperialism with another great call-and-response chorus.

Simon Draper, the A&R at Virgin, asked Mick Glossop to produce that new version. 'He felt it could be a strong single, but not in its present form,' says Glossop. 'And I agreed with him.' The single version is faster, tighter. 'It needed reworking to make it more direct and more commercial. It just needed to make its point.'

Glossop travelled to Scotland to rehearse the song and then recorded it at The Manor in Oxfordshire where, four years later, Big Country would record *The Crossing*. Glossop remembers forcing Egan and Jobson to re-do parts over and over, with the whole band playing along. 'Stuart played his part perfectly every single time across two whole days of recording,' he says. 'He didn't make any mistakes at all.'

'Working for the Yankee Dollar' was released in November and crept to number 20 in the UK charts in January 1980. 'Animation' came out in March and stalled at number 56. In his collection of lyrics, *No Bad Words*, Jobson called it 'a hymn to work – to be proud of what you've achieved – as long as it's the TRUTH'. It's a great track but the lyric was obscure and the chorus wasn't as irresistible as the band's previous singles.

The cover art featured artist George Grosz, a Dadaist German painter famed for his pictures of Weimar Germany that depicted a society falling apart. 'My drawings expressed my despair, hate and disillusionment,' Grosz once said. 'I drew drunkards; puking men; men with clenched fists cursing at the moon ...' Very Skids.

Grosz was left-wing and anti-Nazi, and maybe the sleeve was a subtle atonement for the album art of *Days in Europa*. The cover of the album copied the front cover of a 1936 edition of *Berliner Illustrirte Zeitung* that Jobson had found in a Berlin flea market – Nazi propaganda that put an Aryan spin on the Olympics. Hitler had seen the 1936 Olympics as an opportunity to prove the superiority of the 'Aryan master race' – before the African-American Jesse Owens pissed on the Führer's chips by winning four gold medals.

'The image was perfect for the song "The Olympian",' Richard wrote in his book *Days in Europa*. 'It was a powerful graphic image that stood out from a lot of the sleeve designs of the time. My lyrics have always been anti-fascist. Always. The use of image was meant to be ironic; the song "The Olympian" laughs in the face of the mythic Übermensch.'

But, from the outside, it looked like the Skids had binned the old SS bolts logo and then written the band name in old Germanic type on an example of *actual* Nazi propaganda. There was some outrage in the music press. To Jobson, it was just them dicking around. 'To be fair, I think what had happened is that we'd gone to Europe,' he says. 'We'd gone to Amsterdam and it was such a modern place. Britain during the '70s was still kinda like, post-war, even London – you almost felt like you were still on rations. But Amsterdam felt modern. You had all these Bauhaus buildings and everything – and then you'd go to Germany and it had all been rebuilt and was sparkling and exciting. It made a big impression on me – there was this other place out there that was full of excitement and possibility and much more about the future than the past.'

Nelson disapproved, but put it down to the trend at the time of flirting with supposedly 'dangerous' symbolism. 'There was so much flirting with that sort of imagery amongst that generation of musicians,' he says. 'I don't think there were any Nazi leanings at all, quite the opposite.'

The band had played at benefits for Chilean refugees and at a Rock Against Racism show in Edinburgh. They clearly weren't Nazis. To Bill Simpson, it was another example of music press bias. 'It was garbage. Why are we getting singled out? I mean, Joy Division? New Order?'

The sleeve didn't last too long in the end. With album sales stalling and the singles failing to make a difference, Virgin had the album remixed and reissued with a new sleeve that looks like it came from the Roaring Twenties: a man kisses a partially clothed woman while another woman waits for him. It suggested decadence, sex, the Lost Generation, modernism.

The album itself had been remixed by Bruce Fairbairn, who would later become famous for producing Bon Jovi and Aerosmith.

'They did a remix because they wanted to promote the band in America and they felt that the sound wasn't right for an American audience,' says Bill Simpson. 'We had that lower tone and Bill [Nelson] was very much into echo and such like. There was a perception that it needed to be cleaned up for an American audience.'

No one spoke to Bill Nelson about it. 'I think maybe at the time, they thought that it was too far away from the first album's punky feel,' he says. 'I was completely happy with the album. The band were. It was just Simon Draper at Virgin, I think, who had misgivings about it. I felt disappointed. I didn't see any problems at all with what I'd done.'

It didn't go down very well with the band, either. 'As far as I'm concerned, Bill Nelson is the producer of *Days in Europa*, end of story,' says Simpson, 'and that's the only one I've ever listened to. If they were gonna make another one for marketing reasons ...' He shrugs. 'I was leaving anyway, or had left.'

To do the album justice live, it was decided that they needed a keyboard player. Enter Alistair Moore, from Stuart's hometown of Crossgates.

'Ali Moore was a good friend of mine and Stuart's from school,' says Bill Simpson. 'An excellent pianist, but very much an accompanist with a singer or violinist. More classical. A great guy, but maybe not really the right fit.'

Ali Moore had been given the shit-end of the stick. Bill Nelson had put keyboards on the album, but the Skids' audience wanted a guitar band. 'A lot of people were like: "Who's *this* guy?",' says Bill. They struggled to get the live mix right and, at times, the keyboards dominated.

'A lot of the live recordings I've heard, especially the gig in Edinburgh, all I hear is keys,' says Bill. 'It didnae really work. We should have gotten a second guitarist and worked it out that way. We wanted to do "Pros and Cons" and "Animation" and all that. But it didn't quite work.'

Rusty was leaving. He had loved his time with the Skids ('The only thing I thought was not cool was Albert Tatlock,' he says, 'but saw the funny side once I had played it a few times'), but Visage was calling. Bruce Watson knew Stuart was looking for a drummer and suggested a great local drummer, Mike Baillie. 'We'd grown up together, went to school together, did our apprenticeship together,' says Bruce. 'At the time, Mike was very much intae heavy rock – he looked a bit like Brian May.' He got the gig with one condition: that he cut his hair.

At the last date in Aberdeen, Rusty brought Baillie onstage to play drums on the encore.

Around this time, Bruce Watson gave Stuart a demo of some stuff he'd been working on with his band Eurosect. One song stood out – 'Forbidden Whispers', a track with Bruce on vocals and a driving bass intro.

'There's some really good ideas on that tape,' Stuart told him. 'It would be great to do something in the future. I quite fancy a two guitar kindae thing.'

Bruce was flattered but he didn't take it seriously. It was just Stuart trying to be nice.

Ali Moore wasn't working out and they all knew it. But Ali was a friend and the way it was handled was the final straw for Bill Simpson.

He got a phone call from Sandy Muir. Bill and Mike Baillie were booked on a flight down to London for a Kid Jensen radio session.

'What about the other guys?' says Bill.

'Richard and Stuart are on their way down today – they've got some interviews to do.'

'What about Ali?'

'Oh, Ali's no longer in the band.'

'I took umbrage,' says Bill. 'I'll say no more. I thought, "I've had enough." It could've been done better, that's all I'm saying. I would have agreed with them. I would have said, "You're right, it's not really working." But they didn't even come to me, so …'

Stuart phoned Bill. 'What're you doing?'

'There was a bit of a shouting match,' says Bill. 'So, unfortunately, it didnae end as well as it might've. But that's the way it was.'

'I blame Richard and Stuart for it,' says Clive. 'They gave the instruction.

Working for the Yankee Dollar

I also blame Bill to a point. Bill should've got on the phone to Stuart to *find out* what was going on.' Maybe if they'd all talked more, they could've worked something out. 'Instead, they didn't really talk again.'

It was February 1980. The following week, Stuart was getting married to Sandra and Bill was supposed to be the best man. Richard took his place.

Bill had offers to play in a few other bands, but instead he met up with the girl who became his wife – the girl he'd followed to Amsterdam – and got a proper job and settled down.

'I wasn't a songwriter,' he says. 'I had been with someone who was a fantastic songwriter and musical genius – he certainly evolved into that – and I didn't want to go back to just playing around local clubs.'

Jobson's claim that Stuart wrote all the band's parts, including the 'Into the Valley' bassline, rankles. 'That's rubbish,' he says. 'That annoys me. Stuart was the songwriter and he had a sound in his head, but "Into the Valley" is my bassline, for a start. Stuart would give you guidance, but he didnae show you what to play. Same with drums. Tam was a great drummer, but for fills, Stuart would say, "Try this". He was a *producer*. He wasn't telling us what to play or how to play it, but he had a sound production in his head.

'To be honest with you, because I wasn't a songwriter, I was more than pleased that Stuart had that skill and he was the musical director. Richard has no real musicality, timing-wise and such like. His rhythm's kinda to pot. He's a lyricist, a wordsmith. And the two of them worked great together.'

One day, Clive was in Dunfermline when he heard a commotion. Stuart and Sandra were in the middle of the street, having a heated argument. Clive hid and ducked into Sandy Muir's office.

Sandy greeted him with some news. 'You don't have a job anymore and neither do I.' They had both been let go.

'I thought "Yes!"' says Clive. 'Me and Richard had run our course. I needed an excuse to get out. Nothing against Richard – I think I irritated the hell out of him and he was irritating the hell out of me.'

The Skids were moving up a level and felt that they needed pros. Stuart and Sandra had even considered moving to London. 'We went down to see these properties that we could afford,' she says. 'One house was thirty

Stay Alive

pounds a week.' They stood in a long queue of people waiting to view and, when they finally got inside, it was so bad they turned on their heels and walked right back out again. 'And at that point, the two of us just went, "That's it. It's not gonna happen."'

Everything was moving towards London and Sandra thinks that is probably what they were arguing about that day in the street. Losing Clive was another step away from the security of Dunfermline. 'Clive had been a trusted and dependable friend and he didn't deserve to be told in that way,' she says. 'I felt Clive was important for Stuart, away fae home. Removing Clive left Stuart without their regular piss-taking sessions. It was taking another step towards London.'

Three months later, Jobson was in Dunfermline and asked Clive if he'd like to come back. Clive turned him down.

Did he ever regret that? 'I *do* regret it,' he says. 'I would have loved to have been part of the next tour. But this is when my friendship with Stuart really *started*. We both got married the same year. Stuart was the best man at my wedding.'

REVELLERS Adamson, Jobson and nouveau Skids Russell Webb and Mike Bailey
SPARE DICK AT A WEDDING: Last week we told how Richard 'Dick' Jobson slimmed the Skids by two members. Now, we show the new line-up appearing for the first time at Stuart Adamson's wedding to Sandra Davidson (20).
Jobson, being Scottish, turned up in evening dress, forgetting that you're supposed to wear morning dress to weddings. Our Scottish correspondent reports that Jobbo looks 'a the go. But we still don't know whether Sandra (20) is the new keyboard player.

February, 1980. Bill was supposed to be the best man. When he left, Richard Jobson stepped in.

8
Hurry on Boys (II: England)

*Slave owners and concubines.
Nuns and Nazis. New lives in a dirty
old town. The bumblebee*

Piotr Brzezicki was an orphan. Born in 1922, in a part of Poland that is now part of Ukraine, he never did find out what happened to his parents.

He had vague memories of living with them in the mountains – a log cabin, a cow outside for milk – but then suddenly he was living in a convent, the only child there, raised by nuns. He never saw his parents again. No one ever explained how, why or what had happened.

At the age of seven, Piotr was moved from the convent to a monastery where, once again, he was the only child, this time raised by monks. Eventually, he was placed with a family, but that wasn't his happy ending: the family gave him an education, but they also treated him like a slave. So when Piotr became a teenager, he got out of there.

He ran away – right into the Second World War.

In September 1939, Germany invaded Poland and Piotr joined the Polish resistance, even though he was a pacifist and refused to carry a gun. Captured by the Nazis, he was put in a prisoner of war camp in Hungary where he remained for more than two years before he and a mate escaped under the wire.

The two young men eluded the Germans – if they'd been captured, they would have been shot – and walked from Hungary to France, where

Stay Alive

Piotr joined the Polish Air Force and was trained as a Merlin engine specialist for Spitfire and Hurricane fighter planes. When France fell, he was moved to England, one of 17,000 Polish airmen stationed in the UK, where he joined the legendary Polish Fighter Squadron 303 at RAF Northolt in north-west London.

During the Battle of Britain, it was 303 Squadron – not a British squadron – that shot down the greatest number of German planes.

After spending his early years fighting for survival, Piotr had found a home and a purpose. 'It took him away from the war to a degree,' says his son, Mark Brzezicki. 'There was still a war in Britain, but not like it was raging in Eastern Europe. And it liberated him – it gave him a life.'

After the war, with Heathrow Airport being built nearby, engineers were much sought after, so Piotr got a job with BOAC and settled in the area. As well as being a great engineer, he was a great singer. He loved opera and had a fine tenor voice. He wanted to keep his vocals in shape, so he joined the choir of his local Catholic church in Southall. It was there that he met Mark's mum, Kathleen.

They bought a house in Langley, off the M4, just near Heathrow.

Mark Brzezicki was born in that house and lives in it to this day.

Tony Butler – Anthony Earle Peter Butler, to give him his full name – was born fifteen miles east of Langley, in Queen Charlotte's & Chelsea Hospital, right next to HMP Wormwood Scrubs, the prison that over the years has housed Moors Murderer Ian Brady, serial killer Dennis Nilsen and, for one night in June 1967, Rolling Stone Keith Richards.

Tony was born in February 1957, a few months before Mark. His parents had emigrated to the UK from the Caribbean island of Dominica. But their story starts in Africa and, weirdly, Edinburgh.

Tony's great-grandfather was, he says, on the board of an Edinburgh firm called Mitchells & Butlers. Formed in 1898, Mitchells & Butlers are still going: they're now the owners of big UK pub chains like All Bar One, Harvester, O'Neill's and more.

In Tony's family lore, his great-grandfather moved to Jamaica and made a fortune out of Red Stripe. A lager first brewed in the US by an Illinois company, Galena Brewing, the company sold the Red Stripe brand and recipe to two British investors and it became a huge success as Jamaica's first beer.

So Tony Butler should have been born rich. But nah: the old boy drank all the profits.

Tony thinks his great-grandfather skipped the draft in 1915 and moved from Jamaica, buying land in Barbados and Dominica, where he lived until his death in the 1920s.

Dominica is one of the Windward Islands in the West Indies. Originally populated by the Arawak and the Kalinago – the indigenous people of the area – the stories of their reputation as fierce warriors stem from the arrival of European ships in the fifteenth century. The Spanish, the French and then the British stole their land, setting up timber camps and building sugar and coffee plantations. And, to help them do that, they brought ship-loads of slaves from Africa.

Between 1763 and 1808, the British brought at least 100,000 captive Africans – from Nigeria, Cameroon, the Gulf of Guinea and beyond – to Dominica alone. The importation of slaves was outlawed by the British Parliament in 1807, but the trade continued. Slave revolts across the Caribbean, combined with the influence of abolitionists in the UK, led to the Emancipation Act in 1838. Soon, black leaders were elected to the Dominican Legislative Assembly and the country became the first British colony in the Caribbean to be governed by non-whites.

But the road to freedom wasn't as simple as that. By the end of the nineteenth century, the British replaced that government with colonial rule and the history and power structures of slavery and oppression were still felt across the island.

For centuries, white landowners had taken black mistresses as concubines, the women either forced into sexual relationships with slave owners or tempted by the privileges that such a relationship might offer: money, a rise in status, the promise of freedom. Even after the abolition of slavery, this power dynamic persisted.

Tony's great-grandfather, he says, lived with 'many a concubine' –

possibly as many as fourteen – and one of them was Tony's great-grandmother.

'That's just how things were,' he says.

Tony once saw a photograph of the children of his great-grandmother. 'She had about twelve to fourteen children and eight of them were white. My grandmother – who had my uncle, my auntie and my mother – was one of the darker ones of the tribe. So I come from a multiracial background which began in Edinburgh.'

Tony believes those Celtic genes influenced him in ways that he could never control or explain. When he was a kid, at New Year the TV would feature shows with Scottish performers ('Kenneth McKeller and all these sorts of people' – the same guys who'd driven Ian Grant nuts) and their Celtic music would resonate. 'I'd be attracted and I'd think, "Why? I come from Shepherd's Bush! Why am I interested in this?"'

He's reminded of it to this day, sometimes in the most unlikely ways. 'Anytime I hear a drone,' he says. 'Anything that pitches a note and is constant. I could be doing the hoovering and it hits some pitch, hits a note and I'm gone. I'm in this wonderful place and, before I know it, I've finished my chore.

'I think it's one of the reasons why I was drawn to what kids at the time – when I was twelve or thirteen years old – kept telling me was *white* music.'

Mark Brzezicki was born on the longest day: summer solstice, 21 June 1957. He was the middle child, the third of five children.

With his father's history, and with Heathrow on their doorstep, Mark grew up in love with planes. As a kid, he would cycle over to the airport to watch the aircraft take off and land. 'You could get close to them because there was no real security,' he says. He'd climb through the gap in the fence, watch the planes and his heart would race. He felt overwhelmed – by the size and the noise, by the shape, the engineering.

He had the same thrill when he saw a drum kit.

One day, he was coming home from school, walking down Slough High Street, and he passed the local music shop. 'There was a sparkly drum kit in the window,' he says. 'I was like, "Wow". I'd seen them in pictures, I'd seen them on television, but I had never seen one close up. I thought, "That's like what Ringo uses. There's a *real* one, in front of me". I mean, you would never see a drum kit unless you went to concerts and I hadn't been to a concert.

'And it excited me, like when I saw an aircraft.'

In 1963, Tony was six years old and at home in Shepherd's Bush when there was a knock on the door. 'I was one of those unfortunate people,' he says, 'who opens the door one morning and there's a policeman standing there.'

The policeman told young Tony to go and get his mum.

'And then the bad news came down.'

Tony's father had been involved in a freak accident caused by one of London's rare hurricanes. The car he was in had been thrown into a tree. He was injured so badly that Tony wasn't even allowed to see him in hospital. He died several days later.

For a short time, Tony and his mother lived alone. And then came another life-changing piece of news. Tony had an older brother.

His mum was pregnant with Tony when his parents had moved to the UK in 1956, but no one had told him that they had already had a son in Dominica. 'They'd had to make the agonising decision of whether to bring him or not, and because of costs or whatever, it was decided to leave him behind with our grandmother.'

In 1965, his brother Lennox joined them in London. 'I was eight and he was ten. Our first meeting wasn't pleasant. She was my mum and, all of a sudden, I had to share her with somebody who looked like me. I didn't like that at all. He liked it even less.'

It was something that Lennox never really came to terms with. 'He never knew her,' says Tony. 'He resented her all his life because she abandoned him. I tried to assure him that she didn't, that it was just the way that things were in those days.

'It was weird. We grew up together but not very closely.'

Mark's older brother Anthony bought a guitar. His other brother had a bass. They started rehearsing with a guy who had bought himself a little drum kit. It was an aquamarine sparkle Gigster kit: one tom-tom, no floor tom, one cymbal and a hi-hat. Mark went over to the garage where, he says, they were making a noise.

'It wasn't really music because nobody had any tuition,' he says. 'And the drummer had no idea how to play. I didn't know how to play either, but he said to me, "See if you can make sense of it." My brother was strumming two chords and my other brother was plonking on the bass and I joined in. And it sounded like I could play.'

He was excited. 'And this is gonna sound really stupid,' he says, 'but what excited me was *the look* of it.'

Mark was always very artistic. He was great at drawing. In another life, he could have been an artist or designer of some kind. (He later designed the single sleeve for his band On the Air's single 'Ready for Action'.)

So it was the aesthetics of the drums that first caught him, not the sound. 'I just liked the look of the drums,' he says. 'I had no intention of playing them. It was the thrill of seeing something that I'd only ever seen on TV and in magazines.'

Eventually, the guy offered him the drum kit: 'I don't want it. You have it and play with your brothers.' He set it up in his bedroom and his dad made him put a heavy-duty blanket over it to dampen the sound. 'I was allowed to play for half an hour, after my dad practised his scales – which he did for an hour and a half every single day, never missed a day.'

Piotr – now going by the name Peter – had another stipulation. 'You cannot just *bang*,' he said. 'You have to be trained.' Still, Mark never had an actual lesson. Instead, he trained himself. 'He gave me a book from the Royal Air Force School of Marching Drums – military drums. So I sat down and there it was – "Right-left, right-left, right-left, paradiddle." And I sat down on a practice pad and went through this school of drumming. So that was my starting point. I learned snare drumming – marches – first of all.'

At home, they would listen to opera stuff, classical music, Hungarian gypsy music – 'which I love. Everything else was thought of as decadent. My dad says to me, "unruly music with untrained voices". He couldn't work it out. But my mum loved the modern music of the time. She loved Adam Faith and I liked the drums on his stuff. She liked Motown, the Beatles, Billy Fury, all those things.'

But a couple of records stood out. 'This is gonna sound really crass, but it's true. One was "The Monster Mash".'

A novelty hit from 1962 by Bobby 'Boris' Pickett and the Crypt-Kickers, 'The Monster Mash' opened with a cool descending drum pattern. Mark only had one tom-tom. He could tell from listening that Boris and his Crypt-Kickers had more than one, so Mark made another out of cardboard.

His other favourite song was 'Dizzy', a 1969 hit by Tommy Roe with legendary session drummer Hal Blaine performing a distinctive drum part. 'The drumming stood out,' he says. 'I never listen to lyrics. I can't even sing any of *our* songs. I have no idea about lyrics. I just listen to music in a different way.'

He'd go downstairs, put the record on, listen intently, then go upstairs for half an hour and bash away with that blanket over his kit.

With his brothers, he played at Langley village library in a talent contest, in a band they called New York City Public Library. He was onstage, kit all set up, including his cardboard tom, 'when another act came in and opened the side door not far from where I was drumming, and, to my horror, my cardboard floor tom blew off stage'.

Tony's family moved around west London and the two brothers went to separate schools. Their different upbringings and schooling meant that they didn't even have music in common. 'Lennox was very much into "black music",' says Tony. 'I never referred to it as "black music" – it was West Indian music. Calypso, ska, reggae. That was his thing and what he was getting from his secondary school. My school was more rock- or popular music-oriented.

'I was getting into music that people said wasn't part of what I should be looking like or being like. My family was all about West Indian parties on a Saturday night, curried goat, the whole West Indian thing. But when it came to music, calypso didn't do it for me. When I first heard Deep Purple's *In Rock*, I asked myself, "Why do you like this?" And I just had to say "Because I do!" When everyone was going to parties and skanking and jiving, I was headbanging and listening to Todd Rundgren.'

Tony had a mate at school, Simon, who was a budding keyboard player and guitarist. 'I'd be sitting around his house, getting smashed and listening to all of this music and getting into it and thinking, "I'm not sure I should be enjoying this".'

Tony and Simon started playing music together when Tony was about fourteen. His cousin was in the army and he gave him a bass guitar that a squaddie friend had made out of plywood and papier-mâché. At first, it was just something he used in front of the mirror, but then he found himself picking up notes, accidentally playing a note that was in tune with the record. 'Oh, I see how this works!' And then he'd work out the rest of the bassline.

His cousin came home on leave and took Tony to see the movie *Woodstock* at the cinema. 'The Who came on and Townshend started doing all his antics, and Daltrey had his chest out, like "I'm sex!"' Tony loved it. He had never seen or heard the Who before.

One day at Simon's house, there was an older guy sitting around playing guitar. 'I said to Simon, "Who's that?" He said, "That's my older brother." I said, "He's not very good, is he?"'

And it was then that Simon explained that, actually, his brother Pete was in a band – quite a *famous* band – called the Who. Simon's surname, it turned out, was Townshend.

Mark's older brother had records by Led Zeppelin, Deep Purple and David Bowie, but Mark wasn't impressed. 'That was *his* music,' he says. 'But I kinda liked the drums. I liked *Made in Japan* by Deep Purple. Ian Paice is a brilliant drummer.'

And then he found his music. 'Me and my brother, we got into jazz fusion. Billy Cobham, Herbie Hancock, Chick Corea, anything that didn't have vocals. Vocals meant it was a *song* – and songs meant that it had to have tame drumming on it. Jazz fusion was indulgent drumming. It was incredible stuff.'

Mark started going to pubs where he would 'watch the drummers and then talk to the band. And then they would say, "Why don't you sit in?" And I would be reasonably good.' He was doing an apprenticeship at British

Hurry on Boys (II: England)

Aerospace in engines and airframes. 'My father said, "You must stick it out. It's a six-year apprenticeship. You cannot leave to *bang things*."'

One day, he caught a band called Silver Stream in a pub. 'They were incredible,' he says. He would pick up tips from watching them. 'The drummer, all he did was mic the bass drum up, because that's the only thing you don't hear – low end. That's all I have in my monitors still.'

When their drummer left, they offered Mark the gig. They played weddings, British Legions, pubs. Three gigs a week, playing the top 10. 'We never played the Stones or anything like that. It was always the Commodores, Stevie Wonder – all kinds of muso-y stuff.'

And the rest of the band knew every little nuance: if he played wrong, they'd pull him up on it. 'I loved the discipline. They grounded me. That was my training – my military rudiments, and then playing every song they threw at me, from Latin bossa novas to songs in the charts.' When he was nineteen, somebody invited Mark to his first proper gig: a band called Boxer at the Roundhouse in London. Boxer were a short-lived group featuring Mike Patto, previously of Spooky Tooth, and acclaimed guitarist Ollie Halsall, formerly of Jon Hiseman's Tempest.

'I'd never heard of them,' says Mark. He went along anyway – maybe the drummer would be good. In the end, it wasn't Boxer who would have an impact. It was their support band, Brand X, a newly formed jazz fusion band with Phil Collins on drums.

'It was a life-changing moment,' says Mark. That night, in the Roundhouse, watching Brand X and Phil Collins – the drum kit set up sideways because Collins was left-handed, just the sheer *size* of his kit – he had a eureka moment. 'I knew what I wanted to do.'

'I left there a different guy,' he says. 'I was floored.' It was February 1976 and Brand X were playing the set that would become their debut album, released that June: *Unorthodox Behaviour*. 'To this day, it's my favourite record and I still practise with it. It's a crucial album to me.'

His friend had a connection to Boxer, so they went backstage after the show and Mark met Collins. 'I said to him, "I want to be a drummer one day – y'know, a *professional* drummer."' It was probably the first time the

Stay Alive

thought had formed in his head, let alone had come out of his mouth. 'I want to be like you.'

Collins was kind. 'Well,' he said. 'One day, I hope to hear about you.' Years later, Mark would play drums for Phil Collins.*

Mark went to see Brand X play the following night too and threw himself into the world of drumming: Phil Collins, Billy Cobham, Ian Paice, John Bonham, even Keith Moon ('for his crazy style but great drum sounds. I love good drum sounds especially').

Mostly he heard great drum sounds on those instrumental fusion records, which meant that, as the rest of the world embraced punk rock, Mark fell deeper in love with jazz fusion: Al Di Meola, Billy Cobham, the Dixie Dregs ...

He chuckles at this. 'It'd be completely different if you were talking to Bruce or Stuart,' he says. 'We think of Big Country as being like the bumblebee – it should never have worked. In theory, the wings were too small for the insect. But it worked *amazingly*.'

Tony and Simon Townshend put a few different bands together and, for a while, his brother Lennox joined them too, in a band called Clear Peace, with Lennox on vocals.

When he was sixteen, Tony went to Germany with his cousin, who was in the Signals Regiment, entertaining the troops in a NAAFI (Navy Army and Air Force Institutes) band. 'He was a Ben E. King, Otis Redding freak, and when he performed he did the whole lot – on his knees, begging you please – all that sort of stuff. I was a novice on the bass, but the rest of the guys in the band were really helpful. "Just get into the groove, get into the pocket, follow the bass drum."'

Back at home, Simon had begun writing his own material and Clear Peace became the Simon Townshend Band. Everything started to coalesce. Between the ages of sixteen and twenty, Tony was discovering music,

---

* 'I ended up working with Phil on the Prince's Trust Galas for many years,' says Mark. 'I said to him, "You know I was obsessed about your Brand X stuff." He said, "Oh, that's my crazy period! When I listen to that now, I can't believe what kind of music that was. It was a manic period, manic music."'

instruments, girls. 'And Simon was a big part of that,' he says. 'He was my best friend.'

He was improving on bass and taking inspiration from people like Chris Squire of Yes and Mike Rutherford of Genesis. 'I thought, *This is what you do to be identified.* They all had their own styles and sounds.' Other bass players had no identity, they just played along with the root notes. The players he loved had their own style and he set out to find his.

The Townshend house was at the heart of his growing up. Pete Townshend was sixteen years older than Simon, who had another brother, Paul, closer in age. It was a musical house, a party house, and that didn't start with Pete, or with Simon and Paul – it started with their parents.

'Betty Townshend was an old club singer of yore who was very outgoing, very loud, a complete and utter British character,' says Tony. Her husband Cliff had been a saxophone and clarinet player in the Squadronaires, another name for the Royal Air Force Dance Orchestra, a big band created to entertain the troops during wartime. The Squadronaires became famous after the war, recording for Decca and touring the country.

The house was full of people, music and laughter, and inhabited by generations of Townshends. Tony met his future wife, Jackie Whitburn, at the Townshend house. Jackie was a journalist on the *Acton Gazette* who reviewed a Simon Townshend Band show and then came to the inevitable party back at the Townshend house.

Tony had considered being a journalist himself, 'but I lost that when I got into music, to be honest. And getting involved with one made me realise what a good idea that was. But she was a great journalist, she knows her stuff.' (Jackie would go on to edit Big Country's official fan club magazine, *Country Club*.)

One day, Tony knocked at the Townshend door and Cliff answered. He bent down and picked a letter up off the floor. He said, 'Tony, do you know what this is? This is called a royalty cheque.'

Cliff explained what a royalty cheque was, about how – when you wrote a song or performed on a piece of music – you got paid for it every time it was used afterwards. The royalty cheque Cliff was holding was for music he played on *The Benny Hill Show*.

Piotr told Mark that he couldn't rehearse at home anymore. It was too loud. Other people might have found themselves a rehearsal room, but instead Mark bought himself a 1966 Ford Transit van that doubled as transport and rehearsal room. He would drive out to the Colnbrook by-pass where there are no footpaths, just a busy road with lorries trundling by. There he would pull into a lay-by and set his kit up in the back of the van. Then he would climb back over the seats, stick one of his cassettes in the stereo – Brand X or maybe Jeff Beck's *Blow By Blow* album – listen to a bit of drumming, then climb back over the seats, put on a pair of soundproof BOAC headphones, get behind the kit and practise.

The traffic would roar past, the drivers honking their horns at the sight of a Transit van rocking on its suspension in the lay-by, unaware that inside Mark Brzezicki was just honing his chops.

'I did that,' he says, 'for a long time.'

Tony was hanging out in Soho – around Broadwick Street, where Pete Townshend would soon open his Eel Pie Studios – hustling for gigs, making contacts and then picking up some session work, playing on adverts and jingles. 'I did loads of sessions,' he says. 'Things you never hear. You'd hear something at the cinema, or on an advert, and think, "Oh, I played on that!"'

Tony had discovered he was musically dyslexic. 'Basically, I couldn't read notes on the stave because they kept moving around, a bit like ordinary dyslexia. It became a real problem when I got into session work.'

Tony worked out that if he arrived early at the studio, he could get the music from the producer, sit on the toilet and work out as much as possible before the session started. 'By that time, I'd be 50 per cent literate on the song, and busk the rest.' It worked. They kept asking him back.

Sometimes he'd turn up way too early and rely on the hospitality of Soho's local brothels. A couple of Soho madams would spot him loitering and ask if they could, y'know, *help* him. 'I'd say, "Oh no, I'm a musician and I've got a gig in an hour's time, at the studio just down there."'

And the hardened old sex workers of Soho would take pity on him: 'Aw, come on in, son. Get out of the cold, 'ave a cuppa tea.'

Hurry on Boys (II: England)

Mark moved from drumming in his van to rehearsing at a nearby school, where he met a guitarist called Gary Stevenson, who was working with Richard Drummie and Peter Cox, soon to be famous as Go West, with Stevenson as their producer. Stevenson gave Mark a cassette. 'You should listen to this band,' he said. 'You'll like it. No idea what they're called, though.' Some guy had given him a demo, but there were no contact details on it.

Mark played the tape in his van. It was incredible, like Brand X but with singing. He loved it so much that he rehearsed by playing along with the tape, sitting in the back of his Transit, learning their songs, beat by beat, time signature by crazy time signature.

One day, he was flicking through the back pages of *Melody Maker* – famously, a rich recruiting ground for bands looking for members – when he saw an ad.

It said simply: 'Bill Bruford, Phil Collins-style drummer required.'

The auditions were at Shepperton Film Studios. Waiting outside, Mark realised that it was the mystery band from the tape. He listened to the other auditions, heard drummer after drummer crash and burn after the first ten seconds and thought, *C'mon*.

Finally, one of the band members came out and talked to him. It was Tony Butler. The band was the Simon Townshend Band.

Tony and Simon had been listening to Genesis and Yes, Simon accumulating keyboards – Mellotron, electric piano, all that kind of stuff – and they needed a drummer who could keep up. 'We had about eight drummers audition that night,' says Tony. 'And every now and again, I'd look up at the window and see a certain drummer, ear-wigging what everyone else was doing. At the end of the night, I said to Simon, "Let's check him out."'

They gave him a shot. Mark played his part flawlessly. Simon and Tony were impressed. They started with an easy one and moved on to the more technical tracks. Mark nailed them all. He knew the material backwards and played flawlessly. And then he was checking *them* out. Tony Butler, he realised, was a phenomenal bass player. And the singer, Simon, was great – playing piano and Mellotron when not playing guitar. They were teenagers, but they would have given Rush a run for their money.

Stay Alive

'Mark was absolutely brilliant,' says Tony. 'He played perfectly, played aggressively, played with panache – all the things we wanted. And his syncopation was brilliant. He just fitted the bill. But, more than that, I saw in him what I saw later when I met Stuart – this attractive guy, who looked great and played with incredible prowess.'

So both Tony and Mark were now in the Simon Townshend Band playing those clever, complicated songs, gigging at the Red Lion every week and doing really well. They were writing songs and recording at Pete Townshend's Eel Pie Studios. WEA were interested.

But then something unexpected happened: punk rock. Suddenly, Simon Townshend wasn't into jazz fusion anymore. He was into the Clash, the Pistols, Buzzcocks and the Jam.

Mark and Tony were a bit threatened by punk. They'd been training to be these great prog-fusion players – Mark could even see himself playing disco and soul – and now all that great music was being killed off by this new noise where the whole thing was that anyone could do it, you didn't have to be a great musician.

The Mellotron was out. Simon picked one of Pete Townshend's guitars off the wall and the Simon Townshend Band became a three-piece called On the Air, a power-pop band in the vein of the Jam or the Police. And, slowly, Mark began to like some of this punk stuff. There were some great drummers around. He liked the Clash's Topper Headon and Stewart Copeland of the Police, another skilled drummer who had found himself in a similar position.

'Copeland was groundbreaking,' he says, 'but so were a lot of the punk drummers. I liked the energy that they produced. And it brought out a different side of my drumming.

'I was a musical snob. I didn't like punk at first, but I grew to like it.'

Tony liked bands like Thin Lizzy and Ian Dury and the Blockheads – exciting groups with incredible musicians – but he was starting to get a little disenchanted.

Hurry on Boys (II: England)

There was punk and then there was new wave – every month a new musical fashion to keep up with. A young A&R guy at WEA had Simon's ear and tried to convince him that the band should wear camouflage clothing like Echo and the Bunnymen.

The people around Simon Townshend were obviously just interested in him. Simon had done a couple of solo singles and Tony hadn't been asked to be involved. So he and Mark branched out on their own, selling themselves as a double act called Rhythm for Hire. Mark designed a logo for their business cards and they set out to become the 'Sly and Robbie of Soho' – a killer rhythm section available for session work.

They got a lot of work. Tony had been asked to play on Pete Townshend's *Empty Glass* album and Mark got the call to play on a track too; they then both played on the follow-up *All the Best Cowboys Have Chinese Eyes*. Recording at Wessex Studios and Air Studios, working with production legends like Bill Price and Chris Thomas, it was a trip. 'We played on two and a half Townshend albums,' says Tony. 'You couldn't ask for a better mentorship than that.'

On the Air's manager, with a bit of help from Pete Townshend, got the band a two-single deal with WEA: 'Ready for Action' – for which Mark designed the sleeve, in a parody of the *Beano* comic – and 'Another Planet'. To build some momentum, their manager also got the trio out on the road, doing some support slots for the Skids.

'I loved them,' says Mark. 'I thought they were really innovative. I loved Stuart's playing. He's an unusual guitar player. I called him a great musician and he didn't like that. He used to say, "Don't call me a musician. I'm a songwriter, guitarist, singer, but muso? I don't like that tag." And yet, actually, he was a really good muso. Although he was playing punk, he still really knew how to play the guitar. He stood out.'

Tony was impressed too. 'Not only did Stuart play guitar really well, but he looked good doing it. He had good moves, his hair was great – everything about him was attractive. And I just thought, "He's cool. I like him". And I kept him in the back of my mind.

'I couldn't understand a fucking thing Richard Jobson was singing, but it worked. The interaction between him and Stuart was really great. I found out Stuart was a practical joker. Things like making a hotel bed the wrong way, so when you went to get into it, you couldn't get into the bed. Or you'd go for a dump and all of a sudden it comes back at you because he's put clingfilm across the toilet bowl.

'But I didn't *really* get to know him. He was very quiet and most of the time he wasn't there. It's what he did all the way through my career with him. He wasn't incredibly sociable. And when Sandra was around, nobody saw him.'

Supporting the Skids was a great experience but, when it ended, Mark never thought anything more of it.

He was doing jingles and ad music for a guy called Steve Hall at Hallmark Studios, playing on five or six sessions a week: adverts for Ski yoghurt, Dairy Milk Chocolate, Just Juice, all that stuff.

On 30 May 1981, Tony and Mark played with Pete Townshend at the Rock for Jobs concert at Brockwell Park in south London. Britain was in a deep recession, with unemployment soaring to 2.5 million. The TUC led a protest march from Jarrow in north-east England to London where the prime minister, Margaret Thatcher, refused to meet with them.

Rock for Jobs was a concert in support of the marchers. Pete Townshend & Friends were headlining – Traffic co-founder Jim Capaldi joined them for some songs. Further down the bill were the Members. After the show, this guy came up to Tony and Mark. He was the manager of the Members.

'Hello,' he said. 'My name is Ian Grant. Who are you two?'

9
Goodbye Civilian

*The dark room. A doctor's prophesy.
A cunt of the worst kind. Dodging traffic on
the M3. Mince and tatties and hoovering a hoose*

By the time On the Air supported them, the Skids were hitting new heights – and on their last legs. They had made their best album and were playing to bigger crowds in bigger halls, but personal tensions, illness and alcohol were about to bring them to an end. 'Stuart decided, "Fuck this, I can't take this anymore,"' says Jobson. 'But neither could we.'

With Sandy Muir gone, the Skids hooked up with Arnakata, a management company that also looked after Bill Nelson. To replace Bill Simpson, they brought in Russell Webb, a Glasgow-born bass player who had been in Slik and PVC2 with Midge Ure, and knew the Skids from his time in the Zones.

Webb was in London when he bumped into Jobson on Kensington High Street. 'Richard asked if I would come to the studio because they needed a bass player,' he says. 'It was just one of these sort of magical, miraculous things.'

In the studio, everything just clicked. 'We hit it off,' says Russell. 'Our playing styles really gelled. Mike was making melodies with his drums, I was making melodies with the bass and with Stuart's melodies on the guitar, the whole thing just sounded fucking *immense*.

'I would play harmonies along with what he was doing, and counter melodies along with the vocal. My style just seemed to fit quite neatly into what was previously a really raw approach. The way Stuart and I gelled, we drew out more of the musicality in the songs.'

They played for twenty-six hours straight and wrote 'Circus Games', 'A Woman in Winter' and 'Arena' all in one go. When the session was done, and Russell was leaving for his train, Stuart ran after him and asked him if he wanted to join the band.

'Suddenly Stuart had people around him that were solid musicians,' says Jobson. 'So he didn't have to do everything. He had people he could pass to. He could never do that with me. You couldn't say to me, "What would a D minor sound like there?" But with these guys, he could play around. We changed the way we wrote the songs. We split the credits with everybody.'

With Mike Baillie on drums and Mick Glossop producing, they went back to the studio to record their third album, *The Absolute Game*.

'It's a really good album,' says Jobson. 'You can hear the beginnings of Big Country.'

You really can. *The Absolute Game* is the Skids' one truly great album. Where *Days in Europa* flirted with the new wave, *The Absolute Game* aimed for something more timeless and eternal – the 'open sound' that Stuart had been looking for.

'I started to hear this thing with 'Hurry On Boys' and 'A Woman in Winter' that could take us in a new direction,' says Jobson. 'Even from my own childhood, there was a mixture of the church and my mother singing Irish folk songs – which all had a bit of a political leaning, if you know what I mean.'

Stuart had started leaning into Scottish folk music a little, electrifying it. 'The guitar style had evolved and you can hear it,' says Richard. In concert, Stuart would add 'Will Ye Go, Lassie, Go', a Scottish folk song also known as 'Wild Mountain Thyme' or 'Purple Heather', in the middle of 'Of One Skin'. 'It was becoming part of it,' says Jobson. 'There was a style evolving that would become primarily important to Big Country's identity. But it was evolving *then*.'

Recording at The Manor, Glossop double-tracked all the guitar parts, literally getting Stuart to play the same thing twice, a technique he'd employed on the Ruts' debut album. 'Stuart was a great guitarist,' says Glossop. 'He could play it a second time and it would be exactly the same. It still sounds like one guitar because the two lock together really well, but you get this extra thing, and a wide stereo spread.

'All of his parts were really interesting. Really good riffs. Stuart was on his way to developing that Big Country sound – the sort of slightly bagpipes-y thing that he developed. The sound of *The Absolute Game* is down to the parts – it's what he chose to play. He'd quite often have a melodic riff and he'd be playing it on two strings and one of the strings would be like a drone, which goes back to the ancient days of folk music – pre-folk music to a large extent – the idea of having one note while another melody plays on top.'

Glossop remembers listening to Stuart playing with an MXR harmoniser, probably the M-129, the pitch-changing device that John Leckie remembers him having on 'Masquerade', although Glossop thinks Stuart didn't get it until after they'd finished the album. 'He got that sound using that box. It wasn't on *The Absolute Game* because he didn't have it then. But it was absolutely the Big Country sound, using this rather crude MXR harmoniser. You could do octaves with it as well as slightly detune. He was really into it.'

'The first Big Country album could really have been the album that came after *The Absolute Game*,' says Jobson. 'There's a connection there musically – not lyrically. I don't think I've ever been able to write those kinds of lyrics. I don't have anything against them. I just don't think it's something that I could have written.'

Still, at times the lyrics did seem to match the music's search for something timeless and archetypal. It's not a huge leap from *The Absolute Game*'s best moments to *The Crossing*'s tales of lives lived at the edge, people battling the elements and working the land, of gamblers and houses burning, and unmentionable tragedy. In his book of lyrics, *No Bad Words*, Jobson says that he wanted his writing on *The Absolute Game* 'to be less masculine, less about military conflict and more about people's lives. Big stories that almost had a cinematic feel – a narrative with a drama and more personal type of conflict.'

The characters in the songs give birth, suffer loss, endure. 'Oh, this pain inside me now, it throws me to the floor,' goes 'Happy to Be with You'. 'Out of Town' talks of 'weeping by the river'. 'Daddy's dead, can't understand,' says 'Hurry On Boys'. There's a lyrical theme of innocence lost and children in peril. 'The Devil's Decade' pleads with a higher power: 'Oh mother of mine, your children are bleeding, please show us a sign.' In 'Goodbye Civilian', the boys in the river are 'dying from blows' or 'caught in the tide' with 'nowhere to run'. 'All the boys are innocent,' goes the closing refrain of 'Arena'.

And, throughout it all, Adamson delivers a masterclass in guitar playing. *The Absolute Game* is full of inventive choppy rhythm playing and astonishing licks and solos. 'Out of Town', first recorded for the *Masquerade* EP, is like a showcase, filled with melodic lead lines.

'Circus Games' suggests a story in which an innocent is killed and the child's mother takes her own life ('She sees a heavenly noose'). 'On the surface,' wrote Jobson, 'it's a song about making the wrong decisions but underneath lies a deep sadness that is sometimes lost in the music.' As with Big Country, the anthemic nature of the music disguised the dark subject matter. They got a group of children from a local school to sing on the chorus of 'Circus Games' and Mick Glossop pushed Stuart into 'kind of conducting them, showing them when to start singing, because the timing of the chorus is unusual. He was slightly reluctant – just a bit shy about doing that.' In the finished recording, Adamson's guitar plays a kind of call-and-response with the chorus.

The theme of 'Circus Games', wrote Jobson, is hypocrisy. 'It was our pet hate when we started, but I think Stuart was beginning to see me as a bit of a hypocrite. My dalliances with London life left him cold and what looked superficially as a search for fame on my part was blasphemy to him. It was much more complicated than that, but we never seemed to get around to talking about it. Stuart avoided direct confrontation.'

Jobson was doing spoken word, theatre, poetry readings – he'd thrown himself into the life of a London artist. He shared a flat with Steve Severin of Siouxsie and the Banshees, and played in a football team with Thin Lizzy's Phil Lynott and Sex Pistol Steve Jones. 'I wanted to evolve quick,' says Jobson, 'and I ran around a bit like a headless chicken, grabbing anything that influenced me and using it. I didn't really care about the response to it. It was just the *doing* of it that was exciting.

'Stuart was more measured. I think he thought I was an uncontrollable force at times. We never really had big arguments, we were just different people. He wanted a house and a family, while I didn't really expect to be alive after the age of twenty-five. I'm sure I pissed him off all the time.'

It *did* piss Stuart off. Jobson's life on the London scene was anathema to him. 'The scene was not of interest us at all,' says Sandra. In the Adamson household, 'there was no scene whatsoever. The scene was mince and tatties, hoovering a hoose and getting on with life. And if you're good at songwriting, brilliant. But everything else has to come first. Because if it's not right at home, it's not right *anywhere*.'

Russell Webb picked up on the tensions between the two men. 'Stuart felt that Richard was not always around when you needed him to be. If you were having a meeting or something like that, Richard wasn't always there. Stuart wanted the Skids to be a band that revolved around music – to let the music do the talking rather than, you know, the "big star" frontman. So that was always a tension in the band.'

Stuart was considering leaving – but why should *he* leave the band that he had formed? A different person might have asserted control and sacked the singer, but Stuart hated confrontation. Instead, he decided to wait for Jobson to leave. It seemed like only a matter of time. 'We kept thinking, "He'll get dragged away into something else",' says Sandra, 'and it never happened. I blame myself a bit because I was saying to Stuart, "Hang on in there, keep going." And he was almost in tears. He really *was* in tears. It must have been torture for him.'

Jobson felt it. 'Behind the scenes, maybe Stuart was hankering to do his own thing,' he says, 'write his own songs and fulfil something that he wasn't fulfilling anymore. Because lyrics sometimes impose the identity on a song – what it's about.'

But, meanwhile, the Skids rumbled on. Like the lyrics of 'A Woman in Winter', a song partly inspired by the suicide of a girlfriend of Richard's, 'Winter it just fell some more and I was still alone.'

And then came the rash. Around this time, Stuart became interested in photography. He bought himself a Pentax camera and would develop pictures in a darkroom he made at home. Russell Webb also liked photography and the two of them shot pictures at The Manor during the recording of *The Absolute Game*, some of which ended up on the fold-out sleeve of the 'Circus Games' single.

Not long afterwards, Stuart came out in a rash. 'He was taking photographs, developing them and then this rash happened,' says Sandra. 'It was just before the Skids ended and it drove him to distraction. It was horrendous. He couldnae take his hands off his body. He was itchy from head to toe – and it got worse and worse.'

The doctor prescribed Betnovate – a cream used to treat eczema and psoriasis – and various steroid creams. Nothing seemed to work.

He went to a private doctor in Harley Street in London to get patch-tested. They did forty patch tests on him and produced a long list of the many things that Stuart was allergic to. 'And the one main one,' says Sandra, 'was photo development chemicals.'

The chemicals used to develop photographs are highly toxic and categorised as strong 'sensitisers'. The University of Arkansas defines a sensitiser as 'a substance that causes exposed individuals to develop an allergic reaction in normal tissue after repeated exposure to the substance ... Sensitizer exposure can lead to all of the symptoms associated with allergic reactions, or can increase an individual's existing allergies.'

Stuart's body had reacted to these chemicals and it had triggered a series of allergies. 'The list of the things he was allergic to was *huge*,' says Sandra. 'It was everything – black dye, lanolin. He was allergic to nearly everything you come into contact with on a daily basis.'

Dr Sylvie Marston confirmed by mail more than forty things that Stuart should avoid. They included:

Cement
Ashes
Boiler lining
Anti-rust coatings
Welding
Printing
Paper industry (bleaches and detergents)
Tanning of leather
Glossy paper
Linoleum
Some soaps
Wood polish
Some eye cosmetics and blushers
Paint enamel
Linseed oil
Crayons
Adhesive plasters.

He couldn't wear black trainers or have a black belt, and they couldn't use conditioner in their laundry because it contains lanolin. But Stuart couldn't avoid all of these things and the rashes would often be unbearable – red blotches, cracked skin, tiny itchy pimples. He suffered from it for a large part of the '80s.

'It wasn't until he was about thirty that you noticed he wasn't talking about it anymore,' says Sandra. 'He might say, "I've got a wee bit of rash", but it would only be a couple of blotches and then he would use whatever he had and it would go.'

But it had a huge impact on him. In his book, *Into the Valley*, Richard Jobson talks about Adamson 'disappearing' regularly, without explanation. 'Often, when Stuart did disappear and come home, it would be when his rash was not good,' says Sandra. 'He would just need to come back to his own place, no hotels, get in the shower, calm it down.'

More significantly, his distress over his allergies led him to alcohol.

'Prior to that, Stuart didn't really have any interest in drink,' says Sandra. 'The drinking really started when that rash appeared. And it was because he could not escape from it. I can remember him starting to drink at night – because *he couldn't sleep.*'

The pace was relentless. After recording *The Absolute Game*, the band went to Rockfield to write more new songs. 'I mean, we'd literally just finished *The Absolute Game*,' says Jobson, 'and they're saying, "Go and write more songs"! It was like, "Fuckin' hell!"'

At some point, Stuart went back home. 'Stuart did feel that he needed to be at home a lot,' says Sandra. 'When he wasn't comfortable, or he'd done his parts, or his rash flared up, he went home. He would disappear when he thought he could, when he wasnae needed. Even at times where he *was* needed, he would say, "Fuck it, I don't care. I'm no' going back."'

He would go fishing or get his camera out or go to the football. 'And *then* he would go back. And that's the way he liked it.'

So, in the middle of this writing session, he disappeared from Rockfield, leaving Jobson and Russell Webb at the studio. 'Russell and I had been doing a thing called Cabaret Futura,' says Jobson. 'I'd read poetry and sometimes he'd do this Eno-esque ambient stuff behind me with his girlfriend, Virginia Astley.* So we started to mess around.'

They made weird, discordant songs and pretty, looping instrumentals. 'They were really quite lovely,' says Jobson. 'When Stuart came back, I thought he'd go bananas, but it was totally the opposite. He loved it. He did his own versions of them. On 'Filming in Africa', the bassline was Russell, but Stuart did all the backward vocals, and it was a very elegant, lovely thing. His guitar playing was very Bill Nelson – more the Bill Nelson of Red Noise than Be Bop Deluxe – but it was great.'

The recordings became *Strength Through Joy*, a free album that came with initial copies of *The Absolute Game*, with another bit of inspiration

---

* Virginia Astley was a singer-songwriter who would go on to play with Prefab Sprout, David Sylvian and Dave Stewart, and released several solo albums. Her sister was married to Pete Townshend.

from the Nazis: Strength Through Joy, aka the KdF, was an organisation set up to encourage leisure activities among the workers of the Third Reich. 'I had read about the Strength Through Joy camps,' says Jobson, 'a kind of Übermensch Butlin's. It sounded so ridiculous and at the same time was part of the insanity that the Nazis unleashed on their own country before the beginning of the war.'

The track 'Strength Through Joy' was punk Beefheart: a pulverising riff, with Jobson barking orders over the top. 'We had this crazy riff that we looped around and around so the repetition became an ugly sound,' he says. 'The words I used were a repetitive, percussive and angry blast of commands. A crazy sound for an even crazier idea.

'There can be no doubt that playing with imagery from that period was a dangerous and maybe in retrospect foolish thing to do. The natural irreverence of punk brought into play a juvenile sarcasm and arrogance, but underneath that lay a serious intent.'

There's a Scottish phrase for annoying people: 'noising them up'. It means to wind people up, to antagonise, to get noise from them or maybe bother them with your noise. This was the Skids, noising people up.

The Skids' management company Arnakata was run by a man called Mike Dolan. 'He became Be Bop Deluxe's manager,' says Bill Nelson. 'He was well-known to EMI and good at sorting deals out.'

Russell Webb is more brutal in his assessment. 'Mike Dolan was a cunt of the worst kind,' he says.

Arnakata went into liquidation and left a lot of people out of pocket.

'They were pretty horrible people that looked after Dollar,'* says Jobson. 'They had no interest in us as a group of people. They just thought, "There's money in this."'

With Arnakata gone, the Skids needed new management. Some of the Finchley Boys, the Stranglers' crew, were working for the Skids down at Rockfield and word got back to Ian Grant that they needed a manager.

---

* Dollar were a pop duo who had some hits in the late '70s and early '80s. They were guff.

'I had left the Stranglers at that point,' says Grant, 'and gone into partnership with my old buddy Alan Edwards.'

Alan Edwards had grown up near Grant on the south coast. 'I first met Alan by selling him acid,' says Ian. 'He was a crazy kid who took acid at school. He hitched to Afghanistan when he was fifteen. He got all the way there, got dysentery and was flown back.'

Edwards was five years younger than Grant, but the two men became close friends and when Ian started working with the Albion agency, Alan would come and hang out with him, watching pub rock acts like Ducks Deluxe, Brinsley Schwartz and Ian Dury.

Edwards' friendship with Grant was key to his career and maybe, he argues, it was central to the success of Big Country too. 'Would there have been a Big Country without Ian Grant?' he says. 'Maybe not. Ian was a force of nature. I looked up to him as a kid. He was the wildest, most interesting person on the south coast and he was always in the local papers.

'He's a character. I know so many stories. He always went further than everybody else. He was outlandish. I was the straight guy, really. I'd be going to work on the publicity or the radio and that side of it and Ian would make it work on the road. It was a brilliant partnership.'

Alan had been working for Keith Altham, the legendary music PR, helping out with the likes of the Who when Ian said, 'Do you want to be the PR for the Stranglers?'

So Alan set up his own PR company, looking after Buzzcocks, the Damned, the Stranglers and Blondie, and then he and Ian decided to take the arrangement a bit further. 'I had the publicity thing down,' says Alan, 'and he had the management and live thing down. It was a powerful combination. So we formed Grant–Edwards.'

'Alan had Hazel O'Connor, who was our secretary just before that,' says Grant. 'I got the Members and we wanted one more band. The Skids became a target.'

Alan remembers going to see the Skids at Hammersmith Palais. His then partner Valerie said, 'That keyboard player is really good. He's the talent.' The 'keyboard player' was Stuart.

By August 1980, they were managing the Skids and planning the next album. *The Absolute Game* came out in September and went straight to number 9 in the UK album charts, the band's highest-charting album.

Ian Grant sent all four members of the Skids to a doctor on Harley Street. 'I used to see him myself,' he says. 'He was the kind of doctor, you'd tell him what was wrong with you and he'd say, "Fancy a gin and tonic?" and tell you about *his* problems. So I told him about this band and he said, "Bring them in".'

Afterwards, the doctor told Ian what he thought. 'He said, "Russell Webb will break up this band. He'll get between Stuart and Richard." And he did – not by anything other than his presence, the fact he existed. Russell's a lovely guy now, but he was a bit full-on at the time.'

'Richard wanted me in the band so he could have somebody to be both a go-between and a wedge between him and Stuart,' says Russell. 'In a way, I felt that maybe they were using me so that I could negotiate some of Richard's perspective with Stuart and some of Stuart's perspective with Richard.'

Russell had come in at the end of things. What was about to happen was so inevitable that even a drunken doctor could see it.

'Our job was to try and make it a bit more mainstream,' says Alan Edwards. To do that, he had this mad idea based on the kids choir on 'Circus Games'. Skids for Kids was a mini-tour of schools, playing playgrounds on the back of a lorry – pretty ironic for an album about children in peril. They played Russell's old school, Bellahouston Academy, where he'd once thrown that stone at Eric Clapton.

'It was surreal,' he says. 'Back in the playground of my old school, standing on the back of a lorry. That was funny, really weird.'

'I've no desire to push myself into being a media figure,' Stuart told Ian Penman in an interview with the *NME*. 'I'm quite happy with what I'm doing, creating quietly away in my own corner. I'm quite happy with my cameras and my wife and my guitars.'

Stay Alive

In October, they set off on a sixteen-date tour of the UK and Ireland. By the end of the tour, the band was finished.

It started on the first day, 3 October, at the Edinburgh Odeon. Stuart vanished, says Jobson. 'He fucked off. Didn't want to be around.'

A few shows later, he had a meltdown in front of the band and crew. Russell Webb thinks it was on the way to Plymouth. The bus was on the motorway 'and Stuart just lost it – *completely* lost it – shouting and screaming for the bus to stop'.

Ian Grant remembers it too. 'We were on the M3 and he got out of the van ...'

They pulled over onto the hard shoulder at the side of the motorway. Stuart got off the bus and demanded that they get his bags out of the hold. He was going to walk across the motorway, he said, to get to the other side of the road where he would hitch a lift to London, and then get a train to Dunfermline.

As the bus driver searched for his bags, the tour manager and sound guy argued with Stuart at the side of the motorway. Eventually, they managed to bundle him back onto the bus.

'It was really heavy,' says Russell. 'It scared the shit out of me. I don't know why he did it. Maybe he was still feeling that there was a lot on his shoulders. But it came right out the blue, totally unexpected. I thought he was going to get smacked by a car. It was really scary.'

Their last gig in mainland Britain – before dates in Belfast, Dublin and Cork – was Hammersmith Odeon, 21 October 1980.

It was their biggest-ever show and Stuart disappeared again. 'Hammersmith Odeon,' says Jobson. 'This amazing venue where all of our great heroes have played. He didn't come to the soundcheck and we thought we were going to have to pull the gig.'

Hammersmith, it turns out, represented something else to Stuart.

'This is where it changed,' says Sandra. She and Stuart looked at Hammersmith Odeon and venues of that size and instead of seeing triumph, they thought, '"That's where it ends. With that line-up, it can't go any further". The genuine talent wasnae there.'

The Skids weren't going to conquer America. They weren't going to be the Police. They were going to stay mid-sized and the struggle was going to continue. But the thought of giving it up was equally scary. 'Because you were so *close*,' says Sandra. 'So near, yet so far.'

On the evening of the Hammersmith gig, Stuart phoned Sandra and told her that he wasn't going to play. 'I was horrified,' she says, '*horrified*. You can't just say you're not doing it hours before. Just *do* it and then we'll deal with whatever happens afterwards.

'I think I maybe even said, "Well, you know what you're going to get off me if you don't do that gig." Because there's a responsibility aspect. I was more mature in that way, thinking about the responsibility to everybody who bought a ticket, never mind the band. But, again, I could never ever blame him for the way he felt.'

Hammersmith was full. With no sign of Stuart, the band tried to work out how many Skids songs Paul Fox of support act the Ruts knew, in case he had to stand-in. Steve Jones turned up, but he only knew two of their songs. 'Everybody was panicking, freaking out,' says Russell. 'I was in the courtyard behind one of the dressing rooms, punching the wall – literally punching the walls – my knuckles all fucking cut. I just thought, "Christ – all of this for nothing!"'

Stuart appeared five minutes before they went on stage.

'He said he couldn't find 10 pence for the phone,' says Russell. 'He was in a *hotel*.'

There's a great photograph by Virginia Turbett from that night. Jobson has it framed next to his desk to this day. 'Stuart's flying in one direction and I'm flying the other way. So high in the air, the two of us. If people knew the truth about that photograph, that he turned up just five minutes before the gig ...' He shakes his head. 'And yet somehow this incredible force of nature is there in front of you. I love that photograph.'

Fundamentally broken, but energised by new management, the Skids limped on. They had dates in Europe in November. At some point on tour – maybe in the Netherlands with Hazel O'Connor or in Sweden with

'If people knew the truth about that photograph ...'
© *Virginia Turbitt/Getty*

the Jam – Stuart and Ian stayed up late talking in the latter's hotel room. When Ian fell asleep, Stuart read through his manager's notebooks.

Years later, Grant asked Stuart why he'd chosen him to be his manager and Stuart told him that it was what he'd learned that night. 'I was impressed by your notebooks,' Stuart told him. 'I didn't realise there were so many things you had to do.'

The rash, the drinking, the relentlessness, the touring, the writing, the playing, the being away from home. It was all getting to Stuart.

'It was really, really bad,' says Sandra. 'While he was away, the drinking was getting worse. He knew that there was no longevity with the band line-up. And that's when it came to a head.'

Russell Webb had written a song. 'I wrote "Iona" around about that time,' he says. 'I suppose, subconsciously, I felt the unravelling and I wanted to do something that gave me a chance to have a bigger voice.'

'Originally, I was writing the lyrics,' says Jobson, 'but Russell wanted to have a go and I don't think either Stuart or I cared by that point. So he had a go and ... I hate that song. I hate the lyrics, so sentimental. The one thing we never were was sentimental. I wanted it to be *hard*. Not *that*.'

But, at the time, he saw Russell as an ally. 'What happened was that Richard jumped on it,' says Webb. Stuart wasn't engaged, so Russell filled the gap and Richard encouraged him – which alienated Stuart even further. 'From that point on, it was Richard and me against Stuart,' says Russell. Bill Nelson was lined up to produce and, at Highland Studios in Inverness, everything unravelled.

Bill didn't like the song. He and Russell disagreed. Stuart played his solo, but his heart wasn't in it. Sensing the dynamic, Bill Nelson decided it would be better for everyone if he didn't continue.

'My daughter was born on 14 April 1981,' says Clive Ford. He called the Adamsons to share the news and Sandra told him Stuart was at the studio in Inverness. He phoned the studio and got a rather flustered receptionist.

'I'm sorry, he's not here.'

'Do you know when he's coming back?'

Stay Alive

'I don't think he *is* coming back.'
'What?'
'He left and he took all his stuff with him.'

'We call it "the famous 'Iona' tapes",' says Sandra. 'I was at my mum's and he walked through the door. He had a tape in his hands and he threw it on the couch and he went, "Listen to that pish!" Those were his exact words. "Listen to that pish."'

Sandra pushed the cassette into her mum's tape player and listened. After a minute or two, she looked at Stuart.

'Is it no' about time?' she said.

'Fuckin' right it is.'

10

Wake

*Scottish soul music.
The basement beneath the library.
The new band gets a name. Bottles of pish*

'There's only one way to classify music: it either gives you shivers up the back or it doesn't.'

In June 1981, Stuart spoke to Johnny Waller at *Sounds* about the Skids' split. 'The band's energy is spent,' he said. 'It's just come through a total lack of communication between everyone in the band.

'The distance is a big problem, and I refuse to move to London purely to become more successful. You're always speaking to people on the phone, which is a pain at the best of times.'

With his background on Dunfermline's *Kingdom Come* fanzine, Waller knew Stuart well – well enough to ask him if he was worried about 'the glare of publicity' shifting from Richard to him. 'I don't know,' said Stuart. 'I haven't thought about it that much ... It's something I might have to come to terms with. I was never particularly averse to interviews before, it's just that I don't go out of my way to do things on a publicity level. I'm much more interested in working on the musical side.'

Waller asked him about his immediate plans. 'On a basic level, I'm going to record some stuff on a four-track TEAC machine through there [points to the bedroom]. I just want to make music that's alive and sparkling ...

'I see all the great music as being huge and wide. It releases so many emotions.'

Technically, the Skids *hadn't* split. Jobson and Webb continued without Stuart, finishing the single and working on an album, *Joy*. In an interview, Russell had described the Skids as 'Scottish soul music' and the phrase had stuck with him. 'When we did *Joy*, I went to really dig into that Scottish soul thing,' he says. 'I wanted to use the sound of anvils and hammers and earth and all that sort of stuff.'

When Bill Nelson ducked out, Ian Grant approached Mike Oldfield to see if he'd be interested in producing 'Iona' and playing bagpipes on the record. Russell met Oldfield for a drink and Oldfield said, 'Why don't you produce it and I'll play on it?'

'That was a big shock to me because I saw *The Exorcist* when I was twelve and it marked me for life,' says Russell. The opening theme from Oldfield's *Tubular Bells* album was used in the movie. 'And the music, it also marked me for life. There was a genius there and hearing him say, "You should produce this song but I'll come and play on it" ... Well, I can't even describe what it was like.'

Flattered – and backed by Virgin – Russell stepped into the producer's chair to record a Skids single for which he alone had written both the words and music. From the outside, it looked like he'd staged a coup.

The Skids finished 'Iona' at Pink Floyd's studio in Britannia Row in Islington, using the guitar parts Stuart had recorded at Inverness. 'Originally I thought it would be wrong to include Stuart's parts,' says Russell, 'but the more I heard them, the more nuanced and inspired they sounded.'

To Russell, the solo's simplicity and lack of histrionics showed how musically in tune Stuart was with Bill Nelson. At Britannia Row, Mike Oldfield used a Fairlight to create a bagpipe sound, harmonising with Stuart's parts. 'It made it the actual theme of the song in some ways,' says Russell. 'We still had Stuart on the record and I suppose that made it legitimately "Skids". It was a mistake to put it out as a Skids record – but that's commercialism for you.'

So Stuart Adamson was no longer in the Skids, but Virgin had a single featuring his guitar playing and they kept Russell and Richard on to finish the final Skids album, *Joy*.

Russell has a nice memory of going to Los Angeles to meet with his friend, John McGeoch, the Scottish guitarist from Siouxsie and the Banshees, and playing him the final mixes of *Joy*. McGeoch went to the back of the band's tour bus and emerged an hour later. 'He was sobbing his heart out,' says Russell. 'He was like, "Aw, it's the most beautiful thing I've ever heard!" He *was* pissed, right enough.'

It wasn't as warmly received elsewhere. At the *NME*, Barney Hoskyns stuck the boot in. With *Joy*, he said, the Skids have 'broken all reasonable barriers of taste and credibility … *Joy* is one great idiotic farce of a concept album, an ersatz folk epic of toil and brotherhood, a spurious trek through war and agriculture in quest of the blood and the soil … A more stunted stunt than *Joy* will not be heard this year.'

Joy became the first and only Skids album not to make the UK top 40. (They reformed in 2017 with Bruce Watson and his son Jamie on guitar. Their albums *Burning Cities*, from 2018, and *Destination Dusseldorf*, from 2023, went to 28 and 36, respectively.)

'It wasn't the time for it,' says Russell. 'ABC were about to hit. It was an album out of time.'

Today, *Joy* sounds surprisingly good. It's a bit theatrical, a bit 'Arts Lab' – its weird 'new-wave folk' wouldn't satisfy punks, nor new-wave fans or fans of genuine folk music, a genre that's all about authenticity – but at times it's oddly affecting. Placed at the end of the first side, the epic sentimentality of 'Iona' makes more sense: a hopeful salve to the songs of misery and loss that precede it.

It just didn't sound like the Skids. There was a distinct lack of Stuart Adamson. 'There were some things missing,' says Russell. 'One of them was guitar.'

A couple of years later, writing the sleevenotes of Skids compilation album *Fanfare*, John Peel expressed regret that 'in his search for a Celtic identity and sound, Richard Jobson overlooked the fact that it was precisely these elements that distinguished the Skids from the post-punk herd in the first place'.

Russell Webb has been a practising hypnotherapist since 1992 and works as a mindfulness instructor at a school for kids with additional learning needs ('some social, emotional stuff, autism and whatnot').

'You know what it's like,' he says. 'If I knew then what I know now, things might be different. I could have been a stronger person for Stuart to lean on. We did connect in a fundamental way musically, and we had a kind of shared family history – not identical but very traumatic. I mean, I guess.' Russell is aware of Stuart's father's conviction. 'I'm only guessing that Stuart's was traumatic.'

'Our world views were very different,' says Richard Jobson. 'That really comes through for me when I read the lyrics of Big Country. Those kind of sweeping landscapes. But it's interesting because that's what we were trying to do with *Joy* and we hadn't quite worked it out.

'He was such a talented guy, it was probably time for him to express himself away from me. Certainly, by the time he got into the *Joy* sessions, it was done. You could tell.'

Sometime after the split, Stuart called Russell and asked him to meet him at a hotel in London's King's Cross. There, Stuart asked Russell if he'd like to join his new band. Webb turned him down.

'I really regret not accepting Stuart's offer to go with him to Big Country,' he says now. 'Honestly, the only reason I can think of is that I thought Stuart was just a bit unstable. And with my own background, I found that really quite difficult to be around. It felt as if I was on adrenaline all the time, walking on glass, didn't know when things were going to pop.'

That Christmas, Russell was at home in London when he got a letter from the Skids' new manager. 'Dear Richard,' it said, 'I agree. I'm going to send a letter to Russell and tell him that he's no longer in the band.' The manager had put the letter in the wrong envelope. 'Presumably Richard got the letter intended for me,' says Russell. 'It broke my heart, but hey ho. What a way to go.'

From the outside, Stuart seemed confident and self-assured – a guy betting on his own talent. But leaving the Skids was a big step. It was a band – a business – that he'd built from scratch, and he was leaving it in the hands of others. 'It was very scary,' says Sandra. 'It really was.'

They were living in a flat above a chip shop in Townhill, just north of Dunfermline. Sandra bought the flat. 'In those days, a musician couldn't even get car insurance without paying a massive premium,' she says. Stuart didn't have regular income, so there was no way he could get a mortgage.

'I laugh when folk say "he wanted a mortgage",' says Sandra. 'I bought our first house, I bought the second house, I bought the third house. He never *had* a mortgage! He didn't have that worry. All I ever did was allow Stuart to go and do what he wanted to do and gave him nothing else to worry about.'

Sandra had a well-paid job at the RAF base at Pitreavie Castle. Even on maternity leave, pregnant with Callum in 1981, she still got her wages for eighteen months. She had security. Stuart had been on *Top of the Pops*, had top 10 albums and singles, had toured the UK and played a sold-out Hammersmith Odeon, yet they were *still* waiting for the money to roll in.

'We really were struggling,' says Sandra. 'But we never asked anybody for anything. I just wouldn't have done that. But there were times where I thought, "How are we going to survive?" Because there was nothing. Even PRS [royalties] hardly trickled in much.

'The worry for me was: you've just walked away from something that you put an awful lot into and now we're back to square one. But little did I know the batch of songs that were about to be demoed.

'I knew they would be good. But I thought there would be a link between the Skids' good stuff straight into what he'd do next – and it was nothing like it.'

Back in Scotland, Clive Ford was in touch with Stuart as he planned his next project. 'He wanted to do something that involved Dunfermline – actually, *Scotland*, not Dunfermline. He wanted to do something and base it in Scotland. That was his premise.'

Stay Alive

Clive remembers Adamson travelling back and forth to London – 'because he still had a record deal and a publishing contract' – and spending a lot of time getting to know Ian Grant. 'I think that was the point where Stuart and Ian probably got to understand each other.'

And when he came back, he called in to see Bruce Watson.

It had been over a year since Bruce had given Stuart his Eurosect demo tape. He and his girlfriend – also called Sandra – had moved into a flat together, when one day there was a knock on the door. Stuart came in carrying a crash helmet – he'd bought himself a motorbike.

Stuart: 'Remember that time I said we should dae something?'
Bruce: 'Aye?'
'You still want tae dae it?'
'How?'
'I've fucking left the Skids.'
'Definitely.'

A week later, Stuart, Bruce and his mate Dodds, picked up Stuart's gear from a rehearsal studio in London and Stuart rented the Institute, a space beneath the library across the street from his flat in Townhill.

Bruce was on the dole at the time. 'If you left the dockyard before five years, you got all your pension money back,' he says. If you stayed on for more than five years you didn't get it until you were sixty-five. So Bruce took the lump sum and bought guitars and amps.

'It was just like "Right. What are we gonna do?" And Stuart went "That idea – that one with the bassline at the start, 'Forbidden Whispers'. Let's work on that first."'

So they got the cassette of Bruce's demo and they started re-working it. They re-named the song 'Angle Park' after an old house with high walls in Townhill and the song became so significant to them that the band was named after it for a while.

'I saw the evolution of it,' says Clive. 'Bruce and Stuart that summer, writing in the basement beneath the library. I had Wednesdays off and I used to go there and have a listen to what they were doing.

'The original songs were written on synthesisers. The Yamaha synth that Stuart had with the Skids, that's what he was writing on. And a Selmer drum machine, I think.'

'We recorded quite a few songs,' says Bruce. 'Just pieces of music, all instrumentals. That's the way we worked. We had a drum machine, I'd play bass or Stuart would play bass, the two of us would play guitars. The drum machine did waltz, bossa nova – all push buttons.'

They used the four-track TEAC Portastudio to capture their ideas.

'It was quite intimidating,' says Bruce. He'd seen the rise of the Skids through early rehearsals and support slots, but Stuart had learned from Dave Batchelor, Bill Nelson and Mick Glossop. He used the Portastudio like a pro, capturing the drums, guitar and bass on separate tracks and then 'bouncing' them onto one, leaving three more to play with.

Four-track Portastudios were changing how music was made, giving songwriters the ability to capture ideas and work them up – to add to them, to accompany themselves – without having to go into a studio. The same year that Bruce and Stuart worked on those early Big Country songs, Bruce Springsteen was sitting in a rented house in New Jersey recording what would become his next album, *Nebraska*, on the same machine.

Bruce asked Stuart if he could borrow it. 'Yeah, just take it,' said Stuart. And in his house, mucking around, Bruce wrote what would become the intro for 'Chance'.

For six weeks, they'd start at ten in the morning and work until 4 p.m. At lunchtime, they'd 'go to the pub and get incredibly fucking slaughtered'.

'It was just great,' says Bruce. 'The rules were, there's no rules. But everything was instrumental. We didn't even know who was gonna sing. Stuart had no intention of singing. In fact, when we did "Angle Park", he goes, "Right, you sing the first line and I'll sing the second line, then you sing the third line ..."' You can hear this demo on the deluxe edition of *The Crossing*.

'He didn't want to be the singer,' says Bruce. 'He was thinking about getting a vocalist in. But, in the end, I thought his voice was great. It wasn't the same register it became later. For the first three albums, Stuart's vocals are in a lower register. To me, he's got that naivety and it's brilliant. In later years, he learned to sing properly, but this kinda American accent came in. I preferred how it was originally.'

According to Sandra, Stuart became the singer because he wanted control. After the Skids, he didn't need another ego, another Jobson, to compete with. 'It had to be all or nothing because of what he'd experienced with the Skids,' she says. 'He wasn't going to go there again.'

After six weeks of working on the instrumental demos, Stuart told Bruce to take a couple of weeks off while he worked out what he could do with the songs. Two weeks later, he appeared on his motorbike – Bruce didn't have a phone – and said, 'Right, I've done it. See what you think.'

'I was blown away,' says Bruce. 'He hadn't added anything musically, but he'd bounced it across again and left another couple of tracks, and he'd done a main vocal and a harmony.'

He'd turned the instrumentals into *songs*.

This became the way they worked on most of Big Country's albums: creating a bunch of instrumentals for Stuart to later add lyrics and melodies. Sometimes, that would cause problems. Tony Butler didn't like how one song in particular ended up, and Bruce had to sacrifice a lot of guitar parts over the years. 'He used to drive me crazy. I'd do all these guitar parts, and he'd go, "I've got the vocals but you're gonna have to lose half of those guitar parts because they clash with what I'm gonna do."'

He shrugs. 'Whatever's best for the song.'

But, back then, Stuart had performed a minor miracle.

The music they had been making was a weird mix of punk and progressive rock. New wave and post-punk was at its height and punk's back-to-basics rallying cry was old hat. The songs didn't come out of 'jam sessions'. They were thought-out – music created in isolation at first, and with few rules.

Bruce describes their working method like this:

'Have you got an idea?'

'I've got this riff ...'

'I've got a bit that might go with that.'

'That bit doesnae work, but try this bit ...'

'There was no master plan apart from the fact that we didn't want to do the Thin Lizzy/Status Quo thing,' says Bruce. 'We didn't want to do that blues bendy kind of thing.'

Thin Lizzy's twin harmony guitars and Phil Lynott's Celtic influence seemed like an obvious precursor. 'If you were to pick a song, it would be "Whiskey in the Jar",' says Bruce. 'That would be the one that would fit alongside "Fields of Fire" or something. But it's more of a sound thing – the reverb on the guitars and a melody. There's a lot of melody in what [Thin Lizzy guitarist] Eric Bell's doing, but there's a bit of string bending and we didnae do that.'

So they made a rule. 'Instead of bending, we'll just play the note. We'll slide up to the note, play that note and we'll no' bend up tae it, 'cos automatically you go into blues when you do that.'

The punk rock guitar players – Mick Jones, Johnny Thunders, Steve Jones – had been pretty traditionalist. There was always a guitar solo, string bending, a love of Keith Richards-style rock 'n' roll.

'We didnae want to do that,' says Bruce. They were anti-solo. 'Guitar solos are meant to be almost free form – you wouldnae play the same thing twice – and we wanted to keep everything exactly the same, so that when you played it live, it would be exactly the same as how you recorded it. There was none of this "I'll just do a solo and busk it ..."'

The classic rock guitar heroes were self-indulgent, pleased with their own technical ability and happy to show it off, endlessly. 'It gets a bit boring,' says Bruce. 'I'm no' a soloist anyway. I see myself as more of an accompanist. I used to hate when people said, "Do you want to come round and we'll have a jam?" Fuck off! What would I want to have *a jam* for? That's minutes of my life I'm no' getting back! A jam? Eww, no.'

It was a generational thing. The old guys in bands down the docks, the guys with long hair and duffle coats, they were from the days of jamming. 'They all wanted to be like [Free guitarist] Paul Kossoff or something. Trying to do that nervous vibrato thing that Kossoff had. Not a hope in hell. But before punk, if you were in a heavy-ish rock band, Free were the blueprint.'

Stay Alive

Prog rock had been a dirty word, but things changed a little when John Lydon talked about his love of Hawkwind, Van der Graaf Generator and Can. The impetus of post-punk was to be progressive and original. Stuart and Bruce loved the original Ultravox! with John Foxx.

'That's kind of what I aspired to,' says Bruce. 'I think that's why I didnae want to do cover versions, I always wanted to just go down that avenue. I never, ever wanted to get up and play "96 Tears" or whatever. I love all that stuff, but I just didnae want to do it.'

Stuart took the demos to Ian Grant, who got some interest from Virgin. The label paid for them to go into the studio and do some demos with John Leckie. They did two sessions with Leckie: one at the Town House and one in Abbey Road. On drums was the Jam's Rick Buckler.

Leckie remembers recording in the penthouse studio at Abbey Road, a small studio on the top floor. 'It wasn't very good,' he says. 'It had only just opened but it was small and it didn't have a good sound.'

On top of that, the penthouse studio wasn't built for drums, so there were complaints from the rooms downstairs of sound leakage. 'Can you turn it down? Can you stop that banging?' Rick Buckler had his full kit, with the big tom-toms he used in the Jam. 'He was full-on,' says Leckie.

Leckie says he thought he was recording this new unnamed band's debut single and was disappointed when it turned out to be just demos. Later, when he heard the band were called Big Country, he thought, "Oh yeah, they had a song called that". In fact, the song was called 'Big City', an uncharacteristically catchy pop song about a small-town boy going to work in the city that includes 'comic' dialogue between Stuart and Bruce in the outro.

Bruce remembers messing around at Abbey Road, writing 'Flag of Nations', a bass-driven instrumental that seemed to be drawing from the same well as the then equally nascent New Order. 'God knows how much it cost,' he says. 'We didn't have anything prepared, doing "Flag of Nations", just piddling about with synthesisers upstairs at Abbey Road.'

Virgin passed, and CBS paid for them to go into Whitfield Street studios near Tottenham Court Road. It was mind-blowing stuff for Bruce. The Clash had recorded their debut single 'White Riot' at Whitfield Street, and in the producer's chair was Adam Sieff, the son of Joseph 'Teddy' Sieff, the president of Marks and Spencer. 'Adam was kidnapped as a child,' says Bruce. His dad Teddy had been the victim of an attempted assassination by Carlos the Jackal.

Like Virgin, CBS passed. 'Everyone passed,' says Grant. 'I think the songs were "Heart and Soul" and "Inwards". "Heart and Soul" was *the* song at one point – "This is what we'll get a deal with". Later, it didn't become anything other than a B-side. Polydor passed, Arista passed, CBS passed.'

If Grant was worried, Bruce and Stuart didn't care. 'We were just collecting demos,' says Bruce. 'It wasn't really costing us anything.'

After the CBS demos, they came home and started putting together the band. 'The way Stuart created Big Country was quite extraordinary,' says Peter Wishart. Back then, Wishart was a keyboard player in a Dunfermline band called Subject, with his brother Alan on bass. Peter and Alan had been inspired by the Skids and were amazed that Stuart would turn up to watch them play.

One night, walking back from Dunfermline nightclub Chimes, Stuart said to Peter: 'Listen, I'm putting together a band. I dunno what it's gonna be called yet. Bruce Watson's helping me out with some songs – would you fancy being part of it? I'd like your brother Alan to be in it too.'

'I couldn't believe it,' says Wishart. 'When he could have probably had the finest musicians across Scotland, he went to local guys. The first person he went to was Bruce. Bruce is a great guitarist, but he wasn't the finished product by any means, and he hadn't done anything other than play in a couple of local bands. But Stuart seemed determined that this band, as much as possible, was going to be designed with people from Dunfermline.

'My impression was that he wanted it to be a *band*. Stuart was so immensely connected with Dunfermline. It was like it kept him rooted in something, and there was something that he really valued about living there and being part of the community. So he just had this idea that he wanted the band to be from Dunfermline, with musicians that he felt could hold their own.'

According to Sandra, Stuart was more Machiavellian than that. 'People think he was trying to keep it local. He wasn't. He was just trying to find journeymen that he could orchestrate. Local people would have been easier to control. I don't like using that word, but that is what it was – he wanted to control everything and he wouldn't be able to do that if he recruited the same kind of people that he had in the past. Stuart knew his own strengths, and the depth in his writing, and how it should feel and sound. And he didn't want anybody trying to change anything about it.'

'Every local musician in Dunfermline was considered,' says Clive Ford. 'My brother was best friends with Alan Wishart and he knew that Alan was getting an audition. So he said, "Well, I want an audition too." He just couldn't get a drummer and that's when Ian offered Clive up.'

Clive Parker, formerly of the Members, one of Ian Grant's bands, became their token non-Fifer and the band started rehearsing at the town's Glen Pavilion, knocking the songs into shape. 'We had this collection of demos plus the songs that we recorded on the portastudio,' says Bruce. 'Maybe about twelve songs.' Songs recorded with a drum machine started to develop with a real bass player and a real drummer.

'The first song we ever rehearsed together was "Lost Patrol",' says Peter Wishart. 'We spent ages rehearsing. I think it was September/October when we all got together and we rehearsed solidly until our first gig in February the following year.

'So nearly every day we'd be rehearsing, building up the songs, rearranging, working them out. It was really exciting because the songs were amazing.'

Wishart's contribution, he says, was similar to 'early-ish Simple Minds. I was listening to lots of Simple Minds at that point. I know Mick MacNeil – he's a fantastic keyboard player – so that was the sort of thing I was bringing to the band.'

The sound of the band, on songs like 'Wake', had much in common with post-punk bands like Joy Division, the Sound or the Chameleons, with a Scottish folk influence that made it unique.

'Stuart would always tell you his playing was never inspired by folk music,' says Wishart. 'It was country music. Country was the thing that he always felt influenced his playing more than anything else. But there's a lot of really good folk music in Big Country. I think he sort of stumbled across it a little bit. He realised that people were responding in an emotional way and he knew he was on to something. But I don't think he consciously went out of his way to try and develop a Scottish sound.'

The songs were written, but Stuart encouraged contributions. 'He was quite democratic,' says Peter. 'They were his songs and he had a sense of how he wanted them to sound, but he was open to suggestions. He was easy to work with, for somebody who's a bit of a perfectionist.

'To begin with, we were in awe of him. He was a guy who'd done it and we were just kids. But that sort of went quickly and Stuart made us feel comfortable. And he made us feel part of it. It was never "Stuart Adamson's Big Country". He wanted it to be a *band*.'

But there were some teething problems. 'The bass was really busy,' says Bruce. 'Alan's a great bass player, but he was young and he just wanted to be flash. He wisnae sympathetic to the songs – just wanted to play right through them, no matter if there was a verse or chorus. Clive was pretty much the same – the most important thing in the band was the drums. They wurnae sympathetic. It was just all over the shop.'

The other thing that frustrated Stuart was that none of them could sing. 'He had this image of lots of harmonies,' says Peter. 'I ended up doing harmonies and I can't sing. A lot of the rehearsals used to be just trying to get us to sing proper harmonies to Stuart's songs. It wasn't because he was worried about his own vocals – Stuart always knew the limitations of his voice, but it wasn't something that he dwelt on. I think he just liked harmonies and felt it was an important part of the sound.'

Ian Grant convinced Phonogram A&R man Chris Briggs to come up to Dunfermline to watch this new band in rehearsal. Briggs found some old paperwork recently in which the band was called Angle Park.

'It didn't work as a band for me,' says Briggs. 'I got Stuart and Bruce – I got what *they* were doing. There's a chemistry between Stuart and Bruce, immediately – but it just feels like the wrong rhythm section. Plus, Stuart was new to being a frontman. I thought, "This isn't ready". I told Ian. He wasn't very happy with me about it.'

By the time they did their first gig at the Glen Pavilion on 4 February 1982, Angle Park had a new name: Big Country. 'It just implied a sense of vastness, open spaces,' Stuart said in *A Certain Chemistry*, an official book published by Omnibus in 1985. 'A new sense of discovery. A sense of ambition.'

'It meant a feeling of fresh air and adventure,' he told *No.1* magazine, years later. 'Our music was very optimistic and romantic then.'

'Stuart's idea was that it conjured up wide-open spaces. Adventure. Going on the Oregon Trail, all that kind of stuff,' says Bruce. 'I think it's a great name, but at the time I just thought, "People will think we're a country and western band!"'

The atmosphere at the Glen Pavilion was buzzing. Everyone was interested to see what Stuart Adamson would do next.

'It was all completely new songs, no covers, no Skids,' says Bruce. 'He wouldnae touch the Skids. "That was then." Like Weller with the Jam.'

The sounds of Big Country were different from the Skids. Less punky, maybe even – ulp – a little bit *proggy*. 'The Crossing' was a song in three parts. The first part came from a song Bruce had written for his last band. The ending – which was in a different time signature – had started life in Pete and Alan Wishart's previous band. The middle part was something Stuart had come up with. 'It's just mad prog rock,' says Bruce. 'It's like Marillion before Marillion, you know? It's all 3/4 and waltz and heavy rock ... I think punters were going, "Um, can you play 'Into the Valley' or 'The Saints are Coming'?"'

Peter Wishart was lobbying behind the scenes for the band to do some Skids material. Stuart was adamant: 'We're not doing Skids songs.' Peter campaigned for 'Arena', the closing track on *The Absolute Game*. '"Arena" was brilliant,' says Wishart, 'and actually fitted in with some of the music we were doing in early Big Country. Keyboards, a big atmospheric song. But no – "We're not doing that under any circumstances." I don't think he ever played a Skids song with Big Country.'

The Glen Pavilion was a warm-up show for a support slot on Alice Cooper's Special Forces Tour. Cooper's manager Shep Gordon had a stable of acts that Grant–Edwards looked after across Europe. Shep told them they could pick the support act for the Alice Cooper tour and they chose Big Country. 'Chris Briggs was not convinced,' says Ian. 'He told me not to put them on it, but to me, they'd either sink or they'd swim. And if they sank, we'd learn from it.'

If the pairing looks doomed to failure several decades later, at the time it made more sense. Alice Cooper had been an influence on the punk scene and on the growing goth scene, and his new album was an attempt to court new-wave fans.

But no one had told his audience.

'Everybody had long hair, leather jackets, denim with the patches,' says Bruce. 'And we're doing all this kind of mad punky prog stuff that nobody's ever heard of before.'

'We looked like Duran Duran, with headbands and eyeliner and weird clothes,' says Wishart. 'They wanted a standard heavy metal support and here was us, challenging them with this sort of new-wave Scottish music. It meant nothing to them.'

'You could hear a pin drop,' says Ian Grant. 'In a room of 5,000 people.'

'We got bottled,' says Bruce. 'Bottles of pish. "Boo! Get off, fucking poofs!"'

The following night's gig in Birmingham was even worse. 'We tried a bit harder and they just did not want it at all,' says Peter.

The next morning, Ian Grant got a phone call from Alice Cooper's tour manager, a Vietnam vet. 'A really aggressive guy. He says, "Your band's off the bill. You're not playing again. No arguing." I called Stuart. He was over the moon.'

Sandra had given birth to Callum on 10 February, the night before the first Alice Cooper date. The cancellation meant that he could go home to see his son.

'We were all sharing a hotel room,' says Peter, 'and we were just so down. Stuart shot off back to Scotland and we were all left hanging. "What do we do now?" And the next time I saw Stuart was when he came up to our house to tell Alan he was effectively sacked.'

Stay Alive

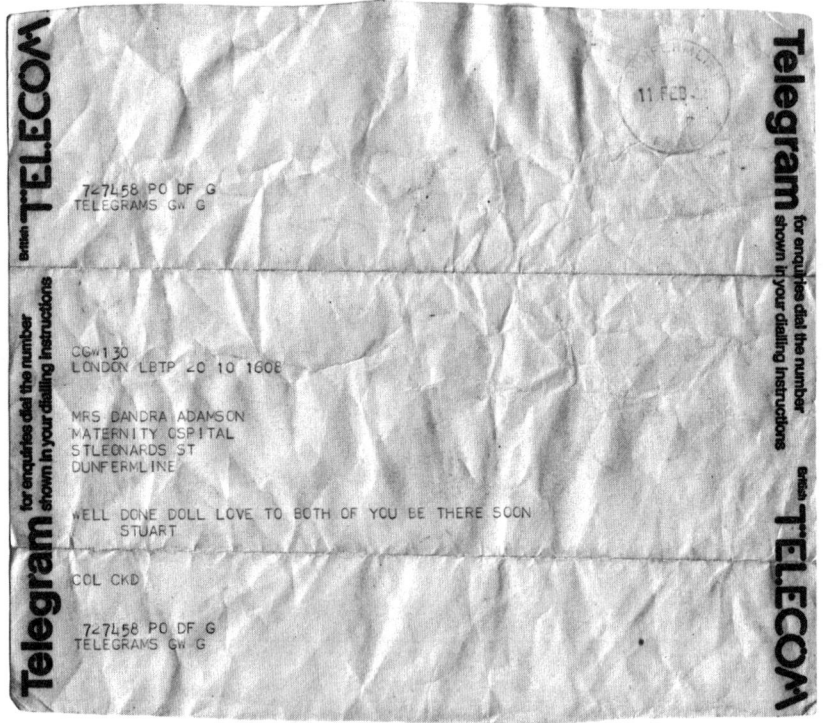

'Well done doll': Stuart's telegram from tour, the day after Callum's birth.

And right here – right where it looks like it's all turned to shit – is when it all starts to click.

Chris Briggs drops in to see his mate Chris Thomas at Air Studios where he's working on Pete Townshend's solo album, *All the Best Cowboys Have Chinese Eyes*, and there's Tony Butler and Mark Brzezicki running through one of the tracks.

'My job is a puzzle-solving job,' says Briggs. 'Ian Grant has planted a puzzle in my head. It's like a football manager: "This number 10 can't time a run into a box. I need a new number 10, maybe two centre halves, and this team might work."'

He looked at Tony and Mark and thought: '*This* could work.'

Briggs chatted with Tony.

'Do you know who Stuart Adamson is?'

'Yeah,' says Tony. 'We supported the Skids. Stuart's a lovely bloke.'

'How busy are you?' says Briggs.

Briggs calls Ian Grant, tells him about Tony and Mark. 'Weird', thinks Ian. He'd spoken to Tony Butler just a couple of months before. He hadn't seen Tony and Mark since the Brockwell Park gig the previous year when Tony had called out of the blue. 'What's Stuart up to?' he'd asked.

A few days later, Grant's phone rings. It's Tony Butler again. 'I've just spoken to Chris Briggs,' he says. 'I hear Stuart needs a rhythm section.'

Ian calls Stuart: 'The way I see it, you've got two choices. You do the right thing and get a new rhythm section – do you remember Tony and Mark from On the Air? They could be interesting. Or – second choice – you take this band and tour it around Scotland and Ireland until it's good enough ... Or you do the right thing.'

'Give me the weekend,' says Stuart.

On Monday, Ian's phone rings.

'I'm gonna do the right thing,' says Stuart.

11

The Days of Promise

'Every day was a curse.'
In the studio with Chris Thomas

This is how Mark Brzezicki remembers it:

Ian Grant told Tony: 'Stuart's left the Skids. Phonogram are interested, but only if they find a good rhythm section. What are you two up to?'

They discussed it.

'Stuart Adamson is a great songwriter,' said Tony.

'And he's a brilliant guitar player,' said Mark.

Tony remembered those nights watching the Skids, his fascination with Stuart's guitar playing, that Celtic music resonating in him.

He called Ian. 'We'll do a session for free and see how it goes.'

Chris Briggs put them in the basement of Phonogram Studios with John Brandt producing. It was the first time Bruce had met Tony and Mark. 'They couldn't understand a fucking word I said,' he says. 'They were like, "Who is *this*?" They were top session musicians. They played on all the Daltrey stuff, all the Townshend stuff. Really, to this day, they should be in the Who. They should be. I could not believe the musicianship. Even Stuart was like, "These guys are fucking amazing!"'

'I immediately gelled with Bruce,' says Mark. 'He came across as a very shy guy, very affable, but from the punk thing – skinny, spiky hair. And we were reminiscing with Stuart. But the great thing was, they let me be *me*.'

'It was funny,' says Bruce, 'because in the Skids, Stuart would always get Tam or Mike, and say, "Right, I want you to play the drums like *this* ..." He did that and Mark said, "Fuck off, *I'm* the fucking drummer! I'm not playing that. It sounds like a fucking drum machine!"'

The results put Stuart's mind at rest. He'd sent the rhythm section a cassette of 'Harvest Home', 'Close Action' and 'Heart and Soul'. Chris Briggs came down and the four powered through the three songs, working for twenty-four hours, playing live in the studio, right through the night.

It clicked instantly. 'John Brandt went on to manage Stereophonics. He was a consummate professional,' says Tony. 'He immediately loved what me and Mark were doing. And then there was the added bonus of Chris Briggs sitting in the studio, smiling like a Cheshire cat. I don't think I'd met Chris Briggs before, but he didn't look like an A&R man to me. All I remember is him sitting there smiling, Ian Grant standing behind him. Even Stuart was a bit amazed at what a great noise we made that day.'

'It sounded like a real band,' says Bruce. 'Like the Pretenders or the Clash. It was like, "Fuck me. We might get *a single* out of this!" It was amazing.'

'"Close Action" was in 3/4,' says Tony, 'but rather than making it a waltz-time thing, we made it swing. We made it dancey. It's a very old-fashioned timing, but it also made it hugely atmospheric. I think it was because they'd used a drum machine to write, and we were able to give it a human feel and, with my West Indian-ness, make it swing better.'

He could tell that it was working by looking at Stuart and Bruce. 'They started dancing around. You can tell what music is doing by the way people react.'

'On the songs they played me,' says Mark, 'a lot of the drums were the same thing: floor tom, snare, floor tom, snare. I just did my thing with China cymbals, roto-toms and proggy drumming. I had a free hand. I would turn it around, make it downbeat, almost like the Police, in a way, with Phil Collins kind of drum fills, the delicacy of the hi-hat that Copeland used. I didn't think a basic rock 'n' roll drum was right, so I brought a lot of different flavours in.

'But the thing that I remember thinking – and this is going to sound terrible – but, I thought it sounded a bit like the bagpipes. I mean, I'm a west Londoner, why did I think that? But it was the way they interacted with Bruce's guitar and the root note was droning, and the fact they didn't play any black notes, so to speak. It was quite triad-y, like you would hear in oriental music.'

The musicianship had jumped up a level. And that was both amazing and terrifying for Bruce. 'I thought, "I'm gonnae get sacked cos I cannae play with these cunts! How the fuck am I gonnae up my game?"'

'Stuart had three albums under his belt, umpteen singles. The two boys had been playing with Townshend and done all those sessions, and I worked in the dockyard on nuclear submarines.'

But what he lacked in technique, he made up for in originality. 'Bruce brought Stuart's guitars alive,' says Mark. 'Bruce came from a more rhythmical side and Stuart would do the kind of lead stuff. They would trade guitar licks, but Bruce had a really great pocket for rhythm and complementing the guitars in a really unique way. You hadn't heard anything like it. Me and Tony loved it.'

'I know my limitations,' says Bruce, 'but I can do a lot of left-field stuff, all your Tom Verlaine, Richard Lloyd kinda stuff. I can make things sound different to what a normal rock band would do. So between making them laugh and being quite experimental, that was me. No one said, "You better up your game – you better learn some more chords or you're out of here, boy!" There was never any of that. Not once.'

When it was over, they said their goodbyes and Bruce and Stuart went back up to Scotland and waited.

Driving home with Mark, Tony was overcome by what had just happened. This weird connection he felt for Celtic music meant that the music they'd made had profoundly resonated with him.

'Stop the van, Mark!'

Mark pulled over. 'What?'

'We've got to join this band!'

'Yeah?'

'Yes! This is something that we can see all the way through. The music's really different. And they're a nice bunch of guys. Well, when you can understand them.'

Tony could *pretty much* understand what Stuart was saying, but he was fucked if he could understand Bruce.

'Well, y'know, let's be careful here,' said Mark, who didn't want to rush into anything.

'What else have we got?' said Tony. 'Sessions? We can do that anytime. And, to be honest, I'm really pissed off with it. I hate doing sessions where the music's crap. Yeah, you get paid, but it's different for you – you're a drummer.'

Drummers will drum on anything, figured Tony. They just sit there hitting things. He wanted some emotional articulation, something with a bit of musical integrity.

His heroes Chris Squire and Mike Rutherford had occupied a big space in the music they made and when he heard what Jean-Jacques Burnel was doing with the Stranglers, he thought it was incredible. He wanted to be part of a band like that. But then he'd do sessions and it was back to 'Do as little as you can, keep the work clean.' He heard that all the time, working with Chris Thomas on Pete Townshend's album: 'Stop playing so much. Keep it simple.'

With Big Country, he thought he could have an impact. 'The music presented me with an area to not just explore, but have fun with,' he says. He didn't want to be just a competent session guy. 'I wanted to be in an *orchestra* where each instrument can have its own space and a reason for being. And I found it in the early days of Big Country.

'Mark's interpretation of the songs gave me space to weave between drums and guitars. And because of the sound that I used, it was toppy enough to be a guitar, but bassy enough to sit with the bass drums. I could work in between those lines to give it a bit more orchestration.'

A lot of the songs from *The Crossing* period had been written on the bass, but because neither Stuart or Bruce were bass players, to hear Tony's interpretation was something else. Bruce was impressed. 'Big Country became my most favourite band in the world,' he says. 'I couldnae stop listening to it. Tony's bass bounces like fuck – it's got nothing to do with the guitar chords.'

'The bass was the third guitar basically,' says Tony. 'It kinda held down notes now and again, but it joined in melodies and counter points. There weren't a lot of people doing that on bass, really.'

Tony played so many melody lines, playing the higher notes so much, that it became an in-joke with the band: we need a bass player!

Word came back: 'Briggsy likes the songs, he likes the rhythm section, he thinks it's a huge improvement. He wants you to come back and do more demos.' So they went back down, to the same studios, with John Brandt again and they did 'Lost Patrol' and 'Inwards'.

'"Heart and Soul" was probably my favourite,' says Tony. It had vocal harmonies, with a verse built around a call-and-response structure. 'At the time, we thought the only thing that wasn't working was the vocal. Stuart hadn't attained that voice yet. And when we went to record it – because people thought it would make a great single – the voice wasn't quite there. But that's because Steve Lillywhite wasn't there.'

Chris Briggs was impressed 'I'm thinking, "This is definitely working".'

Mark Knopfler wandered in with Phonogram PR Mariella Frostrup. 'What's this racket, Chris?' he asked Briggs.

Mark Knopfler didn't like this Big Country, not one bit.

Then came the news: 'Briggsy wants to sign you.'

The deal was with Phonogram label, Mercury. Tony jumped in right away. He said, 'I'm giving up the session work, I'm in this band, I'm going to give it 100 per cent.' Mark, though, was a bit more cautious. 'When I first heard the music, I was so shocked how different it was that I wasn't sure about it. I was so concerned – I was doing a lot of session work – that this would tie me to something and mean I couldn't do sessions. I was being greedy, to be honest.'

'It's not a money thing with Mark,' says Bruce. 'He's always done session work. He likes to be working, keep his chops up. It doesnae matter if he's playing with the Cult, Sting, Big Country or a wedding band – it doesnae matter to him as long as he's drumming. It's just the way he is.'

Stay Alive

Mark didn't sign the contract for almost a year. When it was finally signed and they did a photo op at Phonogram's office with champagne and cake, 'Mark wouldn't join in,' says Grant. 'He refused to do it because he thought he wouldn't be able to do sessions anymore.'

Behind the scenes, the wrangling continued, but as a band they were gelling. Inspired, Stuart was writing again. They'd done a couple of gigs, their first gig at the 101 Club in Clapham, the second in Tony's neighbourhood of Shepherd's Bush. 'And it just worked. There's just lots of smiley faces and everything's great. And then it all went sour.'

Briggs thought that Chris Thomas would be the ideal producer. Thomas's experience and list of credits were second to none. He'd produced some of the tracks on the Beatles' White Album, including 'Happiness is a Warm Gun', and gone on to produce Roxy Music's *For Your Pleasure* (and their next four albums) and several Procol Harum albums, and mixed Pink Floyd's *The Dark Side of the Moon*. When musical fashions changed, he changed with them, producing *Never Mind the Bollocks* by the Sex Pistols, *Power in the Darkness* by the Tom Robinson Band, and the first two albums by the Pretenders. He was now working with rock royalty like Paul McCartney, Pete Townshend and Elton John.

This mix of session musicians and Scottish punks, this collision of prog and new-wave styles, might benefit from a pro at the helm, thought Briggs – and Thomas was ideal, especially as he knew Tony and Mark from the Townshend sessions. But something went wrong. The chemistry didn't work. Chris Thomas rubbed people up the wrong way.

'Every day was a curse,' says Tony.

Here's what went wrong:

1. **There was a feeling that the band weren't getting the producer's full attention**
   Thomas was jetting out to Montserrat throughout the recordings to work on Elton John's *Too Low for Zero* album at the same time. He would come back jet-lagged and exhausted.

2. **He gave Mark a hard time**
'The other thing that disappointed me about Chris,' says Tony, 'was that he had this thing of, "Oh, we can all get on Mark's back because he won't come back at us."' Mark would laugh it off, but it got to him sometimes. Chris Briggs turned up for a session and found Mark in the corridor at Air Studios. 'They'd gotten a decent version of "Harvest Home",' says Briggs, but there in the corridor, Mark told him that something wasn't right. 'Mark is telling me in so many words that Chris has put the wind up him. Chris has said something and it's spooked him.'

3. **He had no affinity with Bruce or Stuart**
'Chris Thomas would openly say "I ain't got a fucking clue what they're saying",' says Tony. 'Now that couldn't have been great. I felt sorry for them – it was just *racist*.'

The final recordings, released much later on the deluxe edition of *The Crossing*, are sterile and flat. There is much more obvious use of studio techniques and Tony's extraordinary bass playing is more to the fore. 'The only person that Chris didn't have a problem with was me,' says Tony. 'I felt really embarrassed.'

4. **And then something terrible happened**
On the 16 or 17 June, bass player Pete Farndon appeared at the studio. Farndon had been sacked from the Pretenders a couple of days previously for his drug use. He'd come to see Chris Thomas with some news.

'Jimmy's just died,' he said.

Pretenders guitarist James Honeyman-Scott had died from heart failure, brought on by cocaine abuse. He was twenty-five years old.

'Chris Thomas broke down,' says Bruce. 'He couldn't finish the session. Just broke right down.' There was no point in continuing. 'Stuart and I just went down to King's Cross and got the train back up the road.'

'Chris Thomas fell apart,' says Ian Grant, 'and the sessions fell apart.'

Chris Briggs called a stop to it all. 'It was probably the best call to stop I've ever heard in my life,' says Tony.

Stay Alive

'It obviously wasn't happening with Chris,' says Grant. 'It was this airbrushed, different-sounding Big Country.'

'We were frightened,' says Tony. 'We were about eight tracks into *The Crossing* and it was all scrapped. Knowing what sort of person Stuart turned out to be, it couldn't have been easy for him.'

With recording stopped and the album canned, Big Country went out on the road that summer. In recordings from the time, they sound unpolished. Stuart's vocals are uneven. They are learning both the songs and how to perform. They went to the US for the first time, supporting the Members.

In New York, Bruce remembers staying in a dive of a hotel with huge cockroaches in the bathroom: 'We used to put Vaseline on the bed legs to stop the cockroaches climbing up.'

In footage of the Peppermint Lounge show on 21 August, you can see Stuart trying to become more of a frontman, swinging his arms around and then baiting an audience who weren't sure what to make of them: 'C'moan then, cheer up! Yeah, cheer up. You never heard that before? It's an old Scottish thing like Hogmanay. You heard ay Hogmanay? I bet ye cannae understand whit I'm saying, right?'

'Wheesht the noo!' he tells a heckler.

On 17 September 1982, Phonogram released the first Big Country single, 'Harvest Home', one of two songs to be salvaged from the Chris Thomas sessions. Led by Stuart's unmistakable guitar playing, the song is a great introduction to the Big Country sound and to Adamson's vision.

Here, at the height of keyboard-driven New Romanticism, was a twin guitar song with impressionistic lyrics about ploughmen and tailors and veiled references to hardship and possibly revenge: 'Just as you sow you shall reap.'

After all those years in the Skids with Jobson as lyricist, Stuart was now in complete control of his new band's lyrics. He loved books and the influence of his reading can be found throughout the songs of Big Country. 'He could read for eight or nine hours without stopping,' says Sandra. 'He would get through several books a week. And he would also have more than two copies – one in the house, one in his bag and maybe one on a tour bus, just in case he lost one. I wish I'd kept his books. You could find Stuart reading anything from Spike Milligan or John Steinbeck, or the philosophers. There wusnae anything he couldn't tackle.'

For the NME, Stuart listed his favourite books as 'anything by George Orwell, Albert Camus, John Wyndham, and DH Lawrence', as well as Michael Herr's Vietnam classic *Dispatches*, *The Dice Man* by Luke Rhinehart, a biography of US motorcyclist Kenny Roberts and 'any of the *Pan Book of Horror Stories*', an acclaimed collection that ran for decades and included writers like Ray Bradbury and Muriel Spark.

'He was clever,' says Peter Wishart, '*really* clever. He was well-read, self-educated. And you can see that with his lyrics – a lot of huge literary references, certainly in *The Crossing*.'

'Harvest Home' is the name of an ancient pagan festival that was celebrated at the end of the harvest season in September across England, Scotland and Ireland. The festival shares its name with an old folk song that could date back to the fifteenth century. A version of it appears in *King Arthur*, an opera by John Dryden and Henry Purcell from 1691: 'Your hay it is mow'd, and your corn it is reap'd/ Your barns will be full, and your hovels heap'd/ Come, boys, come; come, boys, come/And merrily roar out Harvest Home.'

The folk song has a healthy disrespect for landowners and the Church – the people who would tax the farmers back then, taking a tenth of their crop ('We've cheated the parson, we'll cheat him again/For why should a blockhead have one in ten?'). Stuart's lyric also compares the haves to the have-nots: 'How many sheaves were counted ... How did the landlord dine?'

'Harvest Home' was also the title of a best-selling 1973 folk-horror novel by Thomas Tryon about a family who flee the stresses of city life, only to find themselves in a nightmarish small town. Stuart's school friend David Allen remembers him reading it. 'We were both keen readers,' he says. 'I remember us reading stuff like *The Lord of the Rings*, *Harvest Home* by Tom Tryon and *Mad* magazine.'

Stuart might also have been inspired by a collection of short stories with the same name by Scottish writer David Toulmin, published in 1978. Toulmin told stories about ordinary folk in the north east of Scotland and wrote in local dialect. The title story from *Harvest Home* is about a community struggling against the weather to bring in the harvest. The main characters include farmers, blacksmiths and a country vet.

Big Country's 'Harvest Home' appears to be about the nobility of the simple life and the destruction of the highland way of life 200 years previously. 'It's all about the Highland Clearances after the Battle of Culloden,' Stuart told the teenage readers of *Smash Hits*.

The Highland Clearances is the name given to the forced displacement of the Highland people between the years 1750 and 1860 that signalled the end of the Clan structures and the old way of life. Entire communities were forcibly evicted from the lands they had lived on for centuries to make way for sheep – a more profitable use of land to the new landowners. 'Scotland became a wasteland,' said Stuart, 'and the same sort of thing is happening today. The oil boom has burst and now there's a lot of workers up there living in caravans, shivering with nothing to do. Scotland's always been plagued by hardship.'

On the band's second album, *Steeltown*, Stuart's lyrics came in for some criticism for being too serious and political, but the themes were there from the beginning. 'They're pulling everything apart and there's no replacement,' he said in the official Big Country book, *A Certain Chemistry*. 'In this area, the mining is being taken away and the linen industry is dying out and shipbuilding you can almost forget. There's a few rigs being built but that's about it.

'To be out of work for a long time destroys your own self-respect. I know what it's like because I've been on the dole for a long time myself. You draw further into yourself and it does bring that sense of desperation to it. That desperation breaks down a community. Makes people fend only for themselves.

'The age of family and community is being broken down and it is something to look upon with regret.'

The B-side of 'Harvest Home', 'Balcony', is much more contemporary, if nowhere near as exciting. A Bowie-esque, Blitz club knock-off – with Stuart pronouncing 'past' and 'last' in a mannered, English style – its portentous lyrics dwell on a final performance: 'An audience awaits/Heave lads, the final scene is set ... This is my finest hour/Now is your last encore.'

'"Balcony" was called "Abe" to start with,' says Bruce. 'It started off being about the assassination of Abraham Lincoln and then it just moved on.'

On the debut single of his new band, Stuart was singing of death and last chances. As a test of how Big Country might go down, 'Harvest Home' failed badly: it peaked at number 91 in the charts.

Early Big Country promo shot.

The same day that 'Harvest Home' was released, Tony Butler was back in the studio with Chris Thomas, this time with the Pretenders, recording 'Back on the Chain Gang'. With James Honeyman-Scott dead, and bassist Pete Farndon sacked – he would be found dead seven months later, having drowned in the bath after a heroin overdose – only Chrissie Hynde and Martin Chambers remained of the original line-up. 'Back on the Chain Gang' became a tribute to Honeyman-Scott ('I found a picture of you/ Those were the happiest days of my life').

Stay Alive

It was a buzz for Tony. In 1979, he'd been working in distribution for WEA Records in Alperton in north-west London, selling records to record shops, when the Pretenders' 'Brass in Pocket' came out. He loved it and his enthusiasm was infectious, breaking all records for sales reps. Where HMV in Oxford Street might normally take thirty boxes, Tony convinced them to take fifty.

Now he was recording with them. Tony played the bassline on 'Back on the Chain Gang' and sang backing vocals, he and Martin Chambers supplying chain gang-style grunts.

In rehearsals for the B-side, Chambers and Tony started jamming a funky bassline of Tony's and, by the next day, Chrissie had turned it into a song – 'My City Was Gone'. It was a US radio hit and later became the opening music for *The Rush Limbaugh Show*, a nationally syndicated radio show that ran for several decades in the US.

'But somebody forgot to add me to the credits,' says Tony. 'It's not a complaint. I've never been a breadhead, so I never pursued it.'

But experiences like this made him aware of the need to look after his own interests. 'Which is why I became so close with Ian Grant. I thought the best thing to do is to be in touch, keep your eyes open, stay close to the person who's doing all this sort of stuff.'

As 1982 ended, Big Country seemed no further forward: an album that had been canned, a single that had flopped. 'It was a bit of a lousy Christmas going into '83,' says Grant, 'except we had the Jam shows at Wembley.'

The Jam were bowing out at the height of their fame. Maybe Paul Weller was impressed at Adamson leaving the Skids to pursue something new. 'Weller was big mates with Stuart and had a lot of time for him,' says Grant. 'He gave him the shows. It was a fantastic thing to get, even though it was the Jam's farewell, and a significant link in the rise of the band. They won a lot of friends those nights.'

There's a word in this chapter that jumps off the page. You might have noticed it. The word is 'racist'. In telling his side of the Big Country story, it's pretty much the only time that Tony Butler uses the word, or refers to racism at all – and, in this case, it's to describe the attitude of an Englishman to two Scotsmen. Not racism, really – prejudice, bigotry, intolerance, maybe. Patronising, definitely. For a black man in a rock band in the early '80s – with the National Front on the rise and racist policing provoking riots in Brixton and Bristol – it seems extraordinary.

'My colour has never really been a problem,' says Tony. 'Every community that I've lived in has been multiracial. Shepherd's Bush, Chiswick, Ealing ... they're all multiracial areas. And I come from a multiracial background. So I don't see colour, I see people.

'I haven't had a lot of problems with racism, in music or out of music. I think it's to do with the way I was brought up. My mum always made me speak properly. She didn't want me running around with some sort of bastardised Jamaican accent and she always said, "You'll get on better. If you speak properly, people can understand you."'

One time, Tony applied for a job, got through the phone interview stage, and turned up for the face-to-face interview. 'They said, "Oh, can I help you?" I said, "Yes, I've got an interview – Mr Butler." "B-but- *you're* Mr Butler?" I obviously didn't appear to be the person they'd heard on the telephone.

'But apart from that, I was never touched by it. Being involved in music was a kind of shield because I was always with like-minded people. There's very little racism in music. I thought that being more exposed in a group like Big Country, I would probably experience more.

'I won't say who it was, but somebody close to Stuart said, "You're not going to get anywhere with a black person in the band." But I will hold my counsel on that one.

'The only kind of racism I saw in Scotland was at a Protestant march.'

In the build-up to 12 July, to mark the Battle of the Boyne (when King William of Orange's men defeated Catholic forces loyal to the deposed King James II in 1690), 'Orange Walks' – marches organised by the protestant Orange Order – often stir up sectarian hatred across Scotland and Northern Ireland. The Battle of the Boyne was really just a small part of William of Orange's war against the French king Louis XIV for control of 'the Low Countries' – Belgium, Luxembourg and the Netherlands – but centuries later it's still pitting ordinary working-class people against each other (including people who've never been to church and couldn't point to Luxembourg on a map).

'That was racism from a different perspective,' says Tony. 'I went out one night and saw this horrible mess on the street. It was difficult to compute. But hatred has many guises. And when people want to use it, they will use it as hard as they can.'

He mentions some classic lines from the movie *The Commitments*. In the film, manager Jimmy Rabbitte, coaching his Irish band to identify with the sounds of Black America, says: 'Do you not get it, lads? The Irish are the blacks of Europe. And Dubliners are the blacks of Ireland. And the Northside Dubliners are the blacks of Dublin. So say it once, say it loud: "I'm black and I'm proud."'

'I can imagine Scots people feel a little bit like that,' he says. 'Because there's this battering ram that English people can use against people from the colonies or from the other nations. But nobody ever used that stick for the English.'

12

We're Gonna Break Your Fuckin' Goalposts

Kerry-oots. Flicking all night long.
Properly shit-faced.
A whole other Stuart Adamson

'Bruce and Stuart at my mum's house in 1982 were some of the funniest times,' says Tony, 'and also when I realised that these guys *drank*.'

Peter Wishart had noticed it too. 'Stuart drank a lot,' he says, 'but we all did. We were kids. Stuart drank a lot more than the rest of us, but it never seemed out of control at that point.'

Within a short time, he says, it got worse. 'When Big Country had their first success, I saw him in some dreadful conditions with drink, to the point that he could barely make himself heard at all. But we all just thought, "That's what happens when you're famous".'

Rock stars were *expected* to drink a lot back then. 'Keith Richards is the best example of that,' says Alan Edwards. '"Elegantly wasted"? When you look back on it – what, off his head on coke and heroin and whatever, that was *elegant?*'

Back in those early days, though, staying over at Tony's mum's house in Ealing, Stuart wasn't being a rock star. He was just doing what many young Scottish men do: getting wasted.

'Stuart and I used to drink like fuck back then,' says Bruce. He and Stuart had known each other for years, had been working together intensely for months and suddenly they were in a band with two new guys with English accents and totally different backgrounds.

'It was a complete culture shock,' says Bruce, 'from both points of view. Because we were Scottish, at the end of the working day we were like, "Right! Down the boozer!"'

It wasn't a culture familiar to their English bandmates. 'Tony was a moderate drinker,' says Bruce. 'Mark doesnae drink anymore, but back then he was one of those guys that could drink gallons but never be up or down. I've only seen Mark drunk once, something to do with his size. Tony was more of a spirit drinker, Mark was a London Pride, real ale kind of guy, but if we hadn't been there, they probably wouldnae even have a drink. They would have just gone home.'

And the more Stuart and Bruce drank, the thicker their accents became. Their roadie Dodds was Scottish as well so, between the three of them, says Bruce, 'Mark and Tony did not understand a fucking word.'

Tony had been brought up to speak properly and his future career was depending on these incomprehensible maniacs who'd get Dodds to go to the off-licence and get 'a kerry-oot'. Tony and Mark expected him to come back with a bottle of wine and six cans of beer. Instead, he'd arrive pushing a trolley of Tennent's lager.

'What!?'

'That's just for the night!'

They had lager-fuelled, all-night Subbuteo tournaments. 'We'd send the roadies out to get more Tennent's, while we were flicking away,' says Bruce. 'How rock 'n' roll is that?'

So on one hand, it was all quite normal – just what young men do, whether they're students or apprentices blowing their wages down the pub. But, on the other hand, it disguised the fact that Stuart's drinking was getting more serious.

'We wurnae like, "Oh, we're Scottish, we're going to break your fuckin' goalposts",' says Bruce. In 1977, the Scottish football team defeated England 2-1 at Wembley and, during the pitch invasion that followed, jubilant Scottish fans sat on and swung off the Wembley crossbars and broke them.

We're Gonna Break Your Fuckin' Goalposts

'It was never like that. But at that time, there was still a whole Scotland–England thing. "You all right, Jock?" "Whit are you calling me Jock fur?" There was all that stuff still going on. The early '80s was still the end of the '70s, if you think about it. 1981, to me, was still the '70s. There was still a bit of a divide that I don't think exists now. But I think, especially in London, they're maybe – I wouldnae say more *civilised* – but, you know, it's like they have a glass of wine with their dinner and maybe a beer.

'We were like "We're gonnae get *pished!*" But not 'cos we had drink problems ... Or maybe we *did*, I don't know. It just seemed normal to us.'

It was also pretty normal behaviour in the music business at that time. Everyone was drinking. There was coke and spliffs everywhere and a culture that celebrated getting out of it.

'We all drank too much, all of us,' says Chris Briggs. 'You know how some dogs eat like food's going to be made illegal in the morning? We drank like beer was going to be made illegal. We got properly shit-faced. I think that was a weird link between us all. Stuart and myself drank too much, both of us. Particularly after shows, we'd get properly blootered.'

He went to his doctor about it. 'I said, "Look, it's really mad where I work. Every drink's free, all my bar bills are paid and I get free drugs, basically." He wasn't that bothered. It was eleven in the morning. The doctor said to me, "Whisky and soda? I'm gonna have one ..."'

Briggs' drinking started having an effect on his private life. 'I'd got to that point where girlfriends bail on you,' he says. 'I'd say, "I'll be back by nine" and I was back at two in the morning. "I'm just going out for cigarettes" and I was back the next day sometime. I'd reached *that* point. So Stuart and me were bordering on a problem. We both knew it.

'We didn't think it was abnormal, *initially*,' he says. 'But there was a point where we both knew it wasn't normal and we still did it. I couldn't have carried on like that. I'd be dead. All of us would be dead.'

It wasn't normal for Sandra Adamson. Sandra didn't drink and the Stuart Adamson she'd met and fallen in love with wasn't a drinker either. But as soon as Stuart spent time away from home, as soon as Big Country really started to take off, so did his drinking.

Stuart would insist that Sandra came with him to recording sessions or on tours and she'd be surrounded by people off their heads – and a bit freaked out that she wasn't. 'I don't think Sandra approved of us' is a common sentiment voiced by people from that time. And they're *right*.

'It's disconcerting for people when they know you're not a user of any kind of drugs or alcohol,' she says. 'They don't like that. They feel uncomfortable around you.'

To her, music was a job like any other. How could you do business if you were out of it? 'I had no time for it,' she says. 'I just thought it was a real waste of time.'

She was aware of the toll it was taking on Stuart physically. 'You're not able to perform properly. You're in recovery day after day. You think you're okay because you're just going through the motions, but you're not actually.' Sandra ended up making a career for herself in the fitness industry. 'I was the opposite. I was always in the gym or running or doing something healthy.'

Callum had been born in February 1982. Sandra was at home, raising a child and supporting Stuart as best she could. By the time Big Country were recording *The Crossing*, their relationship was tested.

Somewhere on the road, or in London – in the period right before he wrote the lyrics to 'In a Big Country' – Stuart had been unfaithful. 'I don't even know her name,' she says. 'And she was probably one of many, but she was the one I was aware of.'

And so began an unhappy period of her life that ironically would last through some of Big Country's most successful times – a period marked by alcoholism, lies, infidelity and broken promises.

Sandra is not even sure if she should talk about these times. 'The thing is,' she says, 'if I start to tell you, then you're going to have a whole other Stuart Adamson that you don't have at the moment. And it is really what should happen and should be spoken about, but I've got to decide whether I want that.

'Because, for me, it's different too. I've got to be able to live with that.'

Sunset Marquis hotel, 1984.

13

Come Up Screaming

Pain and truth and things that really mattered.
The triumph of **The Crossing**

The writing and the drinking continued throughout those early months. 'They'd be at my house,' says Tony, 'and just sleep on the floor. My ex-wife would come home from work and not be able to get into the dining room because of a pyramid of beer cans reaching to the roof.'

They had started writing together. 'Flag of Nations', an instrumental captured at the John Leckie sessions and released as a bonus track on the 'Harvest Home' 12-inch single, morphed into 'A Thousand Stars' during these sessions, captured on a four-track Fostex machine that Tony sat on his mum's dining table. The table was a bit shaky, so Tony christened it 'Wobbly Studios'. To this day, all of his home studios have been called Wobbly Studios ('I'm on Wobbly 18,' he says).

Ian Grant knew Steve Lillywhite from working with his brother Adrian in the Members. Lillywhite had produced the early Ultravox! albums that Bruce and Stuart loved so much and had gone on to produce Siouxsie and the Banshees, Steel Pulse, Johnny Thunders and more, while his productions for XTC, Peter Gabriel and U2 were defining the sound of the '80s.

'It was the second wave of punk,' says Lillywhite. 'I'd had some success with Siouxsie and the Banshees and the Psychedelic Furs but, to me, punk rock was a springboard to other things. I loved it as an attitude, but as an art form it was very limited. I was never into the UK Subs' form of punk. For me it was *art*. XTC and even the Psychedelic Furs with all their chaos – we considered it art, not just noise. And I'm middle class. I've never lived in a council house or anything like that.'

Chris Briggs was friends with Lillywhite and realised that Steve had a gap in his schedule, having just finished producing U2's third album, *War*. In March 1983, *War* knocked Michael Jackson's *Thriller* off the number 1 spot in the UK and stayed in the top 40 for the rest of that year.

'I was sent a few demos and the Chris Thomas recordings, which I agreed sounded flat and uninteresting,' says Steve. 'So they contracted me to record a single, to see how it went.'

The story goes that Phonogram had gone lukewarm on Big Country after the failure of 'Harvest Home' but, according to Briggs, 'the record company were *never* interested in Big Country. I took a coach-load of people down to Bristol to see them and I could tell. The vibe of the label was "Pfft. Okay." The label weren't all over it, at all. The marketing guy, Bob Fisher, he got it. The plugger got it. But it wasn't a project that everyone at the label thought was a winner.'

This is standard, he says. 'I mean, Robbie Williams at EMI? Mate, 70 per cent of the label thought that I was nuts.* That's normal.'

Chris Thomas had been contracted for a whole album so, with Lillywhite, they were cautious. He was brought on for a single, 'Fields of Fire'. What he produced turned it all around.

'And this is why, when people say, "Who have you enjoyed working with the most?", I always say that Big Country are right up there,' he says.

---

* After his departure from Take That in the mid-'90s, Briggs signed Robbie Williams to Chrysalis, then in the middle of a takeover by EMI, and launched him as a solo artist at a time when his stock was low – famously, he'd been dismissed by Noel Gallagher as 'the fat dancer from Take That'. He is now one of the most successful artists of all time: the solo artist with the most UK number 1 albums and the winner of a record-breaking eighteen BRIT Awards.

They went to RAK Studios, the studio founded by '60s and '70s hit-maker Mickie Most. It was chosen by Lillywhite and Briggs because it had the best drum room in London.

'RAK Studios was incredible for my drums,' says Mark. 'Very different. Steve was a brilliant producer. He would be very quick to recognise character – a hook, a slightly unusual noise.'

The Scottish sounds had made Mark think of marching bands and snare drums. The military drumming style that Steve Gadd used on Paul Simon's '50 Ways to Leave Your Lover' became an inspiration. Where other producers would remove much of the natural rhythm and grace notes produced by a drummer, Lillywhite left them in.

'It blew my mind, what he was doing,' says Bruce. 'This is before computers and flying faders. Steve played the mixing desk like an instrument. You know, faders up and panning and EQ on the fly. That's how he did all those 12-inch mixes.'

Where other producers might just expect a band to lay down the backing track and then focus on the main songwriting talent, Lillywhite spent time with each member of the band, conspiring with them to create distinctive, original parts.

'"Fields of Fire" sounds empty without the bass,' says Tony. 'It's like a third guitar in the orchestration. Steve put every one of us through our paces and I think for the first time everybody felt as though they had been produced. It was a great feeling.'

Stuart's biggest challenge was transitioning from a guitarist who sings into a singer-and-guitarist. 'And that's when Stuart found his voice,' says Tony. On 'Fields of Fire', Lillywhite put the frontman through his paces. Originally written in the key of D to fit Stuart's range, the producer asked them to do it in F instead. They had to tune their guitars up physically to make it work and then Stuart had to sing on top of it, in a key that was way out of his range.

'Steve kept him at it,' says Tony, 'for *a day*. He made him sing and sing and sing and sing and sing. And what you hear on the final record, is this new-born singer. Stronger, more assured. It sounds natural, but it was done incredibly unnaturally. I remember Stuart looking like he was going to pass out at times. But Steve had worked with Bono. He knew what you could do with people.'

It was a breakthrough. As with 'Harvest Home', the lyrics of 'Fields of Fire' are full of repetition – in poetry, they call it 'anaphora' and it brings rhythm and immediacy. 'Between a father and a son/Between the city and the one,' sings Stuart, addressing two of the biggest challenges in his life so far: his relationship with his father and the threat posed by London life.

Stuart once described 'Fields of Fire' as 'thoughts on a train journey' and that journey is almost certainly the one from Scotland to London. 'Four hundred miles,' goes the chorus, 'without a word until you smile.' Dunfermline is 400 miles from London, the city taking him away from his own family, Sandra and Callum ('Between the woman and the boy/Between a child and his toy'). 'I will be coming home again,' he promises.

In a classic Stuart Adamson move, he later suggested that 'Fields of Fire' was partly about the Falklands conflict of 1982, describing train journeys to London in which he and Bruce chatted with guys from the forces. But there's very little in the lyric to support that, beyond the title.

Fields of Fire was the name of a novel from 1978 by James Webb, set in the Vietnam War and exactly the sort of book that Adamson – a fan of Michael Herr's *Dispatches* and Tim O'Brien's *If I Die in a Combat Zone* – would have read. Taken this way, the song's title has a double-meaning. The 'field of fire' is the area that can be reached by gunfire – the danger area – but taken more broadly with the wider lyrical themes of *The Crossing*, it also conjures images of burning fields, of people being forcibly displaced, as in the Highland Clearances – or (more optimistically) fields of gold, a rich harvest.

The song can then be seen as a soldier's feelings on leaving his family. Misdirecting people like this – suggesting that 'Fields of Fire' was about the Falklands and not about himself – was a great way of deflecting people from the personal material in his songs. 'That's how he liked it,' says Sandra, 'because people were left wondering. He would never tell anybody the truth. I still see a lot of crap written about his lyrics and I think, "Oh, if only you knew."'

'In a lot of his writing, he mixed both personal and social and political,' she says. 'It's quite often the choruses that you find the personal stuff.'

Lillywhite brought the song to life. It was dynamic, uplifting, original. Stuart's voice was strong and 'Fields of Fire' introduced a vocal tick that he would become famous for: the exclamation. In karate they call it the 'kiai' – the cry that often accompanies a blow, designed to intimidate opponents, drive confidence and increase power, tensing your body. Big Country's songs are full of kiais: 'Shot!' 'Cha!', 'Haat!' and more. In 'Fields of Fire', it's 'hup' – an uplifting rhythmic 'giddy-up' to the band that in concert would give the audience something to sing along with.

'Fields of Fire' sounded like the work of *a band*, each member heard distinctly as they rolled into the fadeout: Tony's bass soloing, Mark's snare rattling, the guitars skirling elegiacally.

On 26 February 1983, the single went into the UK charts at 64. Seven weeks later, it was at number 10, matching the Skids' highest-ever chart position.

Hup, hup, hup, hup, hup, hup!

The single's B-side was 'Angle Park', the first song that Bruce and Stuart had worked on, and named the band after. Titled after an old house in Townhill, the lyrics imagine what might go on in such a place, alluding to abuse and violence, to children hiding behind their mother ('The beaten cry behind white dress ... While mothers wring their hands of tears/ The spelling books are in arrears'). In the garden, the fountains crack and statues grin menacingly, and the lyric points to the source of this misery: the father. 'The evil genius hugs his wife,' Stuart sings, 'as tiles ring with fear of life.'

Stay Alive

The opening guitar line recalls the melody of Joy Division's 'Love Will Tear Us Apart' released in June 1980, a month after singer Ian Curtis's suicide. Bruce was a fan and Stuart had moved in similar circles to Joy Division. Richard Jobson says the Skids played Manchester's Rafters Club with the Rezillos and Warsaw, an early incarnation of Joy Division, so possibly the melody is a deliberate nod to Curtis.

Deliberate or not, Big Country's first hit single was a song about the anguish of leaving home coupled with a song about domestic abuse that referenced a contemporary who had died by suicide.

On 4 March, the band were involved in a car crash on the way to a gig at Keele University. 'The four of us were in a hire car,' says Bruce. 'I think we were coming from a TV show to go to a gig the same day, and our monitor engineer, a guy called Bob Lopez, was driving us.'

The car was behind an articulated lorry when a huge metal shackle came off. 'We saw it – it was like slow motion. This big heavy metal shackle bounced off the road, hit us and shattered the windscreen. We got showered in glass and every one of us had to go to A&E to get the glass taken out of our eyes.'

They played the gig that night with bleeding eyeballs.

At the end of March, they did several dates supporting U2. At the Hammersmith Palais show, the Alarm's Mike Peters was there. 'In the weeks leading up to the show, I'd taught U2 how to play "Knocking on Heaven's Door",' he told me. 'We used to play it and Bono would come on and sing it with us.'

At Hammersmith, Bono invited both Mike and Stuart onstage to sing it. 'Stuart was in the crowd,' said Mike, 'and he came over the heads of the crowd and over the barrier. I helped pull him up and that was the first time I shook his hand. Bono introduced us then as being "the new breed".'

The new breed were a generation that had neither the aloofness of rock's old guard, nor the nihilism of the punks. After the Hammersmith show, Peters and Adamson stood signing autographs side by side. 'Stuart would always sign "With respect, Stuart Adamson" and I thought that was fantastic,' said Peters. 'It wasn't "Good luck" – it was something deep. It was a very respectful way of doing it.'

In 1976, Peters had gone up to Johnny Rotten and asked him what 'Anarchy in the UK' meant. Johnny told him to fuck off.

'And here was a guy signing autographs *"With respect"* ...'

A change in Steve Lillywhite's schedule meant that he was available to do the album. The 'Fields of Fire' experience had energised Stuart. 'When I'm good, this is what I can do,' says Lillywhite. 'Stuart was inspired by *the sound* of Big Country. We gave them this great spirited, uplifting feeling and, from that, Stuart went off and wrote "In a Big Country". I remember playing Bono the demo of "In a Big Country". I was so knocked out by it. I felt very honoured by that.'

'I think Steve actually burst into tears when he heard "In a Big Country",' says Ian. 'Maybe not "burst into tears", but he became emotional. It clicked with him.'

'I listened to the demo,' Lillywhite told BBC Radio Scotland years later, 'and I remember the chorus came in really quickly and I changed the arrangement. I said, "Stuart, look, let's hold back the chorus to make it pop." I can't believe I said that to him, but it just seemed the right thing to do ...'

The lyrics for 'In a Big Country' were incredible. In the song, Stuart addresses someone – possibly himself, possibly the listener, possibly someone in his life – and asks them to stay strong, despite all they've been through. Written after Stuart's infidelity had come to light, Sandra has wondered if it's partly directed at her. The song is filled with great turns of phrase – 'Dreams stay with you/Like a lover's voice fires the mountainside/ Stay alive' – that are grand and romantic on the one hand, but realistic and grounded on the other: 'I'm not expecting to grow flowers in a desert/But I can live and breathe/And see the sun in wintertime.'

Just 'because it's happened,' he says – whatever *it* is – it doesn't mean your life is over. 'Stay alive,' he exhorts.

Stay alive.

Stay Alive

The signature drum intro of 'In a Big Country' wasn't even part of the song originally. Lillywhite took the drum break from 'Porrohman', the epic album closer that they'd already finished, and turned it into the intro for 'In a Big Country'. 'Steve snipped it, copied it onto another tape and put it at the front of "In a Big Country",' says Bruce. 'It's the same part twice, that's why it sounds weird.'

Drum intros became as much a part of the signature Big Country sound as the guitars. 'From then on,' says Bruce, 'every new song, Mark would be like, "I'm starting it!"'

'The thing about Lillywhite,' says Briggs, 'as much as any producer I've ever worked with, he's really good at removing that sort of "red light fear". He creates an atmosphere in the studio where everyone's comfortable. Over and above his technical ability, he puts people at ease.'

'There are two schools of record producers,' says Steve. 'One will look at a band and say, "Who's the leader? Stuart. OK, I'll go and work with him because he's the creative talent." Whereas I'll go, "Who is feeling insecure? Who do I need to bolster up?" So I look at Stuart and say, "He's fine – I don't need to man-manage him."'

Instead, Lillywhite looked at Bruce. 'Bruce was so nervous,' he says. 'His hands used to shake like crazy in the studio. It's just my natural personality. I try and inspire a sense of teamwork rather than divide and rule.'

'I was nervous as fuck,' says Bruce. 'I was learning, but Steve was great with me.' Lillywhite encouraged his creativity. 'I'm a young musician at my first proper studio session and I've got these fucking mad ideas. I'm thinking, "He'll never wanna try them". But he did. Every idea I came up with got used, unless it clashed with a vocal or something like that. He brought that out in me.

'I'd never done any of that before. But then again, Stuart hudnae done it until he did it with the Skids. You've got to learn.'

The album was recorded at RAK and The Manor, where the Skids had made *The Absolute Game*. It was there that Bruce first saw an EBow. 'Bill

Nelson had one and Stuart had seen Bill using it,' he says. 'I remember opening the boxes at The Manor. That's the first time we used them.'

The EBow later became synonymous with Big Country and the band's use of them popularised the device. 'At the time,' says Greg Heet, its inventor, 'and for a *long* time, people would reference Big Country as their inspiration for getting an EBow.'

But, as with the constant references to 'bagpipe guitars', the band became bored of talking about it. 'The EBow is no' anything to do with the guitar sound,' says Bruce.

They used the EBow on tracks like 'The Storm' to get a long note, almost like a violin. 'But again, it's like bagpipes,' says Bruce. 'On their own, up close, they sound fucking horrible. But when you add effects like your reverb and all that stuff, that's where you get what people call the bagpipe sound. It gives you infinite sustain.'

'We wrote "Inwards" up at Townhill on those early demos,' says Bruce, 'and the arrangement never changed from then.'

The lyric apparently dates from Stuart's first days after leaving the Skids and is possibly a response to the death of his gran. More broadly, it seems to be about trying to keep emotions under control ('I pull everything inwards but everything's loose').

To Tony, it was an opportunity. '"Inwards" reminded Mark and I of our prog days and we thought, "Okay, let's attack this. Let's try to make it cohesive." We got to employ such a range of styles and attitudes towards it. It became something. It was a huge song.'

'Chance' had started life in Bruce's kitchen back in the early days, when he'd taken Stuart's four-track home and messed around with some ideas. Almost two years later, Stuart added the melody, creating a song that truly does fit the description of 'Scottish soul music'.

'All the rain came down/On a cold New Town' go the opening lyrics. When Richard Jobson commented that Stuart's lyrics could sometimes lean towards 'social realist observations of Glenrothes and these New Towns', it was surely 'Chance' that he was thinking of.

It's another song about an abusive father – 'your father's hand that always seemed like a fist' – and a woman escaping an abusive family situation only to end up a single parent, trapped and aging before her time: 'You never knew you were young.'

The songs are full of literary references, apocalyptic imagery and insights into Stuart Adamson's mindset. 'Close Action' took its title from the 1974 novel *Signal – Close Action!* by Alexander Kent, a story of adventure at sea. Stuart sings what seems to be a devotional love song, while the final verse suggests something dreaded arriving from the sea: 'For endless hours the sirens wail/Await the tide that brings the sail/Cling to the walls and close the shore.'

'A Thousand Stars' imagined a nuclear war, referencing the 'Protect and Survive' leaflet distributed to local authorities and police and fire services that outlined the steps to take in the event of a nuclear attack.

'Some say protect and survive,' sings Stuart. 'I say it's over.'

Fear of nuclear war was everywhere in the 1980s, but it was keenly felt in that area of Scotland, with the dockyards and the presence of nuclear submarines. 'We're a prime target here, make no bones about it,' said Stuart. 'If anything does happen, it's going to be bye-bye.'

'Porrohman', a seven-and-a-half-minute-long multi-part epic, was inspired by *Pollock and the Porroh Man*, a short story by H.G. Wells from 1895, about a man hunted and then haunted by an adversary before being driven mad and killing himself.

The lyrics use the same phrase ('tiles ring with fear of life') employed in 'Angle Park', that early song of abuse. 'The fear of life is strong' goes 'Porrohman' and suggests that the course of our lives is just a matter of chance: 'Our fate is in the hands/Of a demon or a god.'

Chance is also a theme of 'Lost Patrol', inspired by *The Lost Patrol* by Dick North. Published in 1978, it's a detailed account of the search for a mail patrol in the Yukon in the early twentieth century. The men died by the Snake River ('We lay the night in anguish/Snakes drawn out by the tide') having taken the wrong path. 'The compass of decision,' sings Stuart, 'falls always on one side.' The cover art for *The Crossing* features a compass, and the 'compass of decision' seems key to understanding the album. It's about the choices we make and the directions we take. Like the men of the Lost Patrol, we could all be choosing a path that ends in death.

'I wanted to go for this big, cinematic sound,' said Lillywhite, totally understanding the brief. 'I tried to make everything larger than life.'

The Crossing was a triumph. It was the 'open sound' that Adamson had been looking for, created by four men of different but fascinating backgrounds: working-class men with family histories steeped in immigration, war and hardship, who had found salvation in the sheer visceral joy of music.

Musically, *The Crossing* was epic and inspirational, as big as the glens, as loud as a cavalry charge. It was rock music, but not the rock music of Led Zeppelin, AC/DC or the Stones. It was modern – with guitar tones and effects that you'd find on records by U2 and New Order – but also harmonised guitar parts that evoked Thin Lizzy and Wishbone Ash.

Sometimes it sounded positively ancient: traditional, eternal. Its lyrics talked of mountainsides and ploughmen and harvests and the westerly winds sighing. It was a guitar player's dream – each song packed with cool licks and counter melodies and inventive rhythm playing – a bass player's nightmare (how could anyone compete with *this?*) and a drummer's delight: a huge, rhythmic, widescreen epic.

In Scottish music, its effect may be unparalleled. In the 1980s, the image of Scotland on TV was one of castles and lochs and Highland dancing at Hogmanay: a world of 'teuchters' and tartan that seemed at odds with the reality of life in 1983. Scotland had not voted for the Conservative government of Margaret Thatcher but got it anyway. Unemployment soared. Traditional industries closed. In the early '80s, Edinburgh became the AIDS capital of Europe. Heroin flooded the estates of Glasgow and Edinburgh, where sharing dirty needles was a way of life. And the nuclear threat felt real.

The music of Big Country seemed to embody both sides of Scotland – a Scottishness that connected to the country's history, but felt modern and vibrant. 'When I first heard Big Country,' said the great Scottish comedian and actor Robbie Coltrane, 'I thought the Clash had high-jacked a pibroch player.'* It was music, he said, that made 'every Scotsman in London eat a bus stop out of homesickness on the way home from the pub'.

'The storytelling is timeless,' says Sandra. 'It's visual. The stories that he tells can be interpreted loads of different ways. If anybody asks me, "What do you think that song means?", if Stuart hasn't already said it, there's no way that I would ever talk about anything that he told me. It's an experience – a Scottish experience or a war experience – a heartfelt experience. But the teuchter thing and the Highland thing – that's something that was really important to me because I was immersed in bagpipe music. So that conjures up loads of stuff for me and it did for Stuart as well, it really did.'

Many of the song titles on the album are obscure and not featured in the chorus. Even its most commercial song, 'Chance', takes its title from a line in a verse: 'You played chance with a lifetime's romance/And the price was far too long.' The idea of 'playing chance' – any game that involves luck and risk, usually involving dice – might have come from another source.

Peter Wishart remembers Stuart recommending a book to him. 'Stuart said, "You have to read this",' says Peter. 'One of his favourite books was *The Dice Man* by Luke Rhinehart. It was a book that actually changed my opinion and philosophy on life.' Published in 1971, *The Dice Man* became a cult sensation. It's about a man who feels suicidal and – instead of killing himself – puts his fate in the roll of the dice. The opening lines of the book are: 'In the beginning was Chance, and Chance was with God ... All things were made by Chance.' The word 'chance' appears eleven times in the first two paragraphs.

It's tempting to read more into this, to see Big Country and *The Crossing* – an album filled with songs of depression, loss, abuse, persecution and death; an album that begins with a plea to someone, possibly Stuart himself, to stay alive – as Stuart Adamson's last roll of the dice. (Think of the lyrics of 'Balcony': 'The final scene is set ... This is my finest hour/Now is your last encore.')

---

* 'Pibroch' is the Gaelic name for a piece of music written for the bagpipes.

If Big Country's music had been sombre, like Joy Division's, then it would have been more obvious. But, instead, the lyrical content was wrapped up in music so passionate, so uplifting and beautiful, that its message was obscured.

Some people heard it differently. When Skids drummer Tam Kellichan heard 'Chance', he thought it was a suicide note. 'When I first heard it,' he says. 'I thought he wrote it for his own death. It was all in the chorus, all this, "Oh gawd, help me now." I thought, "Fucking hell, he must have been in a bad state". I thought it was the last song for him.'

The album took its title from one of the songs written by the first line-up, with credited contributions from Peter and Alan Wishart. 'The Crossing' had also been one of the tracks that had excited Mark and Tony: an ambitious, proggy epic. Tony later acknowledged it as 'the track that set the sails for this ship ... The track where we discovered a shared interest in a musical style.'

The song never made it onto the album, so why did it become the title? What is the significance of 'The Crossing', as a song or a phrase? A 'crossing' can be another name for a crossroads, a place where roads intersect and 'the compass of decision' is needed: which road will you choose?

A crossing is also a journey by boat or ship and there are several references to the sea in the song and on the album. As a merchant navy seaman, Stuart's dad would have made many crossings. The song 'The Crossing' – and that phrase isn't used anywhere in the lyrics – seems to be about someone's return. On the face of it, they are returning triumphant ('Your islands are conquered and you are returned/To the throne') but, as on 'Close Action', their return is also dreaded: 'Martyrs take penance and fill up the mattress/With stones'. The returning person 'wears out their welcome again'.

There is what could be a description of abuse or fear in the night, someone becoming alert in the dark as feet creep to their door: 'Mornings hit hard with an uncontrollable light/Piercing the senses that click deep in the night/Crouched in a pillow of straw, feet on the floor/Creeping a path to the mat that holds back the door.'

Stay Alive

'The crossing' could also refer to the threshold of a door, maybe a door that you have no business crossing. You cross boundaries. You can cross people – double-cross them – betray people who trusted you.

In a room, sings Stuart, there are 'scratches on walls' that 'draw out your loss' – symbols of the damage caused. The chorus, meanwhile, suggests an escape from this returning threat, this thing that creeps into your room at night.

'Pull straws with holy men,' sings Stuart.

They could pray, but it's just another game of chance.

'Stain the atlas pink.'

Destroy the maps so they can't be found.

And, finally, run away: 'Find a beach/where we can cross our hearts.'

And what do you do when you cross your heart?

You hope to die.

Maybe Stuart Adamson saw Big Country as his last chance, a final roll of the dice, and he constructed the band's material – from their very first song, 'Angle Park', to their first album – to tell a story about abuse.

Maybe he couched these tales of frightened children, beaten women, these references to suicide, to the effort required to stay alive, in songs that were so life-affirming that their message – although right there in plain sight – wasn't obvious.

Maybe talk of 'Jock rock' and 'bagpipe guitars' trivialised his grand artistic statement.

Maybe he was such a charismatic performer and his talent so huge and obvious that we were blinded to what he was saying all along.

Or maybe it's a mistake to read too much into things.

'Heart and Soul' – another song that never made the album – could be a sister song to 'In a Big Country'. It is a plea to someone to forget the past ('cast out all of the devils you hold') and throw themselves into the thing that inspires them.

'To the dream that fires the furnace,' sang Stuart, 'give all your heart and soul.'

Come Up Screaming

He had given it his all. On 6 August 1983, *The Crossing* went into the UK album charts at number 4, rising to number 3 the following month. It spent thirty-nine weeks in the top 40 through 1983 and into '84, and had gone platinum by February 1994.

Big Country were big time.

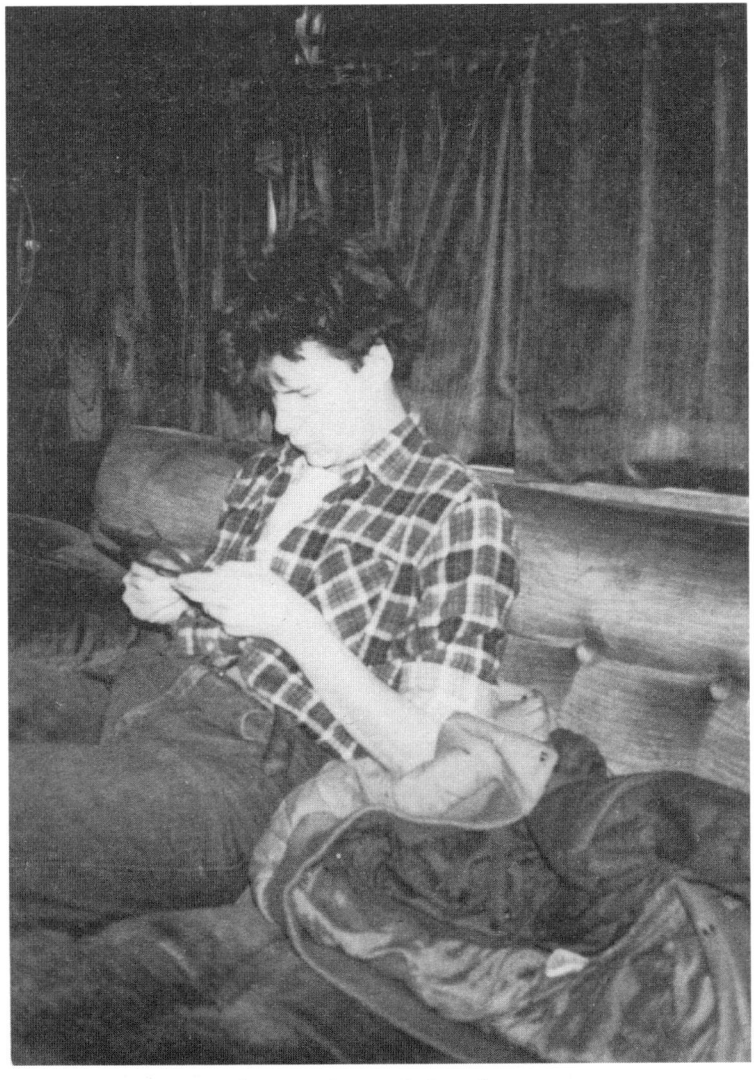

Stuart on his Gameboy, early '80s. 'He never went anywhere without a Gameboy,' says Sandra.

13

Everything You Ever Might Have Wanted

Success. Reading Festival. The US. Play At Home. Triumph at Barrowlands. Wonderland. The Dean Ford Experience

When they make a six-part Netflix series about Big Country, this part of the story will be a whirlwind of fast-cutting, feelgood triumphs. This is when flashes pop and crowds explode. This is a whirlwind of TV appearances and magazine interviews, of photoshoots and chart positions. This is international flights and Californian sun and women and tour buses and hi-jinks and lines of coke being chopped and champagne corks ricocheting off ceilings.

Sure, there will be tearful phone calls home. You will see the wife at home with the baby. You will see flashes of guilt in the eyes of the singer as a body moves under the sheets next to him. But this, finally, is success. This is what we want for our heroes. This is encores and crowds chanting their name. This is fleets of trucks and catering crews and lighting rigs and cash being counted. This is peak Big Country, with walk-on parts for Michael Jackson, Bubbles and Brooke Shields, with Bob Dylan at the door being refused entry to *their* party.

This is *it*.

In July '83, before the album was even released, Big Country toured the UK, playing six nights a week. 'In those days, you did gigs to create an audience,' says John Giddings, Big Country's agent and a legend in the British music industry. 'You didn't just release records. You did a live show and people reacted and more people came to see you next time.' In August, they played just two big dates: one at Phoenix Park in Dublin, fourth on the bill after U2, Simple Minds and Eurythmics; the other at Reading Festival, where they were second top of the bill below the Stranglers.

'The Reading Festival,' says Giddings, 'was one of the big moments. That's what turned them from a pop group into a rock band.'

It almost never happened. Giddings had agreed on the gig with Ian Grant and announced it without Stuart's approval. Adamson was furious: he had August off for a family holiday. He gave an interview to the music press, saying he wasn't doing it. Giddings phoned him. 'I said, "I'll pay for you, out of my commission, to fly out and back because I think it's so important to your career."'

Stuart, impressed by Giddings' conviction, caved.

The band were on second last, after Birmingham reggae band Steel Pulse, who quit their set two songs in, as bottles and cans rained down on them. The barrage didn't stop for Big Country. Memories of the festival captured online are of a band converting an aggressive audience within minutes.

'Big Country met by a hail of cans yet three songs later had everyone in the crowd going mad for them. I've never seen such a volte-face in my life. Brilliance ...'

'The unexpected pleasure of the show was Big Country, who braved the hail of bottles and played a killer set. My recollection has the bottles stopping after two songs, then a song where the audience stood quietly, unsure how to respond, then for the rest of the set they went wild ...'

'Big Country getting canned and then adulated in the space of four minutes ...'

Giddings was vindicated. 'After that performance, they became a real rock band,' he says.

A real rock band – but one that didn't have any eyebrows for a while, thanks to the Stranglers' pyrotechnics guy Martin Blake. At Reading, Big Country were billed as 'special guests' of headliners the Stranglers and Martin Blake was a pyro legend, a pioneer of flame-related shock and awe. The band met Blake backstage before the show.

'We shook hands and his hands were *slimy*,' says Bruce. 'He'd burnt them so much that he had to keep them moisturised. And his face was a bit, y'know, *crispy*. Pyrotechnics guys have orgasms when they set them off. They always use too much.'

On 'Fields of Fire', Blake tells them, he's got pyros set to go off next to their microphone stands. 'So when Stuart sings "... On fields of fire!",' he says, '"*run like fuck*. Get at least four feet away from the mic-stand because it'll get quite hot."'

Quite hot? 'It was like a fucking napalm attack,' says Bruce. 'We had to run back behind the Marshall stacks, the heat was so intense. It took all the hair off our faces – our eyebrows, everything. When you looked up, there were riggers and lampies jumping fae the scaffolding to the ground to get away from the heat.'

The band dived behind the Marshalls, laughing. And then their faces started burning. 'We went down to the St John's Ambulance tent, and they were like, "Oh my god! What did you *do*?" Everybody had bright red faces and singed eyebrows.'

Big Country had the chops – a powerful rhythm section, songs packed with riffs and licks, tailormade to get a crowd moving – but didn't look like a typical rock band. They looked like a pop band.

'At that time, all the bands looked like a gang from [1979 movie] *The Warriors*,' says Bruce. He points to the bands they played with on their first *Top of the Pops*: Dexys Midnight Runners had looked like New Jersey longshoremen, with donkey jackets and woolly hats, before unveiling their Celtic Soul Brothers 'gypsy' look. The JoBoxers looked like a gang from the Bronx. Culture Club, Twisted Sister: every band was distinct. 'They all had a look,' he says. 'U2 had a look, the Bunnymen had a look. So our look was the checked shirts and these Italian army trousers.'

The checked shirts came from outdoors store Millets. 'Right from the word go, there was this idea of Stuart's for us to look in a certain way,' says Tony. 'Kind of a Venture Scout, Boy Scout thing: Big Country, the outdoors.'

On a visit to London, they went to Laurence Corner, the army surplus store near Euston Station that had inspired the Beatles' *Sgt Pepper* uniforms and was later frequented by Vivienne Westwood, Jean Paul Gaultier and

Katharine Hamnett. There, Stuart found some distinctive Italian army trousers that cut off at the knees.

Tony wasn't as enthusiastic. 'I remember getting these fucking Italian trousers and thinking, "Have you seen how short my legs are? You want me to wear these? They look like baggy longjohns!"'

'It was a cheap look,' says Bruce, 'but when we got to *Top of the Pops*, the record company went, "No fucking way!"' They brought in stylist Jackie Castellano. 'She organised for us to get proper haircuts – I think that's when Stuart first got his spiky haircut – and Phonogram gave her money to take us shopping and buy clothes.'

They went to cool shops in London and bought clothes that they had never had the money to buy – '50s-style suits from Johnson's or gear from LaRocka on the King's Road. Out went the short trousers. 'For some reason we kept the checked shirts,' says Bruce. 'Maybe Jackie thought that they looked good with the suits. And then that became fashionable and everybody started wearing checked shirts.'

After 'Fields of Fire' hit, club gigs were moved to bigger halls and the whole production grew. 'The bigger venues didn't have their own PAs,' says Bruce, 'so you had to hire them. That's why all the bands had big artic lorries.' Stuart had been through some of this with the Skids but, for the rest of them, it was all new. They'd rehearse in London and then meet up with lighting designers, sound engineers, PA companies. Where previously they had toured in minivans and Transits, suddenly they had tour buses. Pete Barnes – the guy who designed the famous bomber lighting rig for Motörhead – came on board for lights and design, adding atmospheric back projections of mountains and storms and clouds.

From depending on their PDs to survive ('per diems' – 'Ten quid a day to go and get yourself some grub,' says Bruce), suddenly they had their own caterers. 'You'd see these flight cases coming out with washing machines and tumble dryers and cookers ...'

They had their own security and, much to their surprise, they *needed* it. 'The bigger you got, it just got fucking silly,' says Bruce. 'Nowadays, everything's health and safety, and there's Mojo barriers [the stage barrier systems

Everything You Ever Might Have Wanted

that control crowds]. Back then, you didn't have organised security. You had to bring your own. Even at a place like Hammersmith Odeon, there would be thousands of people outside the stage door. You needed security to get out.'

Hammersmith Odeon was a highpoint for Tony. 'It was where I saw my very first gig – Chuck Berry supported by the Animals,' he says. 'I'd seen so many bands there, so to play there was absolutely fantastic. In fact, on the "Wonderland" single sleeve, there's a picture of me shaking my brother's hand there. That was a great moment.'

'You could play for three hours back then,' says Bruce. 'You could do as many encores as you like, stay on all night.' Nowadays, curfews are tight and bands get fined for over-running. In smaller venues, bands have to be finished by 10 p.m. and do the 'disco load-out' to make way for that evening's club night. 'Back then, you could play for hours. I've seen us doing it.'

Seemingly overnight, Big Country were huge. 'It was a shock to the system,' says Bruce. 'It's what you secretly want but don't expect. I'd thought, *Maybe we'll get a John Peel session, maybe a single out.* That was enough. But things changed.'

'The money starts coming in a year later,' says Bruce. 'I could afford to buy Sandra a car. It was like, "Ooh, this is new".' Sandra and Bruce Watson.

Stay Alive

'It's all about team players, always,' says Ian Grant. 'It's never about just the band, or the manager. It's about *everybody*. We had such a fantastic team. At that time, Mercury were on a roll – Briggs and Brian Shepherd, the managing director. Tony Powell, head of marketing; Julian Spear, the head of promotion. They were on a roll with Dexys, Tears For Fears, ABC – just constantly churning them out. So there was a great vibe there.

'Then you've got a great live crew. The agent, John Giddings. The promoters, Peter Irvine and Barry Wright of Regular Music and Marcia Vlasic at ICM – they all got it.'

'Everybody was on the same page,' says Bruce. 'There was no negativity, even at the record company. Everybody working at the label, management, the band, everybody. It worked. You cannae just say it was just the band. Everything worked and it wisnae 'til afterwards that it fucked up.'

TV wanted a piece of them. They were on *Top of the Pops*, *Cheggers Plays Pop*, *Crackerjack*, *TV-am* and many more. A new British TV channel had launched in November 1982 – Channel 4 – with a remit to provide an alternative to the BBC and ITV. Music show *The Tube* was one of their earliest successes, recorded live in Newcastle and hosted by Paula Yates and Jools Holland. Big Country appeared on it, and its sister show *Switch*, several times.

'I loved *The Tube*,' says Bruce. 'Apart from the fact that it was a great show – and it was complete mayhem and funny – it meant I could get the train home from Newcastle to Dunfermline and get to the pub for a couple of pints.'

'It made us realise how different we were from other groups,' says Tony. 'I never realised how fucking namby-pamby a lot of these other groups were. When you're doing the promotional circuit – radio, TV and all that kind of stuff – you tended to bump into similar bands. Duran Duran, Culture Club, all these groups. And sometimes – well, most of the time – we didn't really associate with them, purely and simply because they behaved like *twats*.'

Another Channel 4 programme, the youth magazine show *Whatever You Want*, hosted by comedian and actor Keith Allen, used 'Harvest Home'

Everything You Ever Might Have Wanted

as its theme tune. Channel 4 even gave the band its own documentary, *Play at Home*, in which they attempted to show the behind-the-scenes workings of the music industry: where the money comes from and where it goes. John Giddings, Chris Briggs, Ian Grant and promoter Paul Crockford all explained their part in the Big Country operation.

At one point, Ian breaks it down like this: 'The total cost of the tour is around £39,000. The PA is £7,500. The lights are £7,350, the trucks are £6,400, catering is £300 a night – that comes out of the promoter's costs. At the start of this tour, if you didn't break any percentage, if you didn't take a lot in merchandise, you'd have lost £12,000. By the time we've finished, we should make two or three thousand pounds profit.'

Three thousand pounds in 1984 is the equivalent to £12,500 today. How does *he* make money? the band ask. 'Our commission comes off the top,' says Ian. 'When the first royalty cheque comes in, apart from you getting some money, we will claim back monies that we've advanced you. Our commission is 20 per cent.'

'Les, the roadie, is the funniest bit,' says Bruce. 'Our stage manager Les was an ex-con. He was a cocaine dealer as well and, fucking hell, the minute you see Les on the screen in the background, you hear this guy going, "Chop 'em out, Les!"'

Les shared a flat with his girlfriend in King's Cross and Stuart and Bruce would stay there when they were in London. The area has been gentrified now, but back in the '80s, King's Cross was notorious for homelessness, prostitution and drugs.

'Les used to rob post offices,' says Bruce. 'His girlfriend worked in one of the post offices that Les held up. It was love at first sight.'

The first time they stayed at the flat, Bruce noticed that the kitchen was full of scales, with flour on every surface. 'Does your girlfriend like baking or something?' asked Bruce. Les told him to fuck off.

It wasn't flour. It was cocaine.

Their local was the Skinner's Arms. Actor Phil Daniels – famous for the lead role in the Who's *Quadrophenia* movie – lived above the pub. 'It was a real boozer, a fucking mental place,' says Bruce. 'So we used to drink with

Phil Daniels and Les and some other guys from King's Cross that were all criminals. They became our road crew. There was Big John, Little John, Medium-Sized John – all these fucking lunatics, but great guys – and they used to terrorise everybody.'

One time on tour in America, Bruce was standing outside the venue and noticed an upturned car in the car park.

'What happened to that car?' Bruce asked Les.

'Promoter didn't bring the fucking cocaine, did he?' said Les.

Another time, Bruce went into Ian Grant's office on London's Edgware Road. All the women were crying.

'What's going on?' he asked.

'Les came round,' they said. 'He took all the word processors and the phones 'cos Ian hasn't paid him.'

'Granty had been late with the wages, so Les took a fucking squad round,' says Bruce. '"You won't be fackin' needing that then! You'll get them back when you fackin' pay us!"'

Stuart and Bruce stayed with Les because they still had no money. From the outside, you would have expected them to be rolling in it: they had hit singles, a hit album, they were playing big halls, they were on TV. The truth was a little less glamorous. 'You had to wait a long time for the royalties to come in,' says Bruce. 'At the time we were doing *Top of the Pops*, we were still skint. When Briggs signed us, we got put on an 80-quid-a-week wage. You survive by doing the gigs.'

At one point, Mark and Bruce were looking to get not a flat, but a *squat* in King's Cross. It 'belonged' to a local sex worker or a pimp, but one of their King's Cross crew was going, 'We'll facking sort 'im out for ya.' They decided against it.

'Eventually, the money starts coming in, maybe a year later,' says Bruce, 'and I could afford to buy [his girlfriend] Sandra a car and put a deposit down on a flat. It was like, "Ooh, this is new".'

In September, they played Belgium, then two nights in New York – where Bill Nelson and Pete Townshend came to the shows – before returning for fifteen dates across the UK. In October, they went to Germany for a week of back-to-back gigs. In November, with *The Crossing* going top 20 in the US, they toured North America.

Bruce has memories of eating at Barney's Beanery on Santa Monica Boulevard, staying at the Hyatt House in LA, and the Sunset Marquis, back in the days of the Sunset Strip, the Rainbow, the Roxy and Gazzarri's. The legendary promoter Bill Graham came to see them in San Francisco. 'I loved being in America,' says Bruce. 'Because I was a big movie fan, to just *be* in America, every second was amazing. I didn't want to go to sleep because I could look out the tour bus window and see the badlands. Deserts. A cactus. It was my favourite place in the whole world.'

But it was intense: sometimes six days on and one day off. 'It was the never-ending tour.'

They flew back to the UK before Christmas and rounded off the year with two Hogmanay shows at Glasgow's Barrowland, their first gig at the famous Scottish venue.

'That was a great show,' says Bruce. 'Definitely one of the highlights.' In the afternoon, they did a matinee show for under eighteens. Steve Lillywhite came up and mixed the live sound out front. He brought his girlfriend, Kirsty MacColl, who he'd met while recording Simple Minds' *Sparkle in the Rain* album. At the second show, Big Country played until just before midnight, before leaving the stage for a pipe band to come on and play 'Auld Lang Syne'. Backstage, Lillywhite proposed to Kirsty and then the band came back on for another hour or so.

'The audience were just unbelievable,' says Tony. 'That sprung floor has never sprung as much as it did that night. You are talking about the heyday of the group's existence – coming back to do Barrowlands, New Year's, getting the pipers on at midnight ... And then to walk off and see Lillywhite on bended knee proposing to Kirsty. It was just the height of emotion, a fantastic thing to be part of. When I sit back in my big armchair up in the great studio in the sky, I can look back at those times and go, "Glad I was there".

'If I was to write a book, I wouldn't write about it, because I couldn't capture the feelings that we all had at that particular time. To see this guy propose and then go back out on stage and play ... You can't write about

Stay Alive

it. The atmosphere of the Barras – this sticky, steaming atmosphere – was just incredible. I never felt prouder to be in this band.'

'What a gig,' says Bruce. 'It's still one of my favourite gigs of all time.'

Afterwards, they went back to Jim Kerr's house for a Hogmanay/engagement party. There's another scene for that Netflix series.

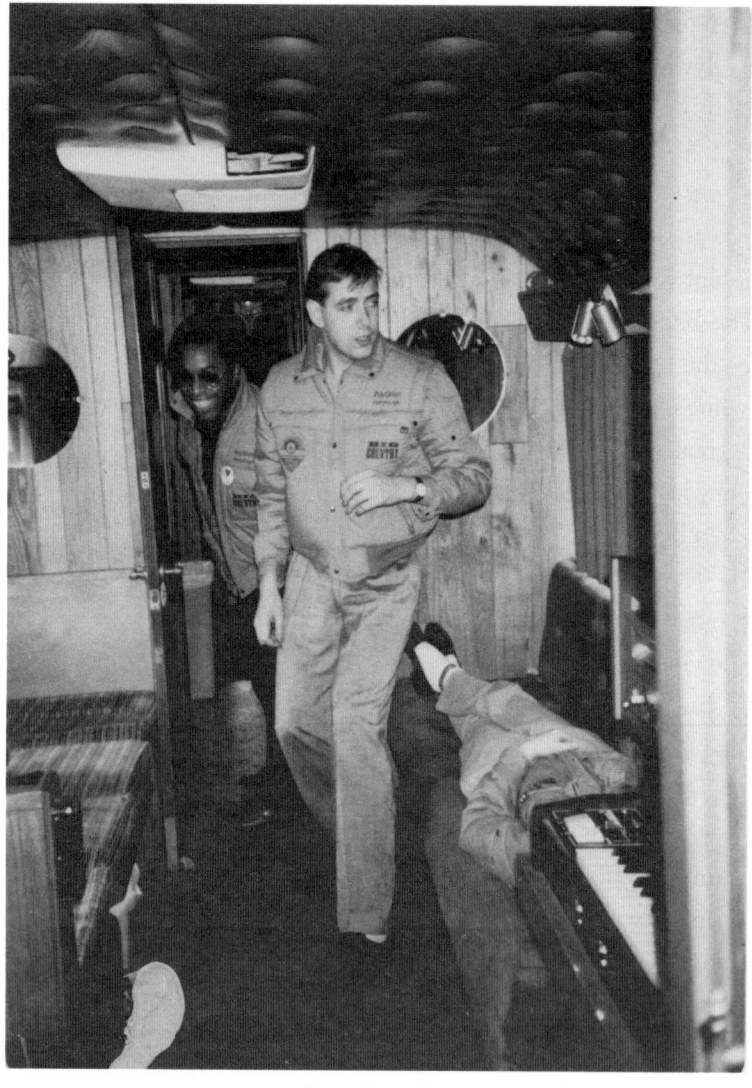

Tony and Mark on the tour bus.
'And then,' says Tony, 'then it all went flat.'

Big Country were on top of the world. On 13 January, they released a new single that seemed to sum up where they were in their career: 'Wonderland'.

'"Wonderland" was the bridge between *The Crossing* and *Steeltown*,' says Bruce. The germ of the song started with Bruce – a funky Prince-style riff that he'd captured on his portastudio at home – and had worked up with Mark. On a rare day off from touring, the two of them knocked it into shape and then presented it to Stuart and Tony. The band went into RAK Studios with Lillywhite to record it.

By this point, Bruce was a natural. '"Put 250 milliseconds on that side, Stephen. And put 375 milliseconds on that side. We'll get some mad fucking criss-cross delay thing." "Yep, no problem!"'

'It was almost like it wisnae me, like, "How the fuck am I doing this?" One point you're learning and the next it becomes second nature.'

The band weren't around when the single was mixed. Somewhere out on the road, at a hotel in America, they took delivery of a cassette of Lillywhite's 12-inch mix. 'And it was fucking amazing,' says Bruce. 'It's one of the greatest 12-inch mixes I've ever heard.'

They had shot the 'Wonderland' video on their jaunt across the States in November, the snow scenes filmed up Mount Hood in Oregon, where Stanley Kubrick shot the exterior shots of the Overlook Hotel for *The Shining*, and then the desert scenes in 'Denver or somewhere like that'.

The video is about extremes: the band are in either the icy cold or the desert sun. This was the 'desert sun' part of their career. 'Wonderland' was their highest charting single so far, reaching number 8 in the UK singles chart. They were unstoppable.

Big Country went back to the US at the end of February for the Grammys, where 'In a Big Country' was nominated for Best Song and they were also in the running for Best New Artist. They flew the band out to Los Angeles on Concorde. At LAX, Bruce was picked up by limo. The chauffeur was an older Scottish guy. 'You might have heard of me,' he says to Bruce. 'My name's Dean Ford ...'

'I was like: "Fuck. *Off* ..."'

Stay Alive

Dean Ford had been the singer for Marmalade, the first-ever Scottish group to top the UK singles chart (in 1968, with a cover of the Beatles' 'Ob-La-Di, Ob-La-Da'), and the co-writer of 'Reflections of my Life', a number 3 hit in 1969.

'It really upset me,' says Bruce. 'He's written all these great songs and here he is with the hat and the uniform, driving a fucking taxi. I'm thinking, "This could happen to me". And, of course, it *did* ...'

They did a full rehearsal, playing 'In a Big Country', running through the process of what would happen if they won an award, with Grace Jones and Alice Cooper presenting it. 'Alice is like, "Not you guys again, fuck me,"' says Bruce. And even though it was a rehearsal, as Big Country walked to the stage, the orchestra played a version of 'In a Big Country'. 'We must've won it!' they thought. 'Why else would the orchestra have learnt it?'

In the end, the Police's 'Every Breath You Take' won Best Song and Culture Club took the honours for Best New Artist. Still, Big Country played live with Michael Jackson and Brooke Shields sitting right in front of them.

At the aftershow, Michael Jackson was in the green room with Bubbles the chimp, while Bob Dylan was refused entry because he was wearing a denim jacket.

'It was funny as fuck,' says Bruce.

They moved so fast that the next day they landed in New York and, because of the time difference, caught themselves on the show in the arrivals lounge. People crowded around, high-fiving them: 'Hey man, Big Country!'

It felt as though they were on the verge of something.

'And then,' says Tony, 'then it all went flat.'

15

Wonderland

You are living the dream

You are in Vancouver or Seattle or San Francisco, in LA, in Phoenix, in Tucson, in Denver

You are on a bus, rolling around in a tiny bunk, a half-bunk in a half-sleep, conscious of brakes being applied, of the bus bouncing on its suspension, your half-dreams interrupted by passing sirens, half-wondering if you need to piss. You are relieved when morning comes, although it's really just a half-morning, and you are at a hotel in Cincinnati – or is it Detroit or Cleveland? – and you drag yourself out, half a person, barely able to say good morning, barely able to look at anyone

All you want is some time to yourself but no sooner are you checked in and heading for the lift than you are being told:

> OK you've got press from 11 o'clock 'til 12, and then you've radio 'til two, it's on the other side of the city, so we'll need to watch the traffic, and then the local what's on guide want to preview the fall tour, that's at three and then we'll grab a quick bite, and then it's TV, and it'll be a rush for soundcheck, so see you down here at 10, yeah?

And you go to your room and you work out what time it is in Dunfermline and you write a letter and you fall asleep mid-sentence and the next

Stay Alive

thing you know someone's banging at your door 'cos it's half ten and fuck me

And you are in the lift and a guy says 'What floor?' and you tell him, and the guy says, 'Gee, I love your accent! What part of Australia are you from? No way! *I'm* part Scotch! My great grandfather was from Edin*boro* ...' And you smile and you talk shit with the guy and then you are hurriedly swallowing some omelette and

And this might be Boston, or Lawrenceville, or Pennsauken

And there's a kid, I mean, he's eighteen if he's a day, and he's asking you these questions, and he's looking at a notepad and pushing a mini-tape recorder across the coffee table

> *How do you like it here so far, how long have you been playing guitar, I read that you weren't born in Scotland, my great grandfather was Scotch, how did you invent the bagpipe sound, when did you first play the EBow, have you got anything special planned for tonight's gig, can I get a photograph?*

And you reply and he speaks in a sing-song voice and he's smiling but frowning

> *I'm sorry, I never caught that*
> *I'm sorry. The what? Is that a place?*
> *How are you spelling that?*
> *I'm sorry–*
> *The what, sorry?*
> *I'm sorry—*

And then you are in a cab and you feel hollow and the cab driver is saying, 'Hey, is that an Irish accent? Ah, *Scatland*, that's part of England, right?

Wonderland

I always wanted to go …' and you are in a radio station and some guy is walking you through the offices and everyone is staring and they all stand as you pass and offer their hands, and you say hiya, hiya, hiya, hello, you awright, and he's introducing you to the head of promotions and the assistant programmer and the VP of sales and the head of sales and the station manager and he's part Scotch and he loves your music, man, that bagpipe thing just sends him, one day he'll get himself to *Scatland*, and then you are on the air and the DJ is telling you that he was the first person at the station to play 'In a Big Country', first in the city, maybe first in the state, he knew it was a hit as soon as he heard those bagpipe guitars, 'cos he's part Irish, not Scotch, but it's the same, right?

And you are in Nashville or Atlanta or Daytona or St Petersburg or Boca Raton or New Orleans and you are in make-up and someone has their hand up your shirt and is pinning a mic to your collar and they're buffering your face with powder and the lighting is fucking blinding and they sit you in front of the mirror and you look like a ghost of yourself and you are three-two-hand-signal LIVE and

> What is 'Chance' about, and can you play the bagpipes, and ain't it funny because Scatland is actually a small country, like, the state of Florida has actually five times as many people, and it says here that you play the EBow, is that like the fiddle and Big Country play tonight at the Fox Theater, don't miss 'em

And words come out but you have no idea what you said and

You are in a cab and you need to piss but at the venue you are shaking hands with the promoter and the venue owner, who's brought his family and his kid is learning the *geetar*, aren't you son, and it would be great if they could have a photograph and you can hear Mark's drums at soundcheck, and you chug some piss-poor lite beer and when was the last time you ate

Stay Alive

And the guys look at you at soundcheck and you're so pleased to see them but you're wiped and you down another beer and you just want to decompress, you wanna lay on your bed and just watch some shit on TV – a crap fucking game show, anything – 'cos your mind is blown but you are fucking trapped 'cos that bed was yesterday and you have a gig and a bus and then you are in San Francisco or San Luis Obispo or Santa Barbara, moving west, further from home

And there is a gig and the gig makes you feel alive and afterwards you hit the whisky and shake more hands, and you repeat yourself and you repeat yourself and you repeat yourself and then you are on a bus, in a half-bunk in a half-sleep, dreaming half-dreams, half-a-person and

16

Where Did the Feeling Go?

Kamikazes in California.
Sword fights on the Bullet Train.
The Love Phone

At the height of his success, Stuart Adamson was falling apart, crumbling under the pressure of being the frontman, the centre of attention, the guy everyone wants a piece of.

'I don't think Stuart was prepared for the success of *The Crossing*,' says Tony. 'He'd sold a lot of albums in the past, but to have something that sold as much as *The Crossing*, and then go straight out on the road for two years – and in his new guise as a singer-guitarist – it was a lot for him.

'He wasn't "showbizzy", and because of that he took it too seriously – far too seriously – which made him recoil and added to his social discomfort. The fact that he was now the *focus* – as opposed to just somebody in the band – that got to him.

'He was forever saying, "I'm just a poor Crossgates boy. I can't be dealing with all this stuff. I just like going to the football and down the pub with my mates." I said to him, too many times, "That's gone. And you got yourself into this. You're doing something that you love, but you can't stand the consequences?"

'We had *many* conversations about this.'

'You had people who were much more ambitious than Stuart, like Bono and Jim Kerr,' says Bruce. 'Stuart didnae have that ambition. I think Ian was pushing Stuart down that avenue – Bono, Jim Kerr and Stuart – but Stuart just wanted to play guitar, sing, write his songs and then fuck off home to see his missus and watch the football.

'It's not like he was being lazy. When you're the frontman in a band, you've got to spend all day doing promotional stuff. Bono and Jim Kerr were fucking *great* at it. Stuart was crap at it.

'The minute you get out of your bunk in the morning, you get checked into the hotel: "You've got press from 11 o'clock 'til 12, and then you've got such and such 'til two, and then such and such 'til three and time for a quick bite to eat and then you've got a radio station." And it's the same questions all the time and you've to fucking shake hands with all these people. Every DJ you meet says, "I was the first person in America to play your song" – *everybody* says that, you've heard it a fucking million times – and after a while, it just fucking gets to you.

'I think it was one of the reasons that Geldof never made it in America – and possibly Paul Weller – they just didn't have the patience to deal with that kinda stuff. But if you want to be U2 or the Rolling Stones – the biggest band in the world – unfortunately, you gotta do it. Stuart didn't want to and quite rightly so. I wouldn't want to do it either. I just wanted to be the guitar player. I don't mind doing a few interviews but, you know, eight hours a day on your day off?'

'You want to be building as many bridges as you can,' says Alan Edwards. 'Every promoter, every radio station jockey, everybody. You wanna make friends everywhere you can. But Stuart could be very moody. You'd be in America, in Indianapolis on a wet day, and you'd go into the dressing room, and Stuart wouldn't say a word. It could be really hard.'

They'd be talking about him behind his back: 'Is Stuart up? How is he today?' 'He was a lovely guy,' says Alan, 'really special and really sensitive – a really, really nice guy. But I think we all realised that he *just wasn't built for it*. There are other artists like that. I mean, Nick Drake, y'know. There's a whole list of people with great talent who weren't really built for the media cycle, the touring cycle. It's physically and emotionally gruelling, and it's a lot easier when you're the drummer. People aren't looking at you every night. You can get away with having an ordinary gig. But when you're the frontman, you have to be 100 per cent every night. And when it came to interviews, however much we might try and put the band in the interview, Stuart had to carry it. I wouldn't have fancied his job. It's hard.

'He connected in America extremely well with what they call the blue-collar guys – guys that maybe worked in a factory or whatever, regular guys. Stuart had that Springsteen-esque everyman vibe about him. You would think he was a tough guy from watching a show. But the real Stuart behind all of that was clearly fragile – even more so than I realised.'

It's hard to believe that Stuart hadn't seen this coming. Richard Jobson had been all over the music press when they were in the Skids. He knew the attention that singers and lyricists got. 'Stuart was very, very shy – or *private*,' says Alan Edwards. 'He was never one to curry favour. He knew he had a talent – a lot of talent – and he knew who he was. He was confident in himself as an artist. He wasn't a pop singer who needed to get in the tabloids every five minutes. He looked at it as a means to an end. He'd do interviews when they were helpful, but it wasn't what got him out of bed in the morning. Whereas Richard loved the social swirl, being in all the magazines and hanging out.'

Jobson's exposure in the press had been one of the things that had frustrated Stuart. But now the same thing was expected of him: always be available, always be interesting, always have a quote at the ready. Surely he knew that was part of being the frontman in a band?

'I don't think you do,' says Alan. 'I think it just happens. At the beginning, it's quite exciting. You get a review in the *Melody Maker* or the *NME*, and then a couple of journalists come to gigs and then you do your first front cover and that's quite thrilling. All your mates see you on the cover of the *NME*.

'That's the easy part. Suddenly, you've got to live up to that every day of the week. And then you've got to go to countries all around the world, and suddenly there's *hundreds* of NMEs. And it's like a machine. You've got to feed them. They want more and more – different angles and a different look and a different hairstyle, a different quote. I don't think people necessarily understand what it's going to be like.

'How can you be prepared for that? You could say the manager, or managers, should prepare you but, like with a lot of bands, it happened very fast for Big Country. One minute, there was a hundred people at the gigs and suddenly, there were thousands.

'In a way, the Skids was the right set-up for him, where he could just write the songs. He would have been an incredible songwriter – he would have made millions. He would have been writing hits that would have been played on American radio every day of the week. He just wasn't a frontman. And if you look at a lot of frontmen – Richard, you could say, is one – they have the fame and this and that, but they can't write the songs. The two jobs are entirely different.

'Daltrey/Townshend is not a bad sort of parallel. Roger is one of the great frontmen. Loves touring. He really is *made* to be on the road – I mean, he's on the road at eighty. Whereas Pete is the mercurial genius songwriter. Not that he's not a good performer, but he's still probably happier creating. So they're a heavenly partnership – they play to each other's strengths, they complement each other in the most wonderful way. Stuart didn't have anyone to share the load in the band. He just didn't. Everyone in the band was good, don't get me wrong, but if he'd had a Roger Daltrey on vocals, then it could have worked. He could have had days where he could be in the shadows. But he couldn't. And it's really easy to be wise years later, but in a way, I suppose, it's sad, even tragic that we all put him in that position. But nobody knew. You take someone at face value. Stuart wanted Big Country to be majorly successful. You only analyse it afterwards.

'He was great on stage. So why wouldn't he be a big star? He was writing great songs and he was a handsome guy. It wasn't like he needed to be in the shadows. He ticked every single box. So on the face of it, everything made sense. The only box he didn't tick was the one that we couldn't really see – inside his head.'

Stuart was losing his grip. He had always put pressure on Sandra to come with him – on tour, to recording sessions – and that increased. He would flatly refuse to go somewhere unless she came too, or he would call her from the road and say that he was coming home unless she came out. It was the last place she wanted to be, but she would go to keep the piece.

'It was always quite difficult,' she says, 'because I knew that Stuart wasn't being 100 per cent honest with the rest of them about it. Stuart was a great liar in his drinking days. But I would hate to think that the band thought that I was the conductor of the show in any way because I was there. I absolutely *hated* being there.'

The US tour started a few days after the Grammys: Philadelphia, Charlottesville, Fredericksburg, Winston-Salem, Indianapolis, Champaign, Madison, Ann Arbor, Nashville, Atlanta. It was a grind.

Sandra and Callum came out for a bit of the tour and the atmosphere changed a little. Stuart behaved differently to the rest of the band.

One night, Tony got back to the tour bus to find he had no bed. 'I didn't feel very well that night,' he says, 'and we did the gig and I got to the tour bus to find out that not only had we been joined by Sandra and Callum, but Stuart had commandeered my bunk and put Callum in it.'

Tired and feeling like shit, Tony kicked off. I mean, someone could at least have *asked* him. 'I found my bag and got off the bus,' he says. '"If that's the kind of respect that I command around here, fuck you!" I got off. That bus didn't move until I got back on it. I wasn't gonna get on it, not until they moved Callum. But that's band life.'

Stuart and Callum on the bus.

Stay Alive

Sandra, meanwhile, got an insight into what life was like when she wasn't there. There were women around – groupies, girlfriends. She knew the partners of the band and the crew and it didn't sit right with her. One night, she demanded that the girlfriend of a married member of the entourage not be allowed on the tour bus. She could see herself being put in an awkward position: later, the wife might ask her if she'd seen anything and she wasn't going to lie. 'I won't tell her if she *doesn't* ask me,' she said, 'but if she asks me, I'll tell her the truth.'

Eventually, it would get too much. 'I would just think, "I need to get home. I've done my stint". It wasnae good for my sanity. And it would go tits up after I left. Because he wouldnae drink when I was there.'

'I never came home with Stuart, when I think about it,' she says. 'Never. I was always back before him.'

On 3 April, the band woke up in Davis, California. They had played there the night before and had a day off. Stuart and Bruce were sharing a room.

'What do you want to do today?'

'There's a Mexican bar down the street – maybe get a bit of grub and have a couple of drinks?'

'Sounds good.'

Big Joe Seabrook – who had worked with them since the Skids days – had been brought in as security, with Ian asking him to keep a close eye on Stuart's drinking. Normally, he would have gone with them, but they sneaked out to let him have the day off too.

The two of them were in this Mexican bar – 'a shack,' says Bruce – 'And we're blethering away, coupla drinks, and we looked behind the bar and it was happy hour.'

Included in the happy hour was a drink called a Kamikaze.

'What's in them Kamikazes?'

'Vodka, lime and triple sec.'

'I'll get the first twelve, you get the second twelve.'

So they had twenty-four Kamikazes on top of whatever else they'd already had to drink. 'They were so easy to drink,' says Bruce. 'We got fucking *hammered*.'

Where Did the Feeling Go?

And then Big Joe Seabrook turned up. It *wasn't* a day off. They had read the itinerary wrong. It was a gig day.

Bruce was so drunk that he only knows what happened next because Mark, Tony, Ian and the crew told him. Big Joe slung Stuart over his shoulder, grabbed Bruce by the belt and he carried them both back to the hotel where he threw them in a cold shower and forced coffee down their throats.

'I was fucking burst,' says Bruce. 'Completely incapable of doing anything. I remember *waking up* on stage, halfway through the gig.'

He'd been in an alcohol-induced blackout. 'Tony says I was doing some kind of one-legged movement, trying to play the guitar but just hitting open strings and not using my left hand.'

Onstage, incapable, he got so frustrated that he threw his Yamaha SG into the air, where it hit the lighting truss. The guitar neck smashed and as it fell back down it snagged onto their backdrop, and tore it all the way down 'like a pirate with his sword in a sail in some old movie'.

Next up: Japan.

'After two years of touring The Crossing,' says Tony, 'we were going to Japan, and then we were supposed to go on to Australia. But Stuart basically broke down. He burned his fuse.'

'Japan was fucking horrific,' says Bruce. 'It was just a blur of alcohol abuse. I'm talking about myself as well. Stuart and I were sharing rooms. I started drinking whisky because I was twinning up with him. I haven't touched whisky or spirits since 1984, I think, but when you share the room with someone, you just tend to go along with them and join in.

'Stuart was a fucking mess. You'd wake up in the morning and he'd be drinking. Crying. He couldnae bite his nails.'

Japan started badly and got worse. At the airport, Bruce got detained after customs officers found a suspicious substance in his toilet bag. 'In Japan, they would go through all your stuff – get your toothpaste and squeeze the tube to see if there's any drugs in it,' says Bruce. In his toilet bag, he had a Vicks Inhaler, a menthol product that helps you breathe easier. 'I've always been bothered by my nose,' he says, 'I've had operations and stuff on it.' The customs officers eyed the inhaler suspiciously. 'They said, "What is this?" and I went [mimes sticking something up his nose and sniffing]. And they took me away.'

After a few hours of questioning via a translator, he was let go. 'It was one of those Spinal Tap stories.'

The shows were part of a package tour with the Style Council, INXS, the Motels and the Romantics called FM Live '84. Big Country were on stage every night around 6 p.m. and finished by 7 p.m. Which left a lot of time to hit the bar.

'Stuart was drinking heavily,' says Ian Grant. 'Arrived in Tokyo drunk, having started drinking in Glasgow.'

'I never drank before a gig – apart from that once,' says Bruce, 'but the minute I came off stage, it was like, "Where's the Black Label?" After the show, we'd go back to the hotel and it was like being in the Beatles – wall-to-wall girls, up and down the corridors, in the reception area, banging on your doors, trying to get in. Girls wanting your autograph all the time. And very subservient – giggling and bowing and all that. It was an unreal situation to be in. I'd wake up the next morning and Stuart would be already up, drinking.'

The distance meant his relationship with Sandra was fraught. Stuart didn't share any details with Bruce, but he often saw the aftermath. With no mobile phones, Stuart would call home from the hotel room. 'He'd say, "I'm just going to phone Sandra",' says Bruce. 'He called it "the love phone". He'd say, "Could you fuck off for half an hour? I'm on the love phone." He *called* it the love phone, but sometimes I'd come back in the room and he'd be in a foul mood and he'd booted chairs about the room because him and Sandra had had an argument.'

The arguments were about drinking and everything that brought with it. 'I wouldn't talk to him when he was drunk,' says Sandra. 'The first two words out of his mouth would tell me. I knew him that well.' She would either just hang up on him – and then have to keep the phone off the hook to stop him calling back – or she would say, "I know you've been drinking" and stay on the phone to work out how bad things were.

'If it became too much, I would just say, "Ah, I'm not talking to you." And often that would be when he would want to come home. I never threatened him with anything. I just said, "I'm not speaking to you." He would know that if he kept going, it was not going to be a good outcome. There were a lot of times that I asked him to leave because I wasn't going to live my life like that, with an alcoholic.

'I had Callum at that time, so my focus was elsewhere, not on what was happening in Japan. But I didn't realise that he trashed rooms when things like that happened. I didn't know he'd ever done that. But I didn't really care – I had a kid to look after. He came first.'

One day the band, crew and the Japanese promoter were travelling between gigs on the Bullet Train. Someone had given them big Samurai Katana swords and Stuart and Bruce decided to have a sword fight on the train. 'We were pissed up,' says Bruce. 'It was a day off and we were fucking wrecked, the two of us. And we started having this sword fight in the middle of the bullet train. It was fucking nuts.'

The swords were blunt, although a blow from one could still do you some damage. The two of them were jumping over chairs and swinging swords around when, somewhere between Tokyo and Kyoto, Bruce noticed Stuart's expression change. 'Oh,' he thought. 'He's gonna puke.'

Adamson tried to make it to the toilet, but it was too late. He vomited all down the back of the Japanese promoter.

There would be chaos and drama like that, but the next day it would be like nothing had happened. 'It was just weird,' says Bruce. 'You're dealing with a Jekyll and Hyde character. That's what [Robert Louis Stevenson's book] *Dr Jekyll and Mr Hyde* is about, y'know.'

Bruce was no stranger to this. He had been brought up around alcoholism. 'My mum was an alcoholic and then she became a recovering alcoholic, so I know a little bit about it. It's not the same person. It *looks* like the same person, but it's not. It's like they've had a blackout. They don't realise. All this devastation and mayhem they caused and they're like, "Oh, I don't remember."

'The next day, he's back to normal Stuart, he's had a blackout, and he doesn't remember having pissed in the corner or whatever, and you don't want to bring things like that up. You don't want to have a post-mortem about the night before, because that'll just cause more problems. So you don't mention it. He's had a blackout and it's quite *good* because he won't remember what he's done.'

Things came to a head during an interview at a Japanese TV station. Tony was there, but his memory of the incident is vague. 'He just collapsed,' he says. 'He broke down. Joe Seabrook slung Stuart over his shoulder and carried him out of the studio.'

It was obvious to everyone that they couldn't continue. Ian Grant cancelled the Australian leg of the tour. 'I told Michael Gudinski, the biggest promoter in Australia, by fax, I guess,' he says. 'There was no email or mobile then. He went apeshit. Still hadn't forgotten it when I saw him in New York a decade later.'

They went home. 'When he came back, he was a complete mess,' says Sandra. 'I remember getting him in the shower, turning the tap on, and then him, in his drunkenness, telling me.'

He'd been with women in Japan.

He hated himself. He couldn't help himself. He was drunk. He would stop drinking. It wouldn't happen again.

You might expect that the end of the Japanese tour and the cancellation of the Australian leg could have resulted in a falling-out between the band members – in arguments and raised voices, fists thrown, fingers pointed – but, in fact, the whole incident in Japan was never really talked about. 'There were never any bust-ups,' says Bruce. 'Never. Never any bust-ups or fights, with any of us.

'But you can't help an alcoholic. An alcoholic can only help his or herself. They've got to want to stop drinking.'

They went home and, even though Stuart and Bruce lived in the same town – with just a railway track separating them – they never even went to see each other. When they hooked up again – with Ian Grant keeping them busy with the Pinkpop Festival in the Netherlands in June and a big support slot for Elton John at Wembley Stadium at the end of the month – no one mentioned it. It's a good example of how men, especially then, didn't talk about emotions or share problems. But it's also an example of the band respecting each other's privacy.

They wondered if Stuart's drinking was connected to problems in his marriage, but talking about that was off-limits. 'You couldn't talk to Stuart about that sort of thing,' says Tony. 'His personal life was personal and he wasn't going to share it. Not at all. He had plenty of willing ears if he'd wanted to.'

'They were frightened of Stuart,' says Sandra. 'They all knew he could turn on them. He could fly off the handle if things weren't going his way professionally. So, on a personal and social level, they wouldn't have dared enter that space.

'I guess we both believed that it was none of their business,' she says. 'We didn't know them. They were your workmates. Nobody was allowed in, really, because we were too busy being a family.'

In interviews, Stuart would say that Big Country were a group of people with real chemistry. 'It was good flannel, but not particularly true,' says Tony. 'We had the same ideas about what we wanted to be as a band, but it wasn't the genuine boys club that he sometimes tried to portray. It wasn't that at all – and that was because of him. The rest of us were eager and willing to make it like that, but he didn't want to.

'I only spoke to Stuart twice on the phone in our whole career,' he says. 'I probably only met his sister three times and only by chance. He wouldn't say, "Oh Tone, this is my sister." None of those sort of niceties. If I had children or friends of mine backstage, I'd go, "Oh Stuart, this is my brother" or whatever. But it was one-way traffic.'

So nothing was talked about. The rest of the band gave Stuart space and respected his privacy, and when they got back together, it was like nothing had happened. The Elton John Wembley show was last minute – they replaced a sick Paul Young – and Elton flew Stuart and Bruce there and back on a private jet.

Stay Alive

'I can remember Stuart coming back,' says Sandra. 'I never had drink in the house, but this bottle of wine miraculously appeared and got slugged. He used flying as an excuse to drink. He didn't like flying, so he'd say, "I have a fear of flying so I have to have a drink."'

'Stuart would sit next to me on planes,' says Mark. 'He was a very nervous flyer and he would sit next to me to reassure him.' Because Mark was a plane nut, Stuart could turn to him if there were weird noises or unexpected turbulence. 'He would always play a certain song on his Walkman – I think it was a Roxy Music song. He had a few little rituals.'

It was one of the ways he revealed his vulnerabilities, says Mark. 'He wasn't as confident as you might think. I don't think a lot of people understood that. He didn't show it on stage, but there was a shyness about Stuart that was quite charming, actually.

'There was Stuart Adamson: a very together guy, incredibly intelligent, incredibly logical, amazing wordsmith, sang from the heart, great poet, brilliant musician. But there were so many insecurities lying in the background. He was vulnerable – and he became vulnerable to drink, which was tragic.'

After Wembley, their gear was packed off and shipped to Stockholm where they were going to record the next album, at ABBA's studios, Polar.

They were back on the treadmill: rehearsals for *Steeltown* in June, recording in Stockholm in August, with the first single, 'East of Eden', out in September. The pace was insane and Big Country were in the classic second-album situation: they had been so busy, they'd had no time to write new songs.

'The first album is always the songs you've played for ages,' says Bruce. 'You've been playing them live for years before you even got signed. Then you record the first album, you tour it and then it's "Right, time for album number two!" Apart from a couple of riffs that Stuart and I had, we had nothing. Absolutely fuck all.'

17

Out of Lightness, Dark

Raking around in ABBA's cupboard. Husbands and wives. A journey to the Land of Nod. Making the difficult second album

This is Ian Grant responding to a claim made by Dave Bates – the guy who would replace Chris Briggs as Big Country's A&R man – that Big Country's decline started as early as *Steeltown*.

'Well, it went straight in at number 1,' said Ian, as though Bates was delusional. But then he backtracked: '... which it would have done anyway, because it was off the back of the first one.' Then he was defensive again – 'Some fans would cite that as their favourite album' – before conceding some ground: 'I think it was rushed,' he said. 'No one had their eye on the ball and there were internal problems. Problems *within* the problems: Husbands and wives, babies, Lillywhite getting married to Kirsty. The session broke down, everyone went home, Steve was doing it on an SSL [Solid State Logic] desk for the first time and I know it gave him a problem because he was experimenting. The album was never brought to its conclusion.'

He could have added to that list of woes: Record company pressure, alcoholism, infidelity, internal tensions, the miners' strike – and an 'I ♥ New York' Zippo lighter sailing out of a recording studio window and denting a car below.

Steeltown was a joyless album made in a joyless time.

No one wanted to record *Steeltown* in Sweden, but they all wanted Steve Lillywhite to produce – and that meant going to Stockholm. Lillywhite was on a creative and commercial high – he'd produced U2's *War*, *The Crossing* and Simple Minds' *Sparkle in the Rain* in a twelve-month period – and, as the royalties rolled in, his accountants had advised that he work abroad for a while to avoid an enormous tax bill.

So the option was that they could either do it in Sweden or do it without Steve. It wasn't ideal. 'We'd been away from home for over two years,' says Tony. 'It had caused problems and now you want us to go away for *another* long period of time?'

Because of this, says Sandra, 'Me, Sandra [Watson] and [Tony's wife] Jackie got dragged there as well.'

Stuart wasn't in a great place. 'Ian felt he'd gotten Stuart back to work too soon,' says Tony. 'But he was under pressure from the record company – "Let's get the second album out, let's make sure it's like *The Crossing*" and all that kind of stuff. When we weren't working, I never saw Stuart. He'd be in his room. I always thought, "He's probably writing lyrics". I kind of wrote it off like that.'

'*Steeltown* was a hard record to make,' says Briggs. 'But the pressure is on once you're up and running and you've had hits …'

In August 1984, recording began in ABBA's Polar Studios in Stockholm. Opened in 1978, Led Zeppelin had recorded their final studio album, *In Through the Out Door*, there. In 1981, ABBA's album *The Visitors*, one of the first-ever digitally recorded albums, was captured on a state-of-the-art 3M digital recorder there. And there was an unlikely ABBA connection: earlier in 1984, Steve Lillywhite had produced ABBA singer Frida's fourth solo album, *Shine*. It had been a family affair: Kirsty MacColl and Stuart Adamson contributed songs (Stuart's is Celtic-tinged and Big Country-related right down to its title: 'Heart of the Country'). Mark Brzezicki played drums.

In what could be a little in-joke, the verses of the song 'Steeltown' are written in enclosed rhyme, using the rhyme scheme ABBA, where the first and fourth, and the second and third lines rhyme. ('He would have done that deliberately,' says Sandra. 'Absolutely.')

To begin with, says Bruce, the making of the second album was great. He remembers late-night drinks with Stuart where they stumbled across a cupboard full of ABBA's old stage costumes. 'It had the star-shaped guitar, all these costumes and the platform boots.' Predictably, they put them on

– 'Well, you would, wouldn't you?' – or tried to, at least. 'You couldn't even wear them because they were so small.'

But the second half of the recording? 'It kind of went tits up,' he says.

The songwriting started at the rehearsals. Mark brought a ghetto blaster and they sat it in front of his bass drum to record ideas. 'That's how we did a lot of demos back then,' says Bruce. 'It was really low tech – just for rough sketches – the kind of thing you would do on your phone now.'

'I would record *everything*,' says Mark. 'I've got hundreds of tapes. I'd record the whole day and I'd label them all.'

Where Stuart and Bruce had worked consistently on the songs for *The Crossing* for months, trading ideas, working up parts alone, swapping instrumental passages from one song to another, *Steeltown* was cooked up by all four members in the Edinburgh rehearsal rooms and then in the studio in Stockholm.

'We wrote a lot when we were in Sweden,' says Tony. 'This is the beginning of everybody bringing in musical ideas. We'd worked together long enough to be able to jam – and that's not something that Stuart and Bruce really grew up doing – so we were jamming stuff and it felt quite encouraging.'

Bruce agrees. 'This was probably the first – and maybe the only album, actually – where the four of us were in one room from start to finish, for all the songs.'

They pressed 'record' on Mark's ghetto blaster and started jamming any ideas they had. 'So maybe Stuart's got a guitar riff,' says Bruce. 'We'll cycle on that riff for a while, and then somebody will take it to another place that could be like a verse to a chorus. All the music was done like that. They were jams, ideas. Some ideas would get bolted on to another.'

Tony and Mark had contributed to *The Crossing*, but the songs had already been written. This was a genuine collaboration.

As a session drummer, Mark was used to understanding arrangements quickly, working out the architecture and dynamics of songs. 'As a drummer, you hear arrangements,' he says. 'That's kind of what you do. You're an observer. I was always instrumental in saying, "I don't think that's a chorus. For me, it sounds like a bridge, we haven't got a chorus." Stuart would say,

"What do you think?" and I'd go, "Well, that section ... can't we bolt it onto *that* song, slow it down a bit? That could work."'

Big Country had always played fast and loose with traditional song structures, but this method of working, with a rhythm section in love with prog rock, pushed it even further. The title track 'Steeltown', for example, has a verse, then a pre-chorus, then a verse, then an instrumental break, a pre-chorus, then two verses. It's not until two and a half minutes into the song – where other songs are often ending – that the actual chorus arrives.

'I think that was bolted together from a couple of ideas,' says Bruce. 'It does take ages to get to the chorus, but that might also be for technical reasons. "Steeltown" is way out of Stuart's register for singing, so it's possibly arranged that way so as not to kill his vocals too soon.'

The album slowly began to take shape. 'It was going well,' says Bruce. 'It sounded different to what we were doing with *The Crossing*, taking on a – heavy metal's not the word – but a *harder* edge.'

When the music was done, Stuart would take the tapes away, come up with the lyrics and turn them into songs. They were songs about the state of the nation – and the state of Stuart Adamson.

The recording of *Steeltown* came at a tumultuous time in the UK. In March 1979, the people of Scotland had voted in a referendum on devolution: on whether or not they were in favour of a Scottish Assembly, with law-making powers of its own, devolved from the British Parliament. Fifty-one per cent voted in favour, but it wasn't enough: a Labour MP called George Cunningham (born in Dunfermline) had introduced an amendment to the bill that required that 40 per cent of the Scottish electorate – that is, everyone eligible to vote – would have to vote in favour for it to become law. While the 'yes' vote had won the referendum, only 63 per cent of the electorate had turned out to vote, and that meant that only 32 per cent had voted 'yes'.

There was a feeling that the Scottish people had been cheated out of devolution on a technicality.

The referendum triggered a vote of no confidence in the Labour government and, in May 1979, the UK elected the Conservative leader Margaret Thatcher as prime minister. (The Conservatives won 43 per cent of the

Out of Lightness, Dark

vote, but only 76 per cent of the electorate turned out, meaning that they also won just 32 per cent of potential electoral votes. Sadly, there was no amendment to stop them from taking power.) Thatcher would remain PM for the entire 1980s and her rule was marked by greater divisions between both the rich and poor and the north and south of the country.

The number of children living in poverty went from 1.7 million in 1979 to 3.3 million in 1990 – almost double. In the same period, the number of pensioners living in poverty went from 3.1 million to 4.1 million. Between taking power in 1979 and 1984, the year of *Steeltown*'s release, the UK's unemployment rate under Mrs Thatcher rose from 5.3 per cent to 11.9 per cent.

It was the end of the 'post-war consensus' – an agreement between the major political parties that government had a duty to raise living standards by caring for the people through a robust welfare state and National Health Service. By contrast, Thatcher believed in small government, a lack of state intervention and the privatisation of state-owned properties. The government's lack of support for traditional industries like shipbuilding, steel-making and coal mining was combined with an attack on trade unions, seen by Thatcher as 'the enemy within': powerful left-wing organisations that could mobilise the working class and bring the country to a standstill.

When the band returned to the UK in May 1984, the country was three months into the miners' strike, a year-long industrial dispute scarred by violence and division. The mining communities around Dunfermline and across Fife were deeply affected.

Big Country had finally started earning money and it brought guilt and resentment. 'It was horrible for me,' says Bruce. 'My dad was a miner. I was earning good money from the tours and getting royalties, and there's my dad and all his mates on strike.'

'It fucked my head up a wee bit,' he told *Melody Maker*. They'd been living it up in Japan and 'then we came home to see all the miners in the high street with their [collection] boxes for the fund. My dad's quite old, he's in his fifties, so he doesnae picket. But he's getting on alright. I'm bringing money in, and I dinnae mind. When I was on the dole, they helped *me* out.'

Bruce's dad would go down to the miners' welfare hall and sweep up or do the dishes, just for something to do. Meanwhile, his son was on TV and touring the world, with money finally coming in. 'That was a horrible time,' says Bruce. 'Me and Stuart got resented so much 'cos at that time we were never aff the telly, obviously earning a bit of money, and everybody here was on strike. We couldnae go oot half the time. We'd get abuse. We'd go down to Asda. "There's that cunt fae fuckin' Big Country." "Oh, fuck's sake, I'm outta here." You couldnae even go out for a couple of pints because anything could get said.'

If the history of ancient Scotland had provided lyrical inspiration for *The Crossing*, the state of modern Britain inspired *Steeltown*. The title track itself was named after the town of Corby in Northamptonshire. Back in the 1930s, a Glasgow company called Stewarts & Lloyds had established one of Britain's biggest steelworks there. Thousands of Scottish workers moved to the town over the following decades – the 1961 census revealed that a third of Corby residents had been born in Scotland. Upon their election in 1979, the Conservative government announced the closure of the Corby steelworks – now in state ownership under British Steel – at a loss of 11,000 jobs. Unemployment in the town rose to 30 per cent.

'All these Scottish guys went there for work,' Stuart told Carol Clerk of *Melody Maker*, 'a travelling population who no longer have any work at all. Norman Tebbit said "Get on your bikes and find work." Six years later, the mill's closed down.'

Big Country weren't the only band inspired by the plight of Corby's workers. In June 1984, Hull band the Red Guitars released a single called 'Steeltown' that went to number 2 in the indie charts. 'I hear the steeltown is closing down,' it goes. 'All the mills are rusting/Everybody's got a new car/ With the redundancy money they pay.' The Alarm were also planning on calling their second album *Steeltown*, but it was changed to *Strength* when they heard about the Big Country album. (The Alarm's song 'Steeltown' was renamed 'Deeside' – it was about closure of the Shotton Steelworks in Deeside, north Wales, the largest single-day industrial redundancy in Western Europe at the time, with 6,500 jobs lost.)

'They're pulling everything apart and there's no replacement,' said Stuart. 'Okay, let the heavy industries die out because they're not cost-productive, but what the hell are people meant to go and work at? Where are they meant to earn a living wage?' *Steeltown*'s title track, he said, was 'about how new towns are built around old industry. But with old industries dying out, these places become ghost towns.'

It's a bleak vision. There's a sense that the album *Steeltown*, with a cover seemingly inspired by Russian propaganda art, is about the nobility of the workers, but Stuart's lyrics are far more conflicted. 'Steeltown' conjures a vision of industrialisation as bleak as William Blake's 'dark Satanic mills': 'All the landscape was the mill/Grim as the reaper with a heart like hell/ With a river of bodies/Flowing with the bell.'

This, after all, was the same Stuart Adamson who had written 'Charles' about the bleak future awaiting those drafted into factory life. Now, a few years older, he seemed to be confessing that even mechanised, mindless work was better than no work at all: 'Who could know we built on sand ... There is no miracle in ruins.'

Like many of Stuart's lyrics, it's tempting to assume that his words might also reflect his own mindset. 'Steeltown', for example, opens with lines that could be about a worker in Corby, but could also be about his feelings as a successful artist with a hit album who still hasn't found peace: 'Here I stand with my own kin/At the end of everything/Finally the dream is gone/I've had enough of hanging on.'

'They're kind of open to interpretation a lot of the time,' says Bruce. 'I tended not to read into Stuart's lyrics too much. Some are quite personal to him and I would probably take them the wrong way. So I tended not to over-analyse his lyrics too much. "Tall Ships Go" could have been about his dad, but it could have been about a fictitious person.'

'Tall Ships Go' could be about anyone, but if it is about his dad (and the words 'If you're an enemy/Then you look a lot like me' support that idea), it's yet another vision of dread. His father's voice, says Stuart, 'keeps me from sleeping' and fills his sleep with dreams: 'I dreamed you sailed me to the swamp/In a black boat/You spoke to me of things/Of the shame that years will bring.'

Again, it's tempting to make sense of this lyric with what we know now, and assume it's a reference to abuse. But, like Bruce says, it could have been about a fictional person. Or, says Sandra, the lines could have been inspired by a story he read. 'He could have read a book the night before. He had four books on the go at once sometimes. Books mattered to him, stories mattered to him. You can't start imagining, because of what we know now, that that's what it was about. That's the danger.'

Steeltown's first single, 'East of Eden', unveiled the album's new sound. It's more complex, less Celtic, a musically dense song about searching for salvation: 'I was waiting/I was watching/Would it ever be there for me?' Luck and chance – fast becoming a theme of Stuart Adamson lyrics – are all there is ('I found that hope and a lucky card/Were all I had to walk with me'). He looks to capitalism for answers and sees slavery. He looks to communism and sees misery. It's all pointless. 'Why care about the weather?' he sings. 'It always ends in dark.'

Stuart claimed that 'East of Eden' came out of 'living alongside the unemployment and anger in the dockyards and factories' – and it *could* be the thoughts of any working person having an existential crisis, but it seems like a way of deflecting people from a very personal lyric.

East Of Eden is the name of a 1952 novel by John Steinbeck that was made into a film starring James Dean – and Sandra remembers Stuart reading it – but the lyric seems to have been inspired by a much older book: the Old Testament. The plot of Steinbeck's novel is a retelling of the biblical story of Cain and Abel. In the Book of Genesis, Cain is exiled to the Land of Nod, east of Eden, as punishment for the murder of his brother, Abel. The Land of Nod is said to be outside the gaze of God, a lawless wilderness where Cain goes to lead a wandering, rootless life.

In 'East of Eden', Stuart is imagining himself (or his narrator) as Cain, carrying enormous guilt and wondering if he can ever find salvation. Some days, he says, he needs to push dark thoughts away, possibly by drinking ('I need to bury/The very depths of me').

On other days, he 'calls upon' those depths. Stuart once commented that 'East of Eden' was 'a questioning song. A song about always having to look for any hope or inspiration'. Maybe that is what he means by 'calling upon the depths of me': the guilt, the darkness of the past or his alcoholic present, is something that he can draw on for inspiration to create songs like this. Some days that darkness consumes him: 'I *walk into*/The very depths of me.'

A powerful song about guilt and hopelessness, it was an unlikely hit single. 'East of Eden' went to number 17 in the UK charts in October 1984.

If Stuart was feeling guilt and hopelessness, it might well have stemmed from his drinking. Sandra Adamson had left the recordings pretty early on and Stuart immediately went back on the booze. 'I didn't want to be there,' says Sandra. 'I was only there because, again, he dragged me there. I knew he would not fulfil if I didn't go.

'He had been sober the whole time I was there. Afterwards, I would phone and say, "Is Stuart there?" and Steve was always put in a position because Stuart had started drinking the minute I left.'

But it wasn't just Stuart and Sandra who were having problems. Someone in the camp had a girlfriend in New York. His other half found an 'I ♥ New York' Zippo lighter in his pocket, put two and two together, and an argument broke out. As voices were raised and allegations flew, she opened the window of Polar Studios and threw the Zippo out into the Stockholm sky. It fell several storeys and hit a car. It all kicked off.

They shut up shop for a couple of weeks and everybody went home.

'Everybody had personal things going on,' says Bruce. 'Everybody left the session, apart from Mark, myself and Will Gosling, the engineer. It was left to us three to finish it. The bass had been done, all Stuart's parts had been done and his vocals had been done. We finished off all the overdubs.'

When they all reconvened, says Tony, the atmosphere was a lot better – but coming back to the material with fresh ears also gave them new perspective: 'People were beginning to realise that the album was very, very dark. It certainly gave the idea that we weren't living in a very good time empirically, let alone within the microcosm of the band. Something that was touching all of our lives was very bleak and it was being represented through this concept of a steel town that was going through crap. Everything was in minor keys.'

The album was released on 19 October. The opener 'Flame of the West' lays out an apocalyptic tale of a charismatic leader leading people to an uncertain fate. It was about the US president of the time, former movie star Ronald Reagan, but it could easily be about Donald Trump. 'It's about certain people in the West who hold power over the whole world,' said Stuart. 'The way they use that power could be dangerous for all of us.'

'The very people who are involved in politics,' he said in a radio interview, 'are, by the very nature of the beast, people who would want to hold power over others – people who would see themselves as being leaders and the rest of people as followers. I don't know if that's a very admirable trait in a person, to want to hold people under that kind of subjugation. And, unfortunately, those are the very people who end up in power.'

'Where the Rose is Sown' and 'Come Back to Me' are the same story shown from two different perspectives. Loosely inspired by the Falklands conflict, 'Where the Rose is Sown' is more generally about a young man going off to war. The verses feature two alternating voices: one, the voice of establishment propaganda, and the other the voice of the boy. 'Leave your work,' says the government. 'I just left school,' says the boy. It was a scene that played out in the films and books about Vietnam that Stuart was watching and reading.

'Both of us got seriously into Vietnam stories,' says Bruce. '*Apocalypse Now* and all that kind of stuff. He liked to use a lot of images from that. "Where the Rose is Sown" uses a lot of Vietnam stuff. That line "If I die in a combat zone" is the title of a Tim O'Brien book and the song they would sing in basic training. It's an Americanism – the British wouldn't say that. We used to like Michael Herr's *Dispatches* and all those books about Vietnam. So a song could have something that had a factual event in it, but then it goes into something fictitious.'

On the album, Mark's martial drumming segues right into 'Come Back to Me', sung from the point of view of the young man's wife, watching as other people return from the war, while she sits pregnant with a child he 'will never know'.

'Girl With Grey Eyes' and 'Rain Dance' can also be seen as two takes on the same story: his marriage to Sandra. 'Girl With Grey Eyes' is a song of longing and desire, while 'Rain Dance' – on the face of it, a jollier, uplifting song that most sounds like the Big Country of old, with harmonising guitars – is a complicated tale about dependency and alcoholism.

'Girl With Grey Eyes' had started as an idea of Tony's which Stuart developed. When he heard the finished lyrics, Tony wasn't happy. 'I thought, "I'm not in this band to play love songs to his fucking wife". John, Yoko and the Beatles came into my head. Me and Stuart had a huge row about it.

'I said, "Look, we're here to write stuff that represents us all. Why are you writing about your wife? This is not a solo album. I don't want you to do this." He ended up winning.'

On phone calls home, Stuart told Sandra about it. 'I agreed with Tony,' she says. 'I didn't think it should have been on the album. It's shite. In fact, I think it's the worst song he's ever written.'

It rang hollow. 'It didn't mean anything to me because of what was happening at the time,' she says. 'Meant nothing. It felt insincere. You cannae write like that and behave a different way.'

The song does strike a different note to the songs of war and strife that surround it. The chorus references the apocryphal line that Napoleon was supposed to have used to reject his wife's advances: 'Not tonight, Josephine.' Stuart uses it in a slightly ham-fisted way to talk of the distance between him and Sandra.

'Tony always hated that line, "Just like Josephine, it will not be tonight",' says Bruce. 'It *is* a bit corny. But that's what Stuart wrote. If you think you can improve on something, you do it better, y'know?'

It's not one of Bruce's favourite songs either. 'I don't think the songs breathe enough on *Steeltown*,' he says. 'They're all in your face. It's like a rollercoaster ride – it's too fast all the time. The only relief you get is "Girl With Grey Eyes". It was one of the last songs to be written and, to me, it disnae really fit musically or lyrically.'

The song includes Sandra's full name, Alexandra. Tony asked Stuart to take it out. 'I could have handled it if he did,' he says, 'but it was like Palestine–Israel. It was going nowhere. So I had to swallow it because I wasn't the writer. I never, ever felt like I would disown something that I helped create.'

'Girl With Grey Eyes' made Sandra feel 'a bit exposed and embarrassed. I didnae particularly like that feeling. I preferred the more subtle ways that

Stay Alive

he used to pop me into lyrics, even in "Rain Dance" when it's not, y'know, *smoochy* kinda stuff.'

'"Rain Dance"', she says, 'is more sincere, better than that schmaltzy crap'. It seems to be about Stuart acknowledging his struggles and asking for help: 'If I hold my hand to you/Though you never asked me to/You will know it's time for the rains to come/And you must help me through.'

It could be a reference to the cycle of drinking he would go through when he came home. 'The drinking would stop for a while,' says Sandra, 'but I always knew – maybe three or four days before a binge – that it was about to happen because the behaviour changed. The agitation was evident. It's hard to describe, but when you know somebody that well, you know that they're struggling.'

The lyric suggests that he is also wary, scared of the power she has over him ('I fear you like the frost that the spring can bring/Or the fire of a cattle brand') – most likely, an expression of Stuart fearing Sandra's disapproval. He was messing up a lot and she was the one person he wouldn't want to let down.

Sandra can't really say for sure because Stuart and his wife never had a conversation about the lyrics for 'Rain Dance' – or *any* of his lyrics.

She never asked him what his lyrics meant?

'I felt that it was important not to,' she says. 'The lyrics were his and his alone. He would never explain because they belonged wholly to him. He'd rather have folk interpret them for themselves.'

Sandra would hear the songs develop 'from the first riff, from when he was sitting on the couch with a guitar'. But she would never pry or ask what they meant.

'I would never want to say, "Give me a read of that". We didn't treat each other like that. It was almost impersonal, his writing. It didn't mean anything to me. As far as I was concerned, he was writing songs to release an album, to try and make some money, to put a roof over his head. That was all really – no other reason.'

The music of 'The Great Divide' started life as part of 'Wonderland' and then took on a life of its own. Stuart told *Rolling Stone* that the song was about 'the delicate, dangerous balance between unions and management' and was 'inspired by a friend who was employed at the same dockyard where Bruce Watson used to work'.

The song shares some of 'Steeltown''s imagery – fire and noise and sweat and steam – but you would be hard-pushed to understand it as a song about a specific labour dispute. As in 'Porrohman', work provides some salvation or distraction: 'Here comes a sign of hope, a length of rope/To measure all our living.' But as the song continues, it seems more and more conflicted. 'And suddenly I find the truth,' he sings. 'And all it is is sighs and youth.'

The great divide itself seems to be between the need to work and the life of hopes and dreams: 'Here comes the great divide/Here comes a sign of hope ... And I know all my dreams.'

'Just a Shadow' ends the album on a grand and depressing note. It's a state-of-the-nation song, the first verse about a man who seems to be doing well but is driven to violence, the second verse about a woman who is the victim of violence and needs 'a place to run', and the final verse about all of us – struggling through life, chasing money and the promised land, and left frustrated and angry.

We are, he says, 'just a shadow of the people we should be' as guitars shimmer elegantly before building to an epic climax.

'I love "Just a Shadow",' says Bruce. 'It's depressing as fuck, but that's one of the things that I love about what we do. A lot of Stuart's lyrics were depressing – right down into the depths of Leonard Cohen – but the music was so uplifting. And all the music was done before the lyrics – they were instrumentals. They could almost be like miniature theme tunes for movies. Stuart and I would fill it up with guitars, and then he'd take it away, and come back with these really down, depressing lyrics. But that's why it works.'

Steeltown went straight to number 1 in the UK album charts in October 1984, knocking U2's *The Unforgettable Fire* off the top spot. But where the U2 album would go on to stay in the top 100 for 132 weeks, *Steeltown* stayed there for just twenty-one weeks. *The Unforgettable Fire* sold more than 3 million copies in the US. *Steeltown* never made the US top 50.

Stay Alive

Today, the album is loved for the very qualities that stopped it from becoming a mainstream hit. *Steeltown* is Big Country without the pop sensibilities of 'Fields of Fire' or 'Chance'. Where the music of *The Crossing* ran counterpoint to the lyrics – uplifting where the words were downbeat – *Steeltown* is dark throughout. It is intense, relentless, adult, and filled with layers of guitars. If Mark Brzezicki's drums were one of the standout features of *The Crossing*, Tony Butler's bass playing takes centre stage on *Steeltown*, right from the first notes of the opening track. It's a great album – a bitter, bile-soaked, whisky-drenched comedown, full of guilt and anger, a lonely album about people locked in their own private hells, battling a cruel world. But it's not for everyone.

The *NME*'s review mocked them: 'Every instrument and voice has been put through their unique "Cavalry Charge" effect unit ... Nothing has changed.' It was the era of the Smiths and R.E.M. Guitar music was changing slightly and Big Country were criticised for being 'old school rock', part of a movement whose music was bombastic and overblown. As *Melody Maker*'s Carol Clerk commented, 'the inevitable backlash has begun with a vengeance, tying the group up with U2 and the Alarm and accusing them of pomposity, emptiness, deception, complacency, pop star posing, rockism ... All the things, in fact, that Big Country have consistently stood against.'

In a feature for the *NME*, Danny Kelly was similarly sympathetic and astute. 'I think that the Adamson predilection for elemental imagery, erotica, and the yearning for the big country, the wonderland East of Eden, is misunderstood. Those who see it as mere chest beating, empty baying for an unreachable moon, forget that the Celtic culture has responded to its historical subservience to its Anglo Saxon neighbour by invoking heady dreams, by eulogising its heroes.'

'It didn't seem to quite click the way the first album did,' says Lillywhite. 'You don't have as long to write a second album. Then again, "In a Big Country" was recorded in no time at all.

'It's a bit dense and a bit muddy. Hindsight is a great thing, but maybe we were trying to put too much on because we trying to cover something up. Who knows where our heads were at at that time?

'Maybe Stuart's writing had become more political and even if people are living in a steeltown with no work, they wanna lose themselves. They don't want to be told that their life is shit. Maybe they need the big dreams even more. No fault of Stuart's – he was doing it for the best possible reasons. But maybe the working man needs aspirations rather than reality.'

It was a criticism that Stuart heard often after the album's release. 'It's a sad indication of the state of the other music around us that what we do is too real,' he said in an interview with *Rolling Stone*. 'Popular music can never be valid and worthwhile unless it reflects the environment that it comes from. I think it should be more like folk music in that I can talk about these situations.

'Music of any kind should be a working, living, breathing part of a community, something that is everyday and completely natural for people to think and feel about, not something tied up in a fantasy-island world of sex and drugs and fast cars. That, to me, is all the bullshit of modern music.'

It was the era of MTV and videos that offered dreams of Club Tropicana and yachting in Rio. Big Country were a universe away from all that. 'It's pathetic for musicians to portray an image to people that says, "Hey, your father's on the dole and your mother's pregnant again, but we're out here in Sri Lanka being glamorous!"' Stuart told the *NME*. 'I couldn't get away with it and I wouldn't want to. I'm just a bloke with a wife and a bairn.'

'I think the album was too dense,' says Tony. 'There was no immediate singles on it. It certainly wasn't *The Crossing*.' For a while, he wondered if the band would get the blame. 'I was waiting for somebody to say, "Well, you *did* let the rest of the band in on the songwriting." I was waiting for that, but it never came.

'But Stuart wasn't writing singles. Stuart was writing "Tall Ships Go". It's a great piece of music, but it's not a hit single. Attitudes were changing in how the band was seen – because it wasn't really accepted by the Americans – and how it was being regarded from within.'

'We got by because we were on a high,' says Ian Grant. 'We were rolling off the first album. Some fans would cite *Steeltown* as their favourite album. But there were no hits on it. I hate that phrase – no *classics* on it.'

Stay Alive

The production came in for some criticism – the sound and the problems caused by recording to digital. 'I thought the songs were very good,' says Chris Briggs. 'But there's something *sonically* not quite right and I knew it at the time. Things you regret – not saying, "Stop – we need to go to another studio and remix this. This isn't right." Those 3M digital machines were a nightmare. I think if you talked to Steve now, he'd say he regretted recording it digitally. I remember thinking, "God, I wish we could mix this again". It wasn't quite right. You learn with experience. The right thing to do is to say to the record company, "No, fuck off. We're gonna get this right."'

'It was nothing to do with Steve's ability or our ability,' says Bruce. 'It was just the time. CD players were just coming out and everything was going digital. It's a dense album and there are too many overdubs, too much going on. It's the only album that I would ever go back and revisit and maybe do a remix. The album's great, but it's hard and digital and nasty sounding – which, actually, is part of the charm of it.'

Stuart wouldn't let the producer carry the can. Shortly after the release, he told the NME that 'Steve Lillywhite gets lots of shit but I think he did brilliantly. We wanted it to be less melodic, a hard bastard! ... I think it's one of the finest albums I've ever heard. I'll not be small about it.'

Later, in his sleevenotes for the CD version of the album, Stuart wrote that the songs were 'dark and dense' and came from 'hard times, fearful places', and that the production reflected that. 'This is the sound of frustration, the words of the powerless, it is hard and brittle, cornered.'

'Hope is replaced by fear,' he wrote, possibly referring to the uplifting qualities of *The Crossing*. On 'In a Big Country', he sang that 'dreams stay with you'. On *Steeltown*, he says, dreams have been replaced by 'survival – most of us get by'. Just enduring is enough.

And, in an admission that the album is also about his own thoughts and feelings, he says that *Steeltown* 'is my home movie, my video diary, where I am from, where I am. Out of lightness, dark. The circle closes.'

He was heading deeper into alcoholism. The first period of Big Country was about to end.

18

Sometimes a Landslide Comes

Brutal news in Hammersmith. Dirty deeds in Liverpool and Nottingham. 'I don't think I know you.' The night it all changed

Just ahead of the album's release, Big Country went on a tour of the UK throughout October. Sandra came along with them and, says Tony, 'whenever Sandra was on the road, there was a problem.'

The problem came to a head on 13 October, the night the band played Nottingham's Royal Concert Hall. This is what Tony remembers of that date.

'In Nottingham, at the Victoria Hotel – it's indelibly printed on my brain – Sandra and Stuart had a row. And this row went through the hotel, running up and down corridors, shouting and screaming.

'It took Joe [Seabrook] to get them both, throw them back into the room and get them to behave. When Sandra was around, Stuart didn't see anybody else. His focus was her – that was it. Nothing else existed. We knew that every time she came out, there would be some sort of incident.

'It wouldn't be something I would've talked about, but it became public that night. It was awful. I was in the next room. And I'm sitting thinking, "What do I do? Do I go in and interrupt?" Then it spilled out into the corridor, shouting and screaming. They were just so cruel to each other.'

To understand what happened at the Victoria Hotel, we have to go back a few days to 2 October and the launch party for *Steeltown* in London. Under pressure to join Stuart – he said that if *she* didn't go, *he* wasn't going – Sandra came down to London with Callum.

And there, in a Holiday Inn off Sloane Square, where Belgravia meets Chelsea, Stuart confessed that there had been more women.

It was the drink, he said. Women threw themselves at him. He couldn't control himself. He hated himself. He'd never do it again.

He'd never drink again.

Understandably, Sandra was getting sick of this.

'It was one thing after another in that period,' she says. 'I was like, "I can't do this any longer. It's insult after insult". It was really difficult.

'He's a grown man, so my way of thinking was, be a grown man. Don't use excuses that you're a musician or a pop star, or whatever the hell you think you are when you're pissed. You know what you are when you're not. So *don't drink.*'

She was pretty sure these relationships were not serious – they weren't *love* affairs. Stuart was never away somewhere: there were no mysterious stopovers or weird weekends away. 'He was always trying to get back, more than he was trying to stay away,' she says. 'I knew deep down that if he wanted to walk, he could – and he never chose to.'

He pleaded with her to come on the tour. If she didn't come, he wouldn't do the tour. If she was there, he wouldn't drink. He needed her.

Eventually, she gave in.

Newcastle, 9 October

'There was a football match on TV,' says Sandra. Sandra is sports-mad and, like Stuart, loves football. Sandra told Stuart that she was going down to the hotel bar to watch the match. But Stuart didn't want her to go. He was adamant: they'd watch it in the room.

'Stuart always gave himself away by his behaviour, which was bizarre at times, but I always knew there was a reason behind it.'

Stuart's refusal made Sandra all the more determined to watch it in the bar. She went down and Stuart followed. Tony was there, watching the football. Stuart wouldn't let up. 'Let's watch it in the room,' he said. But Sandra was determined. The volume increased. 'Let's watch it in the room!'

Eventually, Tony stepped in. 'What's wrong? Let her stay. Why won't you let her?'

'I remember a big shouting match,' says Bruce. 'I saw Stuart getting up and he fucking booted the table with the drinks on it and just stormed out.'

'Tony was angry at Stuart because he was roaring and shouting at me,' says Sandra. 'Tony would probably have *known* why Stuart didn't want me there – there would have been a woman he knew in the bar. There were women everywhere. Nothing happened in the bar, but I knew the reason I was not wanted.

'He knew that if something happened, it would make me want to leave. I don't know how the rest of the band weren't on edge the whole time about him walking off.'

Liverpool, 12 October

'I was *dragged* to Liverpool,' says Sandra. She was watching the band soundcheck when somebody came down and said, 'There's a phone call for you, Stuart.'

Stuart says, 'I'm busy.'

The guy says, 'It's somebody that's on the guest list.'

Stuart put his guitar down and walked off stage to sort it out. When he came back, Sandra took a look at the guest list herself. On it was a name she recognised: the name of someone she knew Stuart had had a one-night stand with.

'I thought, "Right."'

Later, she asked him who'd been on the phone earlier. Stuart didn't try to hide – he said her name.

'But I told her I couldn't see her because my wife's here.'

'Is that the *only* reason you said you couldn't see her?' said Sandra.

But nothing much happened apart from that. He was drinking, but not too heavily. 'I didn't particularly like it,' she says, 'but he wasn't drunk. He was trying, really trying, to control it.'

Stay Alive

Nottingham, 13 October

But by Nottingham, it was all becoming a bit too much. Sandra knew that there were women – groupies – in Nottingham that Stuart had been with. 'I didn't want to be confronted with anything else,' she says. 'I said to Stuart, "I've had enough now. I'm going home."'

They argued about her leaving, she asked sound engineer Sheds Jackson to keep an eye on Callum and then she went down to reception to see if they could help her find a flight.

Stuart followed her down, shouting all the way. At the desk, 'he was standing behind me, grabbing the phone off the receptionist, slamming the phone down, and I was standing there, trying to be all respectable and polite. Then I was trying to get him out of the way so I could get it done. He was going mad because I was trying to leave.'

Rather than continue to argue in a public space, they went back to the room and continued the argument there.

And in the end, after all that? She didn't go. Stuart said, 'If you go, I'm coming with you' and he meant it. So she was trapped.

'The next day,' says Tony, 'bang – everything was okay. I saw it as life. But unnecessary. If it was going to carry on, we would have had to say to Stuart, "Look, we can't carry on like this."'

'On the other hand,' he says, 'if we had said that to him, he would've fucked off. We wouldn't see him again. It was a knife edge.'

'I know Ian had a lot to deal with when he ran the Stranglers, but I think he found it really difficult when it came to Stuart and Sandra because you don't feel as though you can intervene. It's personal, it's a married couple.'

You can't blame Tony for thinking that Sandra's mere presence caused problems – in a way it *did* – but equally she was holding it all together.

'There's so much I don't know about Stuart,' says Tony. 'He just didn't divulge any of it. In the first touring season with *The Crossing*, we all experienced some brilliant highs as a band. But that's where it stopped. We didn't enjoy each other or certainly not with him, because there wasn't a lot that he would get involved with.'

'The only times that we actually spent any time together outside of the band was when we went to a football match. Stuart loved his football, I loved football and Ian loved football, and we went to games. But all these things had a disconnect, all these things kept other subjects at bay. Anything deep and personal he would avoid like the plague.

'There's a lot I don't know. In all the years we spent together, sleeping in the same room, sleeping in hotels, a part of him didn't trust us with too much information about himself.'

It was a different time. Nowadays, people are more open about rehab and able to talk about mental health issues. Alan Edwards had suffered a breakdown in 1982 after an intense tour with the Rolling Stones. 'But in those days, I couldn't tell anyone,' he says. 'You couldn't say, "Oh, I'm having a bit of a breakdown." You'd lose your business. You wouldn't have any clients. And, don't forget, we all went to a lot of football. Sometimes when it was hard to talk to Stuart, I'd say, "Man United looked crap as usual at the weekend, didn't they?" and we were off.

'That was a way of engaging. That was what blokes did. We all acted. We talked about football and had a beer and we were all very tough and no one had any nervous breakdowns or mental health issues at all. It didn't exist. But of course it *did*.

'If you went to the label and said, "I'm having a nervous breakdown", they'd drop you. There wouldn't be any sympathy. And if you went down the pub, and said, "I'm feeling a bit weird, mentally", people would laugh at you. You didn't really talk about things like drinking because we were all "blokes" and we all drank. So the problem would be, well, you haven't had *enough* drink. Today, people would have a lot more sympathy and understanding. But they didn't then.

'He would have been much happier now, I think, wouldn't he?'

In November, the band travelled back to Sweden for some shows. This whole period – from here until June 1985 – is 'the worst part', according to Sandra. 'I remember that flight to Sweden. Stuart said he'd phone when he got there. But there was no phone call that day, or the first half of the next day.'

Sandra called and eventually got Joe Seabrook. She said, 'I take it that he's lying pissed somewhere?'

'Joe, being Joe, said, "He's in a bit of a state – but it's because the plane was hit by lightning." The excuses started wearing thin and just got ridiculous. And it was then that I realised that he was probably with another woman.'

How did she know? 'Women just know,' she says. 'And when he came back, I asked him and he admitted he had been. So, again, it was just boom, boom ...' One thing after another.

Missing that first phone call was weird because Stuart had made a big deal about calling home. He had gone to Europe without Sandra on the condition that they talk by phone every night – and *stay* on the phone all night.

So every night Stuart would phone her from a hotel, and reverse the charges. It would be late at night and they would chat for an hour or so, and then – instead of saying goodnight and hanging up – they would fall asleep with the phone by their ears.

'I can't remember what happened when we woke up,' says Sandra. 'If I didn't hear anything, I think I would put the phone back down, but then it would ring again, before he left to go to the next place.' They were on the road in Europe – Sweden, Denmark, Germany, France, the Netherlands – for two weeks. 'I can't really remember how many days we did it for,' she says, 'I just remember the bill.'

British Telecom sent them a phone bill for £2,000. Luckily, someone from BT called and said, 'We think there must be something wrong with your phone line', so most of the charges got scrubbed.

'Stuart would have known that the reverse charges would probably be a fortune,' says Sandra, 'but he just didn't care. As far as he was concerned, it was worth it. He knew there was a possibility we were going to separate at that point.'

And there was an added complication. Sandra was pregnant.

Bruce remembers those dates as a difficult time. 'His drinking was getting worse,' he says. 'That tour was really fucking bad. I think that's when he was drinking during the day on the tour bus. When somebody's an alcoholic and they're drunk, you cannae speak with them, you cannae help them. They're Jekyll and Hyde. It looks like that person, but it's not.

'There would be other people that would take advantage of that – like when people would see George Best in a pub and they'd want to go up and buy George Best a pint and hang out with him so they can say they've done that. There was a lot of that with Stuart as well. They would see Stuart drunk and – "Oh, there's Stuart Adamson!" – and they would hang out with him and buy him drinks and stuff, which I fucking hated.

'In the end, you have to walk away because you *can't* help. You're just wasting your time. It was getting really bad.'

Even Joe Seabrook found him difficult to control. 'When you've got an alcoholic, they're cunning,' says Bruce. 'They're sneaky fuckers. You blink and they're gone. It was a horrible time.'

Stuart started to look rough. 'He had this big green parka,' says Bruce, 'like a mod parka, but he didnae have it done up like a mod. He had the parka, a pair of Levi's and monkey boots, and he kind of lived in those for ages. He was always falling and he'd always have a hole in his trousers, a skint knee or a mark on his face where he'd fallen.

'The touring was not enjoyable. It was unpredictable. Some nights were great and usually he wouldn't have a drink before he went on. That was probably 99 per cent of the time. It was just afterwards. It was horrendous. He wasnae violent or anything. But that was definitely a low point and it certainly could not carry on.'

The band were back in the PR grind: interviews, radio, TV. 'Stuart was shy, believe it or not,' says Bruce. 'I mean, I've been told that *I'm* shy, I probably am. But Stuart was *really* shy. Like if somebody gave him a compliment, he hated it. I'm like that as well.

'All Stuart ever wanted to do was write his songs, play guitar, do the show and then fuck off. But obviously that's not enough. Your arse belongs to the record company and they need you to do all kinds of stuff.

'Stuart was not interested, one little bit, in how the mechanisms of the music business worked. He probably was to start off with, with the Skids, and then he didn't like what he saw, he didn't like what Richard became. There's nothing wrong with that – it just wasnae Stuart. Stuart didn't like the business that he was in.'

They toured the UK and Ireland in December, supported on some dates by the Cult, a new signing to the Grant–Edwards stable. The tour ended with a run of Scottish gigs, from Glasgow Apollo on 21 December to a Hogmanay gig at the Edinburgh Playhouse. Alan Edwards remembered that 'Stuart was not at his most communicative – burnt out and just about had enough of it.'

Sandra went to the Glasgow show. 'I remember being pregnant, we were in the hotel and I felt a real disconnect with him. I knew he was hiding stuff and things were escalating. I think he felt guilt and knew that things were not good between us.

'I remember being in the hotel and feeling a bit sort of disconnected myself because of everything that had happened. The two of us went to the train station and I remember looking at him and thinking, "I don't think I *know* you".'

In January 1985, the band went back in the studio to record the soundtrack for a new Scottish comedy movie, *Restless Natives*.

'*Restless Natives* still kind of leaves a sour taste in my mouth,' says Tony. 'I felt the recording was horrendous. I thought what was committed to tape was horrible.'

Tony felt that the writing process of *Steeltown* had set a benchmark – a new way of working together – and now he was being presented with a project written completely by Stuart. 'I think we thought that *Steeltown* was something that we'd move on from,' says Tony. 'But I had no knowledge of this thing called *Restless Natives*. The next minute, we're recording a soundtrack. I got that kind of stomach ache I had back in the early days of contracts. I didn't know who to trust.'

Confusion reigned. The project wasn't sold-in to the band very well. Bruce remembers getting a call from the office explaining that the engineer, a guy called Geoff, was on his way up to Scotland and was calling in at his house first. It wasn't until he got there that he realised it was Geoff Emerick, the engineer on the Beatles' *Revolver, Sgt Pepper's Lonely Hearts Club Band* and *Abbey Road*.

To Tony, it all felt like things were unravelling. Adding to his paranoia was 'Winter Sky'. The B-side of 'Just a Shadow', released as a single on 11 January, it had been recorded without the band's rhythm section. The record company had needed it urgently, so Stuart and Bruce had written it quickly and recorded it in a little studio in Edinburgh.

'All of a sudden,' says Tony, 'we were doing *Restless Natives* in a pokey little studio in Glasgow with Geoff Emerick, recording all this stuff that Stuart had written. My god – Geoff Emerick worked with the Beatles and this thing sounded horrendous. I remember watching it in the cinema. It sounded awful.

'And my next memory is sitting down watching the film and seeing "Music written by Stuart Adamson". At that point, I thought, "Maybe we're being squeezed out".

'It started to feel like it was becoming the Stuart Adamson show.'

Stuart's drinking probably added to the confusion and lack of communication. Sandra felt like the whole thing was a bit loose. 'I didn't feel that the work had been really put into *Restless Natives*,' she says. 'The drink was taking priority over everything at that point.'

Stuart went on his motorbike to catch a flight to London for a meeting with Ian Grant. Ian called later: Stuart hadn't arrived.

They found him in the airport lounge, with his motorcycle helmet on, sleeping it off.

Management wondered if they had made a mistake. 'Stuart was sick and tired,' Alan Edwards said in the book *A Certain Chemistry*. 'In hindsight we should have realised how totally exhausted he was.'

Ian Grant says that when he and Alan were on holiday in early January, 'the film producer got directly in touch with Stuart and cajoled him into the studio. There developed a tug of war between the film people and the band. It was particularly stressful for me ... Stuart would have nothing to do with me ... Wouldn't even speak to me on the phone.

'The extra pressure was the last thing Stuart needed,' said Edwards.

Stay Alive

The filmmakers had done a rough cut of the movie and used music from *The Crossing* and *Steeltown*. 'So they'd asked Stuart to write some songs that were a bit "sound-alike",' says Bruce, 'in the same tempo and very similar in sound. There are two or three songs on the soundtrack – one of them sounds like "Come Back to Me", one of them sounds like the song "The Crossing" – because they had edited the movie to that.'

The film was a success in Scotland but it never took off outside the country. The music didn't come out on a soundtrack album at the time, but was released as B-sides on the 12-inch singles of 'Look Away' and 'The Teacher' in 1986.

The promo schedule for *Steeltown* ended with an appearance on the *Oxford Road Show*, a music TV show filmed at the BBC's Oxford Road studios in Manchester. The band were scheduled to perform – miming to 'Just a Shadow' – and Stuart was the guest presenter, hosting the show and interviewing guests. It was a disaster. 'He was so fucking nervous,' says Bruce. 'He shouldn't have been in that position, being a TV presenter. That is not Stuart.'

Usually, the two of them would have travelled together, but when the taxi arrived to take Bruce to the airport, Stuart wasn't in it. Bruce called Sandra who told him that Stuart was still in bed – 'in no fit state' – and would get the next flight.

In Manchester, the BBC weren't pleased. They did a rehearsal with Bruce's guitar tech Gerry ('Gerry, the secret sherry drinker,' says Bruce. 'That's what we used to call him. He was a tea-time tippler, this guy') filling in for Stuart. When Stuart arrived, 'he looked like shit', says Bruce. 'He was always a smart dresser, but he turned up in this old sweater that it looked like he'd been digging the garden in.

'The drinking was getting more noticeable at this point. Alcoholics are very clever at hiding, but when they're about to reach rock bottom, they just don't give a fuck. So he was doing it in front of people now and people were openly saying, "What a fucking mess that guy is."'

Stuart had to interview Scottish footballing legend Tommy Docherty and singer-songwriter Joan Armatrading. 'I could see him splutter and getting tongue-tied,' says Bruce.

'I can remember being horrified watching it,' says Sandra. 'I just felt like he'd let himself down so badly. He wasn't in control of what he was saying. I just remember holding my breath and going, "Jesus Christ".

'That was the period where he was trying to stay sober, but he couldn't. He really was trying. I mean, I wouldn't have stayed with him if I didn't feel that he was trying. At home, he was sober, so it was tolerable. You could live with it. And he was alright for a certain period and then he would have to have a drink.'

One time she saw it coming on and – pregnant and with Callum to look after – she took their dog round to the Watsons' house and asked them to look after it for a few days. It was just all too much. Even walking the dog was one job too many.

According to Ian, it was around this point that he arranged a meeting with Stuart to discuss the forthcoming US tour with Hall & Oates. Stuart didn't turn up. 'Instead, he rang and said he was quitting,' said Ian.

'He was always quitting the band,' says Bruce. 'He would usually quit the band after the last gig of the tour. Stuart was constantly quitting the band and then starting it back up a couple of weeks later.'

Stuart would phone and calmly, matter-of-factly, say it was over. 'Or sometimes Ian Grant would phone me saying, "Stuart's quit the band."' One time, and it might have been this time, Grant called, furious. 'He went crazy at me,' says Bruce. '"He's your fucking singer! Fucking speak to your fucking singer! He's your fucking mate!"

'He didn't even call him by his name. "Your fucking singer." I was kinda taken aback.'

Ian Grant remembered this moment in *A Certain Chemistry*: 'Stuart's got a pregnant wife and he doesn't really like the rock 'n' roll trip, the rollercoaster he's been on for so long. He wants to get off that rollercoaster and here's me trying to keep him on it.

'The way he was brought up, not really seeing his father much until he was twenty, and being away from his son Callum, and the thing about being anti-rock star. This pressure on him gradually built up ... I could see what Stuart was going through. He'd been on a spiral and he wanted to get off but couldn't. So because he didn't get off, it became worse and worse. And his way of dealing with it was to ring me and say, "I'm finished. I'm out of the business."'

Ian says he went to Scotland and they went to the pub and smoothed things over. 'He's fine. He just needed that break. I think I got the best out of him, without wanting to sound manipulative. And he may have gotten the best out of me.'

The Hall & Oates tour was cancelled 'at about seven days' notice', according to Alan Edwards ('which didn't endear us to their management'). It had been touted as the tour that would help Big Country break America – a chance to play to huge crowds across the States. Hall & Oates' manager Tommy Mottola 'was desperate to get involved with the band,' says Ian Grant. A few years later, Mottola became the CEO of Sony Music, so he would have been an influential person to have onside. Instead, Big Country never toured *Steeltown* in the US and didn't return to the country until the summer of 1986.

'Hall & Oates was the tour that the record label and management said, "This is the one that's gonna help you make the next leap",' says Bruce, 'and obviously that never happened. And that's when the American label went off us. "We're not dealing with these bunch of fucking lunatics." We kind of got dropped after that. It was completely fucked.'

Grant–Edwards decided to go on the front foot. 'We also took the initiative to attack Polygram because we thought they had done a bad job on *Steeltown*,' said Alan Edwards. 'We felt they hadn't promoted the album efficiently and hadn't been behind the band. We wanted out.' Polygram weren't happy and threatened a court battle 'which would have destroyed the band'.

'In the end, we got a lucrative deal which guaranteed to pay, even if the album sold no copies whatsoever. The deal was worth a quarter of a million dollars.'

Chris Briggs was done with the record label too. 'Phonogram was becoming a bit toxic,' he says. 'We were working all the hours God sent, making them a lot of money and I just thought, "We're not really being looked after here."' He left to go to A&M.

So Big Country didn't do anything for six months.

Grant-Edwards turned their attentions to the Cult. At the beginning of sessions for their *Love* album, they had fired their drummer Nigel Preston, so Mark sat in for the rest of the album. That same year, he also drummed on albums by Midge Ure, Roger Daltrey and Pete Townshend.

With the band in limbo, Stuart was at home for the birth of his daughter, Kirsten, in June.

On the day of the birth, Sandra started going into labour, but kept it to herself. She had a regular day, timing her contractions by herself and, around dinner time, went for a lie-down. She watched the clock, noticing that the contractions were coming closer together.

Around 11 p.m., she told Stuart, 'We're going to have to go to the hospital.' They dropped Callum off with Sandra's mum, went to the hospital and Sandra gave birth to Kirsten an hour and a half later. Stuart left after the birth, picking up Callum and going home.

By morning, Sandra was determined to leave the hospital. She'd had two uncomplicated births, so at 8 a.m. she asked to see the doctor and set about discharging herself. Around nine o'clock, she phoned the house.

Someone answered the phone but didn't speak and then hung up. She called back. The same thing happened, except this time she heard Stuart saying, 'Callum, stop playing with the phone' before the phone went dead again. She phoned back. This time Stuart answered.

'What's going on?' she asked.

'What do you mean?'

'Nothing,' she said, because she already knew. There was something weird going on and it probably involved alcohol.

'I said, "Come for me when you're ready."'

Stuart arrived in a car full of fishing gear, with no place for Sandra and

Kirsten to sit. She stood with the baby outside the maternity ward as he made space. 'I was raging,' she says. 'The nurse looked at me as if to say, "What's going on here?" I was always in a state of embarrassment.'

At home, as soon as she walked in, she clocked them: two empty bottles of champagne on the mantelpiece. It was at that point that Sandra told Stuart that she wasn't going to let him hold Kirsten.

'I didn't know when he'd stopped drinking,' she says, 'and I'd made my mind up that this was it. I didn't feel that things were going to go well. I don't know why, but I just got the feeling that things were going to change from that day on.'

So things were already tense when, half an hour later, the doorbell rang. It was Sandra's mum. She came into the house furious and started shouting at Stuart. 'Where were you last night?'

Sandra said, 'What are you talking about?'

She said, 'He's been out all night!'

And then, says Sandra, it all kicked off.

Sandra's mum had had a phone call in the middle of the night from Sandra Watson. 'Is Callum staying with you?' she'd asked. He wasn't. Stuart had taken him home.

'Who's looking after Callum, then?'

'Well, Stuart.'

'No, he isn't.'

Sandra Watson knew that Stuart wasn't home with Callum because he was round at Bruce's mum's house, drunk, in the dark, shouting and throwing stones at her window.

Bruce's mum, Mary, had been freaked out by this drunk rock star on her lawn and had phoned Sandra Watson, and she in turn had phoned Sandra's mum – a small network of women looking out for each other and their children.

Sandra took all this in and – appalled that Stuart had left their three-year-old son alone at home – asked him to get out. But Stuart wouldn't leave. 'I couldn't get him out the house. I phoned his mum and dad, told them to come and get him.'

By the time they arrived, Stuart was roaring and shouting.

'He told his mum to stay the eff out the house,' says Sandra. When Stuart's dad tried to come in anyway, Stuart dropkicked him. 'He kicked him right out the door, literally.'

William Adamson picked himself off the ground and gave up.

Sandra's mum phoned her doctor who arrived within minutes. He was there to see Sandra, who hours ago had just given birth, but he brought with him a bunch of AA leaflets and literature.

'He knew,' she says. 'Just from talk around town, probably. I'd had the same doctor since I was ten, so he knew bits and pieces. He said, "Sandra, you've just had a baby. You need to take these tablets, it'll calm you down."'

But, says Sandra, she was already calm. She was reconciled. She knew what had to happen. The doctor insisted she take Valium. 'I took two and it made no difference because I was wired and ready for anything.'

Sandra told her mum to go home and she sat down with Stuart. 'I said to him, "This is it. This is actually *it*." And he'd never heard me say that before. I'd always just said to him that he was free to go any time he chose. But this was different. I said, "This is it and I'm really sorry."

'I knew that he felt safe with me and I could see the fear in his face when he knew I meant it. Normally, I would've caved at seeing that fear, but because of what he'd done with Callum, I didn't care anymore. My son came before anything, so I had to just try my best not to feel that I had to save Stuart too.

'At that point, he said to me, "Give me the phone book." I said, "Do what you like, but you ain't staying here."'

But by late afternoon, she says, 'he managed to convince me that he was going to AA that night and then any meetings thereafter that week.' Sandra's brother Jamie was there. Stuart told him, 'I'm doing this. I'm going to AA and I promise this is the end.'

He got on his motorbike and he went to the local AA meeting. Jamie followed him in his car. Sandra says, 'I said to Jamie, "If he doesn't walk into that meeting, I need to know."' So Jamie followed Stuart and watched as he went into the meeting, and stayed to watch him come out later.

'And then every night– I think every night for maybe two or three weeks, and then every alternate night after that – he went to meetings. We just had to go hour by hour.'

Why did Stuart go to Mary Watson's house? Was it because Bruce had told him that his mum was in AA and could help him? Had Stuart already decided that the drinking had to stop?

'I don't know what he thought,' says Sandra. 'He was drunk. I have no idea. That's what it must have been, but it didn't matter to me.

'It was days before I let him hold Kirsten. And meanwhile, he was detoxing.'

Denied alcohol, an alcoholic's body starts to suffer withdrawal symptoms. 'It was terrible,' she says. 'There were hallucinations, lots of sweats and feeling ill and stomach cramps. And it seemed to get worse, weeks in.

'The meetings were what he relied on – and his sponsor, a guy called Phil. I don't know where he is now. He had the same guy for a long time. This was the point where Stuart realised he loved his kids, he was all about family life and he knew he was going to lose that if he continued. He had to dig deep and figure things out.'

Stuart Adamson would be sober for the next fourteen years of his life.

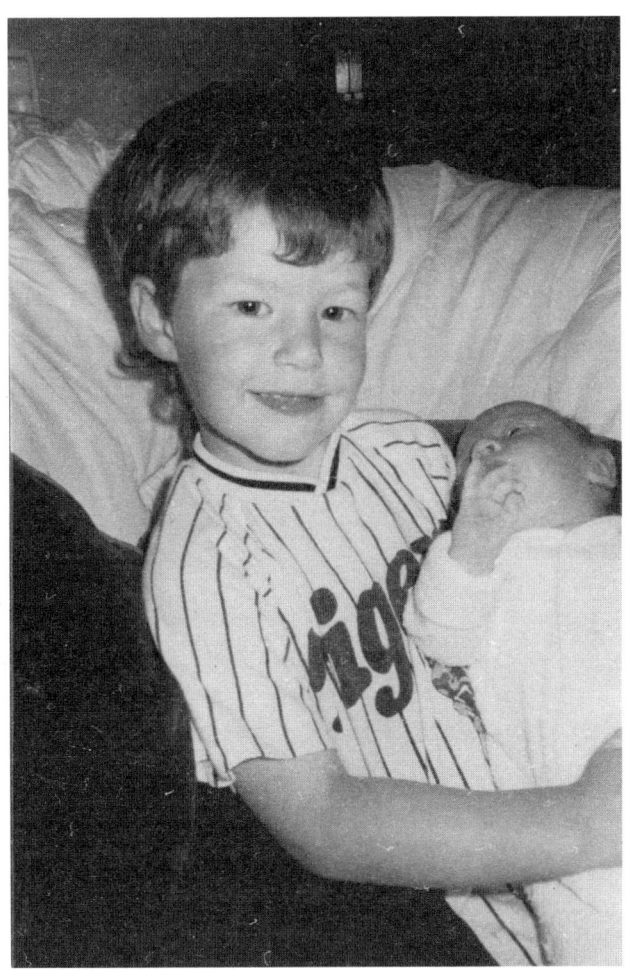

Callum and Kirsten, summer 1985.

19

The Caledonian Antisyzygy

Live Aid. Dave Bates. 'Just let him dae it.'
The conflict at the heart of The Seer

A month after Kirsten's birth, Wembley Stadium played host to the biggest musical event of the decade: Live Aid. According to Ian Grant, Stuart's drinking, and his temporary departure from the band, probably cost them a spot.

The band's PR at the time was Mariella Frostrup, who 'worked at Phonogram where [Live Aid organiser] Bob Geldof was a lot of the time'. Geldof's band, the Boomtown Rats, were also on the label. Frostrup, married to Richard Jobson, 'knew all the Dunfermline gossip', says Ian. So Geldof and promoter Harvey Goldsmith thought the band had split and didn't invite them.

'I thought they'd broken up,' confirmed Geldof in *A Certain Chemistry*. 'I really did, or I probably would have called them. The decision as to who should appear was nothing to do with my own personal taste. It was current popularity and availability – more to do with how many people would watch them. I think Big Country are a great group. I just thought they'd broken up.'

According to Alan Edwards, 'there was talk of Stuart performing with U2 for the whole of their set. These plans didn't materialise and instead Big Country were invited to join in the finale. Live Aid actually brought the group back together again.'

Stay Alive

The way Tony Butler remembers it, he was having a party at his house in Ealing the night before Live Aid when his phone went. It was Geldof. 'He said, "Are you guys available to play tomorrow?" I said, "No – the boys are up in Scotland and we're kind of off the road at the moment."'

It might sound unlikely that Geldof was still looking for bands the night before, but he *was* having to deal with the threat of last-minute cancellations. U2 had threatened to pull out at the last minute because they couldn't soundcheck. Either way, Ian Grant recognised the PR value of being involved and persuaded the band to come to the show at Wembley.

Stuart, just weeks sober, didn't want to go. 'He wasn't going to go to Live Aid unless I went too,' says Sandra. 'I'd never left the kids before and Kirsten was just weeks old. But, again, I knew how important it was for him to be visible there, even though they weren't actually playing.

'He was pretty fragile, but it was great because I felt that I had my pal back, and we were having the same kind of laugh we used to have when we were younger.'

Stuart was interviewed on live TV with comedian/singer Tracey Ullman. Interviewer David Hepworth, discussing a rumour that the Beatles might reform for the finale with Julian Lennon, asked Stuart: 'What do you think they might play?'

'Instruments,' said Stuart.

Just before the show ended, Big Country were standing by the back of the stage when Tony suddenly thought, "I want my mum to see me!"

He grabbed hold of Stuart's jacket, got Mark and Bruce and dragged them to the front. 'And that's why you see the pictures of us standing at the front,' he says. 'Because I wanted my mum to see me.'

It became another on a long list of what-might-have-beens for Big Country. Live Aid transformed U2's career – their performance helped break them in the US and returned all their albums to the top 40 in the UK. Simple Minds appeared in Philadelphia – their album *Once Upon a Time*, released three months later, went top 10 in the US, becoming their most successful album.

For Big Country, says Tony, 'it was a missed opportunity – an opportunity to be on the same level as all these other bands. I think we would have been up there with the rest of them. But I've seen some photographs recently. Stuart doesn't look right.'

Bruce agrees: 'Stuart wouldn't have been in a fit state.'

Stuart was only a month sober. Playing for a global television audience of two billion people might not have been the most helpful thing at that point.

'He had other things to deal with,' says Sandra, 'and they were more important than performing at Live Aid. He knew that. So he didn't care about that at all. He just knew the first step was to stop drinking and recover whatever he's lost of *himself*, never mind what he'd lost professionally.'

Chris Briggs was still drinking. 'Live Aid was a bit of a turning point for me,' he says. 'I was absolutely shit-faced.' He took himself off home early. 'I just didn't want anyone to see me in the state I was in. I surprised myself how out of it I was, so early in the day. So I kept a really low profile. I saw Stuart in the street, coming in, and he went, "I've stopped drinking, Chris. You've got to try it. It's fantastic."'

Briggs gave up that day.

The rest of 1985 was spent resting and writing. 'Stuart was at AA meetings quite regularly,' says Bruce. 'He was getting his life together.' Work began on the next record. For this one, Stuart reasserted himself as the lead songwriter.

The Adamsons moved house in December that year. They had moved from the flat above the chip shop, to another flat in town, to a new Barrett house and then to Balmule, a huge eleventh-century house in the countryside to the north of Dunfermline.

'This is the first house that Stuart was able to get a mortgage on,' says Sandra. 'Because he'd had some success, and he had some money, the accountant did a good job, so he was eventually able to get a mortgage. We bought that as an investment.

'I think we had about twenty-six acres, of which there was six acres of lawn and he was never happier than when he was on the ride-on lawnmower, cutting the grass.'

Stay Alive

They turned the basement into a studio and he wrote there. He had a strict routine, going down at a set time and coming back up at tea time.

'*The Crossing* was Stuart and I, and then Tony and Mark came along,' says Bruce. '*Steeltown* was written as a combined effort with everybody in one room. On this album, Stuart took himself away and started writing on his own. I think that was his way of dealing with it. He was getting himself sober, getting his life together. It wasnae like, "I'm taking control!" It was just his way of dealing with it.'

Bruce would occasionally go and see him. 'He'd say, "You got any ideas?" "Aye, I've got this mandolin riff…" So we recorded that and it became "The Seer". But for that album, Stuart probably wrote just under three-quarters by himself. That was part of his healing process.'

Bruce also stopped drinking a month or so after Live Aid. 'I was just getting sick of it. When Stuart stopped, I had naebody to drink with. I was getting bad with the drink. The problem was whisky. It turns me into a nightmare. If you'd say black, I'd say white.

'So I quit for a few years and Stuart and I used to go to meetings together in Dunfermline.'

In September, Mark played on Roger Daltrey's album *Under a Raging Moon* and Daltrey asked if all of Big Country would play on the opening track, 'After the Fire'. Tony and Mark did their parts, Bruce added EBow parts but 'Stuart just didnae want to dae it', says Bruce. Pretenders/Paul McCartney guitarist Robbie McIntosh did the rest of the guitars.

In December, Big Country played two gigs in the US with Daltrey, in Boston and New York. Roger wanted Mark to come on for his set and play on the song 'Under a Raging Moon', but Stuart said no. Ian backed him and there was a bit of a bust-up between Grant and Who manager Bill Curbishley in the dressing room.

Maybe Stuart felt that the Who connections were over-shadowing the band a little. When they did interviews in the US, journalists would ask Tony and Mark about playing with Townshend or Daltrey. 'It used to piss Stuart off,' says Bruce. 'But they'd never heard of the Skids, y'know?'

At the end of '85, they went into the studio with Robin Millar. Millar had produced *Diamond Life*, the multi-platinum-selling debut album by Sade, as well as a series of sophisti-pop albums by Everything but the Girl, Fine Young Cannibals and Scottish band the Bluebells. His success changed the kind of work he was offered.

'I'd started off as a guitarist,' he said later. 'And then, because Sade, Everything but the Girl and Working Week were sort of moody, soully, intimate – with a complete absence of rock guitars – that was the area that I was being offered work in.'

Millar mentioned this in a magazine interview. 'I said, "I'm basically a rock artist and I'd love the chance to produce a rock album."' Stuart read the interview and got in touch. 'Alright, mate. *We'll* give you a chance.'

The two met up and Millar asked Stuart to play him some of the songs on an acoustic guitar. Listened to like that, said Millar, 'he sounded more like a folk singer, so I wanted to bring a sort of intimacy and a simplicity.'

In Millar's words, he wanted to 'move away from the industrial '80s to a more human, organic approach. The intention, nine months before the release of [U2's] *The Joshua Tree*, was to move into the area of simple realism, letting the drama and emotion of the song – the lyric and the performance and the musicianship – replace the drama of digital '80s reverb.'

Stuart had said similar things after the release of *Steeltown*. 'Music used to be a thing where working people got together on a Saturday night and played some songs,' he told the *NME*'s Danny Kelly. 'Someone'd play the guitar or the fiddle or an accordion. No bastard'd play the synthesiser! It's a shame that people see pop as something separate from that.'

He wanted his music to have a human connection. 'Have you ever been in a pub when some old woman just gets up and starts in on some old ballad? Oh, it tears your heart out ... Music must be a human thing if it is to survive, it must communicate and it must send that shiver down your spine. That's when music's being human. That's what we're trying to get back to.'

Robin Millar's productions were timeless – beautifully produced records full of space and separation. After the density of *Steeltown*, it sounded ideal.

'Unfortunately, another problem arose,' says Tony, 'and it was called David Bates.'

Stay Alive

With Briggs gone, Dave Bates was Big Country's new A&R man. He had an impressive resume. Bates had signed the Teardrop Explodes, Tears for Fears and Def Leppard. He'd signed Scottish artists Hipsway and Texas, and discovered future hitmakers Wet Wet Wet. And there was a Stuart Adamson connection: Bates had signed Bill Nelson to Mercury to release the *Quit Dreaming and Get on the Beam* album, the one that featured Tam Kellichan, and the track 'Living in My Limousine' that had so impressed Rusty Egan.

On the face of it, it was a great match. Spoiler alert: it fuckin' wasnae.

'Dave Bates was never a fan of Big Country,' says Bruce. 'He inherited us and he wasn't quite sure what to do with us. It's not his *fault*, but it didnae help us either.'

Bates had big shoes to fill. The band had enjoyed a close relationship with Chris Briggs and it was hard to replicate. 'Briggs was our mentor in those days,' says Tony. 'He was a great A&R man, had great vision, and when he left, we were signed to a company with nobody who liked us. We got taken over by Dave Bates and it was nothing but grief from that point onwards.'

'I think bands should have a Key Man Clause,' says Bruce, 'and if the A&R guy that signs you goes to another label, you should be able to go with them. I've not got any malice against Dave – and I've had a few bust-ups with him – but he wasn't interested in Big Country.

'We had three hit singles with Dave,' he says, 'so he obviously did something right. But he had his ways. Him and Ian Grant fucking *hated* each other.' Bruce didn't get on too well with him either. 'In the end, Batesy banned me from the studio one day.'

'Dave was full of it,' says Ian. 'For a start, he was competitive with me – he didn't like there being a manager involved. With Tears for Fears, they just let him get on with it, but I've always been hands on – it's how Stuart wanted it. Dave would be the first person to say to Stuart, "Go and write a hit single"' – and he did with "One Great Thing". Not my favourite.'

'Our first thought was, "How do we make them successful again?"' Dave Bates told *Record Collector*. 'How do we get them back in the charts?'

The performance of the last few Big Country singles told their own story: 'Wonderland' had gone to number 8 in January 1984; 'East of Eden' reached number 17 in September; 'Where the Rose is Sown' peaked at number 29; and 'Just a Shadow' reached number 26 in January 1985. They had gone from top 10 to top 30 in twelve months.

But if the record company were concerned, the band weren't. 'I don't think the chart numbers bothered us really,' says Bruce. 'We were still having hits and it was good to be seen as an "album band".'

The chart hits, the *Smash Hits* coverage, the *Top of the Pops* appearances, the checked shirts: Big Country had been marketed as a pop band, albeit one with significant rock muscle. 'Most people in serious bands want to be seen as serious artists,' says Bruce. 'So it was fine to have top 30 hits, as opposed to being like Wham! or Duran Duran or something.'

In fact, it felt weird doing songs like 'Where the Rose is Sown' on *Top of the Pops*, he says. 'I was kicking about with Fish from Marillion at the time and they were in a similar position. They had a big hit with "Kayleigh" but they were an album band, really. So it didn't bother us. From an artistic and creative point of view, I think we were quite happy.'

The record company thought differently. 'We needed to listen to the material and try and steer and find and identify a hit single,' Bates told Allan Glen for his book, *Stuart Adamson: In a Big Country*. 'There was a real rethink at this time. They just couldn't come up with the same thing again. The sound that they had done on the last album obviously hadn't gone well with the public and we were looking to – not turn them into a metal band, or turn them into a folk band – but try and move them and their sound along.'

The recording ran from November 1985 to February '86. Stuart transformed Bruce's mandolin riff into the album's title track, 'The Seer'. Adamson was a fan of Kate Bush and inadvertently – or maybe even deliberately – 'The Seer' had a similar rhythm to her song 'The Dreaming'. Stuart mentioned that it would be good to have Bush sing on the track, so Robin Millar got in touch with her label and, much to everyone's surprise, she agreed.

Stay Alive

'The central character of the song "The Seer" is a woman,' Stuart told *Record Mirror*, 'so I thought it would be good to get a woman's vocal point of view. I have a lot of Kate Bush albums and I like her voice. There's a lot of variety and texture in the way she sings, and she's always coming up with something different. She's a perfectionist.'

'It was unbelievable,' says Bruce. 'She was in the studio for five hours. She was really nice, really quiet. Robin had sent her a cassette of a rough mix and she'd done all these vocal arrangements.' The band sat upstairs in the control room at The Power Plant with Kate downstairs in the studio doing take after take. 'She would do a take, then maybe double it, and then she would do a counter thing, and then something else. It was fucking genius,' says Bruce.

'And in between takes, you could hear this noise.' The noise was a match being struck and a long, satisfied exhale.

'She was smoking dope all the way through,' says Bruce. 'She had what looked like a little Bible – a book that was cut out in the middle with a tobacco tin in it with whatever she was smoking.

'I've never been a dope smoker, but Tony liked to smoke every now and again, so Tony got a toke off her and it knocked him for six! She was just chain-smoking it all through the recording.'

'I wanted it to be like a conversation between Stuart and Kate,' Robin Millar told Tim Barr. 'The mandolin and bodhran were in the middle, totally dry, with Stuart's vocal to the left and Kate's to the right. My starting point, as always, was remembering him sitting on the little corner sofa in Studio 1 with a borrowed acoustic, singing these songs to me on his own.'

Having Kate Bush guest on a track was such a coup that they considered 'The Seer' as a single. The story goes that at five minutes and twenty seconds, it was considered too long, but it's more likely that it just wasn't deemed commercial enough: After all, the fourth single from the album, 'Hold the Heart', was more than six minutes long, but – in theory – a much more chart-friendly ballad.

By the time it was mixed for release, Kate Bush didn't actually have much of a starring role on the track. 'On the Walter Turbitt mix, her vocals are buried a wee bit too much,' says Bruce. 'You can hear them, but I remember them being a lot more prominent and dynamic on Robin's mix. It's almost relegated to a backing vocal. It should be like a duet.'

In the end, they didn't need Kate Bush to have a hit single. Stuart had written and recorded a demo of a song called 'Look Away' on his portastudio. 'He just had the basic chords and the vocals,' says Bruce. 'It just sounded like another Stuart song – great – but it was just like a continuation of what we were doing.'

The lyrics were inspired by a 1982 movie, *Harry Tracy, Desperado*, starring Bruce Dern. The film was based on a true story: Harry Tracy was allegedly a member of Butch Cassidy's Wild Bunch – a robber and killer. The subject of a huge manhunt after he escaped from prison in 1902, he killed ten men while on the run. Eventually surrounded by a posse, he shot himself rather than be captured. 'Harry Tracy had a great sense of his own destiny,' said Stuart, probably talking about the movie character, rather than the historical figure. 'He knew he was out of his time.'

The song was uplifting, with a huge pop chorus. They worked it up in the studio, Robin Millar mixed it and it was released quickly, on 12 April 1986. Three weeks later, 'Look Away' was at number 7 in the UK singles chart – the band's highest-charting single.

It remains the only song produced and mixed by Millar to have been released. The very same week that 'Look Away' became the band's biggest hit, Dave Bates rejected his finished album mixes. 'And then him and Robin had a proper falling out,' says Bruce. 'I know that Robin is very vociferous about Bates. He fucking hates him.'

There had been some signs that Bates could be difficult. When a vinyl record is cut, the pressing plant sends a test pressing to the record company for approval. Bates sent the test pressing back and had them recut it. He didn't like the next cut either, so had them do it again. And again. In fact, says Tony, he made them recut it *forty-two* times.

'They went back and forth forty-two times,' says Tony. 'Now I was suggesting to him, if he would deign to listen, that probably the mix wasn't right. But no, he spends the band's money cutting it forty-two times. And these things aren't cheap.

'The guy has no perception of what we do. You don't waste money like that. You come back, ask the band. There was no communication whatsoever.'

Big Country had gone on the road and left Millar in the studio to finish the mixes. Then Millar was removed from the process. 'The next minute they were putting bloody guitar parts on stuff and trumpets and shit,' says Tony. 'The whole thing was just taken out of our hands for some reason. It was bizarre.'

Bates brought in Walter Turbitt to mix the album. Turbitt had been assistant engineer on the Cars' fourth album, *Shake It Up*, and remixed the single 'She-Bop' by Cyndi Lauper. He didn't have a long list of credits or a history of hit singles behind him.

Turbitt and Bates flipped Robin Millar's intentions on their head. The mixes were less organic – less about the performance and the musicianship – and *more* about the artificial drama of '80s production techniques.

'I did mix the record in my own quiet way,' said Millar. When he heard the new mixes, though, 'my hair stood on end. I thought, "What on earth? What have they done to my record?"

'I didn't criticise the record company for wanting to play safe. But I hadn't recorded the record in a way that *suited* that kind of mixing. So I think you've got the worst of both worlds.'

'A lot of the mixes are a bit dated,' says Bruce, 'with the big gated reverb drum sound and horn stabs. We were on tour and they were doing all these mad 12-inch mixes with trumpets and trombones and Fairlight synthesisers over the top. "The Teacher" had Mark King-style bass on it – Tony never played it. "Look Away" had these synthesised horn stabs – one mix had a freeform avant-garde saxophone all the way through it.'

'You've got to be careful with trends,' says Mark, 'because they come and go very quickly, and they can really date a record. I think they were looking to push more into areas where we weren't selling – more middle of the road, more poppy. At that point, everyone had saxophone. I didn't like it, to be honest, but it wasn't for me to say.'

During a gap in the tour, the band went to Maison Rouge in Fulham to mix the album. Bruce arrived to find Walter Turbitt adding guitar parts ('easy barre chords, anybody could've played them') to 'The Teacher'.

In the control room, Stuart Adamson was sitting, watching. He saw Bruce's reaction and confusion: there they were, the two guitar players for Big Country watching some guy play on their track. And Stuart Adamson – the same Stuart Adamson who, just a few years earlier, had walked out on two recording sessions because *he'd* been asked to do overdubs – rolled his eyes and shrugged.

'Just let him dae it,' he said.

'The Teacher' became the follow-up single to 'Look Away'. It stalled at number 28.

Compromise was the order of the day. 'I Walk the Hill' – the only track on the album credited to all four band members – was a deliberate attempt to 'write a Big Country song'. 'I think Bates said, "Have you got another 'Fields of Fire'?"' says Bruce. So the four of them mockingly jammed one out in rehearsals. 'It was like Big Country by numbers.'

A third single, 'One Great Thing', was a more obvious choice for a single than 'The Teacher'. A plea for peace in our time, that opens with Big Country's trademark 'bagpipe guitars' and goes straight into the chorus, it made it to the top 20 – for a single week. Soon after, they were approached by Scottish brewery Tennent's to use the song in an advert. It was good timing.

'We needed the money,' Stuart said on Irish TV show *Beatbox*. 'We were skint. It was right in the middle of all our business troubles.' They had to consider it, he said, not out of greed but because of the wider Big Country operation. 'Not only do we have to be responsible for ourselves, but there's other people who rely on us for their living as well.'

'We weren't going to do it,' says Bruce, 'but then we found out how much money they were going to pay us. "Really? Fuck it."'

They re-recorded it for the advert because the record company owned the original – and because Tennent's wanted some of the lyrics changed. 'We thought they were going to come back with "one great pint" or something,' says Bruce, 'but it wasnae as bad as that.'

'For when you taste perfection/Then nothing less will do' goes the brewery version. In the advert, a Stuart Adamson lookalike switches his TV off and goes out into the night while a cross-section of Scottish stereotypes sing the words: miners, farmers, fishermen, golfers. Seen now, it's a cute reminder of corny '80s advertising. Then, it seemed like Big Country were leaning into a clichéd vision of Scotland.

The advert soured Stuart on 'One Great Thing'. Even though it was a hit, he felt stupid singing it and they dropped it from their set.

'I keep wanting to sing those horrible words I didn't write,' he said.

They never played it again.

The next single, 'Hold the Heart', also felt straight out of the record company playbook: a ballad, with a distinctive EBow intro, it became Big Country's lowest-charting single since their debut, 'Harvest Home'.

Lyrically and thematically, Stuart had been inspired by Scottish poet Hugh MacDiarmid. MacDiarmid was a complicated and contrary figure who was a part of the Scottish Renaissance, a loose collection of modernist Scottish writers that included Lewis Grassic Gibbon, Nan Shepherd, Neil Gunn and Edwin Muir. MacDiarmid helped found the National Party of Scotland – the first Scottish national political party and a forerunner of the current SNP – but was expelled from it for being a communist. Later, he was expelled from the Communist Party for being too nationalist.

He could start a fight in an empty hoose, that guy.

'Reading his poems gave me the idea for "The Seer",' said Stuart. 'He had this idea for a Scotland that was modern and vital and outward-looking and not one that was just a sentimental picture of clans, whisky and bagpipes – a country that was part of the world.'

MacDiarmid invented his own kind of Scots language, claiming it as an act of resistance against the occupying English culture. He also espoused a theory known as 'The Caledonian Antisyzygy' – the idea that the Scottish psyche is fractured by the nation's history and language, creating an internal warring of opposites within all Scottish people: the oral language of Scots vs the written English, the Protestant vs the Catholic, the Highlands vs the Lowlands, maybe even the sober vs the drunk.

You could say there was an 'antisyzygy' at the heart of *The Seer* too. The album had warring opposites at its very core: Millar vs Bates, the organic vs the artificial, art vs commerce, the contemporary vs the timeless, the cynical vs the sincere.

To the people who had followed Stuart Adamson's career from the Skids and been with Big Country from the beginning, you couldn't miss the signals. The cheesy disco remixes, the horns and keyboards, the TV advert, the ballad – they felt cynical and slightly desperate.

By 1986, the music scene had changed substantially. A new breed of Scottish bands had appeared: the Jesus & Mary Chain, the Soup Dragons, Shop Assistants, Primal Scream. The music press's albums of the year included the Smiths' *The Queen Is Dead*, and records by Sonic Youth, Throwing Muses and REM.

Left to their own devices, with a sympathetic producer and A&R man, Big Country had produced *Steeltown* – a dark and grown-up album for the band's maturing audience. Now on the back foot, the record company was trying to position Big Country as a safe pop band. With Stuart navigating sobriety and under pressure to make it work, *The Seer* was mired in compromise. It went to number 2 in the UK album charts and stayed in the top 100 for sixteen weeks – performing worse than *Steeltown*.

Maybe the more organic Robin Millar mix would have produced a more credible and timeless album to stand next to the production styles of other 1986 albums like R.E.M.'s *Lifes Rich Pageant* or Elvis Costello's *King of America*. For years now, fans have clamoured for a release of the Millar mix. 'There is a Robin mix somewhere in an archive,' says Bruce. 'They're trying to release it, if they can find it.'

For Bruce, the experience of *The Seer* was eye-opening. 'You realise you're just a product at the end of the day,' he says. 'You've got no say.'

There was material on *The Seer* for the hardcore. 'The Seer', 'The Teacher', 'Remembrance Day' and 'Red Fox' were all huge Celtic rock songs, while 'Eiledon' seemed directly connected to the *Restless Natives* material.

Stay Alive

'Remembrance Day', said Stuart, is about 'learning from things gone past. This is the underlying theme and the key that the whole album revolves around.' Similarly, 'The Teacher', he said, was about 'learning from my past and a certain quest for knowledge, finding out and understanding.'

In an interview with Stuart for the *NME* in January 1987, writer Stuart Cosgrove grouped the band's first three albums together as a trilogy. 'The sense of community evoked in Big Country's albums is a coherent statement about the contradictory places that make up Scotland,' he wrote. '*The Crossing* with its open spaces and romantic stirrings is an image of the Highlands, *Steeltown* with its images of decline and urban disenchantment is the industrial cities of central Scotland, and *The Seer* with its images of visionary nature is the rural geography that dominates Scotland: the rivers, the border lands, the islands, the historical crofts.'

'The clearances in the Highlands were just a dress rehearsal for today and clearing Scotland of its industry,' said Adamson. 'Never underestimate the links between the Highlands and the cities. I would like to think that what we do in music has roots not only in thirty years of rock 'n' roll but roots that are much older and more solid than that.'

He wasn't interested in all the shite of stardom and *Top of the Pops* and the trappings of fame. He was trying to carve out a new role for himself: the songwriter, the performer, the family man, more tied to generations of folk singers than to rock 'n' roll stars.

'The star thing is well and truly over for me,' he said. 'One of the biggest things I've achieved is to convince people in Dunfermline that stardom is a myth. Strangely, it gives me a sense of vanity to think Big Country has managed to ignore the star system. It's really about putting music on its proper pedestal, neither as an elevated or a degraded thing. It sounds pretentious, but our music is a breathing part of a real community – a place whose people deserve respect.'

In an interview included as a B-side of the 'Hold the Heart' 12-inch, the interviewer asked: 'Is there anywhere that you'd particularly like to go?'

'I'd like to play behind the Iron Curtain,' said Stuart. 'I think I'd like to do that.'

20

Another Season

*Sobriety. The anti-rock star.
A meltdown avoided. Dancing with David Bowie*

Stuart might have talked about playing behind the Iron Curtain, but the truth was that he didn't really want to play *anywhere* around that time. And that was tough luck because, in 1986, Big Country toured *everywhere*: the UK, Europe, the US and back around again. From March to December, they played more than eighty shows, including two nights at Glasgow Barrowland, two nights at Wembley Arena and a support slot to Queen at Knebworth.

'During that period,' says Sandra, 'he still didn't want to be away. He didn't feel good about being in a band and being away. He was just doing it because it was his job.'

He was coping with sobriety. 'He was picking up AA meetings everywhere he went,' she says. 'There was a period where Bruce was going to meetings too and I think they went together.'

Bruce's son 'Wee Bruce' was born while the band were in Toronto in August and Bruce remembers going to a couple of meetings on the road. Their tour manager was in Al-Anon, an organisation that supports friends and families of alcoholics, and was understanding. 'We employed a few new crew guys that were in the fellowship and that kinda helped,' says Bruce.

With Bruce having given up drinking, the two of them went back to sharing a room on the road. At the end of the night after a gig, they'd go up to the room with coffees and bottles of fruit juice instead of a bottle of Black

Stay Alive

Label. 'And I'd help him tie his fishing flies,' says Bruce. 'I quite enjoyed it. It was different.

'And then, as time went on, I just turned into a boring bastard.'

AA didn't seem right for him. 'You'd listen to people's stories about reaching rock bottom, guys who had lost limbs because they'd set the hoose on fire. I couldn't identify with that sort of thing. I had a drink problem, but I don't think I'm an alcoholic.'

One night, after a couple of years of sobriety, he was out with his wife Sandra for a meal and he ordered a beer. 'I had one bottle and that was it. Didn't even have another one. And I've just had beers ever since. I will not go near any kind of spirit.'

Stuart couldn't afford to be as casual about it. He would phone his AA sponsor, telling him what meetings he was going to, and call home every day. 'I guess it was to let me know he was okay,' says Sandra. 'He knew that I would know if he'd been drinking straight away by his voice.'

He got himself into a good routine. 'He went running in the morning, or he would go to the gym. He took care of himself after that.'

'There was a change in him,' says Bruce. 'I think he could tolerate people a bit better – he was still crabby as *fuck*, he was the world's crabbiest man – and his body changed completely because he was going to the gym. Sandra was doing aerobics and Stuart got into the whole keep fit thing. He went from being skinny, tae fucking abs and muscles an' that. Every time we were in a hotel, he'd be doon the gym.'

At one point, the band came up to Dunfermline for rehearsals. Balmule House was so big that not only could they rehearse there, they could stay there too. 'Tony, Mark and Ian and some of the crew guys all stayed at the house,' says Bruce. When he saw them the next day they were like, 'Aw, it's terrible, we need to find a hotel.'

'What's wrong?' said Bruce.

The ballroom of Balmule had been turned into a gym and Stuart and Sandra had made it part of the band and crew's daily schedule that they all had to do aerobics classes to keep fit.

'All the guys were like, "Get us into a hotel! We can't stay here!"'

'Stuart went from being skinny, tae fucking abs and muscles an' that.' Stuart and Sandra flex.
© Lesley Donald

In June, they played the Provinssirock Festival in western Finland. Ian Grant had hired someone from Stuart's past to do their sound: *Scared to Dance* producer Dave Batchelor. Batchelor hadn't seen Stuart since they'd fallen out over the overdubs back in 1978. 'I remember sitting in a caravan in Finland,' says Dave, 'and it was one of these moments, you know. "How's this going to go?"'

There were ominous signs. Just weeks before, a reactor at the Chernobyl nuclear power plant in northern Ukraine had exploded and burned for weeks, blowing radioactive material all across northern Europe. 'I remember thinking, "What's coming through the clouds?"' says Dave.

As the isotopes rained down, Stuart appeared. 'I can't remember his exact words, but it was just like, "That's past. Let's move on." He touched on it, but in a very gentlemanly way. And I loved their music, so it was a good match.'

The show went well and Batchelor joined them on the road, glowing in the dark all across the US, UK and Europe. Did he see a change in Stuart from the young man of the Skids? 'I think he was probably more energised,' he says. 'He would take command in situations – soundchecks or rehearsals, stuff like that. There was a really good vibe between the guys, Mark, Tony and Bruce, so that always helps.'

Physically, Stuart was strong. Mentally, he still had his dependencies.

In August, Big Country played at Knebworth for what would be Queen's final gig with Freddie Mercury. Privately, Stuart told Sandra he wouldn't do it unless she came with him. 'I was only there,' she says, 'because otherwise he wasn't going to go. Of course, nobody else would know this, but I had to go so that he wouldn't cause mayhem. He was capable of doing that even sober. He would just say, "Well, I'm not doing it."'

By Knebworth, she'd had enough of these demands. 'I didn't even go to the gig,' she says. 'I stayed in the hotel. I just wanted out of there. I'd had enough of the lifestyle and getting dragged away.

'I'd done it with Callum because I had to – because I was *forced* to – and I wasn't going to do it with Kirsten.' So she found herself at Knebworth and she thought, 'Enough.'

For the first time, she was able to prioritise herself rather than Stuart 'because he was alright by then, y'know? He was fine.'

His dependency on her wasn't a mental health thing, she says. 'He was never depressed, absolutely not. Never suffered from depression. It wasn't that. He was just like anybody else who's doing a job they don't want to do. He didnae want to be in a band, didnae want to be tied to the band and, at that point, he wanted to just *stop* the band. He just didn't particularly like his job. He liked his songwriting and creating, but he didn't like everything else that went along with it.'

He went to the doctor just once, she says, back in the days of the Skids, when he had nervous exhaustion from being in the studio, back when he had to do all the parts. 'So that was understandable,' she says, 'but that only happened once. He was never depressed, ever. He always could find his out, y'know, the best place for himself – in a book, at the football, at the motorbikes, fishing.

'He was happy as Larry for all the years he was sober.'

He did interviews, this guy who had hated talking to the press, and flatly refused to act like a rock star, stressing how ordinary and down to earth the band were. 'I don't think we're any different from somebody doing a nine-to-five job,' he told *Record Mirror*, 'or from somebody standing in a dole queue. We just get on with the job. If you're in a band, it doesn't mean you have to lose control. It doesn't mean you have a craving for self-publicity and the more outrageous things pop stars are traditionally supposed to do.

'I've lost track of how many dates we play in a year and I'm terrified of flying. No matter how many times we go up, it still scares me awful. But I still enjoy touring. I feel excited and humble at the same time when I'm on stage. It's a bit emotional. No matter how many shows we've played, a concert is always special to us. It's the ultimate proof of what we're trying to do.

'We will never lose track of the fact that those people have paid their hard-earned money to come and see us. We have to be good.'

'I'd like to see music come down to earth and be more level-headed,' he told *Creem*. 'I don't even like the word "fan", because it implies a second-class citizen, which is wrong. You've got to give your audience credit for having at least as much intelligence as you have. If more groups did that, music wouldn't have to be a star-making thing. It would be more human.'

He was entering into a new kind of stardom and looking for new ways to deal with it. 'We'd go to Edinburgh and people would recognise him,' says Sandra, 'and that kind of attention didn't sit well with him. As far as he was concerned, it shouldnae matter. You know, "I'm just a normal human being with all the flaws that goes with being a human being. Don't think I'm some kind of hero."'

He spoke about it in interviews and people started to understand. 'Then they were very dignified about how they went about talking to him,' she says. 'They wouldnae approach him in the same way. And once that happened, he was more giving.'

He would go to see Dunfermline Athletic and people would leave him alone. Some people would bump into him on a grass verge at a reservoir, fishing. 'He would pop in and out of the shops and nobody would bat an eyelid, really,' says Sandra.

Occasionally, some smartarse would shout or sing something from the other side of the street. 'He always had a great comeback,' she says. 'He was never nasty, but he never failed to have a really good comeback. I just remember pishing myself laughing and thinking, "I bet you wish you never said that, pal".'

It's a side of Stuart that could be forgotten in all of this, says Sandra. He was complex and could be difficult, but he was funny too.

'I hope they all haven't forgotten about how funny Stuart was,' she says about the other members of Big Country. She knows that there is bitterness and pain and confusion, all these years later. 'I don't want them to forget how much fun it was to work with him. He really was a funny, funny person. He would have me in stitches all day. He was a great mimic and he could shoot you down really quickly. He was so fast. He loved having fun. And he really *did* have fun.'

Rather than play into the star system, Adamson was relishing treating music as his job and settling into the life of an ordinary working man. 'We have two children,' he told Max Bell of *No.1* magazine. 'Callum, our son who is five, and Kirsten, she's eighteen months. I space out my life so I'm at home a lot. Sandra always accepted my lifestyle, but roots are important. I reckon I see my kids more than people in nine-to-five jobs.'

He substituted drinking with his hobbies: fishing, football, going to the gym. Football was an obsession and an escape. Sandra's brother Jamie took Stuart down to a regular five-a-side football night at the Bruce Street Hall in Dunfermline where he met three guys who would become friends for the rest of his adult life: Bobby Drummond, Pubsy (aka Garry Purves) and Big Slap (aka Bruce MacKenzie). Bobby had known Stuart from hanging out with Richard Jobson's brother, John, 'but then he stairted coming to play football,' says Bobby, 'and he just latched on tae us.'

They played every Thursday night and then walked down the hill to the Bruce Tavern. 'But Stuart never drank,' says Pubsy. 'He hud what he called "a pint a pish". Soda water and lime. It looked like a pint of pee.'

They knew that he'd been a drinker and had gotten sober and respected that. 'People would say, "Want a drink?" and he'd say, "Aw, you wouldnae like tae see me wi' a drink."'

Bobby and Pubsy managed an amateur Sunday league team that Stuart joined. He was a good guy to have on your team: he attracted all the other good players who liked the idea of hanging out with Stuart Adamson, and he was an aggressive player who lived for the match. 'He was fiery on a football park,' says Bobby. 'He was nice off the park – but in a game, he was a man possessed.'

Once he got a red card for a bad tackle, right in front of the manager of Dunfermline Athletic, Jim Leishman, causing Stuart much embarrassment and everyone else much hilarity. 'We used to ca' him Inspector Gadget,' says Pubsy. 'His legs would be wrapped around people everywhere.'

'If we ever went to a studio,' says Bruce Watson, 'like Rockfield, for instance, and we were there for six weeks, Stuart would always find a local pub team or something to play with. He liked playing football. He was actually a good player. He was good, but he was dirty. Very, very competitive. He'd bodycheck you.'

Stuart got deeper into bikes, sponsoring the Big Country motorcycle racing team. 'I love motorcycling,' he told Max Bell. 'I don't quite know

Stay Alive

Stuart, at one with a machine, 1986.

why, but it must be the feeling of speed coupled with being at one with a machine. It's a touch of the *Zen and the Art of Motorcycle Maintenance* and a touch of the "pushing yourself to the limits" that Hunter S. Thompson wrote about in *Hell's Angels*. Maybe if I wasn't a musician, I'd have visions of being a motorcycling champion.'

Big Country ended 1986 with a gig at the Birmingham NEC, two nights at Wembley Arena and another at the Brighton Centre. 'I never get tired of the actual physical act of going on stage,' Stuart told *Smash Hits*.

But privately, says Sandra, he *was* tired of it. 'He didn't find it interesting in the slightest,' she says, 'and he much preferred having fun back home.' With the kids at school and nursery, they were out running in the morning, or at the gym, doing the things they enjoyed. Being on tour, staying in hotels – it was a grind. 'Every spiel in between each song was the same every single night,' she says. 'I could tell what he was going to say, word for word. He was bored. Not so much with the *performing*, but definitely just being away. He just couldn't handle it.'

Stuart wasn't religious, says Sandra, but sometime in 1987 he asked her to come with him to church meetings every Sunday so that he could get baptised. 'He got baptised as an adult,' she says. 'Kirsten would have been about three at the time and they got baptised in Townhill church. We went every Sunday and then, when he was baptised, he was quite happy. He never went before and then never went again after.' She just put it down to getting sober. Just another part of the journey.

In the *NME*, Stuart Cosgrove had asked if he was religious. 'Not in that sense,' said Stuart. 'The church is still very strong in Scotland, too strong. I hate that tight reformation morality. "Dae this or it's the fiery sword for you." Older people seem to fear not being in control. People in society seem to think that when they get to a certain age, it means they have passed the test and can control the younger generation. Religion becomes a way of controlling.'

In Scotland, religion is sometimes an excuse for sectarian bigotry, says Cosgrove. 'That's true. I hate to think about Scotland polarising about religion. The village I was brought up in had a really healthy mixture of Catholics and Protestants. I can honestly say I never saw one religious fight. I saw people have fights coming out o' pubs and people moaning about no' having enough money, but never religion. It was a case of "We're aw in the same boat, we're aw Jock Thamson's bairns."'*

In June 1987, the band went out on the road, supporting David Bowie for five stadium gigs. Alan Edwards was doing press for Bowie, who was a fan of *The Crossing*.

'We had a great time,' says Bruce. 'We went down well. Roker Park in Sunderland was a great gig. But Bowie admitted later on that it was the worst tour he'd ever done.'

The Glass Spider Tour became infamous as a folly of over-indulgence, with an over-the-top stage show. 'We called it "The Inflatable Spider". It was one of those tours where he didn't play anything recognisable.'

---

* That is: We're all the same, just ordinary folk.

Stay Alive

When it was over, Bruce's wife Sandra danced with Bowie at the after-show party while he stayed at the hotel looking after Wee Bruce.

After the Bowie dates, Big Country started writing and demoing songs at REL Studios in Edinburgh for what would become the album *Peace in Our Time*. In December, they headed out on the Under Wraps Tour – a series of small gigs supported by the Wonder Stuff, where they road-tested the new material to smaller audiences.

'I remember it kinda backfired on us,' says Bruce, 'because at one point we didn't play stuff like "Fields of Fire". Stuart was like, "I'm fucking sick of it – I'm no' playing it!" and the fans got really pissed off. I think we were just trying to get back to being like a cult band again – which is what Bowie probably did with the Glass Spider tour.'

Back in 1983, *Record Mirror* had asked Stuart if he could imagine still doing this in ten years' time. 'Do I still want to be doing this when I'm thirty?' he said. 'No, I don't think so. I think I'd feel pretty stupid if I was playing "Fields of Fire" onstage when I was thirty.'

Big Country had become so famous, so quickly, that it was the first time the band had played smaller venues like Nottingham's Rock City or the Astoria in London. In the *Melody Maker*'s weary review of the Astoria show, the reviewer referred to 'a batch of newly hatched songs, all given long-winded explanatory introductions, most of which seem to explore themes and sentiments worked to a pulp already. "Peace in our Time" is the only one that stands out and that's simply because the key words are repeated again and again.'

The album hadn't even been recorded and the songs were being dismissed already. The review ended on a question: 'Just how much longer can it go on?'

According to Sandra, the band were asking similar questions. 'I know there had been discussions about U2 manager Paul McGuinness and making a move away from Ian. I remember a bit of a heated discussion in the garden at Balmule. Sandra [Watson] was there too. We didn't have much influence, but we knew that it didn't look right.'

The band couldn't agree on what should happen next. 'Too lazy to do anything, to be honest,' says Sandra. 'It was easier just to stay where you were and hope for the best.'

This is how Bruce remembers 1987: 'We did all the demos, we were happy with them. Then we went to LA – and Stuart had written a whole other bunch of songs that we had never even heard.

'Then we went to pre-production in LA with Peter Wolf, did the album with him, then we went to Australia to shoot two videos, and then we launched the album at the Russian Embassy and we went to Moscow.

'And at the end of it, I went: "How much has that just cost us?" And that's when I realised: I'm going to be doing this for a very, very long time.'

21

Paid in Tractors

*Bland in the USA. Bugged in the USSR.
The Hard Luck Café. Combine-harvester racing
from the Ukraine. More crusading porridge*

In October 1986, Ian Grant was flying from London to New York when his plane flew over Iceland. Beneath him, he knew that US president Ronald Reagan was meeting with the leader of the Soviet Union, Mikhail Gorbachev, at the Reykjavík Summit.

Gorbachev was different from previous Russian leaders. In 1984, Margaret Thatcher had hailed him as a man she could work with. 'We can do business together,' she said. 'We are never going to change one another, but we should both do everything we can to see that war never starts again.'

The Cold War was ending and a new world order was coming.

Ian Grant had a feeling that Big Country's world was changing too. Something that Keith Altham had said to him had stuck. 'It's that time, Ian,' the veteran PR man had warned him. 'Your band's gone cold, the honeymoon's over. It's coming to an end – you have to reinvent.'

Altham was a legend in PR, and a mentor to Alan Edwards, so Ian took his advice seriously.

He looked down on Iceland and a thought began to take shape.

In 1987, he worked on the reset. He saw *Peace in Our Time* as a chance to take on America, with a new record label. Ian had called a meeting with the big wigs at Polygram – Dick Asher, Maurice Oberstein and David Simone – and he told them, 'We're outta here'.

'I demanded we get off the label,' says Ian. 'It had all fallen apart in America, Polygram was going down the tubes, the whole thing was a disaster area.'

Polygram released them for the US and Big Country were put out to tender. 'Everybody was interested,' says Ian. 'Virgin, EMI, A&M, CBS before the Sony takeover – they thought this was their U2.

'The money started off at £200,000 and went up to a million, and they were outdoing each other in the end. It was Sony vs Warners. The Cult had already signed to Sire on Warners, so I had relationships with [CEO] Mo Ostin and [Warners/Reprise president] Lenny Waronker because of that. I went with Warners and they matched a million – we probably should have gone with Virgin because I had a great relationship with Richard Branson.'

Stuart and Ian went to LA for a meeting with Waronker, the guy who had signed Jimi Hendrix and the Kinks in the US. 'We took him *Restless Natives* and he sat and listened to it full blast in his office at Burbank, me and Stuart sitting opposite him.'

They listened to the whole thing and then Russ Titelman walked in. Titelman had produced records by Randy Newman, James Taylor, Rickie Lee Jones and more.

'Russ! Listen to this!' said Waronker and he played all forty-six minutes all over again. 'It's genius!'

Waronker suggested three producers for the next album: Titelman, Ted Templeman (Doobie Brothers, Little Feat, Van Halen) and Peter Wolf, an Austrian-born musician who had played with Frank Zappa and moved into production for the likes of Jefferson Starship, Heart, Wang Chung and Kenny Loggins.

Ian and Stuart met with all three and Stuart picked Peter Wolf. 'I didn't think Peter was the man,' says Ian. 'Where it went wrong is that Pete had his own agenda and Lenny Waronker left him to it.'

'Mo Ostin and Lenny Waronker wanted us to sound more American and that's why we got Peter Wolf,' says Bruce. 'It was at the time when he was doing Starship's "We Built This City", and Heart when they went pish. Stuart had written all these songs in that kinda vein.'

It was a world away from their post-punk roots. In 1988, U2 were working on *Rattle and Hum*, a combination live and studio album that came with a self-mythologising documentary, casting them as a modern band carrying the torch lit by the early blues, soul and rock 'n' roll pioneers. The Waterboys were blending traditional Scottish and Irish music with rock 'n' roll on *Fisherman's Blues*. R.E.M. were preparing *Green*, an album that would help define alt-rock and bring it further into the mainstream. The Pogues had just released the Steve Lillywhite-produced *If I Should Fall From Grace With God*.

The music press were falling over themselves to praise debut albums from Pixies and the Sugarcubes. Happy Mondays were blending guitar music and dance grooves. Soundgarden and Dinosaur Jr were pioneering what would be called grunge. And Big Country were heading into the studio to make an album with the guy behind 'We Built This City'.

'There was a sound developing at the time, songs in the charts Tony and I thought were really great records,' says Mark. 'Whether it suited Big Country's production is in hindsight. I thought we were starting to sound a bit like [Yes hit] "Owner of a Lonely Heart". That was all done on the Synclavier and comes out very processed. So that became, you know, less organic, more processed, which was the kind of sound of FM radio in America.'

The songs they had road-tested on the Under Wraps tour were mostly discarded. 'It was almost like there was nothing left of the sound of Big Country,' says Bruce. 'And Stuart's voice had changed.

'He went for singing lessons – I think it was more vocal exercises than singing – and his voice went up. By the time we did *Peace in Our Time*, he was singing in an almost American style. If you listen to *The Crossing* and then *Peace in Our Time*, it's like two different vocalists.

'You have this naivety and charm when you're still learning,' he says. He compares it to playing guitar: by this point, he was a better player than in the early days, but the rough edges had become something more slick and professional. 'You lose all the charm that you had, all that originality.

Stay Alive

You've become part of the mainstream and you've got to have hits. You can't be leftfield anymore.'

Def Leppard's *Hysteria* album had come out the year before. A huge worldwide hit, and one of the biggest-selling rock albums of all time, the production methods had been unorthodox. Producer Mutt Lange had recorded individual parts separately – beats, notes, chords, everything – and then comped them all together.

Peter Wolf worked in a similar way. 'The fashion at the time was for the Synclavier,' says Bruce, 'which was like an early sampler. Mark would play the drums and Peter would sample every drum. Snare drum, bass drum – he'd sample everything and then play it in time like a computer – quantised. "Broken Heart (Thirteen Valleys)" is a simple guitar part, an arpeggio thing – he made Stuart play it and he sampled every note.'

Effectively, he says, what you hear on the record is not Stuart Adamson playing it on the guitar, but Peter Wolf playing Stuart's parts. 'And it sounds shite. And I'll tell you what's wrong with it – it's too precise. I said, "Get him to play it again, but to just move his finger so that you get the string buzz." It made it sound a bit better.'

The imperfection made it sound more human. 'But it still sounded shite,' says Bruce, 'and the whole album was like that. You could not play it live. It sounded amazing if you were a hi-fi buff – really pristine and full of separation – but it didn't sound like Big Country.'

The same thing happened with all of their parts. Peter sampled Mark's snare, instead of having him play it. 'Peter Wolf had a brief to make the sound a bit more affable for American radio,' says Mark. 'Not that we didn't sound good on American radio – we'd had a hit with "In a Big Country". But what do I know? I liked Peter Wolf. I always embrace new producers. I don't question them as such, because you're hiring them to be the referee. You're hiring them for musical guidance and input. You have to let them do their job.'

Tony remembers the initial sessions for the song 'Peace in Our Time'. 'We were in a small rehearsal room and all of a sudden there's this very *massive* piece of music coming out of the four of us,' he says. 'Just this huge barrage of melody, power chords – without being over the top – and volcanic thuddering of drums. But by the time we recorded it, it was just *bleurgh*. It just became a drip. His production techniques were *a crime*.'

'It became keyboard-based,' says Ian. 'If you listen to the original demos, some of the songs are much better in demo form than they ended up. It gave them a new sound.'

'The organic side was missing,' says Mark. 'It was too processed. And the songwriting – I don't think it was developed enough.'

'Anyone that's ever done that with Big Country, it's never worked,' says Ian. 'They're missing the essence of what the band are about. But Stuart let it happen. He could be weak in not standing up for what he believed in. They were so desperate to crack America.'

'The whole idea of *Peace in Our Time* was to sort of elevate the band,' says Tony. 'Catch up on what we've missed out on with Live Aid and Red Rocks [U2's live mini-album *Under a Blood Red Sky* was recorded at Red Rocks Amphitheatre in Colorado. It went to number 2 in the UK charts and helped position them as an exciting live act] – to sort of catapult the band up. It just wasn't happening for us in Britain.'

They felt like they had some catching up to do. They might have had a new deal, but they had a bad reputation to repair, says Bruce. 'We hadn't really toed the line with Polygram – we didn't want to do certain things, we were pig-headed. So we got told that this time we had to be good boys and do as we were told.'

They had to play the game. Peter Wolf, Lenny Waronker – these guys were hit-makers. They knew what they were doing.

And it wasn't all bad. They were living in Hollywood – on Larrabee Street, just off the Sunset Strip – and Peter Wolf was strict about working hours and refused to work weekends, so they had free time. They were there for three months and threw themselves into LA life. Mark recorded his drums in the first week and would drive everyone around.

'We'd go to the Rainbow, Roxy, Gazzarri's, Barney's Beanery – we were out every night,' says Bruce. 'It was brilliant. I was down the Comedy Store all the time. I saw Sam Kinison there. Another night, Robin Williams turned up, unannounced, and did a completely impromptu set.'

Their image changed accordingly. 'I had been happy to get out of the checked shirts after *The Crossing*,' says Tony, 'and then to get out of the garbage that we had to wear – facilitated by U2's dresser – around *The Seer*. I just thought it was hokum. Nasty.

'But every now and again, I thought Stuart wasn't taking any interest in his own image. On *Peace in Our Time*, Bruce was cultivating a rock star image for himself. He was beginning to look the part: growing his hair, cowboy boots, the whole lot.'

'My hair was way doon to here,' says Bruce, putting his hand to his shoulder. 'People were like, "Why have you gone all heavy metal?" But I didn't want to go to an American barber and come out with a mullet or something.'

Tony also got himself a new hairstyle. 'I went down to this place in South Central and had these big dreads put in. I remember turning up at the studio and everyone asking me, "Are you Tony's brother?" "No! It's me – look at all this hair!" I got into the rock star thing in LA. It was part of the atmosphere.'

If they were going LA rawk, Stuart never got the memo. 'The next minute Stuart turns up with a fucking GI Joe haircut,' says Tony. 'Cut all his hair off. It was like, "*Okay*. What are you doing? Where is your head? Do you not care about how you look?" We did a photo session for the album and Stuart looked like he was in a country and western band, not a rock band. It just looked weird.'

To Tony, it added to the confusion about what kind of band Big Country were. 'I worried about that,' he says. 'The people who were supposed to be representing us, and investing in us, weren't 100 per cent sure about a part of what they were investing in.'

To be fair to Stuart, he looks great in the photoshoot by legendary photographer Terry O'Neill. His hair is shorter than the others – not in a crewcut, but a classic kinda James Dean quiff – and it sets him apart from the rest of the band.

Which was possibly – probably – *exactly* what he was aiming for.

Paid in Tractors

'We wouldn't see Stuart for dust,' says Tony. 'There was something incredibly unsociable about him.'

In Tony's memories, Stuart was a bit distant during this period. 'We were staying at some apartments in LA,' he says, 'and we wouldn't see Stuart for dust – just for the studio time. Bruce got married on the roof of the apartments we were staying at and Stuart wasn't there. There was something incredibly unsociable about him.'

Sandra and the kids came out for a bit, which could explain some of it. 'I was out there for the first part,' she says. 'I think I was there for three weeks. I couldn't stand it.' She entertained the kids at Disneyland and Knott's Berry Farm, and, when she flew home at the end of the school holidays, Stuart hired a motorbike and went on a road trip. It meant he missed Bruce's wedding.

Stuart wasn't impressed by life in LA: the schmoozing, the egos, the posing. He was trying to make his life in the band work for him. He wanted to go to baseball games and rodeos, to see a bit of real America.

Stay Alive

And if that meant giving up an LA party that would be full of record company people and drinking – even if it was Bruce's wedding – then that's what he'd do.

Bruce was cool about it. It was what Stuart was like. They had an understanding. 'We always had this thing,' says Bruce, 'that if somebody felt uncomfortable, just do what you think's right and there's not gonna be any sort of comeback or big discussion about it.'

Maybe Tony felt the lack of connection with Stuart because he was going through a hard time himself. At the end of the '80s, he says, 'a horrible thing befell my family. My wife went down with something called ME – myalgic encephalomyelitis. It threw my family life into turmoil. You're absolutely exhausted, debilitated, but you look normal. My ex-wife had it for four years, but the real crunch came when my daughter got it when she was eight years old. It was soul-destroying.'

They'd moved from Surrey to Cornwall to get away from people invading their privacy and now, with Tony touring and recording away from home, he was having to depend on people to look after his family.

To add to his woes, 'I got hit for a tax bill for ninety-five grand. And I just thought to myself, "Why am I doing this?" The band never seemed to make lots of money.'

From decadent Los Angeles at the heart of the American dream, a couple of months later they were in the communist German Democratic Republic (GDR) for the 'Peace Concert' – an event organised by the East German authorities to seemingly counter a concert on the other side of the Berlin Wall. Cue Big Country vs Michael Jackson.

The year before, West Berlin had hosted a festival in front of the Reichstag building. On the west side of the wall, 60,000 people came to see David Bowie, Eurythmics and Genesis – and on the other side, around 3,000 East Germans gathered to listen. In response, the East German police dialled up the aggression, checking IDs and putting up fences to contain them. The fans broke through, only to get clubbed and arrested for their trouble. Things escalated. By the end of the weekend, as Genesis played, thousands more came to hear the music, chant anti-wall slogans and throw bottles at the police. The police got out the water cannons and arrested around 200 people. They had managed to turn a group of intrigued music fans into an anti-Soviet riot.

So when Michael Jackson was booked to play the following year, the East German authorities were spooked. So threatened were they by the thought of kids driven wild by insurrectionist anthems like 'The Girl is Mine' and 'The Way You Make Me Feel' that they put on their own series of gigs on the eastern side of the wall.

They invited a selection of approved artists to play in East Germany – and Big Country got the nod. Going into the Eastern Bloc was a culture shock. 'West Berlin is like a circus or a fairground,' says Bruce, 'and you go over the wall and it's like low-wattage bulbs in comparison.'

But they connected. Big Country lit East Berlin up and had people singing along with songs they'd never heard before.

'This festival represents the spirit of peace between all nations,' said Stuart. 'One of the ways we can bridge those gaps is through music, because music touches everyone, no matter who you are.'

A low-wattage, Soviet-era lightbulb flickered above Ian Grant's head.

Keith Altham's words ('You have to reinvent') were still ringing in Ian's ears. Ian had secured them a new US deal, their sound had become more American (for better or for worse) and, finally, he had a plan that could take it to the next level.

Peace in Our Time's songs – like 'River of Hope' and the title track ('A very '60s-feel protest song,' said Stuart. 'Naive but I did it anyway') were idealistic pleas for a better world. They appealed to Ian's background in '60s radicalism. What if they took this American album to Russia and symbolically brought East and West together? With the Stranglers, Grant had launched the *Black and White* album in Iceland, and the follow-up in Portugal. It was a way of generating press enthusiasm. But no one had been to the USSR – not really. The likes of Elton John and Cliff Richard had played there at the invitation of the government, but no one had done it as free enterprise.

Stay Alive

Something like that could make headlines. It would make history. It would give the band a cause. At the very least, it would be a pretty impressive way to launch an album.

He pitched it to Stuart. 'Your grandad was the chairman of the Scottish Communist Party. Are you a socialist?'

'Yeah.'

'Think about it. Bono – Amnesty International. Sting – the rainforest. You – culture. East–West. You could be a figurehead.'

Stuart went for it. He probably regretted it pretty quickly.

In August, Big Country played Glasnost Rock '88, a rock festival in Tallinn in Estonia, then part of the Soviet Union. 'Glasnost' was the name given to the spirit of openness and transparency that Mikhail Gorbachev was introducing to the USSR as he tried to take it out of the oppressive, regressive policies of the 'Era of Stagnation' that had begun in the '60s under Leonid Brezhnev.

In a *Melody Maker* piece at the time, Steve Sutherland captured the moment that Ian announced his Russian plans to the band. 'Big Country's manager Ian Grant, arrives from Moscow with the news that seven gigs have been set up for late September.' The news is not greeted with enthusiasm. 'Stuart jokes that he'll gladly tour America for a year, he'll even play Pittsburgh, to get out of it.'

The band were not enjoying their time in the Soviet Union. Sutherland describes a country awash with food shortages, prostitution and desperation. 'It's fucking terrible here,' Stuart tells Sutherland. 'I'd rather be on the dole in Hull than have the very best job and have to live here. We have to tell the kids, Steve! We have to! I mean we're always reading in the tabloids about how dull and repressive Russia is and, y'know, "If you want to vote Labour, go and live there and see how you like it." And I always thought, "Come on, leave it out, it's not as bad as all that". But it is! It *is* as bad as all that!

'The people are desperate for change. They need Glasnost and they need Gorbachev and I really hope the man gets his own way because if he achieves what he wants to achieve in the lumbering beast of the thing that is the Soviet Union, it will be one of the greatest political feats of the twentieth century.

'I think it's pretty neat that everyone's in a job and everyone has cheap housing and there's hot water and electricity and stuff like that ... But it seems to have equalised everyone *down* instead of equalising everyone up!

'I despise all political systems. I think politics is bullshit and it's fucking wrong to impose your will on others.'

After the festival, though, Stuart was moved by the connection Big Country had with an audience hearing their music for the first time. 'When I was singing "Just a Shadow" and "Chance" and "King of Emotion" – God! The lyrics felt really close to me, I remembered why I wrote them ...

'It's a pretty spectacular thing to be able to stand onstage and share your moods and emotions and your hopes and your fears directly with people who you know are identifying with it and understanding it and feeling it. And it didn't make me feel big and strong and powerful and godlike. It made me feel very small and insignificant, like standing in front of an absolutely spectacular piece of scenery and thinking, "Christ, that's really amazing. I can tap into this and feel it!" It *is* there, that bond between people – that spiritualism is a tangible thing.'

The album launch was at the Russian Embassy in Bayswater at the end of September. For an attention-grabbing move, it didn't get off to a great start. Stuart was interviewed for ITV's *News At Ten*. 'And you couldn't understand a word he said,' says Tony. 'It was so *dull*, that I'm not surprised no one took any notice.'

They flew out to Moscow a few days later – the band and a huge posse of journalists. 'You have to give all the credit pretty much to Ian,' says Alan Edwards. 'He created it and it was a genius idea. And somehow he persuaded Phonogram to put in a lot of money. I think it was about a quarter of a million – I mean, a *lot* – to make it happen.

'Then, of course, we all go out there and it's a bit out of control, truthfully. You've got hundreds of journalists – it was gigantic – and Moscow at that time. No one had ever done this before.'

Stay Alive

The journalists flew out Friday and back on Sunday. 'There were hundreds of them,' says Bruce, 'and the minute they got on the plane, they just got pissed.'

They stayed at the Hotel Rossiya, at one time the largest hotel in the world with almost 4,000 rooms. 'It was like a spy movie,' says Alan. 'You weren't allowed a key to your room. There was a lady on each floor, an older lady sitting there and she would give you a wooden key.

'I checked into my room and it was like a cell. Tiny. I switched on this flickering black-and-white TV and the only channel had live combine-harvester racing from the Ukraine. It was another world.'

Bruce, meanwhile, was far more suspicious. 'The hotel rooms had old record players in them. It was like, "Why? You can't even buy records here".' He started raking around in the cupboards and drawers and found 'these little electronic things'. They were being bugged.

'It was like the old Michael Caine, Harry Palmer films,' he says.

The food was so bad that Bruce struggled to eat anything and was delighted when the promoter, a guy called Stas Namin ('He was like the Russian version of Bruce Springsteen') offered to buy them dinner at the Hard Rock Café in Gorky Park.

'We went to Gorky Park,' Bruce says, 'and it was just this big shed with "Hard Rock Café" painted on the side. The food was horrendous.'

'Hard Rock Café?' said Stuart. 'Fucking Hard *Luck* Café.'

Music journalist Paul Elliott was one of the press pack. Elliott had interviewed Big Country for his first cover story for *Sounds* at their Rockpalast show in March 1986 and had gotten to know them a little in the years afterwards.

'Stuart was a delightful bloke who could not have been more friendly to me as a very young writer,' says Paul. 'He was a good laugh, very approachable. He could see the funny side of things. Sandy Robertson was a Scottish writer who gave me my job on *Sounds*. On my first day, I turned up and Sandy was vomiting into a bin. He said to me, "Give me twenty minutes. I've just got to review the singles."'

Stuart had asked Paul: 'Who's that guy, Sandy Robertson? That fucker wrote a three-word review of "Look Away".'

The three words were: 'More crusading porridge'.

'But Stuart thought it was funny,' says Paul. 'I don't imagine Bono would have taken it in quite the same spirit.'

So Elliott was looking forward to hanging out with Big Country. It soon became obvious that there was no chance. The whole thing was a circus – a vodka-fuelled media pile-on. 'Keith Altham was coordinating,' he says, 'and he was a total ballbag to me. He was probably under a lot of pressure and dealing with some of the big beasts of Fleet Street. It looked like Big Country's focus was to get in proper media, not the music press.'

Later, he found a note pushed under his hotel room door. It was from Stuart, saying, 'Sorry I haven't been able to say hello.'

'I think he looked at me and the music press as a sort of friend – a friendly face among a lot of jaded old hacks. The Russia trip was mostly the mainstream media, so he probably just decided to lock himself away. He would probably have preferred to talk to a few people about music, rather than "What do you think about Gorbachev and Reagan?"'

The PR strategy was indeed to get them out of the music press and take it to the mainstream, says Alan Edwards. 'My instincts are "Can we get a *Sunday Times Magazine* cover? Can we get a BBC special?" You always want to see where you can take it, but with Stuart there was nowhere *to* take it. He just wasn't going to play that game. So, after a while, you accepted it. We were all in our comfort zone and we didn't really push it. From my point of view, I wasn't able to spread my wings on Big Country's behalf as much as I would have liked to.'

At the first gig, a few minutes into their set there was a power cut, a frequent occurrence in '80s Moscow. 'Come six or seven o'clock at night,' says Bruce, 'the power goes down because that's when people get back from work and start boiling their kettles and turning their cookers on.'

Unfortunately, it coincided with their first song, 'Peace in Our Time'. Peace was thwarted by 5 million kettles – which was a problem for the guy from the *Daily Star* who had written and filed his review before he had even left London. 'He was like, "What a great gig! It was brilliant ..."' No mention of the forty-five-minute wait until power was restored.

At its root, for all the grand ideas about bringing East and West together, Moscow was just a PR stunt. The people of Moscow weren't going to buy Big Country records afterwards – they *couldn't*. It was purely about the media. 'It was a PR thing,' says Alan. 'There were no record shops in Moscow. So the only advantage would have been the hype, if that's the right word. Publicity in the UK, Europe and America – that was the point. So to make that really stick, you needed a star in the middle of it. I actually remember a lot about the trip, but the person I don't remember much about is *Stuart*. Stuart was probably in his room.'

'He was always uncomfortable in social circumstances because he was the centre of attention and he *hated* it,' says Bruce. 'Even at things like the Prince's Trust. Eric Clapton or someone would be there and Stuart would kind of clam up. Alan Edwards was always like, "Right Stuart, let's get a picture with whoever" and he just hated it because he would have to make small talk. And he was *pish* at small talk.'

'If Stuart had been a different personality, he'd have taken charge,' says Alan. 'He'd have been charming. He'd have thought, "Hang on, I'm hosting 100 media here. Forget the manager, I'm gonna make them all think that I'm the greatest and I've got this perception of East–West relations and I'm an incredible songwriter". That's what a Bono would have done.

'But Stuart wasn't that guy and, in a way, Ian had created that incredible project to compensate for that. In every single part of Big Country's career, it's always the same thing: Was Stuart really equipped for that? Was he built to be the ringmaster and take control? And he wasn't.'

An appearance on BBC Scotland's news programme caused a minor upset back home. 'It was a weird one for me,' says Bruce, 'because I wasn't drinking and I couldn't eat the food. I was actually on anti-depressants and I was basically just out of my head.'

The anti-depressants had been prescribed by his doctor. 'I was just going through a bad patch. I just knew there was something no' right with me and I didnae know what. I never really spoke to anybody about it.'

Reporting Scotland caught him in Red Square. 'The food's been pretty disgusting,' Bruce told the programme. 'Rat meat. Little bits of meat about that size [gestures about two inches].'

Interviewer: 'What about the music? What about the bands who've been supporting you?'

Bruce [laughing]: 'I've never seen them. I couldnae be ersed watching them, tae tell ye the truth.'

'It was a throwaway comment,' he says now, 'but they bloody used it. Some people thought it was hilarious, but I got a lot of stick for it. People thought I was a bit of a ned.'

They interviewed Stas Namin, the promoter. 'How popular are Big Country in the Soviet Union?' they asked.

Stas Namin: 'Not popular at all. It's a very good group, but when I was trying to promote this group, everybody thought it was country music.' And that was a problem because country music was not very popular in the Soviet Union – 'because "big country" is *too much* country, y'know?'

They interviewed Stuart in front of the Kremlin. 'Does this mean Big Country will sell more records in Russia?' they asked.

Stuart was a pro: generous and diplomatic. 'Our records are not available in the Soviet Union,' he said, 'unless through bootleg tapes, so it's done purely as a gesture of friendship and warmth. Hopefully, what it means is that it opens things up – not only for other bands to come here and play, outwith the state organisation – but for Soviet bands to come and play in western Europe as well.'

But the PR battle was lost. 'Somebody took a picture of the head of Phonogram/Polygram fast asleep,' says Tony. 'So we got the headlines for that. It was all about the head of Polygram being asleep. All these great opportunities for maximum publicity and all of them missed.'

In his memoir *I Was There*, Alan Edwards recalls a meeting with the band after the Moscow gigs. 'How much money did we make?' asks Stuart.

Well, explained Ian, Russian laws meant that profits couldn't actually be taken out of the country as money.

'What exactly *can* they be sent back as?' asked Stuart.

'They suggested tractors,' said Ian.

To add to their woes, the Cult announced that they were leaving Grant-Edwards for a big-shot US manager called Howard Kaufman. 'We were really upset about that,' says Alan, 'because we'd taken them from nowhere to being a big American act, only to get dumped.'

Big Country were falling apart. *Peace in Our Time* had gone to a respectable number 9 in the UK album charts but, more significantly, it only managed number 160 in the US, making it their lowest-selling album in the States. By becoming US-friendly, they had lost much of what had made them unique. Moscow had been a costly clusterfuck. And now the Cult were betraying them. Ian Grant flipped.

The Cult's guitarist Billy Duffy had been sent to break the news to Ian. 'And Ian went fucking ballistic,' says Bruce. 'He chased Billy out of the office. He was going to kill him. Billy had left his camera equipment in there, so Ian grabbed his camera bag and chucked it in the toilet – he tried to flush a fucking camera doon the toilet!

'Anyway, he's still raging, so he goes out looking for Billy. Billy had this black Jeep and Ian saw it parked across the road. He went and got something – I would say a cricket bat, but that's Spinal Tap [according to Alan Edwards' book, it was a scaffolding pole] – and he smashes the fuck out of this Jeep.

'But it wasn't *Billy's* Jeep ...'

It was the end of Grant-Edwards. 'Ian and I were sort of done at that moment,' says Alan. 'Everything was falling apart. There was no money. We weren't sure we could pay the rent in the office. It actually collapsed. Ian was struggling with it, so he took time off and Grant-Edwards just fell apart. It was astonishing because we'd been a really successful management company with a PR company. You couldn't have imagined it. It all happened almost overnight.

'Big Country were going down, the Moscow thing had lost money, the Cult had dumped us. I think Ian and I both regretted that we didn't stick it out – we'd have probably ended up managing Robbie Williams or someone. But we didn't. And Ian effectively left the business for a while. John Giddings looked out for me. He gave me a room in his office in Fulham and I carried on and I rebuilt from there.'

Alan's company The Outside Organisation built a client list that included David Bowie, the Spice Girls, Blondie, Prince, Britney Spears, Robbie Williams, Amy Winehouse, David Beckham, Naomi Campbell and more.

In 2024, he was at the Sunset Marquis, the famous rock 'n' roll hotel in Los Angeles, with one of his clients and he thought of Stuart. 'The Sunset Marquis is where we used to stay with Big Country,' he says. Bruce Springsteen was there with his band, now all in their seventies. 'Stuart would have fitted in very well. It would have been a very natural environment for him.'

He compares Stuart's appeal to Springsteen's: a blue-collar musician singing about the working man, unpretentious and heartfelt. 'He could have done Bruce,' says Alan. 'I saw Bruce's first-ever gig in the UK at Hammersmith Odeon. I wasn't that blown away, personally. He's okay. I mean, I *still* think he's okay. I saw him last year [2023] at Hyde Park and he played three hours and it was incredible. But, really, it was just decent songs and a hell of a stage performance.

'Stuart could have easily done that. Maybe he could have done it *better*. And you know what? If you asked Springsteen, *he* would say that Stuart could have done it. He would know Big Country. And I'm sure Bono would say that too. I know he would. I mean, the Edge *has* said it. I'm sure they all say it.

'Everything about Stuart, when you think about it, is so sad because he's a guy out of time. A very nice man, a lovely soul. In those moments when he opened up, a beautiful man. Very talented, but just in the wrong thing at the wrong time.

'And it was nobody's fault. Not his, nobody's.'

22

Life at the Tappie Toorie

The baw bursts. Smashie and Nicey. Acres of pop shit.
The Sheep Shaggers vs America.
Throwing up on Led Zeppelin

One by one, people were giving up on Big Country. First among them was Stuart Adamson himself.

They went out on the road in the first half of 1989, with a bigger band, including two female backing singers and a keyboard player. 'The keyboards overpowered the guitars,' says Bruce. 'Everyone had long, heavy rock hairdos, apart from Stuart. It all got a bit '80s.'

Adamson decided he'd had enough. 'Stuart said, "I'm fucking sick of this. I'm leaving,"' says Bruce. The last gig was in Jersey and he told them all, 'I'm leaving after Jersey.'

'He said, "The ball's burst,"' says Mark. 'He said, "It's gone over the fence and it ain't coming back. I'm done. I can't do any more for this band. It's reached its final conclusion. There's nothing more this band can achieve."'

'We sat there – me, Tony and Bruce – with our jaws dropped,' says Mark. 'He also wrote me a note – I think he wrote one to everyone – saying, "Nothing's going to change. Please don't try and influence me, go ahead and do whatever you want to do. We're done."'

Mark put the feelers out and got session work with Simon Townshend and Fish. It meant that, by the time Big Country got back together, he 'physically couldn't do it. I'd made commitments.'

It wasn't completely upsetting, he told *Modern Drummer* magazine. 'I'd been very disappointed when Big Country split up, but I felt that I'd been to the funeral and I now wanted to look forward to other things.'

They got a new drummer in Pat Ahern and started demoing tracks. Bruce had met producer Tim Palmer in LA and, as a fan of the Palmer-produced Robert Plant album *Now and Zen*, approached him about working with Big Country. They did two singles – 'Heart of the World' and 'Save Me' – with Ahern on drums, produced by Palmer, engineering by Chris Sheldon.

After those, Dave Bates threw in the towel too.

'Dave Bates kinda washed his hands with us at that point,' says Bruce. 'There was a big bust-up at the studio between him and Ian, cursing and swearing at each other. He'd had enough of us.'

Being responsible for Big Country was a thankless task. 'King of Emotion' had taken them back into the top 20, but now the band were struggling to make the top 40. 'Save Me' reached number 41, while 'Heart of the World' peaked at number 50. Bates put a young guy called Russ Conway in charge.

He lasted just months. Phonogram were the next people to leave. In May 1990, the label released a greatest hits album called *Through a Big Country* (which went to number 2 and stayed in the charts for seventeen weeks) and then dropped the band before their next album.

'That whole period was tainted by the shadow of the whole Russian thing,' says Tony. '*Peace in Our Time* really took its toll on the band. We could always tour, we could always sell out theatres, but there was this lack of high-end business motivation. I don't know how Stuart dealt with that. I just see it as a dark period.

'We hadn't progressed like people had expected us to. We were completely derailed by the whole *Peace in Our Time* episode and no consideration was taken into what sort of complexion the next album should take – just "Send them down to Rockfield and see what they come up with."

'There was no interest from Phonogram and it was obvious. I've no idea what happened to the Americans after *Peace in Our Time*. I think they were totally put off by the Russian escapade.

'Managing Big Country at the time must have been a nightmare for Ian. *No Place Like Home* [their fifth studio album] – the whole thing seemed like a non-event. I can't even remember half of the songs, to be honest. We went back to Rockfield to recreate old glories, but what was coming back from the record company daily was just off-putting. There was so much apathy in the air.

'It wasn't a very nice time to be involved with the band. It was just hard work. To be honest, I don't know how Stuart survived it.'

While Ian shopped for a new deal, the band were demoing new material. Bruce had moved to Charlestown on the Firth of Forth. Charlestown had another famous resident – Manny Charlton, guitarist for Nazareth – and the two started working together. Bruce had the music for the song that became 'Republican Party Reptile' and Manny programmed the drums and added its distinctive slide guitar part.

'I had this Billy Gibbons, ZZ Top thing in my head – "I hope you like it!"' Stuart did like it and wrote some verses. The lyrics were inspired by the book of the same name by gonzo journalist PJ O'Rourke, a collection of hedonistic travelogues and piss-takes of a world gone to shit. 'You could never admit to being like that,' Stuart told *Melody Maker*. 'But to know someone like that – someone who just wants to get wasted and laid and wants a career in politics as well – would be brilliant.'

Stuart learned to play slide so he could play Manny's part and, for a while, Charlton was in the frame to produce. The Nazareth man had produced the demos for Guns N' Roses' *Appetite For Destruction* – Axl Rose was a big Naz fan – but he didn't get the gig. *Appetite For Destruction* became the biggest-selling debut album of all time, so it stung. Bruce wanted to bring him in to produce Big Country.

'It would have taken us away from that '80s keyboard thing,' he says. 'Manny would have rocked it. Manny was great at getting a great vocal take. When he produced the Nazareth albums, he really pushed Dan [McCafferty]. So it was a shame. I was like, "What's wrong with Manny? The guy's a fucking genius!" It might have been a label thing.'

Ian got them a deal with Vertigo and they recorded *No Place Like Home* at Rockfield. Things didn't work out with Pat Ahern, says Bruce, so they got Mark back as a session drummer just for the album – 'which was very odd,' says Mark, 'because it was no different to me being in the band except I couldn't commit to doing the tour.'

'Mark came back as a session player,' says Bruce, 'but because he hadn't been involved in the rehearsals, and the songs were done before he got there, he was kind of told what to play. In fact, years later he told me that Ian didn't even pay him for the session.'

The music scene was changing. Acid house had influenced guitar music, with bands like the Stone Roses and Happy Mondays bringing a looser, psychedelic groove to their music. Bruce remembers the A&R guy during the *No Place Like Home* sessions trying to get Mark to change a drum part to make it more 'baggy'. 'He wanted to make it a bit more contemporary, with Mark playing a sort of Stone Roses groove.'

'I would have ignored that,' says Mark. 'I would never be told how to play the drums. The writing was heading in a different direction then, but my drumming was the same delivery.'

Producer Pat Moran had a classic rock pedigree – he had been assistant engineer on Queen's *A Night at the Opera* album, had engineered Rush's *A Farewell to Kings* and had produced Iggy Pop, Robert Plant and more – and that gelled with where the band were at that time. 'He was great,' says Bruce. 'I loved him. A great producer.'

'The Beautiful People' lopes along like a Faces number. 'Republican Party Reptile' is ZZ Top gone feral. 'Ships' is a classic torch song, with Bruce Hornsby-style piano. They recorded it twice: a full-band version and a stripped-down take. The stripped-down version made it to the album.

Overall, *No Place Like Home* feels like an album from the '70s.

'I love the production, I love the songs,' says Bruce. 'The problem is that it sounds like four different bands.'

The way he remembers it, they were influenced by British TV comedy programme *Harry Enfield's Television Programme*. A recurring sketch featured two old-school rock DJs called Smashie and Nicey, played by Harry Enfield and Paul Whitehouse, and there was a spin-off compilation album called *Let's Rock* that the band listened to constantly. 'It was stuff like

Bachman Turner Overdrive, Jo Jo Gunne and Deep Purple, and we used to play it in the studio all the time. So our album ended up a bit like a '70s album – but it sounded like three or four different bands.'

In fact, *Let's Rock* was released in 1992, after *No Place Like Home*, but it probably shows you where Big Country's head was at for a couple of years – defiantly anti-fashion, in love with huge, timeless rock songs. The complete lack of EBow or 'bagpipe guitar' made it look a bit like a band renouncing its past.

Melody Maker's album review painted a picture of a band running, embarrassed, from its roots. 'For the rest of the world, it's a joke,' Caren Myers wrote about the 'bagpipe guitars' tag, 'but for Stuart Adamson, it's an obsession. If Adamson were on his deathbed with the priest approaching, his last words would be, "Don't mention the bagpipes!"'

And then there was three. A Big Country promo shot from the time.

Stay Alive

The review ended with the line, 'No place like the bin.'

No Place Like Home stalled at number 28 in the UK album charts – the first Big Country album not to make the top 10.

Mark had other commitments – he played with Sting on the Soul Cages tour, did an album with Procol Harum – so Chris Bell, the original drummer for Spear Of Destiny, joined them on tour. They knew Chris from way back. 'He had the right attitude,' says Bruce, 'and he comes from that kinda punk background. He's not a technician, just a proper old-school drummer. It was good, it fitted.'

It was an opportunity for another course-correction. Keyboard player Colin Berwick joined at the same time, on Hammond and piano. 'We said, "None of this synthesiser shite,"' says Bruce. '"It's gonna be organic."'

What looks like an unhappy time from the outside – bad reviews and falling chart positions, a band slipping out of fashion – was actually a good time in the Adamson household.

Sandra had gone off to America to earn a qualification in aerobics and fitness, and became the first in the UK to receive it. 'Stuart was coming to all my classes,' she says, 'and we were in the gym a lot. He would come to a lot of Kirsten's dance competitions, literally being the family dad, and enjoying it for a long, long period.'

This is the source of Kirsten's first memories of her dad. 'My mum was away in San Diego at an aerobics convention,' says Kirsten, 'and maybe I remember that because it was the first time she wasn't at home. But we were at Balmule and the memory is just my dad playing with Barbies with me.'

Callum, three years older, has more detailed memories of Stuart. 'I remember a lot of airport departure lounges, saying goodbye,' he says. 'I remember the smell of leather jackets, cuddling him goodbye. I remember the tears in the car park. I still cannot fucking stand those little coffee shops in airports before you go through the security. That is just pure PTSD for me. I remember him making me mow the lawn so that I could earn the money to go get my first pair of football boots.'

All pretty regular stuff – except the lawn to be mowed was the one at Balmule. 'This is the problem with having working-class parents who have working-class values but middle-class shit,' he says. '"You need to earn your football boots." That's fine, but usually when you get a kid to cut the grass, it's a back garden – it's not fucking Wembley Stadium.'

The kids went to regular state schools. On his first day there, someone asked Callum for his autograph. 'I didn't know what an autograph was, so I wrote down my address' (Sandra had made him learn his address in case he got lost). 'When your dad's on *Top of the Pops* and you go to school with scaffolders' kids and plumbers' kids, you get in a lot of fights.'

After school, while the other kids waited for the bus, a big red BMW would come for Callum. He just wanted to blend in. 'It was embarrassing. And we were kind of *raised* to be embarrassed about it. You'd go around your mate's house and they'd have just a normal fucking house, and you'd end up idolising that – like, "Why can't we just live in a normal house and be like everybody else?"

'That was the weird thing about them choosing to stay in Dunfermline. They never took advantage of an opportunity that people would kill for – the ability to get out and stay out.'

Stuart and Sandra sold Balmule at the end of 1989. The market was about to crash and the house was huge – 'We lived in one wing of it,' says Sandra – so they downsized, moving to Old Kirk House, the former manse to Dunfermline Abbey. Richard Jobson visited Stuart there and remembers him seeming happy and content. 'I went to his house with my now wife Francesca,' says Richard. 'He was still in Dunfermline, this lovely house down by the glen. His daughter was doing Scottish country dancing and she did a whole thing for us. It was great. He was very proud and he seemed very much at home. It was the last time I saw him.'

Stuart's relationship with his parents was distant – Sandra comments that she 'wouldn't have him [Stuart's dad] in the house, never in a million years' – but it wasn't a problem because he worked abroad most of the time.

Stuart didn't really visit his parents much. 'He kinda thought of *my* family as his family,' says Sandra. 'He went fishing with his dad occasionally, but they never had their tea at our house. They weren't invited for dinner, whereas my mum would come and she'd *make* the dinner. It was a different dynamic.'

Sandra's mum and dad were a normal family household, says Kirsten. 'My dad loved it there. It was just home-cooked dinners and watching *Blind Date* and they always had country music on. They had hundreds and hundreds of tapes of Glen Campbell and all that kind of stuff.' Kirsten is a singer and songwriter now and heavily influenced by country music. It wasn't until her grandfather passed away that she realised that the country music she'd grown up hearing came from her grandparents' house. 'It wasn't from dad playing it. It was from my mum's mum and dad. I don't remember my dad playing music. I don't think he played music at home.

'He was just a normal dad. He never sat and played the guitar in the living room or anything. He completely switched off from the job when he was home. He was just a funny dad. He used to play this game with me and Callum called "zombies". We would have to hide somewhere in the house and you would hear him coming down the hallway and he would catch us and pretend to eat our ears off.

'He used to give us bear hugs, squeezing us as tight as he could. He was dead affectionate. He was always really engaged with me and Callum. He would never just go off to a room and write or anything like that. I think he just loved being at home.'

Stuart found a good routine. He would be out, walking the dogs. He would go fishing and the guys he fished with, says Sandra, were 'the most normal, ordinary souls, who didn't talk to him about anything other than fishing or football. It was a good period for him. He was very healthy.'

He also played football when he could: five-a-side on Thursdays and Sunday league at the weekend. Bobby Drummond and Pubsy remember a time when Big Country were playing Dublin on the Saturday and the team had a match on the Sunday morning. Bobby was the manager and Pubsy was assistant manager. 'I'll be there,' Stuart had told them.

He got the first flight over that morning and arrived minutes before kick-off. They'd been waiting to see his car approaching on the bypass before adding him to the team sheet. Of course, when he arrived, they told him he was too late. 'Sorry Stuart – the team sheet just went in about two minutes ago. We couldnae wait any longer fur ye.'

'He went absolutely mad,' says Bobby. 'Stairted shouting "I told youse I'd be here in time!" We were like, "Calm doon – here's yer shirt."'

Stuart put on his strip and handed Bobby a jiffy bag.

'What's in this?' asked Bobby.

'Huv a look,' said Stuart.

It was full of money. The Dublin gig had been sold out, but the doormen had said, 'How about we let some more in and split the cash?'

'Stuart had said, "Aye – nothing tae dae wi' me",' says Bobby, 'and he'd come back with this jiffy bag fulla money. I don't suppose you could dae it noo, but back in thae days …'

On Sunday 3 June, Big Country played The Big Day, a free festival in Glasgow city centre with the cream of contemporary Scottish acts. Stuart played a game of football that same morning, as Bobby remembers. 'I says, "Are you sure? What happens if you get hurt?" He says, "I'll be awright." I mean, if he'd got hurt in a tackle and couldnae play … It shows you how much he loved his fitba.'

But he wasn't just one of the lads, says Pubsy. 'He was deep an' aw. He would go to the paper shop and buy half a dozen newspapers, just to get ideas. He was very thoughtful. I think he trusted us, big time.'

He trusted them because they didn't want anything from him. They didn't ask him about the band, or use his friendship to elevate themselves. They were just ordinary guys and, when he was with them, Stuart could be ordinary too.

'Ah'll tell ye whit – he was a great friend,' says Pubsy. 'He'd dae anything fur ye and vice versa. If we could help him out in any way, we would.'

'What did we get aff him?' says Bobby. 'A couple of T-shirts and CDs?'

'Aye,' says Pubsy, 'and a loada lip.'

'You'd say, "Gonnae sign this, Stuart?" and he was like, "Ah'm no' signing that!"' says Bobby. 'He was embarrassed because we're his pals. If it was a fan, he'd be like, "Aye, no problem."

'His brother-in-law said to me, "Bobby, youse are his escape route. You dinnae know nothing about the band, really. You go to the gigs, but you dinnae know these people, you dinnae need to know, and you don't care."

'One time in a pub, there was a guy with a guitar doing a few numbers in the corner. They hassled Stuart to get up and do a few songs and, to their surprise, he gave in. Afterwards, the guy laughed and said, "How am I supposed tae follow that?"

'He always said he would never stop playing,' says Bobby. 'He said that to me. He says, "When I'm older, I'll be singing in the clubs on a Sunday afternoon."'

Callum asked Stuart if he would teach him to play guitar. 'No,' he said. 'I taught myself how to play, so you can too.' Callum asked him if he could have one of his guitars to practise on. That was also a no. Instead, he borrowed a guitar from his Uncle Jamie and taught himself how to play from listening to tapes of Led Zeppelin.

'For like, two years, that's all I did in my room,' he says. 'And yet, Kirsten – fifty grand's worth of singing lessons, just as much on guitar and piano lessons, etcetera. It's one of the most puzzling things about the relationship I had with my dad. He never taught me a single thing on guitar, not one thing.'

They never played together in the house. 'I played all the time,' he says, 'but never with him. Odd, isn't it?

'There was a side of my dad that couldn't relate to me as a young man, or a growing man, or educate me as a man. I was a good proxy friend. I was never really a son because I don't think he ever matured enough, or part of him never matured enough, to be an adult.'

Once, after a gig in Jersey, they spotted former Liverpool and Scotland player Kenny Dalglish on the same flight. Stuart went up to him and said, 'Can I have your autograph for my son?'

'You were brilliant last night,' said Kenny.

'You were *there*?'

'Yeah, I was there. I've been to see you seven times.'

Life at the Tappie Toorie

At a game at Everton, Manchester United manager Alex Ferguson made a point of coming over and saying hello to Stuart. That was the kind of thing that gave him a buzz.

Dropped by Vertigo after *No Place Like Home*, there was some good news: Chris Briggs had a label and wanted to sign them. Now sober and working at Chrysalis, the guys in charge had given him his own imprint, a label called Compulsion.

Briggs had little faith in the management at Chrysalis, but was trying to make the best of the situation. '1990 to 1995 was a very difficult time,' he says. 'I'm sober, so I'm sensible, but it just didn't work. Me going back to Chrysalis was a mistake.'

But he had his own label and Big Country were available. It was welcome news in both camps, but Briggs was under no illusion: Big Country were a band out of time. The week after they released *No Place Like Home*, a little-known American band called Nirvana released their second album, *Nevermind*. Its effect had been seismic.

Briggs was the A&R for Def Leppard, although his fellow A&R man David Rose was much friendlier with the Sheffield band. Rose called Briggs and said, 'Joe Elliott called me last night. He said, "Have you heard 'Smells Like Teen Spirit'? Listen to it. That's the end for us. We're *fucked*. That's rock music as we know it dead in the water."'

'It'd been very difficult for a long time for British bands to do anything that could be called "rock",' says Briggs. 'So if it didn't work in America, you were kind of beached.'

Big Country were exactly that: *beached*.

Still, they had a load of new songs that seemed to fit with this new climate. 'We ended up going quite rock,' says Bruce. 'It was the same time as grunge, so a lot of the songs, like "Alone", ended up being quite heavy.'

Bruce and Tony became a rock bulwark against Stuart's increasing drift into country music. 'Bruce and I got quite close during [sixth album] *The Buffalo Skinners* because we still had a similar musical direction,' says Tony. 'He didn't want to go back into the blues string-bending stuff, and he didn't want to go down the country and western route that Stuart was going in. We just wanted guitars to ring out loud and to be as melodic as possible.'

'The songs Stuart was writing were great,' says Bruce, 'but they weren't Big Country songs. It felt like he should be writing them for other people. There's a country template – the slow BPM, everything's in G – and I think Tony and I sometimes did them a disservice 'cos our heart wasnae in it.'

Bruce was the principal writer of the song 'Seven Waves' and it gave Tony faith that they still had it in them. 'It was almost like getting back into shape,' he says. 'I thought it was a great little song. Stuart played a good part on it and it was great to play live.'

They decided to record *The Buffalo Skinners* at RAK, another blast from the past, but this time self-producing the album with Chris Sheldon engineering. Mark wasn't available, so Briggs suggested Simon Phillips, a fusion drummer who'd worked with Jeff Beck and had just toured with the Who. But Phillips was only available for two or three days, so there was no time for rehearsal. He turned up at RAK and did all the songs, first or second take.

After the drummer had gone and they got further into overdubbing, they hit a technical problem. They were recording to analogue tape and a fault had meant that the guitars had recorded at the wrong speed.

'We had to scrap every guitar, every overdub,' says Bruce. Apart from the drums, they had to re-record the whole album again.

Chris Briggs suggested that they re-record two songs from *No Place Like Home*: 'We're Not in Kansas' and 'Ships'. '"Kansas" was one of his favourite songs and he wished he'd worked on it,' says Bruce. 'And he loved "Ships", but Briggs is a rocker – he wanted us to get the guitars out.'

The newer songs painted a typically bleak Stuart Adamson view of the world. 'What Are You Working For', 'Long Way Home' and 'All Go Together' covered a world on the brink of disaster – corruption, climate change and televangelists – while the more ostensibly personal lyrics are about isolation and loneliness. 'I feel alone inside my head,' goes *The Buffalo Skinners*' opener and lead single 'Alone'. 'Alone inside my tiny little world.'

'The One I Love' – musically upbeat and hooky – is a frustrated love song about love fading and people changing. The person I love, Stuart suggests, is still in there somewhere, 'but I don't have the time that I used to.'

And on 'Seven Waves' he – or the narrator of the song – contemplates suicide. 'The things I hid away for all those years, have faded now or died,' he sings. 'It doesn't hurt anymore, it doesn't get me down, but I might just swim out on the waves tonight, and lay right down and drown.'

Released in April 1993, *The Buffalo Skinners* reached number 25 in the UK album chart, only three places higher than *No Place Like Home*.

'In hindsight, I think we made a great record in the wrong year,' says Briggs. 'People just weren't pointed that way. I sometimes torture myself by watching BBC4 reruns of *Top of the Pops*. I think, "Jesus fuck, it was worse than I thought. Look at this shit. Acres and acres of shit pop music". These things go in cycles. Simple Minds, U2, Big Country – they all fitted together and made sense culturally and then suddenly they didn't.

'Myself and Ian still believed. We put a lot of effort in. We flew to America and I played that album to a lot of people. But people were listening to Nirvana and Pearl Jam.'

In the US, *The Buffalo Skinners* came out on Fox, a short-lived imprint of 20th Century Fox. The band went out on the road, playing Germany and the UK before heading to the US in September.

'They were fantastic live around then,' says Briggs. 'Probably better than ever. But it just seems to edge out of sync with the audience somehow. That's not Stuart's fault. There are some artists who are more market aware – bands like U2 that have the ability to tailor their art to fit the culture. Stuart wasn't that person. Stuart would have to do what Stuart would have to do. He's not studying the culture to work out where he fits into it.

'There was a period in the '80s where what he wanted to do just naturally resonated with an audience. That's rare. He could just be true to himself and there was an audience for it. It had to feel right to him or he couldn't do it. I've met loads of artists like that and they quite often have very successful but quite short careers. It doesn't mean their music's shit. It just means they're not making music that reaches a big audience. Where does it say that you deserve a gigantic audience? Nowhere.'

Mark came back to Big Country. They needed someone who could play like Simon Phillips 'and Mark's the only person that can dae it,' says Bruce. 'Mark idolises Simon Phillips.'

The drummer kept his session career running parallel to the band. They'd tour Germany, come home for a week and, in that time, says Bruce, 'Mark would have done a mini tour with Procol Harum, or Midge Ure or Fish or Bernie Marsden's Whitesnake. It was like, "Is there five Mark Brzezickis?"'

When Mark did interviews, people would ask him why he'd left in the first place. It left him in a weird spot: Ian Grant had asked him not to reveal that Stuart had split the band, so the story became about him having opportunities to play elsewhere. It made him look less committed. 'There was no talk about a break-up,' he says, 'so it was just always on me all the time. I was never less committed. But I wasn't married – the others had families to go back to. And when I stop, I still want to play ... It's always been a little black mark against me. "What did you leave for?" But I never *quit*.'

They played the US for almost three months, basing themselves in New York, commuting to gigs and driving back at night. They played in New Jersey at the Stone Pony and the Wonder Bar, the legendary venues that had helped make Bruce Springsteen. They were good times.

'I loved it,' says Bruce. 'The gigs were just amazing. We kinda got a spark back. We were really on top of our game, doing the earlier songs and the hits, but doing all *The Buffalo Skinners* stuff. And we were doing a lot of sort of things like "Oh Well" by Fleetwood Mac and Neil Young's "Hey, Hey, My My" – stuff like that.'

One night in Detroit, the house PA broke down. They had acoustic guitars that they were using to play at radio stations during the day. 'So we said, "Fuck it, let's just do it acoustically,"' says Bruce. 'Even that worked.' The acoustic sets went down so well that it became a regular thing, captured at the end of the year on the *Without a Safety Net* live album and DVD. 'We thought, "Why don't we support ourselves?"' says Bruce. 'We called ourselves the Sheep Shaggers. We'd do a forty-minute acoustic set and say, "We're the Sheep Shaggers. Big Country'll be on in a minute!"'

It was effortless, fun, and it made Bruce optimistic. 'I just felt like, "Oh, this could happen again",' he says. 'After *The Crossing–Steeltown*, *The Buffalo Skinners* is probably my second-favourite period. Briggs has got a lot to do with that. Ian having a working creative relationship with Briggsy helped. Ian and Bates was just conflict.'

In June 1994, the Adamsons moved from Dunfermline to Orlando, for a year in the sun. Stuart had a US visa, 'so he was literally commuting from the States,' says Sandra. Callum played in a great soccer team that got to the state cup finals, Kirsten was in the Orlando Opera's kids company and going to Disney Club classes, and Sandra was teaching at a local gym. She drove 80,000 miles in a year. 'We were very, very busy,' she says. When Stuart was at home – Big Country were on the road in Europe in June, July and September – they'd get up at six every morning to go rollerblading and then get down the gym.

Yeah, *rollerblading*.

It sounds both comical and idyllic. Callum, then twelve, sees it differently. 'Florida was absolute fucking misery,' he says. 'Completely alienating and psychologically tough. Really, really, really hard. Because my dad wasn't there. None of my friends were there.

'And, probably because of how young my parents were, they never explained anything. Never took the time to talk to us and help us understand why we were doing anything, or how long we'd be there. There's no resentment from me – I'm very grateful for the upbringing I had and the parents I had – but fucking hell, man.'

Their move back to Dunfermline in June 1995 coincided with the release of a new album, on yet another record label: *Why the Long Face?*

The way Bruce remembers it, they did demos of the new album for Compulsion but Briggs rejected them. 'He was quite right,' he says. 'I think Briggsy said, "We need more songs" and Stuart said he wasnae gonnae write any more. Numerically, we had enough songs, but they weren't good enough.'

But it wasn't like that, says Briggs. 'They got dropped over my head,' he says. Management at Chrysalis had changed. EMI had bought the label and they wanted him to work on EMI, not Chrysalis.

'I was the only person in the building who wanted to keep Big Country,' he says. 'I tried to help them for as long as I could with *Why the Long Face?*, but at this point, 1995, I think I'm gonna get fired. It hasn't worked out.'

When the founder of the Ensign label, Nigel Grainge, left, Briggs was given his roster, which meant he had World Party, the Waterboys and Sinéad O'Connor to look after. Maybe the bosses at EMI thought he only had room for one tortured Celt in his roster. Big Country's contract was cancelled.

'Stuart didn't have much showbiz in him,' says Briggs. 'He was a musician – a very talented musician. Maybe in the late '60s, early '70s, you could be like Stuart, with the right manager and still have a career and not be interested in playing the game. But from MTV onwards, and now more than ever, it changed. You get artists now saying, "Do I have to do Instagram?" You do, mate. Stuart is that person, but back then.

'It's not that he's *awkward*. In all the years I've been doing this, "awkward" artists are what they call the ones that can't do media. The TV promotion person would say, "Your artist's awkward." It means they've been on Jonathan Ross, got on the sofa and the chat was a bit stiff. Well, not everyone's good at it. Just because you're a good musician, it doesn't mean that you're Mr Life and Soul of the party.

'Go to lunch with Bob Geldof and he'll entertain the table. It's just who he is. But Stuart was not that guy. Stuart was much more introverted. He'd refer to himself as "Tortured Tommy". He used those words to me – "I'm a bit Tortured Tommy". And he was. But that's not abnormal. You can get to the point where you think it's just you who's like that. But *everyone's* like that. Everyone's riddled with insecurity.

'It's not uncommon,' says Briggs. 'A lot of people get isolated in that and I think Stuart was one of them. Sadly.'

Ian inked a deal with Castle Records. Castle had built their business around CD reissues of old albums the majors weren't interested in. They had reanimated Transatlantic, famous as a folk label in the '60s and '70s, and had some money to invest in what record companies call 'frontline': new releases.

So Big Country ended up on Castle. They had little choice. 'We'd been through all the labels,' says Ian. But it soon became obvious that Castle wasn't quite set up for new releases. 'It was a different science to putting out a catalogue album than a frontline.'

'We ended up with a second-rate record company,' says Tony. 'You felt the empire collapsing. They weren't really a record company – they were just poking their toe in the water by taking us on. *Why the Long Face?* – it was almost like "Why are we doing this?" Big Country was on its backside. The only way that we could have carried on was to tour like we had done in the earlier years. But there was no motivation to do that.'

They recorded at RAK again, with Chris Sheldon co-producing. '"*Why the Long Face?*" is my least favourite album,' says Bruce. 'It's trying to be *Buffalo Skinners Part II* but the songs weren't quite there.'

Stuart suggested the album sleeve and title – a picture of a dog with a long face, presumably a comment on Big Country's reputation among critics for lyrical misery. 'It was quite funny at the time,' says Tony, 'but we grew to hate it. It was an old joke. So you immediately started to dismiss the album because you've lost interest in its physical appearance.

'I can't name one track on it,' he says. 'It was a non-event. I didn't know what to do. I didn't know where to turn. I didn't know whether I wanted to continue being in a band or if it was just flogging a dead horse.'

There was a slight nod to their Celtic rock roots. Bruce put some EBow down on the intro to 'One in a Million', while a member of the Pogues, James McNally, played whistle on the intro to 'God's Great Mistake' and Stuart's voice took on the lilt of a Scottish folk singer.

The lyrics gave more insight into Stuart's internal life. 'The tank is empty,' he sings on 'You Dreamer'. 'A wheel came off/How can someone find me if no one knows I'm lost … Oh you dreamer, is this the way that you believed your life was gonna turn out?'

On 'Far From Me to You', he talks about the distance between people:

'Listening in the darkness, to a voice I call my own, shameful that my emptiness, is turning me to stone.'

'I'm Not Ashamed' conjures with ideas of guilt, broken promises and a tempestuous home life: 'Our little house is where the wind has always blown/Our little garden on a bed of sand and stones … It took too long for me to be who I am, maybe it's enough for me to be it when I can.' And 'Blue on a Green Planet' appears to be about the end of a relationship: 'Some people say you have to change to stay the same/I guess we tried so hard to stay the same we changed.'

It was hard not to see some of the lyrics as a reflection of his home life. Sandra and Stuart had been trying to make things work, but were growing further apart. 'When we moved back from Florida, it was a weird situation,' says Callum. 'We were living in a flat and he didn't move back in. When we came back from Florida, family life had ceased.'

Stuart and Sandra had been leading separate lives for a while. 'The two of us – well, it was me, really – we were drifting apart,' says Sandra.

One incident triggered something in her. Stuart was travelling back from somewhere and wouldn't get home until the early hours. Sandra woke to the sound of a car pulling up outside.

'I looked out the window,' she says, 'and it was a woman dropping him off. I don't think there was anything in it. I said to him, "Who dropped you off?" He said it was one of the air stewardesses from the British Midlands flight.'

She believed him, but it bothered her. It was a trigger.

'I knew then that the damage that had been done in the drinking years was still with me,' she says. 'He knew that he'd done a lot of damage, but I don't think he felt like me.

'It was me, really. We were just doing the best we could from then on.'

Released in June 1995, *Why the Long Face?* went to number 48 in the album charts and, like the three albums that preceded it, stayed in the charts for just two weeks. They hit the road in support of the album, playing a ton of in-stores – appearances at chart-eligible record shops like Virgin Megastore,

HMV, Tower Records – where they'd play acoustically and sign albums. Stuart hated them. 'I used to dread him getting a schedule through or Ian phoning,' says Sandra. 'I can remember the roaring and shouting at Ian and then he would come off the phone and be really mad. The in-stores were the worst.'

Maybe they triggered some bad memories from previous tours of the US. 'We did a lot of in-stores when we went to America,' says Tony. 'It was very Spinal Tap – going to a record store and Artie Fufkin from the record label was there to greet you, trying to shove stuff up your nose and be your best friend, and then there's five people in the store because we're in Bumfuck, Nowhere.'

In July, they picked up some proper dates, supporting Page & Plant for four nights in England and Ireland, including a memorable night in Dublin. Mark had food poisoning. They were halfway through the first song when Bruce heard 'the worst drum fill you've ever heard in your life. It sounded like somebody just chucked a drum kit down the stairs. I turned to look at Mark and he's gone. He knocked his snare drum over and ran like fuck.

'He got as far as Jimmy Page's first Marshall amp and he puked right down the back of it.'

Unable to do the set without a drummer, they got their acoustic guitars and did the show unplugged.

At the end of the night, they went up to Page's guitar tech Lionel. 'Hey,' they said, 'sorry about Mark throwing up on Jimmy's amp.'

'Don't worry about it,' said Lionel. 'Makes a change from Jimmy doing it.'

In August, they picked up an even bigger support slot, touring with the Rolling Stones across Europe. 'It was the best tour I've ever been on,' says Bruce. 'The Stones were great with us.' They knew a lot of the Stones' crew, including Joe Seabrook, with a constant party going on behind the scenes.

Before the show, Keith and Ronnie would be playing snooker, smoking over the table, taking ages to play because they're stoned off their faces. 'It was funny as fuck,' says Bruce. 'Keith's dad, Bert, came to one of the gigs and Keith put his joint behind his back and passed it to Ronnie 'cos he didn't want to smoke a joint in front of his dad.

'It was one of the best times I've had in my life,' he says. 'You cannae get any better than being on tour with the Stones. They're just so normal, y'know? Abnormally normal.'

Back in Dunfermline, Sandra bought a pub in the centre of town and named it Tappie Toories. The name was old Scots for a pinnacle – the very top. The pub itself had no pinnacle – a bit like Big Country, its roof was falling in. 'I could stand at the bottom and look three storeys up at the sky,' she says. 'It needed a total refurb.'

Stuart's mentality had shifted. When he was home and playing guitar, Sandra noticed that it was now in a 'country-rock style'. In his head, the band was over and he was moving into a different stage of his career – maybe less performing, more songwriting.

He wanted to end Big Country completely, but Sandra urged him to keep the door open. Apart from anything, she could see the effect that splitting the band could have on the other members.

'He was all for just finishing it,' she says. 'I said, "Go off and do whatever you want, but don't say it's finished." I was trying to keep it alive as long as possible.'

Their relationship was in a similar limbo. They didn't say it was finished, but they knew it was over.

Ian Grant knew change was needed. 'I was thinking, "I've got to get him out of Dunfermline. He can't get inspired by the same things – his roots, the working class, his wife, he needs a new challenge".'

It's not LA, he thought. It's not New York. Then it hit him.

'Stuart,' he said one day. 'How about going to Nashville?'

Stuart, Kirsten, Callum and Sally, Christmas in Orlando, 1994.

23

The Great Divide

The great rock 'n' roll swindle.
New starts in Nashville. Drinking in Damascus

Stuart and Ian went to Nashville in January 1996. 'I set a load of meetings up with different heads of record companies,' says Ian. 'They all knew who he was. They all knew *the song*.'

They gave them some advice: you're not going to make it in Nashville by putting a cowboy hat on and coming once or twice. You've got to keep coming and do all the songwriters' nights. He would have to consider moving out there.

Another voiced an idea that excited both Ian and Stuart. 'I want to put country and Celtic back together,' he said, 'and see what happens.'

Big Country's next project seemed to reflect that vision. In March, they played a couple of nights at Dingwalls in London. Recorded and released later that year as *Eclectic*, the set was a mix of roots music, a combination of Big Country originals and cover versions, performed unplugged with an extended band that included tabla players Mohammed Toufiq and Hossam Ramzy – who had played with Peter Gabriel and Page & Plant ('We called them the Egyptian Magicians,' says Bruce) – Keith Emerson's son Aaron Emerson on keyboards, violin player Bobby Valentino, singer Kym Mazelle, Cockney Rebel legend Steve Harley and Scottish singer-songwriter Carol Laula.

Stay Alive

For something that had, in Bruce's words, 'kind of evolved out of us being the Sheep Shaggers', the music of *Eclectic* was fun and energised and seemed to point to a way for Big Country to balance its electric rock roots with roots music generally. Later in 1996, they toured the show a little, with a revolving cast.

It would be the last Big Country activity until May 1998.

'We were playing smaller venues,' says Bruce. 'The wages were going down, we were getting dropped by different labels and Stuart was going out to Nashville and writing with other people. The writing was on the wall. Things were changing.

'I didn't do anything to try and make it better,' he admits. He formed a band, the Wild Blue Yonder, but it was nothing serious.

'I was a wee bit lost,' he says.

'This was the period where it looked like Stuart might just be walking away from everything,' says Sandra. When he was home, he was helping out at the pub, Callum was playing football and Kirsten was going to singing lessons and dance classes. But, at the same time, he was planning an uncertain future in Nashville.

'So this is where it gets difficult for me,' she says. 'Because then we get the Nashville-bound Stuart, which is something I encouraged.'

Nashville had become real. His few trips out there had taught him that what they said was true: you couldn't make it there by just visiting once or twice. He would have to move. Sandra supported it. Their relationship was ending, the kids were older and he was used to commuting halfway across the world and living out of a bag. The kids would come over on their holidays and he'd be back regularly. On 'Post Nuclear Talking Blues', ostensibly a fun throwaway number on *Why the Long Face?*, he'd sung: 'I better give myself a talking to/I better work out what I'm going to do/Maybe get myself a wife, better get myself a life.'

He was making the lyric real.

Kirsten has two distinct memories of her dad at the last house they lived in together in Dunfermline. Stuart's friend, the footballer Norrie McCathie, had been found dead, aged thirty-four, along with his twenty-six-year-old girlfriend, Amanda Burns, both the victims of carbon monoxide poisoning. 'It was one of the only times I'd seen my dad cry,' says Kirsten. She got her pet hamster and put it on Stuart's shoulder to cheer him up. 'I remember him saying, "Oh, thanks, hen." That's actually one of the only times I can remember my dad being sad.'

The other memory is from just before Stuart moved to Nashville. 'It was one of the only times I remember him sitting with a guitar,' she says. 'He said to me, "Do you want to write a song?" The two of them sat together and wrote a song, and that same night they went to Tappie Toories and performed it, along with Stuart's song 'Ships'.

Almost thirty years later, Kirsten was listening to a random Spotify playlist when the song she'd written with her dad came out of the speakers. It was only then she realised that they *hadn't* written it – it had existed all along. The song was also called 'Ships' and had been written by former Mott the Hoople frontman Ian Hunter in 1979.

'Honestly,' she says, 'I was convinced that we had written that song.'

Hunter had written 'Ships' about the distant relationship he'd had with his own (Scottish) father. 'We walked to the sea, just my father and me,' goes the lyric, 'I said love's easier when it's far away …'

Love's easier when it's far away. Maybe he was trying to convince himself of that. Stuart Adamson – family man, Dunfermline boy – was moving to Nashville.

Melanie Shelley was a rising star in the world of celebrity hairdressing. She had been brought up Mormon, in small-town Arizona. At the age of seventeen, a punk kid with crazy hair, she drove out of town and never looked back. In New York, she got a job with Oribe, the Cuban-born hairdresser who was doing *Vogue* editor Anna Wintour's hair. Melanie assisted in his salon and then went out on her own, working for magazines and living abroad for months at a time, doing hair for fashion shows in Paris and Italy.

A huge country music fan and a budding songwriter, Melanie started spending some time in Nashville. 'It was so alternative in the '90s to be into country music that it felt like punk rock,' she says. There, she met the photographer Norman Roy and started styling hair on his shoots. He became one of the biggest photographers of the '90s, shooting for *Vogue, Vanity Fair, GQ* and more, and Melanie started working with Nashville stars like Faith Hill, Tim McGraw and the Dixie Chicks.

She was also the hairdresser of a Nashville guitarist called Rick Elias. Elias and Stuart Adamson played together on an album by Randy Stonehill. The album, *Thirst*, came out in 1998 and Stuart's unmistakable lead guitar is all over the opening track, 'Hand of God'.

In March of 1997, Rick Elias called Melanie and said, 'I've got this friend who really needs a haircut.'

Melanie was busy, but when Rick mentioned that he was in Big Country, she said okay. She wasn't a big fan, but she knew 'In a Big Country' and loved it.

The last thing she was looking for was romance. Two weeks before, she had come back from the Grammys to find out that her long-term boyfriend had cheated on her. 'So I was in a very weird headspace.'

Stuart came to the house, she cut his hair and they clicked. He was stylish, he loved the same music as her – two ex-punks who liked country, they also both loved Bill Burr and edgy comedy. 'And,' she says, 'he was one of the most charismatic people I've ever met in my life.'

Rick Elias picked Stuart up and asked after Melanie's boyfriend. Melanie rolled her eyes. 'Oh my God,' she said. 'He just cheated on me so I kicked his ass out.'

And with perfect timing, Stuart turned around and said, 'So – what are you doing tonight?'

On that first night, Stuart told Melanie he didn't drink and was twelve years sober. 'And that was good for me,' she says. 'Being raised Mormon, I didn't have a lot of exposure to drinking.'

Quite quickly, Stuart inserted himself into her life. 'I mean, there's a modern term for it,' she says. 'It's called love bombing.' Stuart would drive past her house and because she would often be fixing something up and doing her garden, he would stop and help. Melanie had some really wild dogs and Stuart started training them.

The Great Divide

At one point, Melanie had to go to New York for work and, suddenly, Stuart turned up. 'And that really freaked me out,' she says. They had a heart-to-heart, sitting on the floor of a hotel room in New York.

'I just don't think this is it,' Melanie told him. 'I don't think we're a thing.'

Stuart took it. 'But listen,' he said, 'I have to be in your life. I don't care what it is. I'll be your best friend.'

Within a month, they were together.

Soon, Stuart asked Sandra for a divorce. 'I was really reluctant,' she says. 'I was still protective of him. I knew that he'd met Melanie Shelley, but I wondered what the rush was. So I said no, because I wanted to make sure he was thinking straight – and I didn't need a divorce. But then he was back again at some point from Nashville, and he said, "D, I want to stay in America, so I need to get married."

'We were still close. Not romantically, but we were close. We were always close. There was nothing ever going to change that. So I reluctantly said okay. I felt I couldn't say no.

'I know 100 per cent that he never took a drink – ever – until that happened. Until he said that he was going to stay in America.'

In March 1997, EMI Music Publishing offered to buy Big Country's entire back catalogue of songs from the band. The deal they proposed was this: EMI would buy out the band's right to be paid royalties in perpetuity. EMI would own the songs, but the band would still be paid their Writer Share (50 per cent) of PRS royalties for their songwriting.

In a letter dated 10 March 1997, EMI's business affairs director, Deborah Harris, confirmed two options: £500k for a 50 per cent interest or £1 million for a 100 per cent interest. As standard, this was all subject to board approval.

Stuart directed Ian to accept. The money would help with his move to Nashville. On 17 March, the band's lawyer David Gentle told EMI that Big Country would accept the higher offer – if the agreement was signed and payment made within that current financial year to avoid a £160,000 extra tax bill.

That meant the deal had to be done by Friday 4 April 1997.

Stay Alive

On 2 April, just two days before it was due to be signed, EMI faxed Big Country's accountant, Lester Dales, and said that the deal had been rejected by their board. If it was to go ahead, they said, EMI would need it to include Big Country's Writer Share PRS royalties too.

Stuart was in Los Angeles. No one could get hold of him. No one thought to tell Bruce, Tony or Mark that the deal had changed.

And so it was that on 4 April 1997, Ian Grant and the members of Big Country, minus Stuart Adamson (but with lawyer David Gentle, acting on behalf of Stuart), walked into the EMI offices and signed away what Tony calls 'the crown jewels' – all of Big Country's hit songs, including their Writer Share PRS royalties.

At the time of writing, that deal still stands.

Big Country's songwriting was split four ways. As the writer of the lyrics, Stuart received 50 per cent of each song and an even split of the remaining 50 per cent for the music. This meant that he owned 62.5 per cent of every Big Country song, while Bruce, Tony and Mark each owned 12.5 per cent. Ian Grant, as manager, would take his 20 per cent off the top of income received from EMI (but not from the Writer Share PRS which the writers received direct).

To Tony, Bruce and Mark, sitting in the EMI office, being told that if they didn't sign the agreement that day they'd lose an added £160,000, it came as a bit of a shock. 'I was seething,' says Tony. 'There wasn't a very good atmosphere in that room. Before any EMI people even turned up, we were firing questions at Ian and the lawyer. "Why is this happening? Why are we selling the band's crown jewels? Why are we getting a million pounds? How much am I gonna get of that million pounds?" – stuff that you would have thought would have been discussed beforehand. It all happened in that room, on that morning.

'You were doing the maths in your head. "Twelve and a half per cent of a million pounds. Oh, hang on, it's not a million pounds, is it? It's less 20 per cent. Twelve and a half per cent of £800,000". So my share of a million pounds is not going to be very much – and you're taking away my pension as well. Excellent.'

But without Stuart, the manager and their lawyer felt that they had to accept what they knew was a bad deal. 'Ian and David felt that the overriding priority for Stuart was the financing of his move to Nashville,' says Stuart Ongley, the manager of Stuart's estate and Big Country's historic music rights. 'To advise Stuart that the deal had been aborted was not a viable option.' Stuart had granted David Gentle the power of attorney, but on the understanding that it was for the deal that had been offered on 10 March.

Meanwhile, the clock was ticking down on the end of the financial year. 'I think it was four o'clock in the afternoon by the time we signed,' says Tony, 'and then we had to run across to Coutts Bank, on the other side of London, to get the cheque into the bank.

'We were *fucked*,' he says. 'The whole thing had fucked me, Mark and Bruce.'

Stuart hadn't come out of it very well either. If Adamson had been there, Ongley is convinced that the outcome would have been different. 'Stuart would never have approved the sale of his Writer Share PRS,' says Ongley. 'He had a long history of never letting money influence his decisions and he had specifically agreed with Sandra at the time of their separation that she would retain the dormant pension policy they had jointly contributed to, while he retained his music career "pension" of the PRS Writer Share income.'

To Tony, it felt like Stuart had screwed them over. 'I didn't know how I was ever going to face Stuart again,' he says. 'He dumped us. No wonder he wasn't around. He couldn't face us. He didn't help himself or us by not being there.'

Bruce felt like the victim of music industry politics. 'I just think we got fucked over,' says Bruce. 'We signed it, but I didn't expect to be signing my PRS away. That was my pension.'

'I'm a bit mixed about it,' says Mark. 'I wasn't keen on selling the publishing, but I was grateful that I received some money. I never really made those big, big decisions. Ian Grant led the charge with that stuff and we had lawyers who would advise us. I wasn't keen to sell my share, but I realised I had to toe the line otherwise it wasn't going to happen.'

David Gentle immediately wrote letters to each of the band members on 7 April (the Monday after the Friday signing), expressing his opinion that the deal was 'less than satisfactory'.

It was an understatement. To Stuart Adamson, says Ongley, 'the loss of his PRS income was ruinous. He no longer had the music career "pension" he would eventually be dependent on.'

At the time of Stuart's death, his *annual* payments in PRS Writer Share royalties were worth around $50,000 in today's money.

He signed all that away. He went to Nashville with around £400,000 and the knowledge that he wouldn't make another penny out of Big Country's songs.

Tony wonders if all of this prompted Adamson's return to drinking. 'It's no wonder Stuart turned to drink after that. He couldn't face anybody,' he says. 'Every time we saw each other after that – and I mean *every* time – he was not there.'

Not that they blamed him, he says. But it could have worked out differently. 'He didn't help himself, or us, by not being there. He should have been there for that most crucial financial decision. If he had been there and he had refused – if he had turned around and said, "No, I didn't ask for *this*" in front of everybody – we would have supported him and it wouldn't have happened that day. Instead, there was David Gentle, acting very, very uncomfortably as his power of attorney.'

He shakes his head. 'From a story of hope and camaraderie and love,' he says, 'to *this*. It's fucking ugly.'

But the drinking hadn't started yet. Stuart was carving out a quiet new life in Nashville. 'I didn't know "famous Stuart" at all,' says Melanie. 'Stuart didn't want to be like that. He didn't want a big life. He wanted to have love and family and a simple life. He didn't want fame. He *hated* that.

'He was like that song, a simple man.' Around this time, Stuart wrote a song with that title, which he later recorded with the Raphaels. 'I'm a simple man, want a simple life,' he sings, but then he admits: 'I got a complicated life.'

The Great Divide

'That was him,' she says. 'He didn't want a complicated life, but he had one because he had a career and an ex-wife, and he wanted to be a good father, but he wasn't around his kids that much. So he was trying to *fix* a lot in Nashville.'

In May 1997, when he heard that one of Melanie's friends was a huge U2 fan, Stuart suggested they go and see them in Memphis and volunteered to get the tickets. At the Liberty Bowl Stadium, they were greeted at the door and then ushered through backstage corridors, like Henry and Karen Hill in the Copacabana scene in *Goodfellas*, finally emerging to a seated area and given the best seats in the house, right in front of the stage.

Melanie and her friend were *freaking out*.

Stuart didn't say a word.

U2 played the show and, when they came back on for the encores, Bono said, 'Stuart Adamson – this one's for you,' and the band played 'One'.

'One love, we get to share it,' sang Bono. 'It leaves you, baby, if you don't care for it.'

Stuart was so touched that he cried. Afterwards, they went backstage and met Bono and the Edge. Bono took Melanie to one side.

'This man is so incredible,' he said of Stuart. 'I'm really happy that you guys are together.' Like Lorraine Bracco's character in *Goodfellas*, she was overwhelmed.

In the summer of '97, Ray Davies got in touch. He'd been asked to play Glastonbury and wanted to play a Kinks set, but didn't have a band. His office called Ian Grant and asked if Mark and Tony were available. 'I said, "You can have all of the band or none of them,"' says Ian. Ray Davies loved the idea.

Bruce couldn't make it because Wild Blue Yonder had been given a slot at the T in the Park festival and he didn't want to let the young guys in his group down.

So Stuart, Tony and Mark played Glastonbury with Ray Davies, and afterwards the Kinks frontman struck up a bit of a relationship with Big Country. 'A very eccentric man,' says Ian. 'You didn't know how much was for effect and how much was real, but he took a liking to them. He couldn't understand why they didn't have a record deal and wanted to sign them to [his label] Konk or have them support him, anything that was of use. They did some demos with him and Stuart wrote two songs with him at his apartment in New York in '98.'

For a while, it looked like Ray Davies – the man who had co-written the first single Stuart ever bought – was going to throw Big Country a lifeline. It didn't work out.

In Nashville, Stuart had started writing with a guy called Jerry Boonstra. Jerry was the singer and principal songwriter for a country band called the Voltaires. Stuart introduced himself after a Voltaires gig and asked Jerry if he'd be interested in writing songs with him.

Jerry was sceptical at first. 'I didn't know if it would work,' he says, 'because he was coming from a rock background, but I thought it'd be fun to try. And, surprisingly, we clicked on every level.'

They had more in common than just their taste in music. 'We both struggled with depression,' says Jerry. 'We were both hurting at that time. We both understood, and it came out in the music.'

'Neither of us really talked about it,' says Jerry, but Stuart had 'a sadness in his eyes. He would refer to his family and I could tell that hurt him. It was just an overall vibe of sadness – and we both tended towards the dark in our writing.

'He would say that he was trying to be more positive – not necessarily in songwriting, but in life. But, invariably, because we liked dark songs, we would always go down that road. I would come up with something and Stuart would always ruefully chuckle and go, "Oh, so you want to go *there* do you, Jerry? Alright, if that's where you want to go …"'

It was different from writing with other guys in Nashville, where rules and formulas dictated how the songs ended up. 'I find the rules to be very constraining,' says Jerry. 'You'd come up with a great idea and somebody would go, "Well, I don't know if that'd work on the radio." And you're like, "Well, screw that, man."'

The Great Divide

With Stuart, that didn't matter. 'We weren't trying to write *hit* songs. We were just trying to write really *good* songs.'

One of the first things they wrote was called 'Sun and My Shadow'. Jerry remembers sitting there, looking for a line and saying, 'So what? So I'm a little drunk.'

'Stuart loved that. He laughed and we started writing from there.' It became a verse of the song: 'So what? So I'm a little drunk/ What's it to you/ I ain't some kind of monk.'

Big Country attempted to record it and two other Adamson/Boonstra compositions – 'Soldier of the Lord' and 'Shattered Cross' – for what would be their eighth studio album, *Driving to Damascus*. '"Shattered Cross" is an incredibly bleak song,' says Jerry.

They were jamming the song and suggesting lyrics, when Jerry came up with the lines 'Don't bring me your tales of temptation and loss/ The rags of your dreams, your shattered cross.'

'I was thinking of somebody who's lost faith,' says Jerry, 'religious faith, maybe, or just faith in life, and someone listening and saying, "I don't want to hear about it". Pretty bleak. Don't tell me your tales, I don't want to know. But then Stuart, he's got to go even further ...'

Prompted by Jerry's words, Stuart added: 'I've heard your confession, I know who you blame/ If you had it all back you'd just lose it again/ You can't bank on redemption if you ain't saved.'

He turned to Jerry. 'It's *God* talking to him,' he said. 'Even God is giving up on this guy.'

'That,' says Jerry, 'is as dark as you can get, man.'

It was around this time that Stuart met Marcus Hummon. Born in Washington DC but brought up all over the world (Saudi Arabia, Tanzania, Nigeria, the Philippines), Marcus was carving out a career in Nashville as a songwriter and solo artist. He had written hit songs for Wynonna Judd, Alabama, the Nitty Gritty Dirt Band and more, and his debut album, *All in Good Time*, had come out in 1995, although Sony had dropped him soon after. 'I was coming off a great time, but a very difficult time,' he says.

He was working on an independent deal, gigging around Nashville and writing songs, and one night found himself being introduced to a charismatic guy with a thick Scottish accent.

'The thing I remember was that Stuart was a kinda dashing character,' he says. 'He was in a black suit and he had that heavy accent and he told me that his marriage was ending. He was very honest. He was still smoking like a chimney stack and he told me right away that he was in recovery. And that was actually – ironically, as it turns out – a real *plus* for me, because I grew up around alcoholism.'

Not only did Marcus have personal experience of growing up in a family with alcoholism, but his wife, Becca Stevens, was the founder of Thistle Farms – *Thistle* Farms! Named after the national emblem of Scotland! – a non-profit social enterprise 'dedicated to helping women survivors recover and heal from prostitution, trafficking and addiction'. To Marcus, Stuart's past wasn't off-putting. It was a *connection*.

'One thing we had in common was addiction,' he says. And the other? Fly fishing. Marcus had a cabin in the Smoky Mountains, about fifty minutes east of Nashville, and the two men started fishing together.

'He was a pretty serious fly fisherman,' says Marcus. 'You can tell when someone's hardcore if they tie their own flies. Music and fly fishing are two of my favourite things in the world, so we hit it off immediately.'

Stuart loved the music that Marcus was making and they started to write occasionally. Marcus had a band called Pretty Red Wing and one night they were playing a gig when Stuart came to the side of the stage and said to Marcus, 'Do you mind if I play guitar?'

'He put on this guitar and he just tore it up,' says Marcus. 'There were Celtic elements and country and folk and roots'. He had such a gift – not to mention the gift of charisma. Immediately, everyone's looking at this guy. It's the rock star thing. Some people, they just have it.'

Darrell Scott was another Nashville songwriter and musician in those circles. He met Stuart at a Marcus Hummon session. 'He was just another guy on the session,' he says, 'except he was cool – y'know, cooler than most. I loved the way he talked. He was a great hang. No rock star bullshit at all, just a guy. It felt like he'd had his rocking times – opening for U2 and the

The Great Divide

Rolling Stones and all the big stuff that he'd done – and Nashville was a "getting simpler" kind of thing.'

To Darrell's ears, Stuart was bringing a folk sensibility to his Nashville sessions. 'It's a small walk between folk and country,' he says. 'It's coming from the same source, which is Scotland, Ireland, England, Wales. That's where country music comes from. So, at some point, it's a mish-mash anyway.'

And that fitted in with Nashville at that time, where there was 'a lot of cross-pollination', says Darrell. 'When it comes down to it, we're all hearing *music* – we're not hearing bluegrass only, or rock only or rockabilly only. It's all music, to a player. And Stuart would have been absolutely in the same boat as that.'

Darrell remembers Stuart as being 'in transition' from his Big Country days. 'It wasn't his main focus anymore. From what I could tell, Nashville was a good fit for him. He wasn't hanging with Johnny Cash or Garth Brooks or anything like that. We were all in the underground of Nashville. None of us were famous.'

When Stuart and Marcus decided to form a band, they initially tried to talk Darrell into being a part, but he was too busy with his own solo career. At their very first session together, says Marcus, they played the Jerry Boonstra co-write 'Shattered Cross' and bonded instantly.

In May 1998, Big Country were back together for some UK dates, which included a night at Tappie Toories. 'We had the whole band and a cast of thousands in this postage stamp-sized area playing Big Country songs,' says Bruce. 'It was great fun but, you can imagine, it was mayhem.'

Melanie was there and met Sandra, and Sandra was nice to her, but Scottish drinking culture was a shock. She didn't drink and people acted like she was insulting them as a result: 'C'moan, huv a drink!'

Marcus Hummon also came over on that tour to see his new friend's band. It was a bit different from the Nashville gigs he was used to. 'Very rowdy and raucous,' he says. 'They started to play – and they rocked so hard – and then the audience are waving Scottish flags, and there's a touch of punk going on, a bit of slam dancing. I was like, *What?* One guy got hurt and they carried him out, but the gig kept going.'

Stay Alive

'It was like being in a war zone,' Marcus said to Stuart afterwards.

'Yeah,' said Stuart. 'What you have to understand about Celtic music: Irish music makes you want to make love, Scottish music makes you want to make love – and then go to war.'

Ian Grant had hit a dead-end. Big Country had become very unfashionable. There was no label interest and he was starting to look at what Marillion were doing with crowd-funding. 'We'd run out of steam,' he says. 'Marillion were doing it themselves, raising the money up front and I thought, *Let's try that way*.' Then he met two people who changed his mind. The first was Chris Stamp, one-time co-manager of the Who and co-founder of Track Records. Stamp suggested that Grant relaunch Track Records, which had been lying dormant since 1978.

The second was Bill Kenwright, the chairman of Everton Football Club and a theatre and film producer. Bill had both a background in music and more money than God. Ian put two and two together. Big Country needed a label and Track Records was available. Track Records needed a cash injection and Bill Kenwright was looking for projects to invest in.

He went to Kenwright and laid out his plan: a relaunched Track Records with Big Country as its first signing. 'It might sound like an act of nepotism,' he told Bill, 'but I know we'd do 50,000 albums in Europe and we've got these Ray Davies co-writes, and the band are in a better shape than they have been for a while.'

In the sleevenotes for a reissue of *Driving to Damascus*, Grant wrote: 'Bill Kenwright funded the making of the album, the making of the videos and provided a publishing advance for the band to live on. It would be considered a "conflict of interest" by music business lawyers, but the only "interest" was Big Country. This was a way of making it happen. Bill was also funding Track Records and, all in all, he made a massive commitment to the band – and me.'

Not everyone was positive about this turn of events. 'There was a sense of impending doom,' says Tony. 'Everybody thought, "How long can we keep this battered old thing going?"'

The band went out to Nashville several times in 1998 to write with Stuart. Tony went with some reluctance.

'I hate country and western,' he says. 'And my marriage was going pear-shaped. I was stuck in a hotel, on Prozac, bouncing around the rooms thinking, "What the fuck am I doing here?"'

To make things worse, Tony was sitting in a diner one Sunday when two squad cars pulled up outside, uniformed officers piled out of the cars, ran into the diner and *physically lifted him* out into the car park. They shouted at him, didn't believe his British driving licence was real ('What's this Mickey Mouse shit?') and kept him there for about fifteen minutes, firing questions at him: Who was he, *really*? Where had he *been*? They refused to believe any of his answers.

I'm gonna get a beating here, thought Tony, *and I don't even know why.*

Eventually, another police car turned up and a more senior officer got out. As luck would have it, this guy was a music fan and recognised Tony. Why, he asked the cops, were they questioning the bass player from Big Country?

They let him go and he went back into the diner, shaking. His food had gone cold. The owner showed him a copy of the local paper, the *Tennessean*. In it was a picture of a black guy with a beanie hat who had robbed a gas station down the road.

'They thought it was me,' he says. 'I had the same hat on. I fitted the bill.'

Back in the studio the next day, he told the guys what had happened. 'Mark and Bruce were like "Really? Oh my God!" Not a peep out of Stuart. Not a peep – not an essence of sympathy, outrage, nothing. I said to Stuart, "You know what? I'm gonna go home tomorrow and I ain't coming back." And I did.

'Ian Grant had the nerve to say to me, "The guys are going back out in three weeks. You going?" I said, "You can fuck off. I'm not going out there." They came back with more demos – all country and western shit.'

Kirsten went out to Nashville in the summer of '98. 'My dad was definitely sober that summer,' she says. She went with one of Sandra's friends. Stuart had an apartment and they stayed there, while Stuart stayed at Melanie's house. They took a speedboat out on one of the lakes in Nashville, and went to Six Flags Over Georgia, an amusement park near Atlanta.

'I feel like that year he was quite happy being out there,' she says. 'He seemed to be enjoying life.'

In August, Big Country went back out with the Stones. The first gig was in Tallinn, Estonia and they were put up in the same hotel they had stayed in back in 1988. No longer part of the USSR, there was a huge difference. 'It was amazing,' says Bruce, 'just completely over the top, luxurious.' They had no album to promote, but the gigs were great.

Mark and Bruce – but not Tony – went back out to Nashville and were there for Thanksgiving in November. Bruce still didn't feel at home in the Nashville music scene. 'They were all going to church,' he says, 'and having business meetings after church. It just felt weird. I thought, "This isnae rock 'n' roll."'

Tony Butler thought exactly the same thing when he heard the Nashville demos. But in rehearsals at Monnow Valley Studios and at Rockfield – in March 1999, when they began to record *Driving to Damascus* – he felt like they began to work some magic on them.

'We ended up crashing some of those songs together,' he says. 'We came up with some fantastic stuff.'

'Somebody Else', one of two songs co-written with Ray Davies, sounded like a mash-up of the Kinks and Big Country. Lyrically, it was a bittersweet take on splitting possessions after a break-up. 'You can keep that crew neck sweater I wore to the Talking Heads gig,' sings Stuart, 'I don't need that angry sex, I can find that for myself.'

Producer Rafe McKenna was the son of Irish actor T.P. McKenna. 'He was a nice, lovely man,' says Tony, 'a musical man and he tried to bring something new into the band, to go back to the original sound but bring some modern concepts into it, like drum loops and stuff.'

'See You' – another break-up song – started life as a 'very dreary country and western song,' says Tony, but was 'tarted up'. They added drum loops and McKenna got in a couple of violinists and cello players.

Bruce used to muck about doing comedy Dylan impersonations; 'Fragile Thing' grew from that unlikely place. 'The chord progression to "Fragile Thing" is basically "All Along the Watchtower",' he says. Rafe McKenna had produced Eddi Reader's 1999 solo album, *Angels & Electricity*, and he invited her to do backing vocals on the track.

Callum and Kirsten came down to Rockfield and Kirsten, then thirteen, added vocals to two or three of the songs. 'I just did the bits that dad told me to do,' she says. 'I don't remember feeling intimidated or anything. It just felt like we were having fun because that's how he made it feel.'

The mood in the camp was good. They felt that they'd made a more modern, grown-up Big Country album. Callum and Kirsten had gone home and, with mixing about to start, Stuart went back to Nashville for a couple of weeks.

The cleaner at Rockfield went into his room to freshen it up and came out with two full bin bags, rattling and clinking.

'I thought he didn't drink?' she said.

The bin bags were full of empty cans and bottles. His room had looked like someone had had a party in it. Stuart had just chucked his empties into the bottom of the wardrobe.

Then Bruce got a call from a mate.

'I just bumped into Stuart at Gatwick,' he said. 'He was pissed out of his face.'

'Naw,' said Bruce. 'He doesnae drink.'

'Aw, I know – but he was fucking rat-arsed.'

'Are you sure?'

'Bruce, trust me, he was *pissed*.'

When Stuart flew back over, they had a band meeting. They laid it all out – not just about his drinking, but also about the band's finances. The EMI deal had made clear the long-standing dynamics of the royalty splits: when it came to songwriting, Stuart was a 62.5 per cent shareholder and that was not sustainable. (Live income, and everything else, was shared equally.) They'd all put a lot of work into this new album – Bruce had co-written a lot of the music as well – and to get just 12.5 per cent each, well …

'I'm no' fuckin' daein' it,' said Bruce. 'It's got to be split equally. Fair enough, I didnae write the lyrics, but I don't think lyrics are actually worth 50 per cent.'

'We didn't gang up on him,' says Bruce. Ian was there and their lawyer, David Gentle. 'If he had said no, then it would have been no.'

But Stuart agreed. 'Aye, fair's fair.' They would split it 25 per cent each.

Mark never got involved in the songwriting, but he did help out with arranging and he was a fucking great drummer, so he got 25 per cent too. It just felt fair. To Tony, Stuart gave in too easily. 'To me, it said he'd had it. His tank was empty.'

Now that Stuart's drinking was out in the open, he didn't try to hide it. Not that he would drink socially. 'He wouldnae come and join us for a pint,' says Bruce. 'He wouldnae have a social drink. He'd go up to his *room* and drink.'

He spoke to him about it. They had been to AA meetings together. Bruce knew it was a big deal, but Stuart played it down.

'Look,' he said, 'there's a lot of shit going on right now. It'll be under control. Dinnae worry about me. I'll be fine.'

The band went back to Nashville to film the video for 'Fragile Thing'. Tony didn't want to be there after his experience with the cops and, to make it worse, 'Stuart was distanced from us. We never even got invited to his house.'

Melanie appears as a waitress in the opening seconds of the video. 'It ceased to be a band then,' says Tony. 'It was all about Stuart – all about what he wanted to do, his new place and impressing his new lady. The notion of a band had gone.'

Kirsten went out to Nashville that summer and Stuart picked her up from the airport. 'I remember getting in the car and thinking, "You're drinking",' she says. 'I don't think he was slaughtered or anything, but I could tell right away. I didn't tell my mum because she would have made me come home. I just wanted to spend the summer with my dad – I was a total daddy's girl – so I didn't even really care what version of my dad I was getting, I was getting to hang out with him for four weeks.'

One day, Stuart dropped her off at a water park. She was fourteen and by herself. He gave her twenty bucks to get pizza and said he'd be back later. 'I think he said he had a writing session,' she says. 'So I was just at this water park all day on my own.' She wasn't scared – it's not a terrible memory. But it was weird. And then, at the end of the day, he came in the car to pick her up. 'I think he was drunk.'

'Fragile Thing' was released in August 1999. A well-crafted country ballad, the single became A-listed on BBC Radio 2 and looked a dead cert to make the top 40 – their first to reach the charts since 'Ships' in 1993. In a move typical of the time, the CD single was available in two formats, with different B-sides and packaging. It made the singles more collectible for fans and boosted the chart position, with collectors buying the single twice. One version of 'Fragile Thing' came in a jewel case, the other in a cardboard 'pizza box' packaging.

The band were doing an in-store at HMV in Glasgow, meeting fans and signing stuff when Ian Grant came over. 'I've got some bad news,' he said.

The chart regulators CIN had decided that the 'pizza box' packaging of the CD2 single had one too many folds in it.* The sales would therefore not be eligible. In the end, the single stalled at number 69.

Stuart was furious. All his career he'd been dogged with similar shit, from Virgin and their Skids singles on coloured vinyl, to this. After years of struggle, it felt like the rug was being pulled from under them just as they were about to have some success.

'I didn't think it would affect him as much as it did,' says Bruce. 'But it really fucking did. It was a real kick in the teeth, one of the final straws.'

---

* As record companies tried to boost sales in the 1990s, with various editions of CD singles featuring different tracks, remixes and packaging to encourage multiple buys from collectors, the chart regulator CIN cracked down. A new rule meant that you could include posters or postcards, but the packaging of CD2 of 'Fragile Thing' was deemed a step too far, despite it not being a 'free gift' and having no other obvious use. 'It's straight off of Monty Python,' said Grant at the time. 'Pure red tape. Is this how the music business should be run?'

Stay Alive

Driving to Damascus entered the UK album charts at number 82 and dropped out of the top 100 after one week.

No one, apart from possibly Bill Kenwright, was surprised.

24

Inwards

Burn out in Music City

In November 1999, Stuart went missing. Or, at least, that's what they told everyone. In reality, the band knew exactly where he was. He was in New Orleans, says Bruce, learning to become a hairdresser.

There had been a TV appearance planned and some support slots on a Bryan Adams tour, and Ian had hoped those UK dates might lead to an American tour. Stuart told him he couldn't do it.

He wasn't really learning to become a hairdresser, but he and Melanie *were* opening a hair salon in Nashville. Trim Classic Barber & Legendary Beauty soon became one of the coolest salons in the city, and the two of them were attending a course for salon owners in New Orleans. Ian thought he could talk him out of it, but he couldn't. So 'Stuart Adamson Goes Missing' became the cover story.

'Singer lost in the big country: concern over Adamson,' wrote Scottish newspaper the *Herald*. 'A mystery surrounding the disappearance of the lead singer of 80s Scottish rock band Big Country deepened last night with the group's bassist claiming he was safe and well in New Orleans.'

'I spoke with him on the phone,' says Bruce. 'He wasnae missing.'

He wasnae *missing*. He just wasnae *coming*.

On the Driving to Damascus UK tour a month later, the four members of Big Country sat in a pub and agreed that it was over. 'Tony wasn't keen on carrying on and neither was I,' says Bruce. 'I didnae like seeing him like that. Looking like him, but not *being* him.'

Stuart suggested that Big Country continue with someone else up front and at some point they had a rehearsal with Simon Townshend and Mike Peters. 'It wasnae an audition,' says Bruce. 'The idea was to have *both* involved. We did one rehearsal and Stuart knew about it, but nothing happened. I don't know why.'

A Big Country farewell tour was planned: The Final Fling.

Stuart and Sandra were officially divorced on 6 January 2000. In March, a month before the final tour, Joe Seabrook died of a brain aneurysm. The story goes that when they moved his body from the house, they found a hand grenade under his armchair.

Stuart and Melanie had the flu. They were sick as dogs, throwing up, shivering – the whole lot. 'We were just gross,' she says. 'Nobody'd brushed their teeth. We'd thrown up. It was the worst it could possibly be.' They were lying on the couch, Melanie had her head on Stuart's chest. He said, 'Do you want to get married?'

'Yeah,' said Melanie.

'Do you want to get married *today*?' said Stuart.

'What?!'

'Let's face it,' said Stuart. 'This is the worst it can get.'

A story in the *Tennessean* reported: 'Mazel tov to former Big Country frontman Stuart Adamson, a Nashvillian for four years, who got married a week or so ago to longtime girlfriend Melanie Shelley. Stuart, who is Scottish, said the two did so on a whim: They put on jeans and baggy sweatshirts, went downtown for a marriage license and headed to songwriter pal Marcus Hummon's house for a wedding. Marcus' wife, you see, is a preacher ... Stuart said the two will have a party later this year for friends. "Then Melanie can put on a wedding dress," he said.'

Marcus's wife Becca is an Episcopal priest. She married them in their front room while Marcus's father played a Scottish air on the piano.

The two men's friendship and songwriting partnership had progressed.

They had a band they initially wanted to call the Blue Healers until they found out that 'there was, like, twelve groups in America already called the Blue Healers and one had already trademarked it. My recollection is that the Raphaels was Stuart's idea. He probably just loved the painter Raphael, I don't know.'

Big Country's Final Fling kicked off in Europe in April. 'I'm doing a Noel Gallagher and giving up the travel,' Stuart told the *Belfast Telegraph*, ahead of the tour. 'I'm not sad about it – I'm quite happy. Don't forget that I spent eight months out of each of those past nineteen years touring. Now I want to be available for people I care about – like my eighteen-year-old son and my fifteen-year-old daughter from my first marriage. They will be spending all summer long with me in my new home in Nashville.

'It was the touring and the music that contributed to the break-up of my first marriage and I will make sure it doesn't happen this time.'

Melanie still had no idea that Stuart was drinking again.

'You have to look at it like time series and temporal effects,' says Callum. 'When an engineering system is going to explode, it starts off as a wave with a large gap between the next wave – and then those gaps start to converge. It starts off calmly oscillating and by the end it's like this [oscillating wildly]. So, at that period, he's probably drinking for a week, then not for a week. And then he's drinking for a day, not for a day, drinking for an hour, not for an hour ...'

Stuart was oscillating.

'I remember picking up the phone one night,' says Kirsten, 'and not knowing who it was. I said to my mum, "There's someone on the phone. I think it's *Dad*." He must have been absolutely slaughtered. It didn't sound like him.'

'He never did anything violent or bad,' says Bruce, 'it just wasnae him. It looked like him, but it wasn't. He was just a guy that pissed you off because he talked constantly, trying to be funny.'

One night in Germany, on The Final Fling, it came to a head. Stuart started drinking during the day and, by the time he got to soundcheck, he couldn't play. 'It's probably one of the worst I'd seen him,' says Bruce. 'He couldn't play at soundcheck. He had the guitar around his neck and he could only hit it with one hand. He couldn't use his left hand to fret.'

At one point, Stuart started walking backwards and almost tripped over the monitor speaker. Bruce grabbed him before he tumbled off the stage, marched him to the tour bus and got him in his bunk to sleep it off. He managed to sober up enough for the gig but, somewhere in between, he'd gone looking for a drink and fallen up the stairs of the bus. He scraped his face along the floor, getting a carpet burn which then became a big scab. 'He was a fucking mess,' says Bruce.

The support on that tour, billed as the Alarm 2000, was Mike Peters. Mike wrote about that night on his website years later: 'I felt for both him and the band as they struggled through the show ... Mark, Bruce and Tony showed enormous professionalism, compassion, courage and understanding to come through the performance when it was so obvious that Stuart could hardly stand and play guitar, never mind sing.

'On the tour bus that night, there was only care and understanding shown to Stuart by the band and management, certainly no blame was attached after what was an incredibly difficult show for them all to play. It was obvious they knew and understood that Stuart was ill.'

Tony went to see Stuart in his hotel room the next day. 'I said, "Stuart, we can't carry on like this. I seriously think we should stop and if it means me leaving the band to force you to stop, then we should."

'He was off his face,' says Tony. 'So we had this discussion, but he still wouldn't open up. He *still* wouldn't. He just stared and nodded at me.'

They still had the UK leg of the tour to go.

'I said, "After this tour, I'm off. You guys do what you want, but don't call me unless you want to do it properly."'

He called Ian and told him he was finished. 'I don't want to be involved in his demise,' he told him.

'But nobody took me seriously,' he says. 'I was horrified.'

So, unwilling but resigned, Tony was still there for the UK stretch in May 2000. Stuart continued to drink, alone, so no one ever quite knew the volume of alcohol he was consuming. One night, though, Bruce saw it up close. On 21 May, they played Wolverhampton Civic Hall and then travelled across town for a radio interview with DJ Janice Long.

They grabbed a bottle of red wine and some bottles of beer for the taxi ride. The two of them sat in the back of the taxi, smoking, and uncorked the wine with a Swiss Army knife. Without a glass, Stuart glugged the wine from the bottle.

'Fuck me,' says Bruce. 'He drank half the bottle in one glug.'

They chatted, had another fag and glug, glug, glug, glug, *gone*.

In the space of ten minutes, he'd finished the bottle. Bruce was still nursing the same bottle of beer.

'If that was me or you, you'd vomit,' he says. 'You couldnae do it.'

The Final Fling ended at Glasgow Barrowlands on 31 May. Melanie had joined them for the end of the tour. At the aftershow, she was stunned to see Stuart with a glass of wine. He played it down: 'Oh, I can have a glass of wine every so often.' Melanie thought it was weird. She didn't want to embarrass him at a party with all his people, but she was thinking, 'Really? Are you *sure?*'

On the plane home, they had barely gotten airborne when Stuart got an itchy eye. He started itching it and scratching and itching and scratching until suddenly he was shouting, 'It hurts so bad! It hurts so *bad!*' And he started kicking the back of the chair in front of him in frustration.

The cabin crew came over. 'Sir, you're going to have to settle down or we're going to have to land the plane.' They were somewhere over the Atlantic by this point.

Melanie was trying to calm him, but his eye was driving him mad. 'He was raging,' she says. 'I'd never seen him like that before or after.' It was a long flight and, to have a break from it, Melanie would go to the bathroom, wash her face and take some deep breaths. On the way back to her seat, one of the cabin crew stopped her.

'Ma'am, I can't serve your husband any more alcohol,' she said.

'What do you mean?' said Melanie. 'He's not drinking.'

'No, *he is*,' she said. 'He's had four wines.'

But Melanie still didn't believe it. 'No, you've got it wrong,' she said. 'He's sober. He doesn't drink.' The air stewardess looked at her like she was crazy and Melanie went back to her seat.

'And, of course, he was drunk,' she says, 'but there's no evidence of wine anywhere, so I'm like, *She's wrong*. I had no critical thinking when it came to him. None at all.'

She asked him, 'Have you been drinking?' Stuart said, 'No – you know I don't drink. I don't feel good. I'm just sick. I'm really sick.' And he slept for the rest of the flight.

When they landed, the police were waiting. Stuart was out of it, stumbling and couldn't speak properly, so Melanie explained to the cops that there was something wrong with him and that she was going to take him to the hospital. They went straight to Vanderbilt Hospital from the airport.

After four hours of tests, the doctor took her to one side.

'Has he been drinking?' he asked.

'That's the crazy part!' she said. 'He *doesn't* drink. He's totally sober. I'm so fucking worried!'

'Looking back,' she says, 'I look like the dumbest girl in the world but, truly and honestly, when Stuart told me he didn't drink, I believed him. Why would he lie to me?'

'You have to believe me,' she told the doctors. 'Keep testing!'

Stuart did have a torn cornea, so they gave him some eye drops.

Kirsten came to stay. Stuart was sleeping and Melanie sat down with Kirsten. 'I think something's wrong with your dad,' she said. 'I think that he might have a brain tumour or something. Don't worry, we'll find it. It's gonna be okay.'

Kirsten said, 'Melanie, he's drunk.' They had an argument about it, Melanie was so adamant. 'Go check his bag,' said Kirsten.

So Melanie got Stuart's backpack and there, inside, was an empty bottle of vodka.

Melanie started going through the house.

There were bottles behind the bathroom towels, bottles behind her spice rack, bottles under her bed. 'And I had never seen *one* bottle in my house!' she says. 'It was like I'd been pushed over into a different dimension, where one minute this didn't exist and suddenly it did.'

Kirsten had seen him take a bottle of vodka out of the bag earlier that day. But even before that, she just *knew*. 'I knew my dad and I knew this wasn't my dad,' she says.

When Stuart woke up, they confronted him. 'This was the only other time I saw him cry,' says Kirsten. 'I remember standing in the bathroom with him and he was crying and saying he was sorry, and that he was going to get help and go to the AA.'

But, even then, she didn't tell her mum. 'I knew that if I let anything out the bag, that was it, I'd have to go home.'

Later that summer, Kirsten returned to Nashville, this time with her friend Dawn, and Stuart seemed in a better place. He and Melanie were in the process of moving to a new house.

Stuart told Kirsten and Dawn that there was a ghost in the old house, a ghost that could, like, only move metal objects. The house had air conditioning grates in the floors and, one morning, they woke up to find one of these heavy grates up against a door.

'Must have been the ghost,' said Stuart.

On the day of the move, they went back and forth to the new house. When finally they had everything, and Stuart was locking the old house up, he stopped and shouted through the front door. 'Are you coming, ghostie?' He waited for a moment and then locked the door.

On that first night at the new house, Kirsten found a bottle of port underneath a bench in the back garden. She asked her dad to come outside and pointed to the bottle. 'Are you drinking?' she asked. 'Yeah,' he said, 'but I'm not drinking as much and I'm going to stop.'

He picked up the bottle and threw it into the trees beyond the garden.

He probably did stop, for a while. This was Stuart's new rhythm: on it, off it, hiding it – until it couldn't be hidden. By the time Callum got out to Nashville, Stuart had already been in rehab twice.

Stay Alive

On Callum's first Nashville visit, he flew out on his own and waited for Stuart to pick him up at the airport. 'And I waited for a long time,' he says. 'I was standing up on the top balcony and watched him stumble through the doors at the arrivals. And I was like, "We're gonna get a taxi home. We'll come back and get the car tomorrow."'

It was the first of many times that Callum had to be the responsible 'adult'. 'Pretty much from as soon as he moved to Nashville, it was interacting with an alcoholic,' he says. 'He'd be drunk. He'd have fallen over, hurt himself. I'd sleep in the hotel room with him overnight. It wasn't really a father–son relationship then. It was a son desperately trying to be close to his dad because they loved them and knew they needed help – but not being grown up enough to *know* how to help.

'And it went on like that for a good couple of years. And then it took me the next ten years to try and get over all that. By the time I was twenty-seven, I was finally at peace with everything. It's amazing the destruction that period created.'

The new century wasn't off to a great start. 'That whole year sucked,' says Melanie. 'I was still trying to run a business and it was new, and it was doing well and then sometimes Stuart would wander in and just sit and *stare* at everybody. It was crazy. No one in the business knew what was happening because I didn't want to tell anybody.'

The new house had two floors and a basement, with an open staircase in the middle of it. Melanie had a little StairMaster walking machine for cardio and she wanted it moved downstairs. She found Stuart and asked him to help, but he was weird about it. 'There was something going on,' she says. 'He was probably drinking.'

So, reluctantly, Stuart started to help – but it was awkward and he got frustrated. Suddenly, he lifted the StairMaster over the edge of the railing and dropped it onto the floor, two flights below.

'It was after that,' she says, 'that our *real* problems started.'

In October 2000, Big Country came calling again. The band had been offered 'some kind of corporate gig' in Kuala Lumpur in Malaysia for

$50,000. They didn't think Stuart would go for it, but he did. 'We could do with some cash,' he said. 'And it's in Malaysia – no one'll know.'

The band arrived the day before the show. Stuart, flying in from LA, did not get off his flight. Or the next one.

Panicking, Ian made some calls. Melanie had no idea where he was. 'It was a mystery,' she says. It was his first real disappearance. 'He just wasn't there and he wasn't calling or answering his phone.'

Eventually they found him. Stuart was meant to go to LA for a connection to Kuala Lumpur, but in a drunken haze – and with pre 9/11 US airport security so lax that you could get on a plane without a boarding pass – he'd gotten on the wrong flight and ended up in Indianapolis. Luckily, he still had a day to get there.

When he arrived, Bruce met him in the hotel bar. 'He was smoking a cigar and drinking a pint,' he says. 'He was exactly like we'd left him. So we did the gig. It was shit.'

'The actual final gig was a travesty,' says Tony. 'It was like being our own tribute band with a singer who couldn't hold himself together. It was appalling, horrible. It was embarrassing to be there.'

The next day, everybody went their separate ways. And that was it.

That was the end of Big Country.

Early one morning, around this time, Marcus got a call from Melanie. 'It was the first time I became aware that he had fallen off the wagon,' he says. Melanie told him that Stuart had been missing for days and had just shown up. On his way back from Kuala Lumpur, he'd gone AWOL and then suddenly he'd arrived home, fallen out of the taxi and hurt himself.

'They had this stone stairwell leading up to the house,' says Marcus, 'and he'd fallen hard on that. So I went over and he was as pale as a ghost. He had cut his head and was bleeding a little bit.'

But, more than that, he says, it was like it wasn't even *him*.

'We've got to get you to rehab,' said Marcus. There was a twenty-eight-day rehab just outside of town. 'I'll drive you.'

Stuart didn't flinch. 'Absolutely – let's go.'

'What I heard later was that he charmed his way out of there in about eight days,' says Marcus. 'Because when he was on his game – when Stuart was sober, which was 90 per cent of what I experienced from him – he was the life of the party. Very funny.'

Afterwards, the two of them talked about addiction. 'I think that he had the worst combo you could possibly have,' says Marcus. 'A straight-up addiction to alcohol and extraordinary levels of depression at times.'

He had a name for his depression: 'the dooms'. In 1999, Stuart had played at a music industry event in Hong Kong. Singer Carol Laula, who had performed on *Eclectic*, was there too. She was feeling low, she wrote on her website years later: 'I didn't know how to explain what I was feeling and then Stuart said something about how he couldn't sleep the night before – that he'd had "the dooms".'

At some point in all of this, and Callum can't be sure when ('Chronologically,' he says, 'it's really hard, because the mind erases trauma for the most part. So it's hard to remember what happened when'), he and his dad went to Memphis together. 'I never saw him drink once,' he says, 'but he was drunk the whole time.'

And that meant that Stuart was quiet. He was trying to conceal his drinking and knew that speaking would give it away, so 'he would just be completely inside his head, not really conversational. Just eating or walking or staring at something.'

They stayed at the Peabody Hotel and went to Graceland, and Sun Records, and watched a blues band play on Beale Street. Callum thought, 'This is really sad, because it's so cool, and you're not here, and I fucking hate that and I can't say it because you're my dad, and you'll get angry at me, or do the other thing you do, which is get really upset. And I'm not ready to deal with either of those things. So I'll just be here.'

'Most of my teenage life is just me being sad, quietly,' he says. 'And it's such a shame. I'd have loved to have shared that with him, but you can't share anything with someone who's not present.'

After an episode, says Callum, Stuart would just act like nothing had really happened. 'You could tell he was hungover – detoxing, in a bad way – but he would do everything in his power to be the Stuart you always knew. Instead of just being like, "This is a fucking mess and I'm sorry", he would just try and click back into normality, like it never happened. But again, he was never a violent drunk, never angry.'

Callum got a job in the salon: 'I shined shoes for tips.' At one point, things got so bad that Callum used his tips money to buy his dad's car from him because Stuart needed the cash.

Stuart see-sawed in and out of rehab. 'Coming out of rehab was great the first couple of times,' says Callum, 'because you got a sober, committed, focused person.'

He picked Stuart up from rehab when the time came. 'He came home and it was always the same. You'd get a good solid two weeks of AA meetings every day, always on the phone to sponsors and all that sort of stuff, and then a disappearance. Something would happen. There was an inevitability to it.

'He'd split up with my mum. He'd fucked his career up. He started to build a life in a country without any semblance of planning or structure or support network or new publisher or a project to work on. Musicians need a project: "I've got my new Nashville deal. I'm gonna go do an EP, I'm gonna get some co-writes." Something. Even a back-of-a-fag-packet plan.'

But he *did* have a plan. The Raphaels.

The Raphaels released an album, *Supernatural*, in May 2001 on Ian Grant's Track Records. It included their version of the Jerry Boonstra co-write 'Shattered Cross', the song about a man that even God has given up on. It was starting to look more and more like an insight into Stuart's state of mind.

The Raphaels flew over to play some small dates in the UK and Ireland. Stuart came over before Marcus and they arranged to meet at a hotel near London to rehearse. 'He started drinking on the plane over,' says Marcus. 'We'd talked about it ad nauseam before we went. He was doing well, I don't know for how long, but he was clean and sober and he was talking the talk. He was ready to do it.'

Mark Brzezicki joined them on drums and was pleasantly surprised when he saw Stuart in rehearsals. 'It really seemed like he'd turned a corner,' says Mark. 'He was sharp as a knife. No sign of drinking at all. It was the old Stuart – but then the drinking crept in. It was very harrowing, to be honest with you. It's hard to remember which date was which. That tour was one long haze of a nightmare.'

'I realised something was wrong on the very first night in London,' says Marcus. 'His game was a little bit off – and I knew his game pretty well, because we'd done some shows, and I knew how good he was. But he didn't look great.' Stuart told him he was fine; he'd come down with a cold, that's all. 'But the next show was when it really hit the fan.'

On the drive to Birmingham, Marcus noticed that Stuart had a couple of bottles of vodka in his bag. When they made a stop, Stuart would stay in the van. By the time they got to Birmingham, he was 'just absolutely shit-faced drunk'. When it became obvious that Stuart 'could hardly move', they had a bust-up backstage.

'We were about to go on stage,' says Mark, 'and Ian said to me, "Where's Stuart?" I said, "I don't know. I thought he was with you."'

They found him in the toilet, sitting on the floor, drunk and upset, complaining that everyone was on his back about his drinking. He wasn't doing anything wrong, he said.

'We're only trying to help you,' said Mark.

'You need to get help,' said Ian. 'We'll *get* you help.'

He didn't want help, he said. He was sorting himself out.

They went on late. 'I could see Stuart wasn't really capable of performing,' says Mark. 'Ian Grant was giving me this look, like "Oh my God, what's going to happen tonight?" But Stuart kind of perked himself up, as he would, and went out there.'

'He was sort of deliriously happy-looking,' says Marcus, 'and he was playing *something*, but it wasn't always what we started out playing.' Eventually, Marcus asked the sound guys to turn Stuart's mic off and they did some songs that Marcus sang lead on, like 'Supernatural' and 'Old Country'. But it was clear to everyone that Stuart was drunk.

'He was right in front of my drum kit,' says Mark, 'and he was talking to the audience, but not into the mic.' His mic was switched off. 'People started shouting, "We can't hear you, Stuart!"'

'People started yelling,' says Marcus. 'It was like a Fellini film. I've never experienced anything like it. People were shouting, "Give us our fucking money back!"'

And then Stuart fell over and couldn't get up.

They stopped the show. It was pointless. They helped Stuart backstage, the club owner right behind them, shouting and swearing.

'This guy's yelling. I mean, *really* cussing,' says Marcus, 'and Stuart is tapping my leg. I'm looking at him, like, "Stop it. Just stop".'

But the club owner was still shouting and Stuart was still tapping his leg – 'Will you *stop?*' – and the yelling is getting louder, and Stuart is still tapping his leg, and, finally, Marcus snaps and says, 'What *is it?*'

And Stuart looks at him and says: 'There was some great moments tonight, wasn't there?'

'Fuck me,' says Marcus. 'But that was Stuart. And, you know, there *were* some great moments.'

The following day, they played Manchester before heading to Glasgow where Sandra arranged to visit him at his hotel. She got his room number and was walking down the corridor when a voice from behind shouted, 'D!' She turned around. It was Stuart.

She'd walked right past him.

'I didn't recognise him,' she says. 'He'd changed so much from the drink. He was massive. He looked really bad, really unhealthy. I got a bit upset when I saw him. I must have looked shocked.'

They went into his room. 'It was a mess,' she says, 'half-empty drinks lying everywhere, and clothes and crockery and stuff like that. He said to me, "Are you going to come to the gig?" I said, "I don't want to. I'd rather talk about what's going on with you right now."'

Stuart assured her that he was fine and said he was on steroids. 'I don't think he was,' she says.

She walked over to the venue. 'The first two people I saw were his mum and dad, and I felt really uncomfortable because I knew he was in a mess.'

Stay Alive

She said hello to Stuart's mum Anne 'and I could tell *she'd* been drinking' and she saw Ian Grant 'and I just thought, "I'm going to lose it with everyone in here".' So she went home. 'I felt I couldn't win in that kind of situation. They needed him to pay their wages.'

Afterwards, Sandra called whoever Stuart was rooming with and lost her temper with them. 'I won't say who it was,' she says, 'because I feel bad about what I did. I called virtually everyone enablers. I said, "The whole band, management, whoever is involved with this band, you included, are enabling this to happen." I went off on one, and I do feel bad about it, but I was so worried and angry that nobody had the courage to say anything to Stuart.

'I remember phoning Ian and going off at him. "Why are you not helping him?" I don't know what I got back. I just felt I had to say something to as many people as possible. But, at that point, I had no power to do anything. I just had to hope that he was going to be alright.'

At the show in Glasgow, Stuart dedicated 'Learning to Row' to his dad who was there in the room. 'I grew up in a coal mining village in Fife,' he said. 'Most people grew up to be coalminers and my father decided it would be a really good idea to go away and be a fisherman. This song is for him.'

'Got to grow up fast, when you don't have a choice,' he sang. 'When the table's bare, and there's no father's voice.'

'In hindsight,' says Marcus, 'after Birmingham we probably should have said, "That's it. The tour's over." But we didn't.'

The next gig was at a club called La Belle Angele in Edinburgh. 'My recollection is that we let him have a little bit of beer because we were worried about how much alcohol he had taken in,' says Marcus. Sudden alcohol withdrawal can produce side effects like delirium tremens (DTs), a severe reaction that can be life-threatening, with increased heart rate, blood pressure and breathing problems, as well as severe disorientation, seizures and uncontrollable shaking.

In Edinburgh, after the soundcheck, Stuart 'went into a kind of shock,' says Marcus. 'He had DTs. His body was shaking. It was frightening.'

'I've never seen anyone like that,' says Mark. 'He was sat there, shaking and shivering like he was cold, hardly able to talk, shaking all over.'

Bruce Watson arrived at the venue to find Ian Grant coming up the stairs with his arm around what looked like 'a tramp'. It was Stuart. 'I didn't recognise him,' he says, 'and he didn't recognise me. He was just completely dishevelled. He said, "I'll be all right. I'm just going through some problems."'

He wasn't all right. They took Stuart to the hospital and Marcus and the band played the gig without him so that the club owner wouldn't lose all his money.

The next gig was scheduled to be in Dublin. 'We were supposed to play at the Gaiety Theatre,' says Marcus. 'I think Bono was coming.'

He went to Dublin without Stuart and then he got a call from Ian. 'He's just too far gone,' he said. 'He can't perform.'

And that was the end of it. Mark Brzezicki never saw or spoke to Stuart again. Marcus Hummon spent three or four weird days in a fog, walking the streets of Dublin, thinking, 'What the hell?'

Marcus and Stuart met up one last time in Nashville. They met for coffee and talked about what had happened. 'He was sort of apologetic,' he says, 'but we both understood that addiction is an illness. You can't sit and judge someone.'

They chatted about the future and about Stuart getting healthy again. But the thing that was so strange about that conversation was this: 'You know, I never told you,' said Stuart. 'When I was a little boy, I was born in Manchester, but I ended up living in Dunfermline and my father was on the boats fishing, so I was actually raised by my grandfather.'

Marcus already knew some of that. But then Stuart said: 'I found him. He hung himself in the family home.'

'It's such a huge thing, when you feel like you really know someone, to suddenly hear them say that,' he says. 'He was saying, "He struggled". His grandfather struggled with some of the same things that he struggled with.

'I remember saying, "Stuart, can you hear yourself? This is life and death at this point." And I'll never forget, he said: "You know I would never do that. Never." He specifically said that to me, the last time I saw him. He said he would never do that – "because I would never do that to my children".'

Kirsten and Callum went out to Nashville again in the summer of 2001. 'He was sober that summer before he died,' says Kirsten. She worked in Melanie's salon, mopping floors and doing odd jobs. She became friends with a girl who worked there and, one day that summer, as she was getting ready to meet her friend at the mall, Stuart got a phone call.

Kirsten's friend had killed herself.

Stuart and Melanie had some bohemian friends and they went to a dinner party where everyone read the Shakespeare play *A Midsummer Night's Dream* around the dinner table. Everyone was given a character and read their lines. Kirsten played the part of Titania, a character with a monologue full of apocalyptic imagery that could have come straight from a Big Country song: 'The ploughman lost his sweat, and the green corn hath rotted ... The human mortals want their winter cheer/No night is now with hymn or carol blessed.'

Kirsten had gone home by the time of her friend's funeral, but Stuart and Melanie went. Afterwards, Melanie was upset by the suicide of someone so young. Stuart comforted her.

'Baby, I will never do that,' he said. 'I will never do that to you.'

The thought had never crossed her mind.

'I won't do that to you either,' she said.

Callum was planning to live in Nashville, so Kirsten travelled home by herself. Stuart drove her to the airport and she got upset leaving him. She walked through security, looking back at her dad, until finally Stuart put his Ray-Bans and his keys in a tray and came through security to comfort her.

He stayed with her in departures until boarding. 'I don't remember saying goodbye or anything,' she says, 'but I guess that would have been the last time I saw him.'

What followed, says Callum, 'was a final six months of just real chaotic shit. I was backwards and forwards, must have been four or five times, picking him up out of rehab, helping him with Alcoholics Anonymous and stuff, and trying to help him navigate what he was going through with Melanie – because it felt like they got married and then were getting divorced four seconds later.'

In September, Stuart went missing in the UK. For a week or so, no one knew where he was. They found him holed-up in a hotel near Gatwick Airport, not far from the home of Ian Grant. He was in a bad way and was taken to hospital. There, nurses found him in a store cupboard. He had been so desperate for alcohol that he'd drunk from a bottle of methylated spirits.

Callum had seen the aftermath of that desperate kind of drinking. 'I never saw him drink, ever,' he says. 'But I would go into his bedroom and see eight empty bottles of fucking mouthwash and, like, aftershave emptied out. The weirdest shit on earth.'

For Melanie, it was all too much. 'Our whole lives are about to be ruined,' she thought. 'I'm going to lose my house, I'm going to lose my salon, I'm going to lose my family …'

She went to Al Anon – for the families of alcoholics – and shared her story with the group.

They said: *'You're not safe.'*

She had no one. She didn't have family in Nashville and she didn't want to tell anyone at the salon what was going on. 'You need some place safe to go at night,' Al Anon said. 'You need some place where everything's okay.'

So she found herself a place and she moved out.

Callum was also in the UK that September. On the day that he was due to fly back to Nashville, Sandra took him to the airport where they heard some shocking news: a plane had crashed into one of the Twin Towers in Manhattan.

'Something is telling me you shouldn't fly today,' said Sandra. They drove back home and put on the TV. The other tower had also been hit.

In Nashville, Stuart was arrested on a Driving under the influence (DUI) charge. 'He was in a car, with a ton of fucking beer bottles, intoxicated,' says Callum. 'He rolled it into a fence down by the gas station. There's not much more to it than that. It's a pretty boring alcoholic story. There's just so many sad stories and they're all like that. They're not rock 'n' roll or cool or edgy or anything. They're just kind of grubby.

'I don't mean "sad" as in "What a sad cunt for doing that." I just mean "What a *shame*".'

Stuart called Sandra from jail. 'At the time,' she says, 'I thought, "Is it still the rule that you're only allowed one phone call?" You would have hoped he'd have someone closer that could've helped. He wasn't incoherent, but it was difficult to talk to him. His brain was racing and it was a mess.

'From then on, I just was in a state of panic for him because I couldn't help. Geographically, it was just impossible. I tried to say to him, "Come back. Buy a flat here", but it's just total chaos in the mind of an alcoholic.'

He was sent to Cumberland Heights, a rehab centre in north-west Nashville. He told Sandra that, while he was there, he'd been diagnosed as bipolar. 'But again,' she says, 'you couldn't believe everything Stuart said when he was drinking.'

Bipolar disorder is a condition that results in extreme mood swings, with periods of mania followed by periods of depression. 'Someone told me later that they were pretty sure that he was bipolar,' says Melanie. 'I think I got it from a counsellor.'

People speculated later that the DUI charge could have been behind Stuart's suicide – a serious charge that could have led to jail time – but no one involved thinks so, including the Nashville detective who led Stuart's missing persons inquiry. It was a first offence, which would be regarded as comparatively minor, he said.

Callum picked up the abandoned car. 'You would not believe the amount of bottles in there,' he says. 'If you saw it you'd be like, "There's no way that one person caused this." Bottles in the backseat, in the boot, in the foot wells. He's drinking and driving literally all the time. Extreme volumes.'

He was a teenager, trying his best to help, and feeling his father slip further away from him. 'It felt like something heavy is tied to a rope and fallen off a building, and the more you try and hang on to it, the more your hands just get fried. It was that sort of feeling. And at some point, you're like, "This is fucked. I *can't*."'

The last time Kirsten spoke to Stuart on the phone, he said he had a new girlfriend. He and Melanie were splitting up and he was talking about a woman called Heidi. 'I can't remember what else we spoke about,' she says, 'but I forgot to tell him that I loved him. And that stuck with me. I don't know how long it was after that that he went missing.'

'This is the saddest fucking story of all time,' says Callum. He's remembering the last night he spent with his father. Stuart was back from rehab and they were together in the house. Callum was in his room and could hear Stuart talking on the phone to, he thinks, Terry Wilson, a friend from Dunfermline who was in Atlanta coaching football.

Callum could hear Stuart on the phone, walking towards his bedroom door. The door was closed. 'Give me a minute,' Stuart said to whoever was on the phone. 'Are you awake, Spud?' Stuart said to the door.

He used to call Callum 'Spud'.

'I *was* awake,' says Callum, 'but I didn't say anything and I don't know why. I never spoke to him again. And if ever there's something that fucking haunts you, it's not saying, "Yeah, I'm awake."'

The next morning, he found a note on the table: 'Gone to Atlanta', it said. 'I'll be back on Sunday.'

It was 7 November. Stuart Adamson did not come back that Sunday.

25

The Land Where I Lie Cold

Stain the atlas pink

You stay in Atlanta and hang out with Terry Wilson. You are in good spirits, thinks Terry, and he leaves you in a bar drinking Diet Coke. Later, he gets a call asking him to come back and pick up his pal.

You are shitfaced. You switched to wine when Terry left.

You watch Ireland play Iran in a World Cup qualifier. Manchester United captain Roy Keane is also captain of Ireland. They win 2–0. You stay in Atlanta to watch the second leg, on 15 November, even though you should have been home on the 11th.

Ireland lose 1–0. Keane is injured, but they still qualify.

Melanie is calling you the whole time, leaving message after message, begging and crying for you to come home or call back. Each one: *Please call me. Please call me. What's happening? Please, just, please, just call me.*

Finally, she is freaked out and she leaves you another message. It is over, she says. I'm filing for divorce.

You play it to Terry Wilson and he calls Melanie and screams at her down the phone. He says that *she is the reason* that you are drinking.

You phone Bobby Drummond. Bobby tells you he's meeting Pubsy and Big Slap the following night at the Bruce Tavern. You tell Bobby, 'I'll phone youse there at nine o'clock.'

Stay Alive

At nine o'clock on the button, you call the Bruce Tavern. You speak to Bobby and then ask him to pass the phone to Pubsy and Big Slap.

When they come off the phone, a guy sitting in the pub says to them, 'Was that Stuart?'

'Aye.'

'That's him saying cheerio to youse,' he says.

In all the years you worked with Tony Butler, you only ever called him at home twice – *twice!* – but you call him now too. Tony is out and his wife takes a message. He never gets a chance to speak to you again. Tony thinks about it later. 'I don't know why he would have called,' he says. 'It was about two weeks before he died.'

You call Bruce Watson. You're just chatting, nothing significant, but as you're about to go, you say something you've never said before.

You say, 'I love you.'

'I love you tae,' says Bruce.

You have never spoken like that to each other before.

It's the last conversation you have with him.

You don't know this, although maybe you could guess, but Callum is looking for you in the bars of Nashville. Nashville is pretty fucking big, though, and it's not like you even drank in bars or had regular haunts.

It's not that type of drinking. You are not Norm from *Cheers*.

You come back to Nashville and check into the Best Western. A worker at the hotel remembers you. You have no visitors, he says, but you sit in the lounge every night and then go back to your room.

Callum is out looking for you, and you are in a hotel two minutes from your house.

Sandra calls you, livid. She leaves a message saying, 'You better get in touch with me. I'm really angry and I'm worried about Callum. What the hell are you doing?'

The Land Where I Lie Cold

You phone her back.

'You know what it's like, D,' you say, 'I'm in a hotel.'

'What are you doing in a hotel?' says Sandra.

You say, 'I'm with a woman.'

'Well, get your fucking arse back to Callum,' says Sandra. She is mortified, but she knows she is talking to a different guy now, that guy from way back, and she has a feeling it's not going to make any difference.

It's the last time you speak to her. She calls your mobile over and over, but you don't answer and eventually she knows you won't.

'And then I was just living in fear,' she says. 'Of what, I didn't know.'

You have withdrawn a load of money from the bank and got yourself some new credit cards. Because the credit cards are new and in your name, no one will talk to Melanie about where you are or where the cards are being used.

You call your AA sponsor. It's 19 November. You are out of it and either driving or sitting in the car by the side of the road.

You tell him that you're going to Clarksville to visit another AA member you know. Clarksville is an hour's drive north of Nashville.

Melanie's birthday is on 20 November. She is thirty-three. You are forty-three. You have been gone for almost two weeks and Melanie thinks, 'Fuck it. I'm tired of living like this. I'm going to have a birthday party.'

She invites people round to her new house and she decorates the stairwell with these wrought-iron candleholders, and they're kinda spiky and scary, like something you would see in New Orleans, with a huge sharp point at the top. She runs upstairs to grab something and, as she comes back down, she slips.

She falls backwards, right on to one of the candlesticks.

It plunges into her back and right through her rib cage.

Melanie is on the floor, impaled. The phone is within arm's reach. She pulls herself across the floor to it, this evil black sconce sticking out of her back, blood smearing across the floor, and she calls 911.

Stay Alive

She lies face down on the floor and tells herself, 'Don't pass out, don't pass out, don't pass out.'

Stay. Alive.

Police and medics get there quickly. She is rushed to ER. Friends arrive for the party. Someone finds out what happened and they stick a note on the door: 'Melanie's had an accident, the party's cancelled.'

Word gets around: Stuart's missing and Melanie's in the hospital with a stab wound.

Everyone thinks *you* did it.

You didn't do it. You don't even know about it and you do not come to her aid. Right now, you're not even officially missing. Right now, you're just another guy with addiction issues who's fallen off the wagon – and you can imagine how many of those there are in Nashville.

Melanie is in hospital for two or three days. Her lung collapsed, but she is lucky. A few inches either way and there could have been major organ damage. Callum visits her, brings her food and helps her to the toilet – the stuff *you* should be doing.

After a few days, her wound is stapled up and she is sent home to rest.

When she is feeling better, Melanie goes round to the house and she and Callum have an argument. Everyone is fraught and burnt out. Decades later, Melanie will remember this as one of the worst nights of her life.

Callum calls his mum. Sandra, freaking out, books him a plane ticket home. When he lands in Glasgow, Sandra sees the trauma written on his face and bursts into tears. 'You look like a skeleton!' she says. She drives him straight to Burger King.

When he gets home, Callum sleeps for twenty-three hours straight.

People are worried about you now. Melanie files a missing persons report on 26 November. This is more than just a drunken bender. This is carnage. There are stories in the newspapers and Ian Grant has hired a private investigator to find you.

The Land Where I Lie Cold

Bruce is quoted in the press: 'If anybody is harbouring Stuart because they think it is helping him, then please think again and turn him in. It could save his life. Stuart's alcoholism is not a cheap publicity stunt, it is a disease and he needs help as soon as possible.'

You leave the Best Western on 3 December. The manager remembers you because you don't check out and you leave the room full of beer bottles.

Later, there's a small mystery around where you go next.

Everyone thinks you fly to Hawaii on 4 December. Everyone says so, but maybe it's just a mistake that was made once and repeated over and over.

Because it doesn't really matter. Either you were drunk in a hotel in Hawaii or drunk in a hotel somewhere *on your way* to Hawaii.

The Honolulu police will later confirm that your hotel room key-cards show that you never left your room. Did you really stay in a hotel room for twelve days?

Ian Grant's private investigator offers a different scenario. On 13 December, a 'William Adamson' – your real name, your father's name, the name on your passport – checks out of the Baymont Inn and Suites in Nashville.

Maybe you fly to Hawaii that day. It is a ten-hour flight. You walk out of the airport and check into the first hotel you see: the Best Western Plaza. You ask reception for three bottles of wine to be delivered to your room.

You do not leave your room. You ask for three more bottles to be sent up.

You watch the sun in winter time. It has hung low in the sky all day and, as it sets, it looks like the heavens are on fire. The trade winds blow from the north east and the sky smoulders with pink, orange and purple.

The light floods your room, warm and golden.

And then everything starts to go grey.

It always ends in dark.

You are in the Land of Nod, carrying the guilt of Cain. You have found a beach where you can cross your heart.

Stay Alive

At around 1 p.m., on 16 December, the day that you are supposed to check out, a maid finds you on the floor of your hotel room closet. You are in a seated position and the electrical cord around your neck is tied to the hanging rail.

But it's not really you. You have long gone.

26

Your Father's Hand

Pain and truth and things that really mattered

A week or so after he returned home to Dunfermline, Callum came downstairs to find Robin, Sandra's partner (then and now), standing there. They looked at each other and – without a word being spoken – Callum knew.

'I think he went to Hawaii because it meant that nobody he loved found him,' says Callum. 'And maybe for a pretty view – the last view that you're ever going to see, the splendour of God or whatever. I think he probably made up his mind, drank himself to a point where he knew it wasn't going to hurt and then off he went.'

Kirsten was at school that morning. She had PE. She and her friend smoked a cigarette in the changing rooms and then went to play badminton. When the teacher pulled her out of the badminton class, she thought, 'Aw shit, I've been caught smoking.' Instead, in the changing room, sat Sandra and the deputy head.

They told her the news right there. Sandra was scared it would be on the radio at lunchtime and wanted to get to Kirsten first.

Stuart had booked the room under the name 'William Adamson'. To aid with identification, Nashville police sent over copies of Stuart's fingerprints to confirm.

The City Medical Examiner's office confirmed that Stuart died from asphyxiation.

Stay Alive

It was Ian Grant's birthday on 17 December. Around nine in the morning, he sat down for breakfast with his family and his mum said, "Have you had any news on Stuart?" As she said it, his phone rang.

'I knew the number,' he says. 'It was Kim, Stuart's sister. She said, "He's died, he's killed himself." I went for a walk.'

Later that day, Ian sat in front of his computer and composed a statement that he published on the Big Country messageboard. 'And then all hell broke loose – Reuters, Billboard, GMTV ...

'I spoke to his AA sponsor,' he says. The sponsor called it a 'black haze'. You function, but it's like when you go on a vacation – they *call it* going on a vacation. You end up somewhere and you don't know how you got there.'

He grew a beard, he says, hardly slept. It was twenty-four-hour stuff, lots of people digging for a salacious angle: 'Is it a Michael Hutchence case? Is sex involved?'*

The Honolulu police dismissed the idea quickly.

Cases like that tend to happen on the bed, they said, and there's usually pornography involved. There was no porn in Stuart's room.

Ian got in touch with Virgin boss Richard Branson and Branson volunteered to fly Stuart's body back to Scotland, and paid for all of the non-Virgin parts of the journey.

Terry Wilson told the *Mail on Sunday* that Stuart played him Melanie's answerphone message, saying she was leaving him. Terry called her 'evil' and blamed her for tipping him over the edge. Big Country fans piled in on her.

'I got the early end of the internet,' she says. 'Super fun. If I ever come to Scotland again, they're going to murder me, that kind of stuff.'

Someone threatened her about what would happen if she came to

---

* A couple of years before, Paula Yates claimed that the hotel-room death of her partner Michael Hutchence, the singer with INXS, was not suicide but auto-erotic asphyxiation gone wrong.

Stuart's funeral, so she stayed away. 'My husband died and I didn't get to grieve and be a widow,' she says. 'It was press and weirdos and death threats from weird fans for years. Even to this day, I get shit. I can't have social media accounts where I post personal things. I just get all these Big Country fans going, "You disgust me."

'It's just wild,' she says. 'I feel so bad whenever some dumb girl gets piled on. It's kept me from actually pursuing a lot of stuff in my life, because I don't want that group of people to just pile in on me.'

At Stuart's funeral, his dad gave Bruce Watson a hard time in front of everyone: 'You should've looked after my son!' and all that.

Bruce was stunned and just took it. He wasn't going to argue with a guy at his son's funeral.

In February 2004, William Adamson was sentenced to four years for sexually abusing three children, aged between seven and ten, over a six-year period from 1997. At the trial, it was disclosed that one of the girls was abused up to 150 times. It came to an end when he was confronted by the girl's mother.

He handed himself into the police. After he was interviewed by them, according to news reports, he tried to kill himself.

He lived. He was convicted and sent to Perth Prison.

When William got out of prison, Bruce bumped into him in the street. William tried to be all pally. 'Hey Brucie! How's it gaun?'

'Get tae fuck away fae me!' said Bruce.

They had to keep moving him from house to house for his own safety – people would find out they had a paedophile living next to them and threaten him. He died in 2023.

Marcus Hummon's wife Becca was abused. Her father was killed in a drunk-driving accident when she was about four or five years old and Becca was systematically abused by an elder within their church for several years until she confronted him as a teenager and ended it.

'I have no idea why no one knew or why I didn't tell,' she wrote in her 2013 book, *Snake Oil*. 'I've since discovered that this is a common experience among abused children. You know it's wrong, but it feels that if you acknowledge it your whole world might fall apart.'

Now she helps women worldwide – women who have been abused, trafficked, women who are addicted – through Thistle Farms. Marcus sees parallels now with Stuart's story. It's a familiar story at Thistle Farms. 'Literally everyone's been sexualised, usually by about the age of eight, and often, by family members,' he says. 'And if you combine that likely trauma and being the first to experience your grandfather dying of suicide.' He pauses. 'I can only imagine those ghosts.'

Marcus suffered after Stuart's death. It derailed him a little and made him see his career differently. Sometime later, he wrote a musical play called *The Piper*. It was set in Boston during the second wave of Irish immigration and the main character was inspired by Stuart. She's called Wilder, a girl with polio brought up in the brothels and slums, who plays a whistle given to her by a father she didn't know. But her whistle-playing is magic. Whenever she plays it, she can affect things that are happening. She can move things, move time, move space. If she wants to, she can make people dance – or walk off a ledge.

'That little girl was, for me, representative of Stuart,' says Marcus. 'He had a terrible disease, an affliction, but he had a gift to shape-shift – he could shape-shift himself and he could do it to people. And that's a very unique thing to have.

'He was playing Wembley as a very young man and he wasn't just saying "do-do-do-do-de-dah-dah-dah". He was using fantastic, really interesting, lyrics. That was the nature of his commerciality. He was able to be openly, flagrantly poetic, joyously artistic. He would go for the jugular. He was a Bob Dylan, he was a Joni – he was that kind of character.

'Over time, what I've come to feel is that he did not commit suicide. I feel that he *died* by suicide, and for me, that's a very big distinction: that he had no intention of doing this to his kids. He said it, and I believed him, and I don't think he did. I think the disease killed him, as it does sometimes. That's how I've come to feel about it.'

'I fully believe alcoholism is a symptom of unhealed trauma,' says Callum. 'There was something there that needed to be resolved. Any obsessive compulsive behaviour is a symptom of something not right.'

The phone calls Stuart made to Bruce, to his friends in Dunfermline, and the attempted call to Tony are all significant to Callum. 'I feel really happy about that,' he says, 'because it means it was a conscious choice. It wasn't a mistake or a moment of panic. If it was *decided*, I'm actually really okay with that. Good on him. Fucking love him to bits, miss him every day of my life, but I'm glad he got to do it on his own terms. It was probably just, "I'm never going to be able to kill this part of me, so I have to kill *all of me*."'

Callum, like many of the people in this book, has been through years of therapy to come to terms with Stuart's death. He is now older than Stuart was when he died and a successful businessman.

'None of these stories are sad,' he says. 'Even his death isn't sad. He tried for a long time to be content and happy and decided to punch the button. I'm totally okay with that. I think it's absolutely fine for someone to make that decision. It's a fucking *shame*. There's loads of shames in it. Like, we'd spent three years talking about the fact that there would finally be a *Lord of the Rings* film and he killed himself a week before it came out! My mum took us to see it the day before Christmas Eve and I couldn't go in because I was like, "We've been talking about this with dad for three years."'

I laugh at this and he knows why. 'Such a stupid fucking thing. But it's the little things,' he says. 'It's the little, little things.

'Music is a shite career. But Kurt Cobain is not Kurt Cobain because he's a good businessman. I think music is the only art form that can't be faked. There are people out there that can do things that are unexplainable. He was one of them. What a thing to be. That's worth a life. Like, I'll be fine, I've got my own set of skills, but I'll never be on a fucking T-shirt.'

But there's a price, he says. 'Want to be Jimi Hendrix? Well, you've got to die alone in a hotel room. It's part of the fruit salad. There's fucking kiwis in there as well as cherries. There's bitter, horrible shit in there too and sometimes it gets the better of you. Some people come through it. A lot don't.

'But none of this is sad. Do I wish he was here now? Every fucking day. But I'm not going to be sad about it, because it's not sad. You're talking about somebody who did something that maybe one in half a billion people get to do. I don't think he's upset.'

Stuart needed guidance, he says. 'He didn't have a relationship with his dad, for obvious reasons. He never found that mentor. I've been really lucky to have two great mentors. He never had that. I don't know if he ever sought out father figures, or mentors, or if there was an overhang of fear from his childhood about that.'

I talk about what a great performer Stuart was and use the phrase 'he had the audience in the palm of his hands'. Callum corrects me. 'He *is* the audience,' he says. 'He feels at home. They're one animal at that point. He's not an entertainer – it's a shared enjoyment.

'And that's who he wanted to be all the time – that calm, that centred, that eloquent, that unafraid. Not scared to be himself and not scared to show off his talent. Not embarrassed by the fact that he was fucking better than everybody. He got to do that unashamedly up there.

'And, I mean, that's *it*. We'll never know peace like he knew peace up there. I think that's the only place it all made sense. "I can do this thing and people enjoy it, and I enjoy their enjoyment, and at some point there's no line, it's all the same thing."

'It's okay to feel pain and sorrow and sadness and hurt,' he says, 'because on the other side of that is freedom and peace. But unless you feel it and live in it, it's hard. You can't get to the other side and you can't see the person for who they were.

'He was *not* great,' he says. 'He was also a *genius*. He was a terrible dad and also one of the best dads that you could ever hope to have. He was all of those things at the same time. And that's what being a person is about and it's super okay. Anybody that says otherwise is not human, because that's what we all are.'

He is quiet for a moment.

'Well,' he says. 'What a thing to be talking about.'

Glossary

Aff: off
All over the shop: an uncontained mess
Auld: old
Aw: all

Backhander: a bribe
Baw: ball
Blether: small talk, talking shit
Blethering: talking, chatting
Blootered: just one of many Scots terms for getting drunk. They say the Eskimos have fifty words for snow. We're like that for drunkenness

Cheerio: goodbye
Cunt: 'cunt' is not a Scottish word, but we do use it differently from other people. In some parts of the world, 'cunt' is literally the worst word you can say. In Scotland, it's tossed around liberally and not always intended as an insult at all. Someone might be a 'funny cunt' or a 'lovely wee cunt'. Equally, someone might just be a cunt. It's a subtle admission, maybe, that – at the end of the day – we're all just a buncha cunts

Dae: do
Daein': doing
Deid: dead
Dinnae: don't
Doin' (a doin'): a kicking, a pasting, battered, assaulted
Doon: down
Donald: 'Donald Duck' = luck

Efter: After

Stay Alive

Ersed: literally, 'arsed' but meaning 'bothered'. For instance, Bruce in Moscow: 'Ah couldnae be ersed'

Fitba: football
Fur: for

Gaun: going. 'How's it gaun?' = 'How are you, my good man?'
Gie: give
Gonnae: going to

He goes: he said
Hen: a term of endearment for a young woman, like 'love' or 'darling'
Hoose: house
Hud: had

I went: I said
Isnae: is not

Jobbie: a shite, a poo, a crap
Jock Thamson's bairns: all the same, ordinary folk. 'We're all Jock Thamson's bairns' means 'We're all the same'

Ken: y'know
Kerry-oot: Literally 'carry out' – similar to 'take-away', but usually applied to the purchase of enough booze to kill an elephant
Kindae/kinna: kind of

Like fuck: an awful lot ('We used to drink like fuck'). Can also be used to mean 'I don't believe you': e.g. 'That Angelina Jolie was coming on to me last night.' 'Aye, like fuck'
Lip: cheeky backchat, banter
Lob: to throw, a looping throw

Mair: more

Glossary

Mortal: drunk. Presumably 'so drunk you might die'

Ned: a lout, a hooligan, a thicko. Allegedly stands for 'non-educated delinquent'
Noo: now

Oan: on
Oot: out

Pish: piss, urine, rubbish. E.g.: 'He talks pish, that guy'
Pished: drunk/pissed
Polis: police

Rat-arsed: see 'blootered'

Stairted: started
Stoap: stop

Tatties: potatoes
Teuchter: an insulting name for Highlanders used by Scottish people in central Scotland and the Lowlands, probably mocking the guttural 'uech' sound of 'loch' etc.
Thae: those
The bells: Scottish name for the strike of midnight on Hogmanay (that is, New Year's Eve)
The-night: tonight
Thrapple: throat/Adam's apple
Thum: them
Toon: town

Wan: one
Wasnae: was not
Wee: small, little, young
Wheesht: shhhh. Be quiet

Stay Alive

Windae: window
Wur: were
Wurnae: were not

Youse: you but aimed at more than one person. Thank youse all for reading.

Sources

This book is the result of more than eighty hours of interviews with more than thirty people. I did the interviews in chronological order so that the story revealed itself to me as I went. I tried not to use too many other sources than the interviews because I was wary of repeating other people's mistakes. Additional material is listed below.

'Classic Scottish Albums #26: Big Country – *The Crossing*', Davie Scott, BBC Radio Scotland, November 2018

'Protect and Survive', Central Office of Information, Home Office, HMSO

'Classic Tracks: The Pretenders, *Back on the Chain Gang*', Richard Buskin, *Sound on Sound*, September 2005

'The Thatcher Effect: What Changed and What Stayed the Same', James Ball, the *Guardian*, 12 April 2013

'Rock Star's Perv Dad Caged', Ian Sharp, *Daily Record*, 18 February 2004

'Respiratory or Skin Sensitizers', University of Arkansas, December 2019

'The Epic Story of Nazareth', Dave Ling, *Classic Rock*, June 2004

Interview, *Record Mirror*, December 1978

'Crazy Skids Stuff', Ronnie Gurr, *Record Mirror*, 17 March 1979

'Two Virgins', Ira Robbins and Dave Schulps, *Trouser Press*, October 1979

'Memories of Reading '83', ukrockfestivals.com

'Schizophrenia on Skid Row', Ian Penman, *NME*, 1 November 1980

'Men With Steel in Their Balls', Danny Kelly, *NME*, 27 October 1984

'Return to Eden', Carol Clerk, *Melody Maker*, 20 October 1984

Sleevenotes, *Skids –The Virgin Years* boxset, Tim Barr

This Searing Light, the Sun and Everything Else: Joy Division: The Oral History, Jon Savage, Faber & Faber, 2019

'The Robin Millar Story', interview with Iain McNay, Cherry Red YouTube channel

'Seer Chart Attack', Allan Glen, *Record Collector*, March 2016

'Hoedown in Steeltown', Jon Young, *Creem*, April 1985

'"Oh Yes, We're Very Deep"', Robin Smith, *Record Mirror*, June 1986

Stay Alive

'Country Life', Max Bell, *No.1*, September 1986
Interview, William Shaw, *Smash Hits*, December 1986
'Scot Free', Stuart Cosgrove, *NME*, January 1987
'Hard Times', Roger Morton, *Record Mirror*, February 1989
Margaret Thatcher, interview for BBC, December 1984
Mark Brzezicki interview, Simon Goodwin, *Modern Drummer*, January 1992
'Rock Music at Berlin Wall Sparks Riot', *Los Angeles Times*, June 1987
'Berlin Whitsun Riots 1987', thewallmuseum.com
'Girl Crush: Life After Loss', the *Nashville Edit*, Volume 3, 2019
'Singer Lost in the Big Country', the *Herald*, November 1999
'Stuart Scores a Big Hit With His New Bride', the *Tennessean*, March 2000
'Stuart and the Boys Say a Big Farewell', the *Belfast Telegraph*, May 2000
'Big Country Blog: Day 10 – Norwich', Mike Peters, thealarm.com
'Big Country Singer Missing Again', BBC News, December 2001
'Big Country's Stuart Adamson Dead in Hotel', Jeevan Vasagar, the *Guardian*, 18 December 2001
'Global Stir Caused By Singer's Death in Isles', *Honolulu Star-Bulletin*, 18 December 2001
Snake Oil: The Art of Healing and Truth-Telling, Becca Stevens, Jericho Books, 2013

Tim Barr's liner notes for Big Country and Skids reissues were an huge help. One of the Robin Millar quotes is taken from the brilliant Big Country podcast The Great Divide. I put off listening to it until I'd almost finished – it was intimidating and I wanted to find out the story for myself. For the same reason, I avoided Allan Glen's book *Stuart Adamson: In a Big Country*, which I had read back in 2011, until I'd finished. He interviewed Dave Bates at length and one of the Bates quotes is from there. The David Allen quotes are from an email tribute sent for Stuart's funeral and shared with me by Sandra Adamson. The timeline at bigcountryinfo.com was invaluable. Richard Jobson's books *No Bad Words: 1977–2017, Into the Valley, Days in Europa* and *The Story of the Skids* are all worth a read, as is his autobiographical novel *The Kreuzberg Sonata*.

All photographs © Sandra Adamson, except where stated.

Thank you

This book could not exist without the thirty or so people who gave up so much of their time to be interviewed. Special thanks to Sandra Adamson for being so open and for trusting me to tell this story. And to Bruce Watson for taking me through the Big Country story, month by month, album by album, over a ridiculous amount of interviews.

Thank you to Callum and Kirsten Adamson for their frankness, insight and good humour. Massive thanks to Tony Butler and Clive Ford, who were among the first people interviewed and who really got me started. Thank you to Marcus Hummon and Melanie Shelley for talking me through a painful period in their lives. Thank you to Stuart Ongley for all of his wisdom, help and advice generally – and specifically for his inside knowledge of the EMI deal. Thanks to Bobby, Pubsy and Big Slap (aka Bruce: I used his nickname because otherwise it was one Bruce too many) – especially for having the patience to be interviewed again when the first recording didn't work. And thanks to Ian Grant who got me into this in the first place.

For their time, patience and stories: Bruce Watson, Mark Brzezicki, Tony Butler, Richard Jobson, Bill Simpson, Tam Kellichan, Clive Ford, Rusty Egan, Russell Webb, Ian Grant, Bill Nelson, John Leckie, Dave Batchelor, Mick Glossop, JJ Burnel, Jake Burns, Cinder, Peter Wishart, Chris Briggs, Alan Edwards, John Giddings, Greg Peet, Darrell Scott, Jerry Boonstra, Russell Mills and Paul Elliott. And, of course, to Stuart Adamson. If only he'd been here to tell his side of the story.

Thanks to Robbie Fraser for being a great sounding board and well of knowledge. Thanks to Alan Niven for reading it over and giving some sound advice. Thanks to Debbie Grant and Sandra Watson for their hospitality. Thanks to Ian Winwood and his wife Ruth for help with a

Stay Alive

pitching document and for introducing me to Matthew Hamilton. Thanks to Matthew for getting me a deal in the face of many rejections. As ever, Big Country just weren't cool enough for some people.

Thanks to David Barraclough for his early support. Massive thanks to Pete Selby and James Lilford at New Modern. Thanks to Nige Tassell for his close edit.

For their help: Sil Wilcox, Adam 'Rad' Saunders and Tito Belis. Thanks to Stuart Williams at Future for being supportive. Thanks to my long-time partner in publishing crimes, Brad Merrett, for designing the cover.

The interviews for this book took place between 2023–25, but I have also included interviews I did with Ian, Bruce, Tony, Mark, Mike Peters and Steve Lillywhite back in 2011. Some of the Richard Jobson quotes are taken from an interview we did in 2007. Thank you to Joe and Alfie Rowley for the half-price (and half-arsed) transcriptions and to Andy McDonald for the real deal. Thank you to Lianne Austin, who transcribed all my 2011 interviews. No thanks to Otter.ai, the transcription service that can't understand Scottish accents.

Thanks to all my old schoolboy muckers in our school band, the Dawn Preachers: Billy Houston (my teenage gigging buddy: I first heard the Skids in his bedroom. After watching our first gig – matinee show, Echo & The Bunnymen, October 1984 – we bought records and went back to his auntie's in Drumchapel where we sat around the stereo, gobsmacked, as we listened to *The Absolute Game*), Ian 'Miff' Smith (who learned to play guitar to *The Crossing* and came with me to see Big Country with Mike Peters at the Barras), and my fellow music nerd, drinking buddy and drummer extraordinaire Findlay MacKinnon. *Slàinte!*

Thank you to Sarah Sweet-Rowley for all the love, support and cocktails in the car park. I couldn't have done it without you. Thanks to Tom Rowley for I'm-not-sure-what but it feels weird leaving him out, the big daft lunk.

Thank you

This is a book about family and is dedicated to Sylvia and Joe Rowley for bringing me and my sister Lisa up in a safe and warm house full of books, movies, music and strong opinions.

The team at New Modern would like to thank the following individuals:

Nige Tassell for copy-editing
Chris Stone for proofreading
Marie Doherty for typesetting
Brad Merrett for cover design
Dusty Miller for publicity
**Marie Lecouturier, Charlotte Rose, Andreina Brezzo
and the team at Simon & Schuster UK** for sales and distribution